Behavioral Medicine Approaches to Cardiovascular Disease Prevention

Behavioral Medicine Approaches to Cardiovascular Disease Prevention

Edited by

Kristina Orth-Gomér
Karolinska Institute, Stockholm

Neil Schneiderman
University of Miami

IEA LAWRENCE ERLBAUM ASSOCIATES, PUBLISHERS
1996   Mahwah, New Jersey

Lawrence Erlbaum Associates, Inc., Publishers
10 Industrial Avenue
Mahwah, New Jersey 07430

Library of Congress Cataloging-in-Publication Data

Behavioral medicine approaches to cardiovascular disease prevention /
    [edited by] Kristina Orth-Gomér, Neil Schneiderman.
        p.   cm.
    Includes bibliographical references and indexes.
    ISBN 0-8058-1820-0
    1. Cardiovascular system—Diseases—Prevention. 2. Cardiovascular
system—Diseases—Epidemiology. 3. Cardiovascular system—Diseases—
Psychosomatic aspects. 4. Cardiovascular system—Diseases—Risk
factors. I. Orth-Gomér, Kristina. II. Schneiderman, Neil.
    [DNLM: 1. Cardiovascular Diseases—prevention & control.
2. Behavioral Medicine. 3. Risk Factors. 4. Health Behavior. WG
120 B419 1995]
RA645.C34B44 1995
616.1′05—dc20
DNLM/DLC
for Library of Congress   95-2986
                                                              CIP

Books published by Lawrence Erlbaum Associates are printed on acid-free
paper, and their bindings are chosen for strength and durability.

Printed in the United States of America
10 9 8 7 6 5 4 3 2 1

Contents

**PART III: BIOBEHAVIORAL AND PSYCHOSOCIAL
           FACTORS IN CARDIOVASCULAR
           DISEASE PREVENTION**

PART IV: BEHAVIORAL INTERVENTION MODELS IN CARDIOVASCULAR DISEASE PREVENTION

PART V: SUMMARY AND CONCLUSIONS

Acknowledgments

We are indebted to the International Society of Behavioral Medicine, the Karolinska Institute, and the Folksam Insurance Company Research Foundation, whose generous contributions provided the means for a teaching seminar, which was the precursor of this book. The seminar, held in Högberga, Sweden, was also co-sponsored by the World Health Organization's regional office for Europe and by the International Association of Epidemiology.

Part I

INTRODUCTION TO CARDIOVASCULAR DISEASE PREVENTION AND BEHAVIORAL MEDICINE

Concepts and Theories of Prevention: Reasons for Soliciting Behavioral Medicine Knowledge

Kristina Orth-Gomér
Karolinska Institute

Cardiovascular disease (CVD) is the number-one killer of men and women in industrialized countries. In men above age forty and in women above age sixty CVD is the most important cause of death (1). In older age groups, CVD is also the most important cause for hospitalization. Furthermore, in many countries, heart disease is an important cause of early retirement from work. Thus, CVD is associated with enormous costs for care and loss of productivity, as well as for disabilities, pensions, and so on. Furthermore, it is the cause of acute and prolonged suffering in many people. All this has motivated clinicians and scientists to develop and implement new methodologies and technologies to better care for patients who are hospitalized for heart disease.

Efforts to improve care in the acute phases of coronary heart disease (CHD), the most common CVD, have been very successful. In the 1960s and 1970s, the initiation of intensive coronary care units (ICCUs) with continuous monitoring of cardiac activity and prompt therapy of life-threatening complications substantially reduced mortality rates. In an early Swedish trial, patients were randomized to intensive coronary care or traditional inpatient care without continuous surveillance. Mortality fell by 50% in the former group (2).

During the last decade, the immediate mortality risk of a patient admitted to coronary care for a suspected myocardial infarction (MI) or other acute coronary syndrome has further decreased to less than 10%. This can be ascribed to various attempts to limit infarct size before the full development of the myocardial damage has occurred. Thrombolysis, beta blockade, angiotensin converting enzyme inhibitors for patients with early signs of heart failure, and acute surgery have all contributed to these remarkable gains in human lives and well-being (3).

Despite these achievements, CVD continues to represent a major threat to the health of middle-aged and elderly men and women. This is particularly true for middle-aged men in high-risk groups. In men under 65, more than half of deaths from CHD are sudden cardiac deaths. This usually means that they occur before the patient has had a chance to be admitted to a hospital and benefit from the technological advancements of modern acute care. Sudden cardiac deaths often come as a complete surprise, without any known or noticed premonitory symptoms. In a few fortunate cases, the patient happens to be in a place where resuscitation competence and equipment are available. Most often, however, these deaths are medically unattended (4). Therefore, to prevent or postpone these deaths, it seems necessary to address the underlying process before it becomes symptomatic. Sudden cardiac death is less frequent in women than in men, and with increasing age its frequency decreases in both genders. However, the total number of sudden deaths is so large that powerful actions and measures are necessary to deal with the problem. Thus, many facts speak in the favor of prevention (5).

It is often said that there is no cure for CHD once it has occurred, and that the lifelong development of atherosclerosis in the coronary arteries—as well as in other organ vessels such as the brain, kidneys, legs, and aorta—needs to be controlled. It has become known through a variety of pathological studies that this process starts early in life, perhaps in adolescence or early childhood. Thus, it seems necessary to influence this atherosclerotic process at an early stage, and to maintain the effects over a long period of time—indeed, throughout the life span.

These and other facts are the basis for a growing public interest in the epidemiology and prevention of CVD. The insight has become widespread that, even if acute care becomes sufficiently successful that it saves the life of almost every admitted patient, this approach will never be efficient enough from a public health viewpoint. So it becomes evident that efforts in acute care have to be complemented by population-based attempts to prevent or at least slow down the atherosclerotic process. In that way, it has been argued, many more people would be able to lead healthy lives until their seventies or eighties, many unnecessary premature deaths would be postponed, productivity would be increased, and the costs of care, disabilities, and pensions would decrease. Most important, perhaps, the quality of many lives would considerably improve.

CAUSALITY AND THE RISK-FACTOR CONCEPT

How could this goal of preventing a considerable number of disease cases in the population be most efficiently approached? If the true causes of the accelerated atherosclerotic process were recognized, it is conceivable that these could be eliminated and the unhealthy development stopped. If CHD, like some other major diseases and threats to humankind, was caused by a single infectious agent that could be identified, modified, or eradicated, its prevention would be technically possible. In the case of many widespread infectious diseases in Third

World populations, it has been estimated, for example, that infant mortality might be reduced by as much as 40% if only proper immunization programs were implemented. In diseases caused by the atherosclerotic process, however, it has proved impossible to identify single causes. Instead, multiple factors associated with an increased risk of an accelerated disease process have been recognized. These factors are referred to as *risk factors*. This does not imply causality, but only that the factors have been identified as related to the disease process.

It is reasonable to question the extent to which one can rely on evidence derived from statistical associations without having complete scientific control over the entire disease process. Therefore, certain criteria have been postulated that may increase the plausibility of a risk factor being a causal factor. If several of these criteria of the risk factor are met (6), the likelihood of a causal relationship is increased. The eight criteria are:

1. *Temporality of events.* If it can be demonstrated in prospective studies that the exposure to the risk factor precedes the disease outcome, the likelihood of causality increases.
2. *Strength of association.* How much of the variance in the outcome variable is explained by the exposure variable? How great is the relative risk associated with the exposure? The greater the risk and the narrower the confidence limits, the more certain is the association.
3. *Consistency of associations.* If several studies demonstrate similar results, the conclusiveness of results is increased.
4. *Biological gradient.* If there is an increased risk of adverse outcome with an increase of exposure to the risk factor, likelihood of causality increases.
5. *Biological plausibility.* Is there evidence of a plausible pathogenic mechanism linking the exposure to the outcome variable? If such mechanisms are identified, associations become understandable and the results are more readily accepted as support for causality.
6. *Coherence.* If several kinds of studies (e.g., animal, human population, human patient) point in the same direction in their conclusions, the likelihood of causality is increased.
7. *Specificity of outcome.* If the effects of risk-factor exposure are specific for a particular disease, the likelihood of causality is increased.
8. *Experimental/intervention evidence.* If there is evidence from intervention studies that the disease can be prevented, more support is provided that the association is based on causality.

Most commonly, the identification of behavioral factors associated with an increased cardiovascular risk has been based on observations of real-life processes. Evidence from experimental studies, in which the entire disease process is kept under control, is usually not provided. Such demonstrations from truly experimental conditions have been carried out using animal models, which are difficult to apply directly to the human situation. Thus, one cannot be entirely sure that the risk factor is a causal factor. Rather, it may be associated with an underlying cause that was not recognized in the observation, but just happened to be associated with both the hypothesized risk factor and the disease outcome. This phenomenon—often encountered in epidemiology and referred to as *confounding*—causes multiple problems in the interpretation of results. In particular, the results from behavioral epidemiology need to be scrutinized as to various possible sources of confounding.

THE APPLICATION OF BEHAVIORAL MEDICINE IN PREVENTION

Ample evidence has been gathered that the rates of chronic diseases, such as CHD, can be reduced. Often, however, it has been found that net preventive effects on disease incidence or mortality have not been as strong as expected. Even if the effects in the intervention group are satisfactory, the net gain of preventive efforts can become small because favorable changes begin to occur in the control group as well. Usually the mechanisms of these effects have been poorly understood. They may have involved unintended dissemination of health knowledge and health practices to the control group as well as the target group. They may involve a change of therapeutic principles and treatment modalities by health professionals, which were not intended in the prevention project. Finally, they may have affected the health concepts of an entire population, although they were only aimed at specific target groups.

In other cases, unexpected adverse effects have occurred, which may unfavorably influence the disease outcome. An example is official policies against cigarette smoking in public places and workplaces. In some groups under specific conditions, this has led to an increased consumption of snuff tobacco because its use is not as visible and it is believed to be less health damaging. A further complication has been noted when preventive measures have led to the decrease in CHD expected, but other concomitant effects of the treatment were so unfavorable that the decrease in CHD became secondary in importance (7). This has been experienced with pharmacological lipid lowering, which in some cases has led to a decrease in CHD incidence, but also a concomitant rise in mortality from violent causes. Consequently, the net gain for patients has become questionable. The reasons for these effects are not known, but behavioral mechanisms cannot be ruled out (8). It is possible that some of these ambiguities in the conclusions about preventive efforts can be explained by the fact that behavioral factors usually have not been considered to any major extent in prevention projects.

It is quite obvious that any traditional preventive program, primary or secondary, that tries to influence CVD incidence will need to include knowledge and techniques for behavior change, and consider the interactions between physiological and behavioral effects that are so commonly present.

HIGH-RISK AND POPULATION-BASED STRATEGIES IN PREVENTION

Two theoretically different approaches to preventive action have been introduced. With the high-risk approach, the preventive efforts are only directed toward individuals or patients identified through screening or health care registers as being at high risk for CHD. Special efforts are directed toward these persons, mostly on an individual or group basis. Behavior change and behavior modification are crucial components among the preventive tools. It is assumed that if one is able to correctly identify the persons at risk in the population and significantly modify their risk-factor profile, a net and substantial reduction of CHD morbidity and mortality will occur in the target population.

The other approach is based on a different assumption—namely, that changing habits of an entire population, including those who are not recognized as high-risk individuals, but make up the majority of that population, will be highly effective in preventing CHD. The preventive techniques are different. They rely on media, community actions, political and community bodies, and institutions to communicate health-promoting knowledge and practices.

Most modern disease-prevention projects use both approaches in combination. However, to disentangle specific effects and possible mechanisms of behavioral methodologies, one needs to make the distinction between the two different concepts. The high-risk strategy was successfully applied in the Oslo Heart Study. It was a study of high-risk men, in whom smoking cessation and dietary change were managed by means of highly skilled dietitians and doctors. The behavioral interventions were quite effective, with strong and convincing effects on lipids, smoking, and CHD incidence. Unfortunately, the behavioral interventions were not described in great detail in that study, so it may be difficult for other groups to replicate the findings (9). Another successful disease-prevention study that has used a traditional risk-factor model, but more consciously applied behavioral techniques to lifestyle change, is the North Karelia Study (see chap. 15, this volume). In contrast to the Oslo Heart Study, this project used a population-based approach, in which it attempted to change lifestyles toward more healthy habits in the entire target population of eastern Finland (North Karelia). These two examples—the Oslo Heart Study and North Karelia Study—refer to primary prevention projects, in which attempts were made to prevent people from acquiring heart disease. In secondary prevention, a field where behavioral methodologies have been extensively used, the target group is patients who are already diseased.

Part 1 of this volume is intended to provide an introduction to CVD prevention (chap. 1) and behavioral medicine (chap. 2). In this chapter, attention is called to the multiple risk factors associated with the acceleration of CHD. Both high-risk and population-based disease-prevention strategies are described, as is the need for attending to the social environment, biobehavioral and psychosocial factors, and behavioral intervention models in CVD prevention. In chapter 2, by Stephen Weiss, the many interfaces and possible interactions between the behavioral and biomedical sciences are explored. These range from epidemiology and public health to clinical patient-oriented approaches, and invoke biomedical, biobehavioral, and psychosocial mechanisms.

THE SOCIAL ENVIRONMENT

Cardiovascular preventive efforts have traditionally focused on the three well-established and major risk factors for CVD: smoking, diet, and blood pressure. Large-scale epidemiological trials have attempted to influence these factors in such a way that incidence and mortality rates would be significantly and substantially decreased. However, it is often found that preventive effects are unevenly distributed in the target groups or populations. Often the necessity to consider the social settings and social environments in preventive projects is overlooked. These aspects have only recently been recognized as relevant for prevention. They are widely described and discussed in Part 2 of this volume, "Behavioral Epidemiology and Public Health in Cardiovascular Disease Prevention."

The important potentials of new models for preventive efforts and projects become particularly evident when one considers the uneven basic distributions of disease among social groups and in social hierarchies. Within industrialized countries, social epidemiologists are almost unanimous in finding that the socially and economically underprivileged are also underprivileged in their cardiovascular health. In addition, preventive efforts seem to be least effective in the poor and socially disadvantaged. Possible explanations speculate about the competence of the better educated to understand and integrate knowledge about health promotion in their daily lives.

Furthermore, when comparing CHD incidence rates in different European countries, an East–West gradient in cardiovascular health is becoming increasingly evident. Eastern European countries generally have higher incidence and mortality rates than Western Europe. Also, in many of these countries rates are increasing, as opposed to most Western industrialized countries, where rates are decreasing. A similar East–West gradient in wealth and assets of individuals and populations is well known. These trends are thoroughly discussed and the causes elucidated in the chapter by Michael Marmot and Amanda Feeney on "Socioeconomic factors in CHD prevention" (chap. 3).

Further characteristics of the social settings that form the basis for populations and groups at high risk for CHD are described in chapter 4 by Leonard Syme (chap. 4, this volume). These characteristics include social instability and insecurity, and the chronic stresses caused by mobility and social turbulence.

However, there are also characteristics of the social environment that may counteract these hardships, and thus provide protection from stresses and ill health. Among these factors are the networks and support provided by the social ties that are part of an individual's social environment and life situation. These may be helpful in meeting crises and coping with stressors. They may increase host resistance against disease agents, and they may provide emotional and practical support to individuals who are at risk or already diseased. These characteristics are discussed in the chapter by Lisa Berkman and Kristina Orth-Gomér, "Prevention of cardiovascular morbidity and mortality: Role of social relations" (chap. 5).

It has become increasingly well established that work environment and work stress are important and potentially noxious components of the social environment. The prevailing theories, which have been corroborated in numerous empirical studies, point to the imbalance between high psychological demand and low control over work and reward for the work performed as the most important components. The strain—caused by high demand and low control—is discussed by Töres Theorell in the chapter on "The demand–control–support model for studying health in relation to the work environment: An interactive model" (chap. 6).

The relationship of these work strain models to the reward and personal gratification obtained by the individual from his or her work is described by Johannes Siegrist in his chapter on "Stressful work, self-experience and cardiovascular disease prevention" (chap. 7). Until now, the empirical evidence and practical experience from efforts to change social and occupational environments have been limited. However, there are indications that these areas carry an important potential for prevention. These issues are addressed and the possibilities for intervention are described in Part 2 of this volume.

BEHAVIOR AND PHYSIOLOGY INTERACTIONS

The important questions of how behavioral sciences can be conceptually integrated into traditional, medically based, preventive efforts are described and discussed in Part 3. In their chapter on "Insulin metabolism, sympathetic nervous system regulation, and coronary heart disease prevention" (chap. 8), Neil Schneiderman and Jay Skyler explore the pathophysiological processes that intervene between psychosocial stressors and disease-promoting lifestyle factors on the one hand, and CHD on the other hand. The possible links described between behavioral variables and biological processes appear to provide a conceptual framework for the further development of interventions aimed at preventing the progression of atherosclerosis and CHD.

The strong and important psychophysiological effects of mental stressors on the cardiovascular system are discussed in the chapter by Andrew Steptoe, "Psychophysiologic processes in the prevention of cardiovascular disease" (chap. 9). Personality and behavioral characteristics that are associated with physiological reactive patterns are described in the chapters by Ad Appels, "Personality factors and coronary heart disease" (chap. 10), and Redford Williams, "Coronary prone behaviors, hostility, and cardiovascular health: Implications for behavioral and pharmacologic interventions" (chap. 11).

The important capacities and abilities of the individual to cope with adverse life situations, with disease and disease risk as well as efforts toward prevention, are addressed in the chapter by Margaret Chesney, "New behavioral risk factors for coronary heart disease: Implications for intervention" (chap. 12).

BEHAVIORAL INTERVENTION MODELS

Both population and high-risk behavioral intervention approaches are addressed in Part 4 of this volume. Based on his experience from teaching behavior change, Gerjo Kok and his colleagues describe in detail "Health education at the individual level" (chap. 13). Brian Oldenburg and his collaborators have developed particular skills in how to make doctors become more efficient in communicating their knowledge about prevention to patients. This is thoroughly described in the chapter "Modification of health behavior and lifestyle mediated by physicians" (chap. 14). Gunilla Burell has long experience and particular skills in teaching coronary patients how to cope with stressors and reduce the stresses in their lives. She relates her and other researchers' experiences to disease outcome in her chapter, "Behavioral medicine approach to secondary prevention" (chap. 15). Kok, Oldenburg, and Burell each have vast experience in communicating behavior change on an individual level, and each is a master of the scientific literature in the field.

Two examples of the community approach are also described. Pekka Puska, initiator and leader for many years of the North Karelia Project, describes the behavioral experiences and new knowledge gained from carrying out this pioneer community project (chap. 16). Michael O'Connor (chap. 17) has gathered experience with community prevention from a different angle—that of politicians. In his chapter on "Health public policy: Getting governments onside," he addresses how public and political structures can be successfully approached so that these potentially powerful forces can be used to improve the health of populations and nations.

In summary, this volume examines the social environment and its potentials for preventive actions, reviews the psychosocial and biobehavioral mechanisms involved in these effects, and describes concrete and practical implementations of behavioral medicine knowledge as they have been applied to CHD.

REFERENCES

1. World Health Statistics. Genève: WHO, 1992.
2. Hofvendahl S. Influence of treatment in a coronary care unit on prognosis in acute myocardial infarction. Acta Med Scand 1971; Suppl 519:9–78.
3. Hurst JW, Schlant RC, Rackley CE, Sonnenblick EH, Kass Wenger N, editors. The heart. 7th ed. New York: McGraw-Hill, 1990.
4. Wikland B. Medically unattended fatal cases of ischaemic heart disease in a defined population. Acta Med Scand 1971; Suppl 524:3–78.
5. Biörck G. Early diagnosis of coronary heart disease—what is it good for? Adv Cardiol 1973;8:25–37.
6. Hill AB. The environment and disease: association or causation? Proceedings of the Royal Society of Medicine 1965;58:295–300.
7. Oliver MF. Doubts about preventing coronary heart disease. Br Med J 1992;304:393–94.
8. Muldoon MF. Lowering cholesterol concentrations and mortality: a quantitative review of primary prevention trials. Br Med J 1990;301:309–14.
9. Hjermann I, Helgeland A, Holme I, et al. A randomized intervention trail in primary prevention of coronary heart disease: the Oslo Study. Presented at the 8th European Congress of Cardiology; 1980 June 22–26; Paris, France.

Chapter 2

Principles of Behavioral Medicine: Implications for Prevention

Stephen M. Weiss
University of Miami School of Medicine

Over the past 20 years, revolutionary changes have occurred in the way we think about chronic disease, how we consider what causes it; how we measure its depth and intensity, how we treat it, and, most important, how we seek to prevent its occurrence in the first place. Historically, attempts by the biomedical and behavioral disciplines independently to investigate these chronic disease issues have resulted in serious errors or omissions, due to an insufficient understanding of concepts within "the other" discipline's purview. It has become increasingly obvious that successful research, prevention, and control efforts require collaborative relationships among the various disciplines that collectively embody the necessary expertise to understand all the dimensions of the problems facing them. Familiarity with one another's terminology, concepts, and perspectives is a prerequisite to model the combination of biobehavioral and sociocultural circumstances responsible for the development of chronic disease (1).

This conceptualization has been most thoroughly articulated by the term *behavioral medicine*, defined by the International Society of Behavioral Medicine as ". . . the development and integration of biomedical, psychosocial and behavioral sciences' knowledge and techniques relevant to health and illness and the application of this knowledge and these techniques to prevention, diagnosis, treatment, and rehabilitation."

The emphasis on "integration" calls for a pooling of talent across many disciplines to capitalize on the synergistic and catalytic potential inherent in such collaborative efforts. Given the major differences in perspective and concept that have traditionally separated the various disciplines, interdisciplinary efforts sought to use those differences as a means to stimulate new approaches to old problems. It encouraged participants to forsake traditional perspectives, and instead focus on the potential inherent in multifactorial approaches. Understanding the role of environmental, social, and behavioral factors as synergistic, catalytic, modulating, and mediating agents in the complex physiological and biochemical reactions that result over time in organ damage has become a significant challenge to the biomedical, psychosocial, and behavioral research communities.

Treatment and prevention efforts to broaden the attack on chronic disease have identified many nontraditional paths for potentially fruitful exploration. For example, diet, exercise, stress reduction, weight control, smoking behavior, and strategies for compliance and adherence have all recently emerged as legitimate areas of research in the prevention and control of chronic disease.

Underlying all these approaches, one needs to consider the dimensions of *interaction* and *variability* as most uniquely characteristic of the behavioral medicine model. *Interaction* refers to the interplay of disciplines, levels of analysis, and effect of combinations of variables "whose whole is greater (and perhaps 'different from') the sum of its parts." *Variability* concerns assessing the range of physiological function in reaction to a broad array of environmental challenges. These measures may allow us to understand and intervene upon biobehavioral processes that, if left unchecked over the long term, could lead to organic dysfunction, disorder, and disease.

Combining these two concepts, one might question whether certain stressors in our environment (e.g., psychological demands, social isolation, natural disasters) might interact with other substances or conditions (e.g., caffeine, nicotine, salt, alcohol) to produce physiological "hyperresponsivity," which could lead to disease in susceptible (e.g., genetically or environmentally predisposed) individuals. One cannot underestimate the complexity of the behavioral medicine model, particularly when the nature of the interaction among variables may be more important than the main effects of the variables themselves.

COMPONENTS OF THE HEALTH–ILLNESS PARADIGM

Let us briefly consider the various components of the health–illness paradigm from the perspective of behavioral medicine. These include etiology and diagnosis, treatment and rehabilitation, and prevention and health promotion.

Etiology and Diagnosis

Etiology and diagnosis of disease have been cornerstones of research and practice throughout the history of the healing arts. Scientists and clinicians concerned with mind–body interaction have traditionally devoted much effort toward understanding the psychological impact on physiological status, how such alterations in physiological function might affect psychological and emotional variables, and so on. Major advances in instrumentation and data processing have created exciting opportunities for psychophysiological measurement. Breakthroughs in the neurosciences have provided new understandings of the interrelationships between the central and peripheral nervous systems and their mediating effects on bodily processes. Lifestyles, including the long-term effects of our attempts to cope with our environment (subsumed under the rubric of *stress*), have been targeted as one of the major factors in the development and progression of chronic disease.

As noted earlier, the biobehavioral approach suggests rather complex scenarios of genetic, psychological, physiological, sociological, nutritional, and environmental variables interacting on many levels, producing variations in physiological responses of such a nature that would predict dysfunction or breakdown over time. All these scenarios contain the common element of human behavior—either action or reaction—which is measurable topographically and/or physiologically. However, rather than confine our analysis to the relationship of behavioral or environmental factors to the development and progression of disease, the biobehavioral perspective requires an analysis of all the factors that may contribute to the condition in question, and how these factors interact in a synergistic, catalytic, or inhibitory fashion. Assessing each variable independently might result in inconsistent or contradictory findings because one is liable to miss what may be the essential ingredient of the clinical event—the interaction among variables.

For example, we are all familiar with the potentiating effects of psychological stress on blood pressure, but only recently have we come to use this phenomenon in a diagnostic paradigm to determine how one's "reactivity" to standardized stressors (physical, psychological, social) compares with established reactivity norms (2). We are also aware of the effects of caffeine, nicotine, salt, and alcohol on blood pressure (3), but only recently have we come to appreciate the interaction of psychological–environmental stressors and these substances, particularly on individuals who are genetically or psychosocially "sensitized" (e.g., "hyperreactors") (4). As diagnosticians and therapists, we must be sensitive to such interactions in our efforts to understand and effectively intervene with the most relevant pharmacological and nonpharmacological therapies.

Treatment and Rehabilitation

The biobehavioral perspective suggests four major approaches to clinical intervention: (a) combined pharmacological–nonpharmacological therapy, (b) combinations of nonpharmacological therapies, (c) nonpharmacological therapy for multiple risk factors, and (d) nonpharmacological therapy for a single disorder (e.g., Raynaud's disease).

Although nonpharmacological therapies have an important role to play in the prevention and control of coronary heart disease (CHD) and hypertension, it is also obvious that multiple factors at multiple levels must be considered in designing, implementing, and evaluating such programs, given the complexities and interactions of the relevant variables. Recognizing the limitations as well as the contributions of these therapies will go a long way toward achieving their acceptance by the entire health care community.

We should be cautious when making clinical claims that have not been fully established by clinical trials research. Although we may achieve promising results in clinical studies, until such findings are replicated in large-scale clinical trials, which are truly representative of the condition we are studying and the population at risk, we must present such therapies to patients as still in the experimental stage. As clinical research documents the efficacy of a technique as well as its specificity–generalizability to some or all individuals with the disease (or risk), we can have greater confidence in applying this therapeutic approach to appropriate patients.

One misperception about the behavioral medicine approach concerns its relationship to the use of pharmacological agents. Sometimes the scientific question has been posed in terms of, Which is better, pharmacological or nonpharmacological therapies? From a biobehavioral perspective, this is the wrong question. How one can maximize the strengths and minimize the shortcomings of both types of therapy through judiciously "combining" them to produce the most effective and efficacious result for the patient is the real issue of concern.

Although essentially all health care providers would agree that a nonpharmacological strategy would be preferable if equally efficacious, nonpharmacological and pharmacological interventions are more often complementary in terms of their short- and long-term advantages and shortcomings. For example, in treating hypertension, one must achieve two goals: (a) reduce blood pressure, and (b) maintain that blood pressure reduction over time. Combination pharmacological and nonpharmacological therapies have been effectively employed to accomplish both objectives, as well as to reduce or eliminate dependence on medication for the majority of patients who have participated in such treatment programs. For example, Patel et al. (5), Green et al. (6), and Fahrion et al. (7) successfully demonstrated that using pharmacological therapies to lower blood pressure and using nonpharmacological (biofeedback-assisted relaxation) therapies to maintain blood pressures at normotensive levels have been effective in reducing and, in most cases, eliminating reliance on medication, using a "step-down" procedure of weaning patients from drugs. Exceptional adherence to the combination program was noted because most of these patients were experiencing undesirable side effects from the antihypertensive drugs, and thus were highly motivated to become involved in a program that offered potential relief from these side effects. Thus, the patients were "rewarded" for diligent practice of the nonpharmacological procedures by medication reduction, which further stimulated their efforts to continue that process even when medications were not completely eliminated (8).

Multifactorial behavioral medicine clinical research programs employing multiple nonpharmacological treatments have produced encouraging findings, particularly in CHD, hypertension, and with human immunodeficiency virus (HIV)-infected persons. Ornish et al. (9) demonstrated reversal of coronary atherosclerosis using a combination of dietary, exercise, stress-management, and social support interventions. Kostis et al. (10) showed similar combinations of nonpharmacological strategies to be equivalent to pharmacological therapy in lowering blood pressure in mild hypertensives, but without the deleterious side effects associated with pharmacotherapy. Burell et al. (11) and Friedman et al. (12) demonstrated significant reductions in postmyocardial infarction (MI) morbidity and mortality in patients treated with behavioral therapies in addition to cardiology counseling, while Schneiderman et al. (13) showed immunologic enhancement in HIV-infected individuals using stress-management and exercise interventions, resulting in delay of onset of acquired immune deficiency syndrome (AIDS) symptoms.

In general, the behavioral medicine approach emphasizes the need to consider both multiple determinants of disease and synergistic treatment modalities (e.g., pharmacological and nonpharmacological interventions; relaxation and cognitive–behavioral stress-management packages). However, it should be pointed out that, just as single-modality pharmacological interventions may be appropriate in the treatment of some disorders, single-modality behavioral treatments may also be useful. Thus, for example, in the treatments of disorders such as fecal incontinence (14) and Raynaud's disease (15), biofeedback training has proved to be clinically effective.

Although many behavioral medicine findings require replication and verification in large-scale clinical trials, they join a growing body of research data that support interventions addressing the behavioral and psychosocial dimensions in conjunction with the biological concerns relevant to the health issue in question.

Disease Prevention and Health Promotion

The ultimate goal of our efforts is not to treat or understand chronic disease, but to prevent its occurrence in the first place. To accomplish this not only involves multiple disciplines, but also multiple levels of analysis (e.g., intrapersonal, interpersonal, environmental) (16).

At the intrapersonal level, for example, the focus is on the individual in terms of genetic background, constitutional factors, developmental experiences, personality characteristics, and so on. We are concerned with issues of biological dependency (in the case of substance use/abuse), family history of hypertension or obesity, ability to successfully cope with life's daily challenges (e.g., self-efficacy measures), and similar factors relevant to assessing predisposition for health-related problems amenable to behavior change strategies and/or predicting outcomes of such strategies.

The interpersonal level addresses all of the social, family, and occupation-related relationships of the individual, and how such relationships may enhance or inhibit health behavior development and/or change and maintenance. Social support, peer pressure, and family environment are powerful reinforcers of behavior throughout the life cycle. Such sociocultural influences must be considered potential agents of change as we come to better understand and define their parameters.

Environmental factors, including characteristics of the physical setting as well as legal and policy issues, are also potent determiners of health behaviors. Access to exercise facilities, health assessment procedures, cigarette machines, the availability of "prudent diet" menus and information at school or workplace cafeterias, ambient air quality, noise level, lighting at work and home, the "corporate culture," the statutory regulations concerning smoking, seat belts, and bicycle helmets all influence health behavior and presumably health outcomes (16).

It has been argued, in fact, that in the absence of environmental changes, the likelihood of maintaining individual health behavior change is quite low (17). Thus, programs that focus on the intrapersonal and interpersonal levels without considering concomitant environmental modification are unlikely to achieve the desired long-term effects.

If this were not sufficiently complex, our model must also differentiate between the processes of health behavior development (e.g., smoking prevention, development of prudent dietary habits), health behavior change (shifting from health-destructive to health-protective behaviors), and health behavior maintenance (adherence, preventing relapse). The technical approaches may be quite different in achieving the objectives in each area. Differences in populations and unique strategies based on the special needs of these populations may also apply.

Our experiences in the fields of learning and behavior modification at the clinical and small-group levels have also entered the public health domain through concepts of *social marketing* (18, 19), *communication* (20, 21), *community organization* (22), and *social learning* (23). These theoretical models designed to influence the lifestyle behaviors of populations (e.g., communities) are presently being tested in several community risk-reduction programs throughout Europe and the United States (24–26).

In summary, there are exciting developments taking place in behavioral medicine—psychologists, physicians, nurses, health educators, epidemiologists, and many others have much to offer each other in seeking biobehavioral solutions to problems of health and illness. Using Neal Miller's classic statement on the subject as our watchword—"we must be bold in what we try, but cautious in what we claim" (27)—we can be sure of a long and viable future for this field.

REFERENCES

1. Schwartz GE, Weiss SM. Behavioral medicine revisited: an amended definition. J Beh Med 1978;1:249–51.
2. Manuck S. Cardiovascular reactivity in cardiovascular disease: "once more unto the breach." Int J Beh Med 1994;1:4–31.

3. The 1988 report of the Joint National Committee on the detection, evaluation and treatment of high blood pressure. Arch Intern Med 1988;148(5):1023–38.

4. Falkner B, Onesti G, Angelakos E, et al. Effect of salt-loading on the cardiovascular response to stress in adolescents. Hypertension 1981;3 Suppl II:195–99.

5. Patel CH, Marmot M, Terry D, et al. Trial of relaxation in reducing coronary risk: four year followup. Br Med J 1985;290:1103–06.

6. Green E, Green A, Norris PA. Self-regulation training for the control of hypertension: an experimental method for restoring or maintaining normal blood pressure. Prim Cardiol 1980;6:126–27.

7. Fahrion S, Norris P, Green A, et al. Biobehavioral treatment of essential hypertension: a group-outcome study. Biofeedback Self Regul 1986;2:257–77.

8. Weiss SM, Anderson R, Weiss SM. Programs for cardiovascular disorders and hypertension. In: Sweet J, Rozensky RM, Tovian SM, editors. Handbook of clinical psychology in medical settings. New York: Plenum, 1991:353–74.

9. Ornish D, Brown SE, Scherwitz LW, et al. Can lifestyle changes reverse coronary heart disease? Lancet 1990;336:129–33.

10. Kostis JB, Rosen RC, Brondolo E, et al. Superiority of nonpharmacological therapy compared to propranolol and placebo in men with mild hypertension: a randomized, prospective trial. Am Heart J 1992;123:466–73.

11. Burell G, Ohman A, Sundin O, et al. Modification of type A behavior pattern in post-myocardial infarction patients: a route to cardiac rehabilitation. Int J Beh Med 1994;1:32–54.

12. Friedman M, Thoresen CE, Gill JJ, et al. Alteration of type A behavior and its effect on cardiac recurrences in post-myocardial infarction patients: summary reults of the Recurrent Coronary Prevention Project. Am Heart J 1986;112:653–65.

13. Schneiderman N, Antoni M, Ironson G, et al. HIV-1, immunity and behavior. In: Glaser R, Kiecolt-Glaser J, editors. Handbook of human stress and immunity. New York: Academic Press, 1994; 267–300.

14. Engel BT, Nikoomanesh P, Schuster MM. Operant conditioning of retrosphinceric responses in the treatment of fecal incontinence. N Eng J Med 1974;290:646–49.

15. Freedman RR, Ianni P, Wenig P. Behavioral treatment of Raynaud's disease. J Clin Consult Psychol 1983;151:539–49.

16. Weiss SM. Health and illness—the behavioral medicine perspective. In: Zegans LS, VanDyke C, edtiors. Emotions in health and illness: foundations in clinical practice. New York: Academic Press, 1983:7–15.

17. Brownell KD, Marlatt GA, Lichtenstein E, et al. Understanding and preventing relapse. Am Psychol 1986;41:765–82.

18. Winett RA, King AC, Altman DG. Health psychology and public health. New York: Pergamon Press, 1989.

19. LeFebvre RC, Harden EA, Rakowski W, et al. Characteristics of participants in community health promotion programs: four-year results. Am J Public Health 1987;77:1342–44.

20. Winett RA, Kramer KO, Walker WB, et al. Effective consumer information interventions: concept, design, and impacts using field experiments. In: deFontenay A, Sibley D, Shugard M, editors. Telecommunications and demand modeling: an integrative review. Amsterdam: North Holland, 1987: .

21. Solomon DS, Maccoby N. Communications as a model for health enhancement. In: Matarazzo JD, Weiss SM, Herd NE, et al., editors. Behavioral health: a handbook for health enhancement and disease prevention. New York: Wiley, 1984:209–21.

22. Rogers EM, Kincaid DC. Communication networks: toward a new paradigm for research. New York: Free Press, 1981.

23. Bandura A. Social foundations of thought and action: a social cognitive theory. Englewood Cliffs, NJ: Prentice-Hall, 1986.

24. Puska P, Nissinen A, Tuomilehto J, et al. The community-based strategy to prevent coronary heart disease: conclusions from the ten years of the North Karelia Project. In: Breslow L, Lave IB, Fielding JE, editors. Annual review of public health. Palo Alto, CA: Annual Reviews, Inc., 1985:147–93.
25. Farquhar JW, Maccoby N, Solomon D. Community applications of behavioral medicine. In: Gentry WD, editor. Handbook of behavioral medicine. New York: Guilford Press, 1984:437–78.
26. Farquhar JW, Fortmann SP, Flora JA, et al. Effect of community-wide education on cardiovascular disease risk factors: the Stanford Five City Project. JAMA 1990;264(3):359–65.
27. Weiss, SM. Health psychology: the time is now. Health Psychol 1981;1:81–91.

Part II

BEHAVIORAL EPIDEMIOLOGY AND PUBLIC HEALTH IN CARDIOVASCULAR DISEASE PREVENTION

Chapter 3

Socioeconomic Factors in CHD Prevention

Michael Marmot
Amanda Feeney
University College–London Medical School

Coronary heart disease (CHD) is the leading cause of death in industrialized societies, and it is rapidly becoming a major cause of death in developing countries, imposing an enormous burden on the social and economic welfare of each country (1, 2). There are two striking features of the epidemiology of CHD that are of major scientific and practical significance. The first is the marked contrast between the countries of Western Europe, where CHD is now showing welcome declines in mortality, and those of Central and Eastern Europe, where CHD rates are rising dramatically. Figure 3.1 shows that countries of the West, with the exception of Ireland, all show decreases; the countries of Central and Eastern Europe, which were at the time all under communist governments, all show increases (3). The second feature is the sharp socioeconomic gradient in CHD (higher rates in lower socioeconomic groups) that is now seen in most Western industrialized countries, but may be different in the countries of Central and Eastern Europe. Understanding reasons for the variations in the socioeconomic gradient in CHD mortality is crucial to public health.

The social gradient in CHD mortality is far from stable. In England and Wales in the 1930s and 1950s, CHD mortality was higher in the more affluent classes, but in the 1970s this gradient reversed toward the lower social classes (4). A similar change has been documented in The Netherlands. One hypothesis is that the social gradient in CHD is related to the stage of development of society. The overall

This chapter is an abridged version of a chapter in *Society and Health*, edited by Amick B, Levine S, Tarlov A, and Walsh D (in press). It is included here by permission of Oxford University Press.

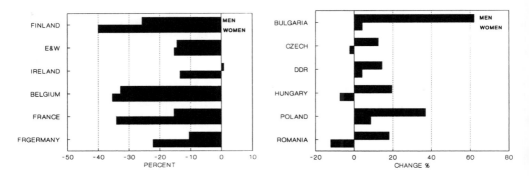

FIG. 3.1. Percentage change 1970–1985 in age-standardized death rates from heart disease (ages 30–69).

pattern can be represented as in Fig. 3.2. As the rate of CHD rises, it appears to first affect those of higher socioeconomic status (SES); at an intermediate stage, there is little social class difference, subsequently there is an inverse association with social position. Data from Hong Kong (5), Puerto Rico (6), and India (7) show higher rates of CHD in higher income groups. They are presumably at the left-hand slope of the curve. Poland, which has also shown marked increases in CHD mortality, also shows a slightly higher mortality rate in groups with more education (8). Between the early 1950s and 1960s, England and Wales were at the flat part of the curve. The social class transition actually began before the overall

CHD MORTALITY

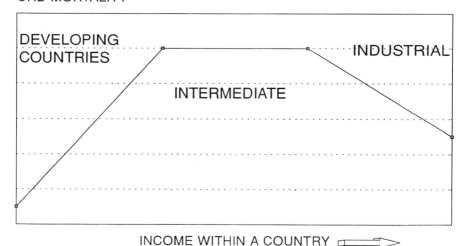

FIG. 3.2. An idealized model of the relationship between income and CHD mortality.

mortality rate began to fall, but the decline in mortality first began in higher status groups (4), similarly in the United States (9).

A comparison of mortality from CHD at one point also supports the pattern shown in Fig. 3.2. In Fig. 3.3, we divided countries into those with gross national product per capita above and below $6,000. As an index of prosperity, we have taken the proportion of total household income not spent on food. For countries with low average incomes, there is a positive relationship between prosperity and CHD rates. Among higher income countries, there is little relationship. These results support the speculation that a common set of factors may relate to inequalities between countries and within countries. It is worth anticipating the discussion of what these factors might be by suggesting a framework for examining these international trends in CHD.

How can we put these results together? If we ask why Central and Eastern European countries should be going through an epidemiological picture, like that of England and Wales in an earlier period, it is perhaps not fanciful to suggest that this reflects the relative state of economic development. Those countries may be at the point in industrialization and economic development that, in the West, coincided with the upswing of the CHD epidemic before it reached its peak (10).

What does *development* mean in this context? Internationally, there is a correlation between CHD mortality and dietary fat consumption, and, to a lesser extent, smoking rates. Certainly, smoking rates are high in Hungary and Czecho-

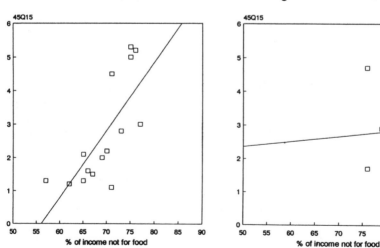

FIG. 3.3. Probability of death between ages 15 and 60 according to level of prosperity in low- and high-income countries. (Low income is GNP per capita less than $6,000.)

slovakia, as is consumption of dietary fat. Data from the World Health Organization (WHO) MONICA study show that Hungary and Czechoslovakia have about 80% higher CHD mortality rates than the western part of Germany (11). Our own calculations from MONICA data suggest that differences in smoking and plasma cholesterol can account for 35% of the excess in CHD rates in Czechoslovakia and 24% in Hungary.

To inquire what may account for the rest, it is instructive to look at what has been happening in Japan. There, over a 20-year period (1965–1986), life expectancy increased by an astonishing 7.5 years—the equivalent to abolishing heart disease and cancer from Britain (12). In Japan, the two major causes of death, stroke, and stomach cancer have declined markedly, and mortality from heart disease, always at a low level in Japan, has continued to decline. The low rate of heart disease in Japan is likely to be related to a low-fat diet. Diet does not offer an easy explanation of the trends, however, because heart disease mortality continued to decline despite a doubling of fat intake. Smoking is an important cause of premature mortality, however, this does not help explain the Japanese mortality record because two thirds of Japanese men smoke. A major change in Japan over the 20-year period is the greater rise in prosperity than elsewhere. Not only has the GNP risen markedly over this period, according to World Bank figures, but this income is more equitably distributed in Japan than in any other Organization for Economic Development (OECD) country.

This suggests three broad classes of influence on the rise and fall of CHD rates: nutrition, smoking, and factors related to socioeconomic level. This is consistent with findings from within-country studies. Our task is to determine what these other factors related to socioeconomic level might be.

THE WHITEHALL STUDIES

We studied morbidity and mortality in two large studies of British civil servants. The first Whitehall study, conducted in the 1960s, consisted of 18,000 British civil servants; a group of people of one predominant ethnic group; all employed in stable office-based jobs; not subject to industrial hazards, unemployment, or extremes of poverty or affluence; and all working and living in Greater London and adjoining areas. The measure of social class used was grade of employment. This is a precise social classification—it corresponds closely to salary, and is related to position in the employment hierarchy. Yet in this relatively homogeneous population, we observed a gradient in mortality—each group with a higher mortality than the one a step higher in the hierarchy. The difference in mortality was threefold between highest and lowest grades (Fig. 3.4). Adjustment for conventional risk factors—blood pressure, blood cholesterol, smoking, and obesity—only reduced this ratio by 30% (13).

The second study, the Whitehall II study, was set up to investigate the degree and causes of the social gradient in morbidity, to study additional factors related

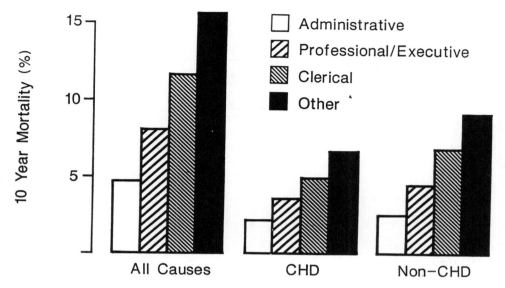

FIG. 3.4. Age-adjusted mortality rates (%) by grade of employment for civil servants ages 40–64 in the Whitehall study.

to the gradient in mortality, and, importantly, to include women. The study examined 10,308 men and women ages 35–55 in 1985–1988, nearly 20 years later. As in Whitehall, the indicator of social class used is grade of employment. Table 3.1 shows the prevalence rate of various indicators of morbidity in the Whitehall II study in different employment grades (14). The two top levels, labeled here as 1 and 2, are the top administrative ranks of the civil service; they correspond to what was labeled *administrators* in the original Whitehall study. In general, the lower the grade, the higher the prevalence of ischemic heart disease. Women report higher prevalence of angina than men, despite the lower prevalence of ischemic electrocardiograms (ECGs). The excess of abnormal ECGs in men is greater for probable ischemia, Q waves, than it is for possible ischemia, S–T- and T-wave changes.

Among men, there is an inverse association between grade and (a) number of symptoms reported in the last 14 days, (b) health problems in the last year, (c) likelihood of rating health as *average* or *poor* as opposed to *good* or *very good*, and (d) prior diagnosis of hypertension or diabetes. This is in addition to the inverse association with prevalence of ischemia and of cough and phlegm. In general, women have a higher level of reported morbidity than men. The relation with grade is less consistent. In addition to a higher prevalence of premenstrual bloating, lower grade women are more likely to report premenstrual irritability and breast tenderness.

For comparison with the Whitehall results from 1967–1969, data are restricted to men ages 40–54, and grades grouped into three broad classes. Figure

TABLE 3.1
Morbidity Prevalence by Civil Service Grade of Employment
(Age-Adjusted Figures)

Variable	Sex	Employment Grade						Total Sample	p
		1	2	3	4	5	6		
Number of men and women	M	1,026	1,627	1,228	1,496	881	642	6,900	
in grades	F	122	264	198	480	660	1,690	3,414	
Age (M)	M	46.9	44.2	43.5	42.5	43.4	44.6	6,900	≤.001
	F	44.1	43.0	42.1	42.9	45.5	46.7	3,414	≤.001
Probable ischemia on ECG	M	1.3	0.9	1.1	1.2	1.4	2.1	6,896	≤.10
(%)	F	0.0	0.0	0.7	0.1	0.7	1.1	3,412	≤.05
Probable/possible ischemia	M	6.4	4.9	5.0	6.5	6.7	10.5	6,896	≤.001
on ECG	F	3.6	3.3	3.0	6.5	7.8	7.3	3,412	≤.01
Angina by questionnaire	M	1.7	2.4	2.5	3.1	1.9	2.9	6,835	>.10
(%)	F	1.8	1.6	2.9	3.3	5.8	4.0	3,351	≤.05
Probable/possible ischemia	M	7.6	7.0	7.3	9.3	8.4	12.3	6,835	≤.001
on ECG or angina (%)	F	4.5	5.0	5.5	9.8	13.3	11.1	3,357	≤.001
History of diabetes (%)	M	0.3	0.6	0.8	0.8	1.7	1.7	6,852	≤.001
	F	0.9	0.6	0.0	0.0	0.8	1.4	3,386	≤.05
Mean number of symptoms	M	2.1	2.4	2.5	2.5	2.6	2.6	5,151	≤.001
	F	3.2	3.3	3.1	3.1	3.2	3.0	2,442	>.10
Self-rated health average or	M	15.3	19.5	21.5	22.8	27.5	33.7	6,874	≤.001
worse (%)	F	26.2	25.5	28.7	28.9	34.4	42.1	3,404	≤.001
Regular cough with phlegm	M	6.7	7.3	6.9	9.2	11.0	10.9	6,850	≤.001
in winter (%)	F	4.2	6.1	10.3	6.4	6.5	8.6	3,364	≤.10
Long-standing illness (%)	M	29.9	30.4	30.1	31.6	31.8	36.4	5,157	≤.01
	F	30.2	35.8	26.7	33.7	31.6	30.5	2,485	>.10
Any health problems last	M	69.0	68.0	67.3	67.7	66.5	70.7	5,148	>.10
year (%)	F	69.8	70.6	73.5	72.3	75.3	75.6	2,463	≤.05
Drug therapy for	M	2.1	2.1	2.1	2.7	4.8	5.2	6,673	≤.001
hypertension (%)	F	3.7	4.4	4.1	2.9	3.5	4.3	3,338	>.10
Premenstrual "bloating" (%)	F	2.2	8.6	9.6	10.9	16.8	19.6	1,939	≤.001

Note. Grade 1—Unified Grades 1–6, Grade 2—Unified Grade 7, Grade 3—Senior Executive Officer, Grade 4—Higher Executive Officer, Grade 5—Executive Officer, Grade 6—Clerical Officer/Office Support. Professional equivalents for Grades 3–5.

3.5 shows prevalence rates for ECG abnormalities, angina pectoris, chronic bronchitis, and smoking in these two cohorts of civil servants separated by 20 years. In the first Whitehall study, limb leads only were used for ECGs, hence a lower prevalence of ischemia would be expected compared with the full 12-lead ECGs used in Whitehall II (14). There is no suggestion of a diminution in the grade difference in prevalence of ischemia over the 20 years separating Whitehall and Whitehall II (14). The relative difference between clerical officers and administrators appears to be greater. For angina pectoris, the questionnaire is identical in the two studies: The difference between grades has changed little in the 20 years.

For chronic bronchitis (i.e., cough with phlegm production), the prevalence rate for men ages 40–54 is considerably lower in Whitehall II than in the first Whitehall study, but the relative difference between the grades is similar. Both the grade difference in chronic bronchitis and the diminution in prevalence rates between the 1960s and the 1980s are likely to be related to smoking. Figure 3.5 also shows that smoking prevalence among civil servants has decreased, but the striking inverse association with grade of employment persists.

POVERTY OR INEQUALITY

Much of the discussion about social inequalities in health has related to the health disadvantage of those at the bottom (15). This is analogous to seeing social problems as a particular problem for a disadvantaged minority. There is little doubt that poverty, or deprivation, is likely to be bad—for health, among other things. The Whitehall data on mortality (Fig. 3.4) and the Whitehall II data on morbidity (Table 3.1) suggest that something other than absolute poverty is at work here. Each grade has worse health and higher mortality rates than the grade above it. Executive-grade civil servants are not poor by any absolute standard, yet they have higher mortality rates than administrators. Even clerical officers who are far from well off, with earnings at or below the national average, are not poor by comparison with England at an earlier period in history, or with developing countries.

The question is not why people at the bottom have worse health, but why social differentials in health are spread across the whole of society. Whether it is relative deprivation or relative lack of access to the fruits of a wealthy society, it is clear that explanations for socioeconomic differentials in Britain in the 1990s must be broader than the notion of *poverty* advanced earlier in the century (15).

POTENTIAL EXPLANATIONS OF SOCIAL INEQUALITIES IN CHD

The remarkable findings on social inequalities is that it applies to most of the major causes of morbidity and mortality. In the Whitehall study, the higher risk of death among lower grades applied to deaths from CHD, cerebrovascular disease, other cardiovascular disease (CVD), lung cancer, other cancers, chronic bronchitis, other respiratory disease, gastrointestinal disease, genitourinary disease, accidents, and violence (16). Potential explanations for the gradient in CHD need to be sought alongside explanations for the gradient in morbidity, and all cause mortality.

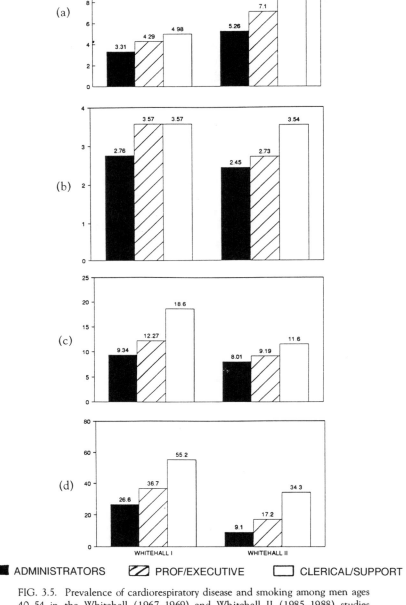

FIG. 3.5. Prevalence of cardiorespiratory disease and smoking among men ages 40–54 in the Whitehall (1967–1969) and Whitehall II (1985–1988) studies (age-adjusted percentages). (a) probable and possible ECG ischemia %, (b) angina pectoris %, (c) chronic bronchitis %, and (d) current cigarette smokers %.

Medical Care

One explanation for social inequalities in health might be inequity in the distribution of medical care. Indeed, the establishment of the Black Committee in the United Kingdom was in response to the apparent failure of social inequalities in health to have disappeared 30 years after the establishment of the National Health Service. Congruent with McKeown's (17) conclusions on the limited role of medical care in contributing to improvements in life expectancy, the Black Committee did not attribute inequalities in health to inequity in the distribution of medical care.

Analogous to the limited role of differences in medical care in generating social inequalities in health is its limited role in generating international differences. When comparing Japan to England and Wales, for example, we noted that Japan, like the United Kingdom, spends a relatively small proportion of GNP on medical care. The decline in mortality in Japan was observed both for amenable and nonamenable causes of death (12). Access to high-quality medical care is a right that should be enjoyed equally by all members of society. It is hard to make the case that it is differential access to or provision of medical care that is responsible for inequalities in health in European countries.

Health Selection

The argument here, in essence, is that health may determine social position rather than vice versa. This was one of the possible explanations considered by the Black Committee report and rejected as a major cause of social inequalities in health (18). There are several periods during the life course when selection could operate, and also several potential mechanisms with a varying degree of plausibility and evidence supporting these interpretations (19).

The most straightforward suggestion is that the sick drift down the social hierarchy, producing social groups at the bottom that contain a disproportionate number of individuals at high mortality risk. Three pieces of evidence bear on whether such intragenerational selection is an important contributor to mortality differentials. First, in the Office of Population Censuses and Surveys (OPCS) longitudinal study (LS), a follow-up of 1% of the population from the 1971 census, social class mortality differentials after 1981 for subjects who were in the same social class groups in 1971 and 1981—and could therefore not have experienced health-related social mobility—were identical to those for the whole population (20). Second, in the same study, mortality differentials between social classes persisted beyond age 75, long after retirement (21). Here, social class is based on last occupation. By definition, health after retirement cannot cause downward social drift because the classification is fixed. Third, in participants free of manifest disease at entry to the Whitehall study, mortality differentials by employment grade are essentially the same as in the whole study population. Because no reclassification of social position after study entry is made, mobility caused by differences in health status, at least as measured, cannot account for the mortality gradient (13).

Recently, there has been much interest in the possibility that selection occurring at an earlier age—between early childhood and labor market entry—is an important determinant of health inequalities (22, 23). This could occur in two ways: if health status in childhood determines both health and social class in early adulthood, or if a common antecedent determines both adult health status and future adult social class. The second way is considered in the next section. There is evidence that ill health in childhood is associated with downward social mobility (24), but the effect is minor. Other studies that can relate health in childhood to health in early adulthood similarly suggest that this cannot account for class differences in health in adulthood (25, 26).

Factors Operating Early in Life

A different version of the selection hypothesis suggests that, although social selection based on health status is not a crucial contributor to health differentials, common background factors determine both social position and health in adulthood. This process has been termed *indirect selection* (27). It recognizes that people bring with them into adulthood the results of influences from their earlier days: genetic factors; biological results of early experiences; and educational, cultural, psychological, and social factors. Because it has been argued that the major influences on health in adulthood operate early in life (28), it is possible that both social position and health in adulthood are determined by common early life influences. The focus on childhood origins of adult disease has been criticized precisely because influences from early life shape the lives people lead and the social environments in which they live and work (29). It may be these conditions of adult life that are related to ill health, and the importance of childhood conditions may therefore be indirect. It is clearly not easy to separate the direct effects of early and later life experiences on health.

One indicator that may help is height. In his studies in Aberdeen, Illsley (30) showed that women who were upwardly mobile—their husbands' social class was higher than their fathers'—were taller than women who married within their class. More recent work, analyzing data from the 1958 birth cohort in the United Kingdom, confirmed that social mobility between birth and age 23 was selective with respect to height, but mobility did not account for the social gradients in height (25, 31).

Whitehall data relating height to mortality provide some insight into the possible separate effects of current and past environments. Height is influenced by environment as well as genes. As Table 3.2 shows, height is related to social status as measured by employment grade. Short height predicts adult mortality independent of grade of employment (16), and it is reasonable to speculate that this may in part be a reflection of a persisting influence from early life. Grade of employment, which is to some extent an index of current social influences,

TABLE 3.2

Physiological Measurements, Health Behaviors, and Family History
by Grade of Employment (Age-Adjusted Figures)

Variable	Sex	Employment Grade						Total Sample	p
		1	2	3	4	5	6		
Physiological Measurements									
Mean cholesterol	M	6.05	5.97	5.93	6.02	6.00	6.00	6,865	>.10
	F	5.79	5.85	5.80	5.80	5.90	5.86	3,375	>.10
Mean systolic blood pressure	M	124.3	124.6	123.9	124.8	125.4	125.4	6,886	≤.01
	F	117.6	120.5	120.6	119.2	119.7	119.5	3,413	>.10
Mean diastolic blood	M	77.6	77.5	77.6	77.9	78.8	79.1	6,886	≤.001
pressure	F	74.0	75.2	75.3	74.3	74.8	74.9	3,412	>.10
Mean body mass index	M	24.6	24.4	24.6	24.5	24.8	25.1	6,888	≤.001
	F	23.7	23.7	24.3	24.1	24.5	25.3	3,412	≤.001
Obese (%)	M	4.1	3.7	4.6	5.1	6.0	10.7	6,888	≤.001
	F	7.4	4.6	7.9	7.8	10.3	13.2	3,412	≤.001
Mean height	M	177.8	177.1	176.9	176.3	174.3	172.9	6,890	≤.001
	F	165.5	165.1	165.3	163.1	162.8	160.7	3,413	≤.001
Health Behaviors									
Current smokers (%)	M	8.3	10.2	13.0	18.4	21.9	33.6	6,892	≤.001
	F	18.3	11.6	15.2	20.3	22.7	27.5	3,408	≤.001
Mean units of alcohol in	M	14.6	12.6	12.9	12.9	11.6	10.1	6,845	≤.001
last 7 days	F	12.1	9.8	9.3	7.0	5.2	3.6	3,375	≤.001
No moderate or vigorous	M	5.1	5.4	4.9	7.5	16.2	30.5	6,662	≤.001
exercise (%)	F	12.0	14.7	10.8	13.2	19.7	31.1	3,221	≤.001
Usually use skimmed or	M	44.2	39.3	35.1	31.8	27.8	21.2	6,869	≤.001
semiskimmed milk (%)	F	39.5	48.3	49.8	46.2	40.5	34.4	3,389	≤.001
Mainly wholemeal bread	M	47.7	45.2	43.6	37.2	37.5	32.2	6,867	≤.001
(%)	F	57.2	52.9	58.2	55.4	43.8	35.5	3,380	≤.001
Eat fresh fruit or vegetables	M	34.0	39.6	40.6	47.9	52.5	61.7	6,881	≤.001
less than daily (%)	F	17.7	20.4	28.4	29.7	36.4	43.6	3,400	≤.001
Family History									
Parent had heart attack (%)	M	26.1	28.1	26.1	26.1	24.0	22.5	6,649	≤.01
	F	39.2	36.4	24.7	29.8	22.6	24.5	3,234	≤.001
Sibling had heart attack (%)	M	2.0	2.3	2.7	3.2	4.4	3.8	5,496	≤.01
	F	0.8	1.7	1.0	4.3	4.8	6.4	2,804	≤.001

Note. Grade 1—Unified Grades 1–6, Grade 2—Unified Grade 7, Grade 3—Senior Executive Officer, Grade 4—Higher Executive Officer, Grade 5—Executive Officer, Grade 6—Clerical Officer/Office Support. Professional equivalents for Grades 3–5.

predicts mortality independent of height. Thus, two sets of influences may affect mortality risk: factors from early life and current influences. As indicated, this is to oversimplify: People's current social situations are influenced by their prior experiences. Nevertheless, it is important to distinguish these two sets of influences because their relative importance is crucial to determining the appropriate locus for interventions, which may both improve overall adult health and reduce the socioeconomic differentials. Current research may reduce the degree to which views are polarized—between those who think future health status is virtually programmed in early life (32), and those who support the current mainstream focus on influences acting in later life (33).

General Susceptibility or Specific Causes?

The striking gradient for all causes of death found in Whitehall (Fig. 3.4), suggesting that there may be common factors operating that cut across known causes of disease, has prompted the speculation that there may be factors that increase general susceptibility to ill health (34, 35).

An alternative to a general susceptibility hypothesis is that a variety of specific factors are operating to explain social class differences in mortality. Support for this view comes from the fact that some cancers—notably those of the colon, brain, prostate, hematopoietic system, breast, and melanoma—do not show the same social class variation as the causes listed earlier (36).

When posed with two conflicting alternatives such as these, a reasonable working hypothesis is that they are both correct. A general susceptibility hypothesis implies that certain groups will be at higher risk of death, whatever causes are operating. It does not deny the operation of specific causes. Diseases linked to smoking—such as chronic bronchitis and lung cancer—show a particularly strong social class gradient—stronger than cancers not linked to smoking. But the latter do show a social class gradient, as do other diseases not linked to smoking. Put another way, the general susceptibility hypothesis means that there are factors operating that cut across our current system of classifying diseases. These will increase risk of death, in addition to the effect of known factors such as smoking. This can account for the fact that an administrator who smokes 20 cigarettes a day has a lower risk of lung cancer mortality than a lower grade civil servant smoking the same amount (16), even after pack years and tar content of cigarettes are taken into account, and for the gradient in mortality that occurs for CHD even among nonsmokers (37).

The production of this apparently increased susceptibility may well be operating at a social level. The whole life course of people in different social locations is different, and insults to health may accumulate over the entire period from birth to death. It is undeniable that these influences on health cluster in such a way as to produce social groups at differing degrees of disadvantage with respect to most diseases. However, our current level of knowledge regarding this general susceptibility allows us to go little beyond this empirical observation.

Health-Related Behaviors and Biological Risk Factors

The possible role of health behaviors and other established biological risk factors in generating social inequalities in health can be illustrated from the Whitehall II study in Table 3.2, which presents differences by grade of employment (14).

Plasma cholesterol levels do not differ by grade, and the small inverse association between grade and blood pressure level in men observed in the Whitehall study is still present, but now even smaller. There is a significant inverse trend of mean body mass index (BMI; weight/height^2) by grade, but, especially in men, the differences are small. The distribution is different, however. The prevalence of obesity (BMI > 30) is greater in lower grades, and strikingly so in the clerical grade. As in Whitehall, the higher the grade, the taller the man and woman.

The most striking risk-factor difference among grades is in smoking (see Fig. 3.5). Women have higher prevalence of smoking than men in all but the lowest (clerical and office support) grade. The proportion of men and women not taking moderate or vigorous exercise in their leisure time is higher in lower grades. As a rough indicator of dietary pattern, consumption of skimmed and semiskimmed milk, wholemeal bread, and fresh fruit and vegetables is higher in higher grades. Average alcohol consumption is reported to be higher among the higher grades of men and, more strikingly, women. Reports of parents having had a heart attack are more frequent in higher grades; a positive family history among siblings is more common in lower grades. This is in keeping with data suggesting a possible social class crossover in CHD risk (38).

Thus, there is a range of candidates to account for grade differences in mortality. Only some of these were measured in the first Whitehall study. As implied previously, the grade differences in smoking are insufficient to account for differences by grade in mortality from smoking-related diseases (16). There are only small differences in blood pressure between grades, and plasma cholesterol levels are higher in higher grades. Therefore, the main coronary risk factors could account for little of the gradient in mortality by grade of employment. It is possible that some of the other factors listed in Table 3.2 may provide part of the explanation.

Material Conditions

The Black Committee Report (18) emphasized the importance of material conditions as an explanation for social inequalities in health. In fact, Black referred to materialist or structural explanations, emphasizing hazards to which some people have no choice but to be exposed given the present distribution of income and opportunity. These can be interpreted as broader than simply material conditions, and include psychosocial influences that are inherent in position in society.

In the working population that makes up the Whitehall cohort, grade is a guide to material conditions because it is a proxy for salary, which in turn relates to circumstances outside work. It is not surprising, then, that the lower the grade in Whitehall II, the greater the frequency of reported financial problems (see Table 3.3). As shown in the OPCS LS, independent of social class based on occupation, other measures predicted mortality: among them, housing tenure

TABLE 3.3
Psychosocial Characteristics by Grade of Employment (Age-Adjusted Figures)

Variables	Sex	Employment Grade						Total Sample	p
		1	2	3	4	5	6		
Work Characteristics (upper tertile of distribution)									
High control (%)	M	59.3	49.7	43.1	31.6	24.7	11.8	6,877	≤.001
	F	51.2	45.4	47.1	31.2	20.1	10.2	3,341	≤.001
Varied work (%)	M	70.5	52.1	41.9	27.1	18.2	3.9	6,875	≤.001
	F	71.2	55.2	40.5	31.7	14.0	4.7	3,356	≤.001
Fast pace (%)	M	58.0	43.6	34.7	27.9	20.8	15.8	6,878	≤.001
	F	60.9	50.3	43.7	31.1	29.7	18.0	3,356	≤.001
High satisfaction (%)	M	58.2	38.7	34.1	29.5	29.4	29.8	6,865	≤.001
	F	57.5	42.2	40.3	36.6	41.6	47.7	3,337	>.10
Social Network/Activities									
See at least three relatives	M	22.1	24.8	29.0	27.2	29.7	30.6	6,426	≤.001
per month (%)	F	18.9	23.7	21.1	24.1	30.4	44.9	3,187	≤.001
See at least three friends	M	65.3	61.3	58.5	58.6	56.4	50.2	5,162	≤.001
per month (%)	F	71.1	62.8	67.1	63.6	52.9	49.0	2,473	≤.001
No hobbies (%)	M	12.4	12.9	12.7	15.0	23.0	25.4	6,453	≤.001
	F	12.5	15.4	11.3	11.9	18.3	27.5	3,044	≤.001
Social Support from Closest Person (upper tertile of distribution)									
Confiding/emotional	M	31.3	33.7	28.3	28.3	34.6	26.1	5,021	≤.10
support (%)	F	37.3	33.8	33.0	32.5	32.9	31.8	2,380	>.10
Practical support (%)	M	41.1	40.0	37.2	33.0	36.4	29.1	5,022	≤.001
	F	21.8	25.9	26.8	17.1	24.0	28.0	2,384	≤.10
Negative aspects of	M	25.0	28.4	31.3	30.9	38.1	39.0	5,010	≤.001
support (%)	F	33.0	32.5	28.3	36.4	28.3	33.8	2,379	>.10
Events and Difficulties									
Two or more major life	M	29.6	31.6	35.1	37.9	39.9	41.9	6,758	≤.001
events (%)	F	41.1	43.6	35.5	42.8	46.5	49.2	3,247	≤.001
Sometimes not enough	M	7.0	12.6	21.5	26.4	34.4	37.2	4,977	≤.001
money (%)	F	7.7	6.9	9.6	13.2	24.4	34.4	2,282	≤.001
Some difficulty paying	M	11.0	16.2	22.8	24.7	29.6	29.6	5,167	≤.001
bills (%)	F	15.2	13.2	11.8	15.7	18.1	26.9	2,490	≤.001
Other									
Type A (defined as upper	M	51.3	40.2	36.9	27.8	20.4	12.8	6,729	≤.001
tertile) (%)	F	62.6	54.6	44.0	39.0	29.0	17.6	3,228	≤.001
Hostility score	M	9.7	10.2	10.9	11.3	12.7	14.7	4,266	≤.001
	F	9.5	9.5	9.4	10.1	10.4	12.3	1,772	≤.001
Believe one can reduce	M	71.6	72.2	70.8	66.8	65.5	52.4	5,136	≤.001
risk of heart attack (%)	F	58.1	61.6	69.7	68.4	65.0	53.7	2,487	≤.001

Note. Grade 1—Unified Grades 1–6, Grade 2—Unified Grade 7, Grade 3—Senior Executive Officer, Grade 4—Higher Executive Officer, Grade 5—Executive Officer, Grade 6—Clerical Officer/Office Support. Professional equivalents for Grades 3–5.

(ownership) and household access to cars (39). These are clearly a guide to material conditions. In the Whitehall study, car ownership predicted mortality independent of grade of employment (40). In addition, men who reported engaging in gardening had lower mortality than nongardening men. The link between gardening and lower mortality is open to a variety of interpretations. Among them is that possessing a house with a garden is a measure of wealth. These data are consistent with the link between deprivation and mortality demonstrated in our geographic-based studies outlined later.

Area-Based Measures of Material Circumstances

A quite different approach to measuring inequalities in health is to classify areas rather than individuals. This has been used to some extent as a proxy for individual-based measures, where these may not be available. The use of these measures has also been justified on theoretical grounds. Townsend, one of the authors of the Black report, developed census-based measures of social deprivation to examine the effect of material circumstances on mortality (41). His index of deprivation was composed of the proportion of households that had access to cars, the percent unemployed, the percent of owner occupiers, and crowding. In the northern region of England, this measure was strongly related to mortality— the greater the deprivation, the greater the mortality (41). A similar measure of deprivation in Scotland was strongly related to area differences in mortality (42).

We applied the Townsend measure of *deprivation* to census tracts (population approximately 7,000) throughout England (43), and related the deprivation scores to CHD, and all cause mortality. Figure 3.6 illustrates the continuous relationship between deprivation and mortality—the more deprived wards have higher mortality for CHD, and all cause mortality. There are alternative ways to interpret this finding of a gradient in the relationship of deprivation to mortality. One is that *deprivation* is a misleading term. As with data on occupation-based social class, we are not dealing with the effects of poverty, but relative position—a gradient in mortality. Most people living in wards that are classified in the second or third quintiles (see Fig. 3.6) are not deprived, yet their mortality rate is higher than that of people in the least deprived quintile. This interpretation suggests relative deprivation, rather than absolute material disadvantage.

An alternative interpretation would be a dichotomy between deprived and nondeprived—above the threshold of deprivation mortality is raised compared with below. This would suggest that each successive quintile contains a greater proportion of deprived households, hence the appearance of a gradient in mortality. It is not easy to distinguish between these two alternatives from ecological-based studies. The studies based on classification of individuals, reviewed earlier, strongly suggest that the relationship between social position and mortality is graded and not a threshold effect.

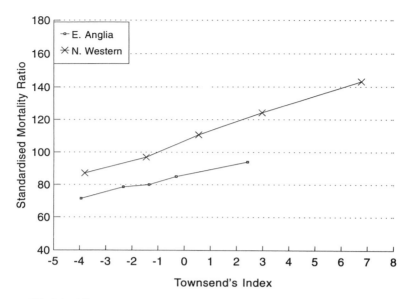

FIG. 3.6. All cause mortality in two regions of England: NorthWestern and East
Anglia. Mean male mortality by quintiles of Townsend index of deprivation. A
high score means greater deprivation.

A second observation from Fig. 3.6 relates to regional differences in mortality
within England. The NorthWestern region has higher mortality than East Anglia
and a greater spread of deprivation yet at comparable levels of deprivation the
regional difference in mortality persists. In addition, the slope of the relationship
between deprivation and mortality appears to differ between regions. This suggests that the meaning of the deprivation index differs depending on the context,
or that there is some other factor(s) that modifies the effect of deprivation on
mortality within region, and contributes to regional differences in mortality
independent of deprivation.

These area-based studies are important because they provide a guide to the
SES of individual residents. In addition, the Human Population Laboratory from
Alameda County, California, showed that people living in poverty areas experienced a higher mortality rate than people living in nonpoverty areas, independent of a wide range of personal characteristics including income and health
behaviors (44).

The difficulty in understanding material explanations is to know how they
operate. At a time when poor living conditions meant polluted water, crowded
unsanitary housing with high rates of cross-infection, and appalling employment
conditions, it was not difficult to see how these could be responsible for worse
health among the socially deprived. This would be additional to the effects of
inadequate diet, which is part of the material conditions of life. As conditions

improved, mortality of all social groups improved. But why do the social gradients persist? Are we to understand that there are residual effects of bad housing with damp and infection, as well as air pollution and other material conditions that, although they affect the lower social groups less than they used to, still affect them more than the higher social strata? If there are such residual effects, it is no surprise that they do not affect all social strata equally. Can this be the whole explanation?

The Whitehall data and Wilkinson's data on income inequalities are relevant here. In the Whitehall and Whitehall II studies, morbidity and mortality varied linearly with grade of employment. It is possible that the worse health of the second highest grade compared with the highest could be the result of worse housing, poorer diet for children, or greater pollution, but it seems unlikely that comfortable, middle-class people in Britain are suffering from the effects of material deprivation. Similarly, comparing rich countries, Wilkinson (45) showed that it was not differences in wealth that predicted differences in life expectancy, but differences in inequality of income distribution.

One is drawn to the view that, in addition to the multiple influences already discussed, there must be an influence of relative position in society. What may be important is not absolute deprivation, but relative deprivation. This would account for a social gradient in ill health because each group, while not necessarily suffering from greater effects of bad housing, and so on, will have less than the group above it. This would account for the widespread finding of social inequalities in health in societies with different levels of health. The social gradient in ill health will vary in magnitude depending on the magnitude of the relative differences in deprivation. In a society that has met the subsistence needs of its members, what do we mean by *less* or *relative deprivation*? In addition to the factors explored previously, we should look to psychosocial factors for part of the answer.

Psychosocial Factors as Potential Explanations

The potential importance of psychosocial factors in explaining social gradients in health may be illustrated from the Whitehall II study. Table 3.3 shows differences in psychosocial characteristics, by grade of employment. Fewer of the lower grades report control over their working lives, having varied work, or having to work at a fast pace. Overall, fewer of the lower grades are satisfied with their work situation.

Social relations can be expressed quantitatively as extent of social networks, and qualitatively as the nature of social supports. More of the lower grades report visiting relatives once a month or more; more of the higher grades visit friends. Fewer of the lower grades are involved in hobbies. Among men, fewer of the lower grades have a confidant in whom they can entrust their problems, fewer receive practical support, and more report negative reactions from persons close to them. Patterns were less clear in women.

The lower grades were more likely to report two or more from a list of eight major potentially stressful life events in the previous year, as well as difficulties paying bills or with money in general. Despite their lower rate of heart disease, more of the higher grade participants have the Type A behavior pattern. It has been suggested that the major component of Type A behavior responsible for the link to CHD risk is hostility. The lower grades have higher scores on the Cook–Medley Hostility scale. As one measure of perceived control over their health, fewer of the lower grades reported believing it was possible to reduce the risk of heart attack.

These findings offer a wealth of potential explanations for social inequalities in health that tie in with other evidence on psychosocial factors and health. Three major hypotheses are: job strain, low social supports, and low control. There is a large body of evidence linking high psychological demands at work and low control to CVD and other diseases (46). The relative disadvantage of lower grades with respect to control could be a factor in the higher rates of disease (47). Similarly, the evidence on low social support and ill health suggests a further contributor to the gradient in ill health (48, 49). Syme (50) suggested that increasing lack of control may be a linking factor that accounts for increasing health disadvantage as the social scale is descended. Whatever else it represents, poverty is lack of control.

This may relate to the international differences in health. Why have the life expectancies of Central and Eastern Europe fallen behind those of the West? It cannot only be a matter of capitalism versus communism. In the early postwar years, life expectancy was not greatly different between the two Central European countries of Austria and Czechoslovakia: One was capitalist, and the other was communist. Later, Czechoslovakia fell behind, as did Hungary and the other countries of Eastern Europe. We have argued that this was in some way related to the relative failure of their economies, compared with the success of Western Europe. How might this operate? Perhaps it does so in all the ways discussed earlier, including psychosocial factors. An economy that fails to deliver an improved standard of living in line with people's expectations may lead to widespread feelings of lack of control. Once the basic material conditions of subsistence are met, the expectation of what is necessary for a reasonable standard of living changes. Difficulty in achieving this for large proportions of the population may lead to widespread feelings of lack of control. This may translate into adverse health behaviors such as smoking and obesity, and it may affect health by more direct stress pathways.

AN EXPLANATION FOR SOCIAL INEQUALITIES IN CHD?

Research on inequalities in health ultimately should determine if these inequalities can be changed. One approach to this problem is political. If social inequalities are reduced, inequalities in health will be reduced. This may or may not follow. What is required is a better understanding of the links between social position and health.

We have argued that a combination of the factors reviewed may account for inequalities in health, both within and between countries. The situation is complex, but not impossibly so. Much progress has been made in sorting through potential explanations. The Whitehall studies have been used to illustrate these possible explanations. There is only a unifying explanation to the extent that social position is related to a number of factors: differences in early life experience, differences in behavior, differences in material conditions, and differences in psychosocial factors. Often investigations focus on just one of these issues, and thus fail to explore the other factors, making interpretation difficult. Although there may be multiple factors operating, one is drawn back to the observation that the social class differences apply to CHD and most causes of death. The challenge for researchers in this area is to develop the methodology for exploring the interrelationships and interactions between the influences on health occurring throughout the life course. Only then will it be possible to separate out the relative importance of the various potential explanations for socioeconomic differentials in CHD and other diseases, which is crucial for planning the strategies to counter them.

REFERENCES

1. Feachem RGA, Kjellstrom T, Murray CJL. The health of adults in the developing world. Oxford, England: Oxford University Press for the World Bank, 1992.
2. World Health Organization. Mortality statistics. World Health Statistics Annual. Geneva: World Health Organization, 1989.
3. Uemura K, Pisa Z. Trends in cardiovascular disease mortality in industrialised countries since 1950. Wld Health Statist Q 1988;41:155–78.
4. Marmot MG, McDowall ME. Mortality decline and widening social inequalities. Lancet 1986;ii:274–76.
5. Wong SL, Donnan SPB. Influence of socioeconomic status on cardiovascular diseases in Hong Kong. J Epidemiol Comm Health 1992;46:148–50.
6. Sorlie PD, Garcia-Palmieri MR. Educational status and coronary heart disease in Puerto Rico: the Puerto Rico heart health program. Int J Epidemiol 1990;19:59–65.
7. Sarvotham SG, Berry JN. Prevalence of coronary heart disease in an urban population in northern India. Circulation 1968;37:939–53.
8. Krzyzanowski M, Wysocki M. The relation of thirteen-year mortality to ventilatory impairment and other respiratory symptoms: the Cracow study. Int J Epidemiol 1986;15:56–64.
9. Feldman JJ, Makuc DM, Kleinman JC, et al. National trends in educational differentials in mortality. Am J Epidemiol 1989;129:919–33.
10. Marmot MG. Coronary heart disease: rise and fall of a modern epidemic. In: Marmot MG, Elliott P, editors. Coronary heart disease epidemiology. Oxford: Oxford University Press, 1992:3–19.
11. The principle investigators of the MONICA project. WHO MONICA Project: geographic variation in mortality from cardiovascular diseases. Wld Health Statist Q 1987;40:171–84.
12. Marmot MG, Davey Smith G. Why are the Japanese living longer? Br Med J 1989;299:1547–51.
13. Marmot MG, Rose G, Shipley M, et al. Employment grade and coronary heart disease in British civil servants. J Epidemiol and Comm Health 1978;32:244–49.

14. Marmot MG, Davey Smith G, Stansfeld S, et al. Health inequalities among British civil servants: the Whitehall II study. Lancet 1991;337:1387–93.

15. M'Gonigle GCM, Kirby J. Poverty and public health. London: Golantz, 1937.

16. Marmot MG, Shipley MG, Rose G. Inequalities in death—specific explanations of a general pattern? Lancet 1984;1:1003–06.

17. McKeown T. The role of medicine: dream, mirage or nemesis. Oxford: Basil Blackwell, 1979.

18. Black D, Morris JN, Smith C, et al. Inequalities in health: the Black report; the health divide. London: Penguin Group, 1988.

19. Blane D, Davey Smith G, Bartley M. Social selection: what does it contribute to social class differences in health? Sociol Health Illness 1993;15:1–15.

20. Goldblatt P. Mortality by social class. Population Trends 1989;56:6–15.

21. Fox AJ, Goldblatt PO, Jones DR. Social class mortality differentials: artefact, selection or life circumstances? J Epidemiol and Comm Health 1985;39:1–8.

22. Illsley R. Occupational class, selection and the production of inequalities in health. Q J Soc Affairs 1986;2:151–65.

23. West P. Rethinking the health selection explanation for health inequalities. Soc Sci Med 1991;32:373–84.

24. Wadsworth MEJ. Serious illness in childhood and its association with later-life achievement. In: Wilkinson RG, editor. Class and health. London: Tavistock Publications, 1986:50–74.

25. Power C, Manor O, Fox AJ, et al. Health in childhood and social inequalities in health in young adults. J R Statist Soc 1990;A153:17–28.

26. Lundberg O. Childhood living conditions, health status and social mobility: a contribution to the health selection debate. Eur Sociol Rev 1991;7:149–62.

27. Wilkinson RG. Socio-economic differences in mortality: interpreting the data on their size and trends. In: Wilkinson RG, editor. Class and health. London: Tavistock Publications, 1986:1–20.

28. Barker DJP. The intrauterine and early postnatal origins of cardiovascular disease and chronic bronchitis. J Epidemiol Comm Health 1989;43:237–40.

29. Ben-Shlomo Y, Davey Smith G. Deprivation in infancy or adult life: which is more important for mortality risk? Lancet 1991;337:530–43.

30. Illsley R. Social class selection and class differences in relation to still-births and infant deaths. Br Med J 1955;2:1520–24.

31. Power C, Manor O, Fox J. Health and class: the early years. London: Chapman & Hall, 1991.

32. Barker DJ. The fetal and infant origins of adult disease. Br Med J 1990;301:1111.

33. Elford J, Whincup P, Shaper AG. Early life experience and adult cardiovascular disease: longitudinal and case-control studies. Int J Epidemiol 1991;20:833–44.

34. Berkman LF, Syme SL. Social networks, host resistance and mortality: a nine-year follow-up of Alameda County residents. Am J Epidemiol 1979;109:186–204.

35. Cassel JC. The contribution of the social environment to host resistance. Am J Epidemiol 1976;104:107–23.

36. Davey Smith G, Leon D, Shipley MJ, et al. Socioeconomic differentials in cancer among men. Int J Epidemiol 1991;20:339–45.

37. Davey Smith G, Shipley MJ. Confounding of occupation and smoking: its magnitude and consequences. Soc Sci Med 1991;32:1297–1300.

38. Marmot MG, Adelstein MM, Robinson N, et al. Changing social class distribution of heart disease. Br Med J 1978;2:1109–12.

39. Goldblatt P. Mortality and alternative social classifications. In: Goldblatt P, editor. 1971–1981 longitudinal study. Mortality and social organisation. London: Her Majesty's Stationery Office, 1990:163–92.

40. Davey Smith G, Shipley MJ, Rose G. Magnitude and causes of socioeconomic differentials in mortality: further evidence from the Whitehall study. J Epidemiol Comm Health 1990;44:265–70.

41. Townsend P, Phillimore P, Beattie A. Health and deprivation: inequality in the North. London: Crom Helm, 1988.
42. Carstairs V, Morris R. Deprivation and health in Scotland. Aberdeen: Aberdeen University Press, 1991.
43. Eames M, Ben Shlomo Y, Marmot MG. Social deprivation and premature mortality: regional comparison across England. Brit Med J 1993;307:1097–1102.
44. Haan M, Kaplan GA, Camacho T. Poverty and health: prospective evidence from the Alameda County study. Am J Epidemiol 1987;125:989–98.
45. Wilkinson RG. Income distribution and life expectancy. Brit Med J 1992;304:165–68.
46. Karasek R, Theorell T. Healthy work: stress, productivity, and the reconstruction of working life. New York: Basic Books, 1990.
47. Marmot MG, Theorell T. Social class and cardiovascular disease: the contribution of work. Int J Health Serv 1988;18:659–74.
48. Berkman LF. Assessing the physical health effects of social networks and social support. In: Breslow L, Fielding JE, Lave LB, editors. Annual review of public health. 5th ed. Palo Alto, CA: Annual Reviews, Inc., 1984:413–32.
49. House JS, Landis KR, Umberson D. Social relationships and health. Science 1988;241:540–45.
50. Syme SL. Control and health: a personal perspective. In: Steptoe A, Appels A, editors. Stress, personal control and health. New York: Wiley, 1989:3–18.

Chapter 4

Social Class and Cardiovascular Disease

S. Leonard Syme
University of California–Berkeley

We are at a crisis stage in the study of psychosocial factors and cardiovascular disease (CVD). Over the last 40 years, researchers in this field have generated a large and impressive body of data on many psychosocial risk factors. Unfortunately, the field operates in a theoretical vacuum. No agreed-on conceptual model or theory exists in epidemiology to guide either our research or the interpretation of findings that have been generated. As a result, the field of psychosocial epidemiology consists of a series of seemingly unrelated findings on a variety of seemingly unrelated topics.

One explanation for this problem is that we have never agreed on the central focus of our work in this field. Is the purpose of our research to explain why some groups have higher rates of disease than other groups? Or is it to explain why one person gets sick while another does not? Or is it to explain why one person gets sick with one disease while another succumbs to another disease? Each of these questions is important, but the research to answer them all involves different training, research instruments, technology, and language. Anyone who has attended an interdisciplinary meeting knows how difficult it is to communicate with people who are asking fundamentally different questions and who do not explicitly recognize this difference. These interdisciplinary meetings tend to become multidisciplinary meetings. We *seem* to be talking about the same things, but we are not. In nursery school children, we call this *parallel play*. Like nursery school children, we often meet in the same room and talk about the same topics, but, essentially, we each do our own thing. My task in this chapter is to discuss findings regarding social class. I do this in a way that is amenable to interdisciplinary collaboration. This may seem odd because social class is a sociodemographic concept that describes group phenomena, but I hope to show that it allows us to work at several conceptual and disciplinary levels.

The first thing to say about *social class* is that, no matter how it is defined, it is an important risk factor for coronary heart disease (CHD). Whether one defines *social class* in terms of income, education, occupation, or residence, or some combination of these, there almost always and everywhere exists a strong relationship between it and CHD (1–6). Earlier in this century, those higher in social class had high rates of CHD. Since midcentury, this relationship has reversed. Today, virtually every study in the industrial world shows a strong inverse relationship between social class and CHD, regardless of how these categories are defined or studied. The question is to explain this phenomenon so that interventions can be implemented.

Although social class is a well-recognized and important risk factor for disease, we know little of the reasons or its importance. There are at least two explanations for this. One is that social class is so powerful a risk factor we almost always statistically control for its influence in research so that we can study other factors of interest. If we did not do this, the effect of social class would overwhelm everything else under study. Consequently, social class rarely is studied as a phenomenon in its own right.

The second explanation is more subtle: We tend to study risk factors that we think we can do something about, and social class seems not readily amenable to intervention. But, of course, it is turning out to be difficult to get people to change their diet, stop smoking, or change their behavior in other ways (7).

This difficulty is dramatically illustrated by behavior changes observed in the Multiple Risk Factor Intervention Trial (MRFIT) (8). This trial was the most ambitious effort ever organized to test the hypothesis that mortality rates from CHD could be reduced if people changed their behavior. After 7 years of follow-up, disappointingly few people had made and maintained recommended changes. These findings are of particular importance because this trial contained all the elements one would desire in an intervention program; for this reason, one would have anticipated better results than were achieved. Three special features of the trial are of special importance. First, the 6,428 men randomized to the special intervention (SI) group had been carefully and clearly informed that they were in the top 15% of risk for CHD. They also knew that their risk was due to high serum cholesterol levels, high blood pressure, and/or cigarette smoking. Indeed, before being selected for the trial, each man agreed to change his eating and smoking behavior, and to take antihypertensive medications if necessary. Thus, all of the men in the trial knew of their special risk, and had volunteered to change behavior to lower this risk. Second, an excellent intervention plan was devised to help people change their behavior. This plan was carefully developed to take account of individual circumstances, and it used a variety of approaches including group meetings, one-to-one counseling sessions, and opportunities to involve family members. Research findings from the behavioral literature were reviewed, and, wherever appropriate, successful strategies were included in the plan. Third, the staffing pattern at each of the 22 MRFIT clinics was designed to enable each participant to have close and continuing contact with well-trained professionals for the entire 7-year study period.

Despite these unique features, the behavior changes observed in MRFIT were of modest proportions. The best achievement was in the SI group—40% of smokers stopped smoking by the end of the trial. Of those SI men with hypertension, 64% achieved control. Only a 6.7% reduction was observed in serum cholesterol levels among SI participants. It should be noted that these results only refer to the men in the SI group, and not to men receiving ordinary care (the usual care [UC] group). The trial's overall objective was to see if those in the SI would have a lower CHD mortality rate than those in the UC group. The mortality results after 7 years of follow-up in MRFIT showed no statistically significant difference between the study groups; this was due, in part, to the fact that many of the men in the UC group changed their behavior on their own. Indeed, they changed to such an extent that the contrast between the two groups was much smaller than had been anticipated. Why men in the UC group dramatically changed behavior on their own is an important topic in its own right; for purposes of the present discussion, however, it is noteworthy that SI men changed much less than was hoped.

In an ordinary study, the results achieved in the SI group would have been quite acceptable. In MRFIT, however, they were disappointing because this trial included so many of the elements needed for 100% success: an informed and highly motivated group of participants, a superb intervention plan, excellent staff in sufficient numbers, and enough time to bring about behavioral change. The less-than-100% success is disappointing because these results are probably the best we can hope to achieve in one-to-one programs; it would be hard to imagine a situation better suited to complete success. Two lessons can be drawn from this experience: we can achieve some success in one-to-one efforts, but, even under the best circumstances, results cannot be perfect or even close to perfection.

Although it is difficult to help people change their behavior, we nevertheless feel it is easier to do this than to intervene on social class. However, it seems inappropriate to conclude that we cannot intervene in regard to social class without first knowing its essential ingredients. On the one hand, if the important ingredient in social class is income, interventions may indeed be difficult. On the one hand, if the important ingredient is education or a way of looking at the world, there may be things we can do. In any case, without an understanding of the components involved in social class, it seems inappropriate to decide ahead of time that interventions are impossible.

One way to study this problem is to focus on social class in some detail as a worthwhile research topic in its own right. The Marmot et al. (5) research on British civil servants provides an excellent example of the power of this type of

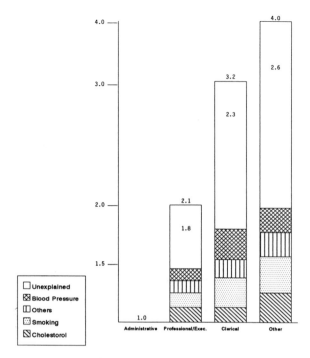

FIG. 4.1. Relative risk of CHD by civil service rank.

research. As shown in Fig. 4.1, British civil servants in the highest civil service grade (administrators) have the lowest rate of CHD, and those in the lowest grade (mainly unskilled manual workers) have rates four times as high. After CHD risk factors—such as high serum cholesterol, cigarette smoking, high blood pressure, insufficient physical activity, glucose intolerance, and lack of social support—were taken into account, the rate of those at the bottom was reduced to three times as high. However, after this adjustment, about 60% of the difference in CHD rates among civil service grades still remained unexplained. More interesting, civil servants in professional and executive jobs (Grade 2) and in clerical jobs (Grade 3) had CHD rates 2 and 3.2 times as high as administrators, respectively.

This finding poses a challenge. Although it is reasonably simple to explain why those at the bottom have higher rates than those at the top, these explanations do not account for the fact that those close to the top have higher rates of disease than those at the very top. Factors such as inadequate medical care, unemployment, low income, race, poor nutrition, poor housing, and poor education may account for higher rates of disease among those at lower social class levels, but they do not explain why professionals and executives in the British civil service have rates twice as high as administrators at the very top grade.

This gradient of disease is not unique to British civil servants (4). It has been observed in a wide variety of populations in many different countries, and it is not confined to a single disease entity or age group. The gradient has been observed for many body systems, including the digestive, genitourinary, respiratory, circulatory, nervous, blood, and endocrine systems. It has been observed also for most malignancies, congenital anomalies, infectious and parasitic diseases, accidents, poisoning, violence, perinatal mortality, diabetes, and musculoskeletal impairments (6). An example of this phenomenon is shown in Figs. 4.2 and 4.3 for morbidity associated with four chronic diseases, and for mortality in infants and adults, respectively.

It is difficult to explain why those one or two steps from the top have higher rates of disease than those at the very top, and why this gradient exists for so many diseases in so many different geographic locations. One hypothesis involves the concept of *control of destiny*. For example, it could be postulated that the lower one is in the social class hierarchy, the less control one has over the factors that affect life and living circumstance.

This hypothesis is general, and it does not specify whether control involves money, power, information, prestige, experience, or something else. Over the years, many social scientists have studied a large number of concepts related to control of destiny, and it may be of value to look for common denominators in

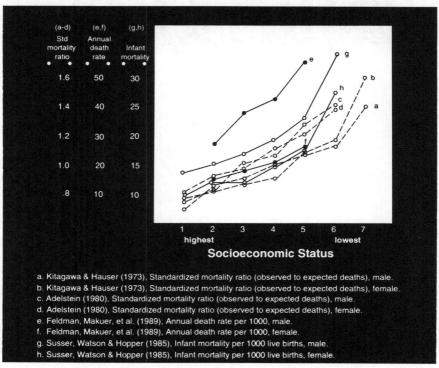

a. Kitagawa & Hauser (1973), Standardized mortality ratio (observed to expected deaths), male.
b. Kitagawa & Hauser (1973), Standardized mortality ratio (observed to expected deaths), female.
c. Adelstein (1980), Standardized mortality ratio (observed to expected deaths), male.
d. Adelstein (1980), Standardized mortality ratio (observed to expected deaths), female.
e. Feldman, Makuer, et al. (1989), Annual death rate per 1000, male.
f. Feldman, Makuer, et al. (1989), Annual death rate per 1000, female.
g. Susser, Watson & Hopper (1985), Infant mortality per 1000 live births, male.
h. Susser, Watson & Hopper (1985), Infant mortality per 1000 live births, female.

FIG. 4.2. Gradient of morbidity rates by social class.

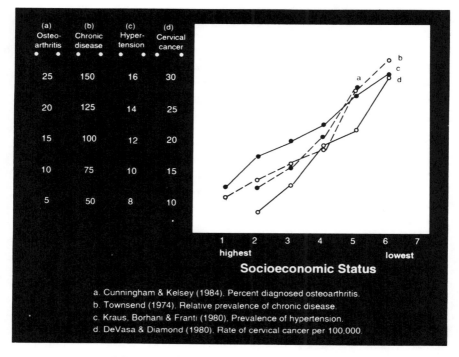

FIG. 4.3. Gradient of mortality rates by social class.

that body of work. The list of such concepts includes *mastery* (9), *self-efficacy* (10, 11), *locus of control* (12, 13), *learned helplessness* (14), *ability to control* (15, 16), *predictability* (17), *desire for control* (18), *sense of control* (19–21), *powerlessness* (22), *hardiness* (23), and *competence* (24). If these ideas, or something like them, are supported by research evidence, an avenue for intervention might become available that is more precise and understandable than simply suggesting that we intervene on social class.

Research on job stress certainly is consistent with this finding. For many years, researchers have tried unsuccessfully to demonstrate the existence of a relationship between job stress and disease. Such a link was shown only after Karasek, Theorell, and their associates added the idea of job latitude and discretion to that of job stress (25–27). These investigators showed that occupational stressors have consequences for health primarily when workers do not have sufficient latitude and discretion for coping with these stressors. When workers have little control over workplace and methods, higher rates of catecholamines are seen, as are higher rates of mental strain, CHD, and other health problems. The implications for prevention are clear when one is able to focus on such concepts as *worker discretion*, *latitude*, and *involvement*, instead of concepts such as *social class* (28).

In addition to job stress, the concept of *control of destiny* is consistent with several other concepts in psychosocial epidemiology. In our work with people undergoing coronary angiography, for example, Seeman and I (29) showed that the important components of social support involve the instrumental dimension. For example, less coronary atherosclerosis was seen among people who had friends to help them with advice, economic assistance, and transportation help. This instrumental support was more important than that of emotional support or network size. One way to interpret this finding is to say that instrumental social support helps people solve problems, influence the events that impinge on them, and control their destiny.

Following this type of reasoning, it is possible to suggest that mobility is a risk factor for CHD because it disrupts social relationships and the help they provide. Life events such as birth, death, marriage, and job loss also disrupt these relationships. Similarly, Type A behavior can be seen as a continuous, but unsuccessful, effort to control events.

There is a growing literature on physiological mechanisms that is consistent with this approach. This literature suggests that animals lower in the social order experience greater threats to well-being. They also exhibit more physiological arousals and poorer health (30–32).

Regardless of whether *control of destiny* is an appropriate concept for our work, we need some idea of this kind to help us integrate findings from research between groups, between people, and within people. We need some theoretical and conceptual integration in our field so that we can better talk with one another and begin to choose important and strategic topics for research, instead of selecting projects simply because they are interesting. Our findings also must be capable of explaining (or at least be consistent with) research observations at the social, individual, and physiological levels.

REFERENCES

1. Antonovsky A. Social class, life expectancy and overall mortality. Milbank Mem Fund Q 1967;45:31–73.
2. Syme SL, Berkman LF. Social class, susceptibility and sickness. Am J Epidemiol 1976;104:1–8.
3. Kitagawa EM, Hauser PM. Differential mortality in the United States. Cambridge, MA: Harvard University Press, 1973.
4. Haan MN, Kaplan GA, Syme SL. Socioeconomic status and health: old observations and new thoughts. In: Bunker JP, Gomby DF, Kehrer BH, editors. Pathways to health: The role of social factors. Palo Alto, CA: H.J. Kaiser Family Foundation, 1989:76–117.
5. Marmot MG, Rose G, Shipley M, et al. Employment grade and coronary heart disease in British civil servants. J Epidemiol Comm Health 1978;3:244–49.
6. Susser MW, Watson W, Hopper K. Sociology in medicine. New York: Oxford University Press, 1985.
7. Syme SL. Strategies for health promotion. Prev Med 1986;15:492–507.
8. Multiple Risk Factor Intervention Trial Research Group. The Multiple Risk Factor Intervention Trial—risk factor changes and mortality results. JAMA 1982;248:1465–76.

9. Perlin LI, Menaghan EG, Leiberman MA, et al. The stress process. J Health Soc Behav 1981;22:337–56.

10. Bandura A. Self-efficacy mechanisms in human agency. Am Psychol 1982;37:122–47.

11. O'Leary A. Self-efficacy and health. Behav Res Ther 1985;23:437–51.

12. Rotter JB. Some problems and misconceptions related to the constuct of internal versus external reinforcement. J Consult Clin Psychol 1975;43:56–7.

13. Wallston KA, Vallston BS. Who is responsible for your health? The construct of health locus of control. In: Sanders GS, Suls J, editors. Social psychology of health and illness. Hillsdale, NJ: Lawrence Elbaum Associates, 1982:65–95.

14. Seligman MEP. Helplessness: on depression, development, and death. San Francisco: Freeman, 1975.

15. Glass DC, Singer JE. Urban stress: Experiments on noise and social stressors. New York: Academic Press, 1972.

16. Sherrod DR. Crowding, perceived control, and behavioral aftereffects. J Appl Soc Psychol 1974;4:171–86.

17. Cohen S. After effects of stress on human performance and social behavior. Psychol Bull 1980;88:82–108.

18. Burger J. Desire for control and achievement-related behavior. Psychol Bull 1980;88:82–108.

19. Langer EJ. The psychology of control. Beverly Hills, CA: Sage, 1983.

20. Rodin J. Aging and health: effects of the sense of control. Science 1986;233:1271–76.

21. Schulz R. Effects of control and predictability on the physical and psychological well-being of the institutionalized aged. J Pers Soc Psychol 1976;33:563–73.

22. Bauman KE, Udry JR. Powerlessness and regularity of contraception in an urban Negro male sample: a research note. J Marriage Fam 1972;34:112–14.

23. Kobasa SC. The hardy personality: toward a social psychology of stress and health. In: Sanders GS, Suls J, editors. Social psychology of health and illness. Hillsdale, NJ: Lawrence Erlbaum Associates, 1982:3–32.

24. Libassi MF, Maluccio A. Competence-centered social work: prevention in action. J Primary Prev 1986;6:168–80.

25. Karasek R, Baker D, Marxer F, et al. Job decision latitude, job demands, and cardiovascular disease: a prospective study of Swedish men. Am J Public Health 1981;71:694–705.

26. Theorell T, Alfreddson L, Knox S, et al. On the interplay between socioeconomic factors, personality and work environment in the pathogenesis of cardiovascular disease. Scand J Work Environ Health 1984;10:373–80.

27. Karasek R, Theorell T. Healthy work: stress, productivity and the reconstruction of working life. New York: Basic Books, 1990.

28. Syme SL. Control and health: a personal perspective. In: Steptoe A, Appels A, editors. Stress, personal control and health. New York: Wiley, 1989:16–27.

29. Seeman TE, Syme SL. Social networks and coronary artery disease: a comparison of the structure and function of social relations as predictors of disease. Psychosom Med 1987;49:341–54.

30. Sapolsky RM. Hypercortisolism among socially subordinate wild baboons originates at the CNS level. Arch Gen Psychiatry 1989;46:1047–51.

31. Sapolsky RM. Adrenocortical function, social rank, and personality among wild baboons. Biol Psychiatry 1990;28:862–78.

32. Manuck SB, Kaplan JR, Adams MR, et al. Effects of stress and the sympathetic nervous system on coronary artery atherosclerosis in the cynomolgus macaque. Am Heart J 1988;116:328–33.

Chapter 5

Prevention of Cardiovascular Morbidity and Mortality: Role of Social Relations

Lisa F. Berkman
Yale School of Medicine

Kristina Orth-Gomér
Karolinska Institute

Social networks and social support have been found, in a number of studies, to predict mortality, especially from cardiovascular disease (CVD). Recently, several investigators have been exploring where along the spectrum of disease social networks and support might have their greatest influence on the disease process. Studies revealing an association between social isolation and increased coronary heart disease (CHD) mortality, for instance, tell us nothing about whether social factors influence: (a) the development of atherosclerosis directly; (b) CHD risk factors, which in turn influence disease processes; (c) the clinical expression of specific CHD endpoints; or (d) survival after the onset of a CHD "event." Although data are still sparse, some important recent studies have shed light on this issue. Most important, because there are now a number of studies indicating an association between mortality and social isolation, or lack of support, it is imperative—if we are to introduce preventive practices and develop successful interventions—that we have a more refined understanding of which aspects of social networks and support are related to specific aspects of CVD.

In this chapter, we discuss the development of measures of social networks and support, and we review the evidence linking specific aspects of networks and support to cardiovascular mortality and morbidity. We conclude with the importance of developing clinical trials to test further hypotheses relating to the effects of social networks and support on CVD.

51

SOCIAL RELATIONSHIPS

Concepts and Theories of Social Networks and Support: The Multidimensional Nature of Social Relationships

To understand the specific role that networks and support play in influencing health and functioning, and to plan effective interventions, it is important to outline the multidimensional nature of social relationships. The three major dimensions of social relationships are: (a) structure (e.g., size and composition of the social network), (b) content and function (e.g., availability, type, amount, and source of social support provided by members of the network), and (c) subjectively perceived adequacy of support or, conversely, amount of conflict and strain produced by members of the individual's network. As Cohen (1) noted, it is likely that aspects of network structure and the support or conflict produced by network members will have specific influences on disease. Their impact will depend on characteristics of the individual's disease status, the specific pathophysiological or behavioral pathways linking a specific characteristic of the network or support to a clinically relevant disease outcome, and the length of time or stability of exposure. For instance, the sudden loss of emotional support due to the death of a close friend may have a critical impact on the health of a vulnerable, frail older person, whereas it may have a much weaker impact on a healthy, vigorous person. Alternatively, an adult who spends 10, 20, or 30 years in social isolation may develop diseases that take a long time to develop (e.g., atherosclerosis). In the first instance, it is unlikely that a relatively short-term exposure could substantially contribute to a long-term disease process. For instance, Cohen and Matthews (2) reported that satisfaction with support or perceived availability would not be likely predictors of atherosclerosis because they tend to be relatively unstable or variable over time.

The Structure of Social Ties

Much of the work uncovering the structure of social ties grew from social-science research in the area of social-network analysis (3–5). Social networks classically were seen as the web of social ties surrounding an individual, and measures were constructed that characterized the links tying people together. Typical structural measures of ties are *size* (number of network members), *frequency of contact*, *geographic proximity*, *percent of network composed of kin*, *durability* (how long members have known one another), *reciprocity*, *homogeneity* (how similar network members are to one another), and *density* (how many network members know one another). Most of these measures focus on actual behaviors (i.e., How often do you see any relatives? How many of your friends know one another?), rather than hypothetical situations (i.e., If you needed a ride, who would you call on?).

  Most prospective community-based studies, in which social ties predict increased mortality risk, have relied on this theoretical base, although most of the summary indices used in these studies do not tap many specific network measures. Rather, they often lump several dimensions of network structure together to form a more global measure (i.e., often measured by items on marital status, number of close friends and relatives, participation in church and group activities), which has been loosely termed *social integration*. Even with these summary measures, studies in Alameda County (6, 7), Tecumseh, Michigan (8), North Carolina (9), and Scandinavia (10–12) have all found lack of social ties to be related to long-term mortality risk, often between 10 and 20 years after baseline assessments.

The Functions of Social Networks: The Provision of Support

The second important component of social relationships is the availability and amount of specific kinds of social support received or provided (i.e., characterizing the types of resources that flow through social networks). Although network measures characterize the structure of ties, they reveal little about whether such ties are actually supportive. A major issue in this field is to understand the conditions under which networks provide support (13). Barrera (14) and colleagues (15–17) described numerous types of support functions in extensive reviews. However, subsequent empirical research (16, 18) suggested that three types of functions capture the majority of types of social support.

The first type of support is *emotional support*—the availability or presence of someone to talk to about personal matters and express comfort and concern for one's well-being. The second type is often called *instrumental* or *tangible support*—having someone available to help with tasks, provide transportation, help with groceries, and so on. The third is *informational* or *guidance-oriented* support—help with information, giving directions, or suggesting action, which may enhance capacities for coping. Often a fourth dimension is referred to as *belongingness*—that is, the sense of being part of a group or community with which one shares values and interests (19). It is likely that this aspect is most closely measured in studies that have used social activity indices as measures of social support (10, 12, 20). In these Swedish studies, this dimension has been referred to as *social anchorage*—the lack of which was found to predict mortality in elderly men. Aspects of support that are important to measure include current availability, availability under hypothetical conditions, and the source (i.e., who provides support). For instance, evidence suggests that *who* provides supports makes little difference in terms of disease risk.

Perceived Adequacy of Social Support

The third major component of social relationship measures is the perceived adequacy of social support. In contrast to the number of providers of support, or types of support, the perceived adequacy of support usually focuses on the recipient's subjective assessment that the support available or received would, or did, enhance his or her well-being (15). There is evidence that at least some of the benefit of social support is cognitively mediated (14, 21, 22), influencing health via the perception and cognitive understanding of its presence. Furthermore, some evidence suggests that not all apparently supportive acts are perceived as supportive (23).

Equally important with respect to perceived adequacy of support are the negative aspects of social relationships: Not all networks provide support, and recently it has been hypothesized that not all aspects of support are health promoting. For instance, support that decreases competence or autonomy and independence may be potentially damaging (17, 24–27), especially when recovering from illness.

SOCIAL RELATIONSHIPS AND CVD

Social Networks, Social Support, and CVD

Many studies on the health effects of social networks and support have focused on mortality, often from CHD. Since 1979, there have been at least eight major longitudinal, community-based studies examining the effects of social isolation on mortality risk. There have been several reviews of the major studies in this area (28, 29). More recently, in the last several years, there have been five studies of survival postmyocardial infarction (MI) (30–34), and a series of studies on social support and recovery from a stroke (35, 36). There have been only one or two studies in which the effects of support have been examined in relation to the incidence of MI (37). In addition to these epidemiological studies, there is a body of experimental work in both animals and humans, in which investigators have studied the role of social relationships in the development of atherosclerosis and cardiovascular reactivity.

Of the population-based mortality studies published to date, virtually all show that social isolation, or lack of support, is associated with increased mortality risk among men (see Table 5.1). Results from analyses of 9-year mortality in Alameda County reveal that, for both men and women, those with no or few ties are at increased risk of dying (6). These findings, along with those from the Swedish population by Orth-Gomér and Johnson (12), show the most robust results for women. In these studies, the relative risks associated with isolation are well over twofold for both men and women. Because there are several detailed reviews of these studies, we do go into them in depth here.

Among these studies, however, one in North Karelia is of special interest (11). In the rigorous study of CVD in men and women in North Karelia, lack of social ties is related to increased risk from all causes of CVD and CHD for men, but not for women. The study is important because, although it does not have a particularly innovative measure of social ties, it measures cardiovascular

TABLE 5.1
Social Network/Support Studies of All Cause or CHD Mortality

Study	Sample Size	Age Range	Outcome	Number of Events	Average Follow-Up
Community-Based Alameda County Berkman & Syme	4,725	30–69	All cause mortality	M: 211 W: 160	9 years
Tecumseh, Michigan House et al.	2,754	30–69	All cause mortality	M: 172 W: 87	9–12 years
Duke Blazer	331	65	All cause mortality	50 total	30 months
Evans County, Georgia Schoenbach et al.	2,059	15	All cause mortality	M: 279 W: 251	12 years
Swedish population Orth-Gomér & Johnson	17,433	29–74	All cause mortality	M: 562 W: 279	6 years
North Karelia, Finland Kaplan et al.	13,301	39–59	All cause mortality	M: 450 W: 148	5 years
EPESE East Boston Iowa New Haven Seeman et al.	3,807 3,097 2,788	65+	All cause mortality	M: 426 W: 466 M: 290 W: 293 M: 417 W: 386	5 years
Swedish Men Welin et al.	989	50, 60	All cause mortality	151	9 years
Survival Post-MI B-HAT Ruberman et al.	2,320	30–69	All cause mortality	184	3 years
Diltiazem Post-MI Trial Case et al.	1,234	25–75	Recurrent nonfatal MI or cardiac death	226 total	25 months
Angiography and CAD Williams et al.	1,368	46–58	Cardiovascular death	237 total	4–11 years
EPESE Berkman et al.	194	65+	All cause mortality	M: 44 W: 32	6 months
Swedish men Orth-Gomér (1988)	150	40–65	All cause mortality	M: 34	10 years

risk factors and endpoints with precision. The reason that social effects were not found for women seems puzzling at first; however, there are very low CVD rates among women in the study. This precludes a meaningful analysis of risk factors. In fact, the age selection of the cohort (39–59 years) is a period of high risk for premature death for men, but is clearly not one for women. Thus, from this well-done study, we conclude that if we are to study CHD mortality in women, we may do well to focus on age cohorts entering the period of highest risk—that is, postmenopausal women. This may explain some of the more disparate findings in Evans County, Georgia (38) as well because it was among the older women that CHD mortality risks associated with social isolation were observed.

The Established Populations for the Epidemiological Study of the Elderly Studies

In the Established Populations for the Epidemiological Study of the Elderly (EPESE) study of older men and women, we have examined the association between social ties and 5-year mortality risk in three communities: East Boston; New Haven, Connecticut; and two rural counties in Iowa (39). This study allows us to examine the effects of social ties on mortality for older men and women using identical measures across three diverse communities. Community differences are not the result of differences in measurement of social ties.

Figure 5.1 shows the estimated relative risks from a series of proportional hazards models in which only age is included as a covariate. In all three communities, for both men and women, people who lack social ties in terms of contacts with friends, relatives, and children; who are not married; and who do not participate in religious and other voluntary activities are more likely to die. The risks for women are greater than those for men. However, when the other covariates are included (Fig. 5.2) in the model, risks are substantially reduced.

The risks remain significant for men and women in New Haven and, interestingly enough, for women in Iowa. Among these three cohorts, it is in East Boston—the most tightly integrated and homogeneous community—that the association between social ties and mortality is nonsignificant; in New Haven—the most socioculturally and economically diverse community—the magnitude of the effect is greatest. It is also important to note that the estimates of relative

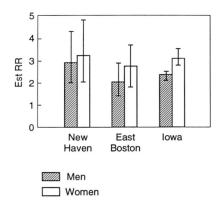

FIG. 5.1. EPESE: New Haven, East Boston, Iowa studies: proportional hazards models (estimated relative risk) for 5-year mortality comparing those with least ties to those with most ties. Age-adjusted models.

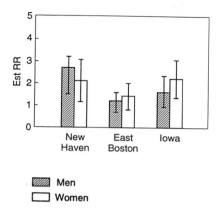

FIG. 5.2. EPESE: New Haven, East Boston, Iowa studies: proportional hazards models (estimated relative risk) for 5-year mortality comparing those with least ties to those with most ties. Full model (age, chronic conditions, body mass, angina, cigarette smoking, physical and cognitive function.)

risk fall the greatest for women, compared with men, when covariates are introduced. For instance, in New Haven, the relative risk falls from 3.1 to 1.8. Similar findings were reported by House et al. (8) in Tecumseh, Michigan.

Such reductions identify a potentially important question. Are social ties differentially related to standard risk factors for all cause or CHD mortality in women compared with men? Most studies have shown weak and nonsignificant correlations among such risk factors for men. But does the same hold true for women? The data with which to examine this question are not plentiful. In the New Haven EPESE (40), the correlations are small for CVD risk factors (e.g., smoking, body mass, diagnosis of hypertension, diastolic blood pressure, angina) and social ties in men and women. The correlations are somewhat higher for women between social ties and prevalent CHD and disability at baseline. Thus, it does not appear that standard risk factors interact with gender and extent of social ties to reduce risks in women. However, the larger correlation between social ties and prevalent CHD and disability at baseline suggests that we pay closer attention to the relationship between prevalent disease and disability because women may be more sensitive to their physical abilities in being able to carry on relationships. Alternatively, it may be precisely at this point in the disease process (with an onset of clinical symptoms and disability) that the extent of ties influences prognosis.

Studies of Recovery From Myocardial Infarction

Although the previously mentioned community-based studies have shown social isolation, or lack of social ties, to be related to mortality risk, these studies have not clarified where along the spectrum of disease social factors might have their greatest impact—that is, do they influence mortality by influencing the onset or progression of clinical disease or survival following an event?

Recently, researchers have begun to address this question by examining the influence of social ties on survival in post-MI patients. In five studies, patients who lacked social support, lived alone, or were never married had an elevated mortality risk post-MI (30–34) (see Table 5.1). In the first of these, Ruberman et al. (30) explored 2,320 male survivors of acute MI who were participants in the beta-blocker heart attack trial. Patients who were socially isolated were more than twice as likely to die over a 3-year period than those who were less socially isolated. When this measure of social isolation was combined with a general measure of life stress, which included items related to occupational status, divorce, exposure to violent events, retirement, or financial difficulty, risks associated with high-risk psychosocial status were even greater. Those in the high-risk psychosocial categories were four to five times as likely to die as those in the low-risk categories. This psychosocial characteristic was associated with mortality from all causes, as well as with sudden deaths. It made large contributions to mortality risk in both the high- and low-arrythmia groups. Although this study may be criticized on several methodological grounds, regarding the inability to determine the temporal association between the assessment of psychosocial resources and the severity of disease, it nonetheless serves as a powerful model for future studies.

In a second Swedish study of 150 cardiac patients and patients with high risk factor levels for CHD, the findings that lack of support predicts mortality were further confirmed (34). Patients who were socially isolated had a three times higher 10-year mortality rate than patients who were socially active and integrated. Because these patients were examined extensively for cardiological prognostic factors at study entry, it was possible to disentangle effects of psychosocial as well as clinical characteristics. In traditional multivariate analyses, three factors emerged as independent prognostic markers for high mortality risk: (a) a high incidence of ventricular ectopic activity (arrhythmia) on 24-hour ambulatory electrocardiographic [ECG] monitoring, (b) a low score on a scale describing self-perceived health (i.e., bad subjective health), and (c) social isolation. When all prognostic factors from univariate analyses were examined in a model of possible pathogenic pathways, using canonical correlations analyses, the associations depicted in Fig. 5.3 were found.

One pathway described mainly cardiological/clinical influences. In that pathway, arrhythmia was influenced by old age, presence of myocardial damage evident as signs of heart failure (left-ventricular dysfunction), and alcohol consumption. This pathway was distinct from the pathway of social isolation. The latter was associated with low social class, so that low-status men were more socially isolated. Its effect on mortality was partly a direct one and partly mediated through hypertension. The third factor, self-perceived ill health, was not associated with arrhythmia or social isolation. Thus, it appears from these analyses

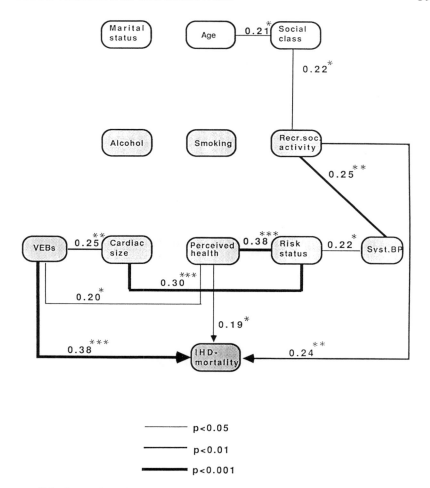

FIG. 5.3. Independent associations between predictive factors and mortality. Canonical correlation coefficients. Only correlation coefficients significant at the 5% level or lower were included. $p < .05$; —, $p < .01$; —, $p < .001$.

that lack of social integration in cardiac patients is not a consequence of their disease status.

In a third study, Williams et al. (32) enrolled 1,368 patients undergoing cardiac catheterization from 1974 to 1980, and who were found to have significant coronary artery disease (CAD). They examined survival time until cardiovascular death through 1989. Men comprised 82% of the sample. In this study, men and women who were unmarried and without a confidant were over three times as likely to die within 5 years, compared with patients who had a close confidant or who were married (OR 3.34, CI 1.8–6.2). This association was independent of other clinical prognostic indicators and sociodemographic factors, including socioeconomic status (SES; in itself an important predictor).

In another study, Case et al. (31) examined the association between marital status and recurrent major cardiac events among post-MI patients enrolled in the placebo arm of a clinical trial, The Multicenter Diltiazem Postinfarction Trial. These investigators reported that living alone was an independent risk factor, with a hazard ratio of 1.54 (CI 1.04–2.29) for recurrent major cardiac event, including both nonfatal infarctions and cardiac deaths. In this study, the condition of living alone was a more important predictor of poor outcome than was having a disrupted marriage (defined as *widowed, divorced,* or *separated*). Although there were not statistically significant gender differences, the hazard ratio was greater for women than for men (2.34 vs. 1.24).

In a fifth study, Berkman, Leo-Summers, and Horwitz (33) explored the relationship between social networks or social support and mortality among men and women hospitalized for an MI between 1982 and 1988 who are participants in the population-based New Haven EPESE. Over the 1-year period, 100 men and 94 women were hospitalized for an MI. Thirty-four percent of women and 44% of men died in the 6-month period following MI.

Among both men and women, emotional support, measured prospectively (i.e., before the MI), was related to both early inhospital mortality and later mortality over a year-long period. Among those admitted to the hospital, almost 38% of those who reported no source of emotional support died inhospital, compared with 11.5% of those with two or more sources of support. The patterns remain steady throughout the follow-up period. At 6 months, the major endpoint of the study, 52.8% of those with no source of support had died, compared with 36% of those with one source and 23.1% of those with two or more sources of support. These figures do not change substantially at 1 year. As Fig. 5.4 shows, the patterns are remarkably consistent for both men and women, younger and older people, those with greater or lesser comorbidity, and those with more or less severe CVD. In multivariate models controlling for sociodemographic, psychosocial, and clinical prognostic indicators, men and women who report no emotional support have almost three times the mortality risk compared with subjects who report at least one source of support (OR 2.9, 95%, CI 1.2–6.9).

The findings from these studies are strong and consistent, although the measures of support and the populations vary dramatically. Although they in no way preclude that these social factors influence onset of CHD, they strongly suggest that they influence survival post-MI.

Progression and Disease Incidence

Data regarding whether aspects of social relationships are related to the progression of atherosclerosis or the onset of new cardiovascular events are much more limited. Available data do indicate that the effects of social relationships may

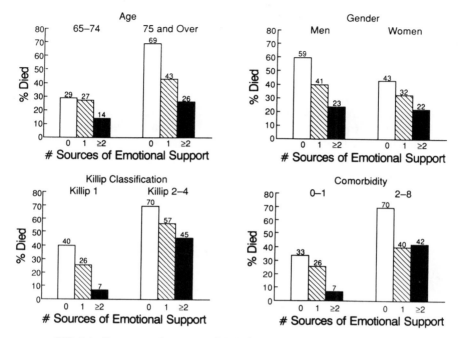

FIG. 5.4. Percentage of patients with MI who died within 6 months by level of social support. Adjustments were made for age (*top left*), gender (*top right*), severity of MI as defined by Killip classification (*bottom left*), and comorbidity (*bottom right*).

operate at several early stages of the disease process. For instance, two studies— one in monkeys and the other in humans—show that aspects of social ties may influence coronary artery atherosclerosis and occlusion. In the first of these studies (41), monkeys were placed in five-member groups, in which the stressed monkeys were in constantly changing groups and the unstressed monkeys remained in stable groups. Both groups were fed a low-fat, low-cholesterol diet. At the end of the 21-month experiment, the monkeys were killed. Coronary artery atherosclerosis in each monkey was expressed as mean intimal area and mean intimal thickness of 15 sections of coronary artery. Substantial differences in coronary artery atherosclerosis were observed in stressed versus unstressed monkeys, and many more stressed monkeys were found to have fatty streaks that had progressed to small plaques than unstressed monkeys.

In a study of men and women undergoing angiography (42), support was also found to be associated with coronary atherosclerosis. In this study, men and women suspected of having CAD who were referred for angiography were given a psychosocial questionnaire. The extent of coronary atherosclerosis was determined from the film of each subject. Evaluations of the three major coronary arteries were done in terms of 15 subdivisions, with each lesion in these segments assessed in terms of percent stenosis of the artery. Occlusion was significantly associated with instrumental, but not emotional, support for men, but not for women. Instrumental support tapped the help the respondent had received with transportation, household tasks, and financial assistance.

In another study on cardiovascular reactivity to psychological challenge, (43) young college-age women were presented to an experimental challenge situation, in which they were either accompanied by a friend or unaccompanied. Subjects who were permitted to bring a friend to the experimental situation showed reduced heart rate (HR) activity and, in some instances, reduced blood pressure responses. These studies indicate that social relations might influence both the progression of CVD and the development of patterns of cardiovascular reactivity, which may be associated with increased risk of disease.

In fact, a recent study demonstrated an association between lack of social support and risk of MI. In a 6-year follow-up of 50-year-old men in the Gothenberg study, MI incidence was more than three times higher in poorly integrated men, compared with well-integrated men (Fig. 5.5). Also, the MI risk associated

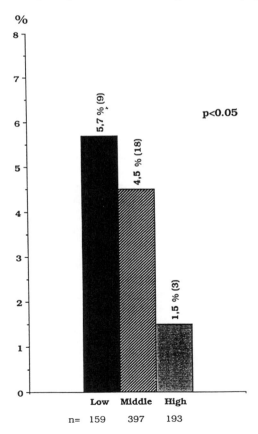

FIG. 5.5. Six-year incidence of MI by social integration score.

with poor attachment to the closest family members was of almost similar magnitude. In multivariate analyses, controlling for standard risk factors, including blood pressure, lipids, coagulation factors, family history, and sedentary lifestyle, two factors emerged as the strongest independent risk factors for MI in these middle-aged men: smoking and lack of social support (37). As far as we know, this is the first study to prospectively link social support to the incidence of CHD. If these findings are repeated in further studies, a new psychosocial cardiovascular risk factor needs to be considered in future investigative, as well as preventive, efforts.

DISCUSSION

Prevention and Intervention Studies

We believe that the evidence to date on the influence of social networks and support on CVD strongly supports a move from the virtually exclusive conduct of observational studies to the design and implementation of clinical trials to investigate the effects of lack of support and social isolation on cardiovascular morbidity and mortality. By far the most consistent and convincing body of evidence relates to the influence of social support on survival and recovery of post-MI patients. In general, early-stage clinical trials are most efficacious when focused on high-risk groups, for whom outcome events are not rare. Thus, it is entirely appropriate to begin development of social support interventions among people with established CHD.

Although clinical trials or intervention studies in cardiac rehabilitation have rarely focused either directly or exclusively on strengthening social networks or social support, clinical approaches to cardiac rehabilitation have, in fact, often included elements of social support from both health professionals and family members in their rehabilitation efforts. Because these effects are not often scientifically evaluated, it is difficult to conclude anything about their magnitude and impact. However, a few studies have deliberately attempted to stimulate social interactions to form new bases for friendships and social ties among participants, and to measure the effects of these interventions on cardiovascular outcomes.

In a study of elderly women in the Greater Stockholm area, 108 women—all living alone—were selected for an intervention group (68 women) and a control group (40 women) (44). Their mean age was 77 years, and they were all rated as being in good physical health. The intervention consisted of organized meetings with other women in the neighborhood, at which specific themes were discussed and new social ties were formed. Measurements of psychological, social, and biological conditions were made at baseline. Six months after beginning participation in the program, the following statistically significant changes were found in the intervention group as compared with the control group: Intervention subjects rated themselves as less lonely, having more social contacts, higher self-esteem, a greater ability to trust others, and lower systolic and diastolic blood pressure than controls. Systolic blood pressure decreased an average of 8.8 mm Hg, and diastolic blood pressure decreased by 5.6 mm Hg. Although these women were not judged to be initially hypertensive, and the main aim of the study was not hypertensive treatment (45), the results show that it is possible to influence a cardiovascular risk factor by altering the social environment and increasing social support. Therefore, the results have great significance for the future development of research and prevention strategies in the field of social support and CVD. Furthermore, many behavioral interventions aimed at changing dietary patterns (46, 47), smoking cessation (48), and increasing physical activity (49) rely heavily on strategies involving elements of social support from either professional staff, family members, or support group members.

Although few studies were explicitly designed to improve social support and increase or ameliorate social networks, some conclusions can be drawn from studies of secondary prevention after MI. For instance in the Recurrent Coronary Prevention Project (RCCP), the attenuation of Type A behavior pattern was accompanied, according to the therapists, by one inevitable consequence—the increase of support from coworkers and family (50). It may be that this change in the social environment accounted for some of the beneficial effects on risk of reinfarction and mortality. If one considers the nature of some of the practices that patients engage in—like expressing positive feelings, expressing gratitude, or giving compliments to significant others—it would be difficult to understand if these changes did not ameliorate patients' social milieu.

A relevant intervention conducted by Frasure-Smith and Prince (51) in Canada involved a psychosocial intervention in a controlled clinical trial of 453 male MI survivors. Patients were randomly allocated either to a nurse-managed stress-monitoring and intervention program or to a usual care group. Patients who reported they had problems during a monthly telephone call by the nurse were then visited, and attempts were made to help the patients cope with identified problems. One-year mortality in the intervention group was 4.4%, compared with 8.9% for control ($p = .05$). Although it is not clear what components of the intervention were most effective, and some imbalances between the treatment and usual care groups existed, this study is nonetheless important because it indicates that straightforward psychosocial interventions can be effective in reducing cardiac mortality.

CONCLUSION

Many studies have revealed strong and consistent associations between lack of social support or social isolation and risk of cardiovascular mortality and, to a lesser extent, cardiovascular morbidity. In addition, elements of social support have been integrated into many behavioral interventions in CVD without fully appreciating or evaluating the intervention components related to manipulating aspects of social support. Based on this evidence, we propose that it is now time to develop and test the effects of social isolation and social support using rigorous clinical trial methods, in addition to supporting continued research using prospective observational study designs. Only through such a dual strategy can we make substantial progress in this area in the coming years.

ACKNOWLEDGMENTS

This chapter was supported in part by National Institute of Aging grant RO1AG11042-01A1. Parts of this chapter and Table 5.1 are reprinted from "The Role of Social Relations in Health Promotion" by L. F. Berkman, 1995, *Psychosomatic Medicine*, 57, pp. 245–254. Copyright © 1995 by Williams & Wilkins.

REFERENCES

1. Cohen S. Psychosocial models of the role of social support in the etiology of physical disease. Health Psychol 1988;7:269–97.
2. Cohen S, Matthews KA. Editorial: social support, type A behavior and coronary artery disease. Psychosom Med 1987;44:325–30.
3. Fischer CS. To dwell among friends: personal networks in town and city. Chicago: University of Chicago Press, 1982.
4. Laumann EO. Bonds of pluralism: the form and substance of urban social networks. New York: Wiley, 1973.
5. Mitchell JC. Social networks in urban situations. Manchester: Manchester University Press, 1969.
6. Berkman LF, Syme SL. Social networks, host resistance and mortality: a nine year follow-up study of Alameda County residents. Am J Epidemiol 1979;109:186–204.
7. Seeman TE, Kaplan GA, Knudsen L, et al. Social network ties and mortality among the elderly in the Alameda County study. Am J Epidemiol 1987;126:714–23.
8. House JS, Robbins C, Metzner HL. The association of social relationships and activities with mortality: prospective evidence from the Tecumseh community health study. Am J Epidemiol 1982;116:123–40.
9. Blazer D. Social support and mortality in an elderly community population. Am J Epidemiol 1982;115:684–94.
10. Welin L, Tibblin G, Svardsudd K, et al. Prospective study of social influences on mortality: the study of men born in 1913 and 1923. Lancet 1985;1:915–18.
11. Kaplan GA, Salonen JT, Cohen RD, et al. Social connections and mortality from all causes and cardiovascular disease: prospective evidence from Eastern Finland. Am J Epidemiol 1988;128:370–80.
12. Orth-Gomér K, Johnson J. Social network interaction and mortality: a six year follow-up of a random sample of the Swedish population. J Chronic Dis 1987;40:949–57.
13. Wellman B. From social support to social network. In: Sarason I, Sarason, B, editors. Social support, theory, research, and applications. The Hague: Martinus Nijhoff, 1985:205–22.
14. Barrera M. Social support in the adjustment of pregnant adolescents: assessment issues. In: Gottlieb BH, editor. Social networks and social support. Beverly Hills, CA: Sage, 1981:69–96.

15. Barrera M, Sandler IN, Ramsay TB. Preliminary development of a scale of social support: studies on college students. Am J Community Psychol 1981;9:435–43.

16. Barrera M, Ainlay SL. The structure of social support: a conceptual and empirical analysis. Am J Community Psychol 1983;11:133–43.

17. Barrera M. Distinctions between social support concepts, measures, and models. Am J Community Psychol 1986;14:413–45.

18. Caldwell RA, Reinhart MA. The relationship of personality to individual differences in the use of type and source of social support. J Soc Clin Psychol 1988;6:140–46.

19. Weiss RS. The provisions of social relationships. In: Rubin Z, editor. Doing unto others. Englewood Cliffs, NJ: Prentice-Hall, 1974:17–26.

20. Hanson BS, Mattisson I, Steen B. Dietary intake and psychosocial factors in 68-year-old men. A population study. Compr Gerontol 1987;B1(2):62–7.

21. Cohen C, Teresi J, Holmes D. Social networks, stress, and physical health: a longitudinal study of an inner-city elderly population. J Gerontol 1985;40:478–86.

22. Antonucci TC. Social support: theoretical advances, recent findings and pressing issues. In: Sarason IG, Sarason BR, editors. Social support: theory, research and applications. The Hague: Martinus Nijhoff, 1985:21–37.

23. Wortman C, Lehman D. Reactions to victims of life crises: social attempts fail. In: Sarason IG, Sarason BR, editors. Social support: theory, research and applications. Dordrect, Netherlands: Martinus Nijhoff, 1985:463–89.

24. Parmelee PA. Spouse versus other family caregivers: psychological impact on impaired aged. Am J Community Psychol 1983;11:337–49.

25. McFarlane AH, Norman GR, Streiner DL, et al. Characteristics and correlates of effective and ineffective social supports. J Psychosom Res 1984;28:501–10.

26. Rook KS. The negative side of social interaction: impact on psychological well-being. J Pers Soc Psychol 1984;46:1097–1108.

27. Pagel MD, Erdly WW, Becker J. Social networks: we get by with (and in spite of) a little help from our friends. J Pers Soc Psychol 1987;53:793–804.

28. Berkman LF. The relationship of social networks and social support to morbidity and mortality. In: Cohen S, Syme SL, editors. Social support and health. New York: Academic Press, 1985:241–62.

29. House JS, Landis KR, Umberson D. Social relationships and health. Science 1988;241:540–45.

30. Ruberman W, Weinblatt E, Goldberg JD, et al. Psychosocial influences on mortality after myocardial infarction. N Engl J Med 1984;311:552–59.

31. Case RB, Moss AJ, Case N, et al. Living alone after myocardial infarction. JAMA 1992;267:515–19.

32. Williams RB, Barefoot JC, Califf RM, et al. Prognostic importance of social and economic resources among medically treated patients with angiographically documented coronary artery disease. JAMA 1992;267:520–24.

33. Berkman LF, Leo-Summers L, Horwitz RI. Emotional support and survival following myocardial infarction: a prospective population-based study of the elderly. Ann Intern Med 1992;117:1003–09.

34. Orth-Gomér K, Unden AL, Edwards ME. Social isolation and mortality in ischemic heart disease. Acta Med Scand 1988;224:205–15.

35. Glass T, Matchar D, Belyea M, et al. The impact of social support on outcomes in first stroke. Stroke 1993;24(1):64–70.

36. Colantonio A, Kasl S, Ostfeld A, et al. Psychosocial predictors of stroke outcomes in an elderly population. J Gerontol 1993;48(5):S261–S268.

37. Orth-Gomér K, Rosengren A, Wilhelmsen L. Lack of social support and incidence of coronary heart disease in middle-aged Swedish men. Psychosom Med 1993;55(1):37–43.

38. Schoenbach VJ, Kaplan BG, Freedman L, et al. Social ties and mortality in Evans County, Georgia. Am J Epidemiol 1986;123:577–91.

39. Seeman TE, Berkman LF, Kohout F, et al. Intercommunity variations in the association between social ties and mortality in the elderly: a comparative analysis of three communities. Ann of Epidemiol 1993;3:325–35.
40. Berkman LF, Vaccarino V, Seeman T. Gender differences in cardiovascular morbidity and mortality: the contribution of social networks and support. Ann Behav Med 1993;15:112–18.
41. Kaplan JR, Manuck SB, Clarkson TB, et al. Social status, environment, and atherosclerosis in cynomolgus monkeys. Arteriosclerosis 1982;2:359–68.
42. Seeman TE, Syme SL. Social networks and coronary artery disease: a comparison of the structure and function of social relationships as predictors of disease. Psychosom Med 1987;49:340–53.
43. Kamarck T, Manuck S, Jennings JR. Social support reduces cardiovascular reactivity to psychological challenge: a laboratory model. Psychosom Med 1990;52:42–58.
44. Andersson L. Intervention against loneliness in a group of elderly women: an impact evaluation. Soc Sci Med 1985;4:355–64.
45. Andersson L. Intervention against loneliness in a group of elderly women: a process evaluation. Hum Rel 1984;37(4):295–310.
46. Brownell KD, Stunkard AJ. Couples training, pharmcotherapy and behavior therapy in the treatment of obesity. Arch Gen Psychiatry 1981;38:1224–29.
47. Brownell KD, Kramer FM. Behavioral management of obesity. Med Clin North Am 1989;73:185–201.
48. Mermelstein R, Cohen S, Lichtenstein E, et al. Social support and smoking cessation and maintenance. J Consult Clin Psychol 1986;54:447–53.
49. King AC, Taylor CB, Haskell WL, et al. Strategies for increasing early adherence to long-term maintenance of home-based exercise training in healthy middle-aged men and women. Am J Cardiol 1988;61:628–32.
50. Friedman M, Thoresen CE, Gill JJ, et al. Alteration of type A behavior and its effect on cardiac recurrences in post myocardial infarction patients: summary results of the recurrent coronary prevention project. Am Heart J 1986;112:653–65.
51. Frasure-Smith N, Prince R. Long-term follow-up of the Ischemic Heart Disease Life Stress Monitoring Program. Psychosom Med 1989;51:485–513.

Chapter 6

The Demand–Control–Support Model for Studying Health in Relation to the Work Environment: An Interactive Model

Töres Theorell
*National Institute of Psychosocial Factors and Health
and Department of Occupational Medicine,
Karolinska Institute*

The relationship between the psychosocial environment and cardiovascular illness risk has attracted considerable attention during recent years. In modern Western societies this seems to be logical, because physical demands are diminishing and the increasing complexity of a modern society is increasing the demands on psychosocial interaction. In several countries, an increasing number of employers' unions and trade unions have realized that a functioning psychosocial work environment heavily depends on good work organization.

Another reason that development in this field is accelerating is that methods for monitoring physiological and endocrinological processes, which are consequences of a bad psychosocial work environment, have become cheap and practically feasible. When mechanisms in the interplay between the environment and bodily function become known, the medical occupation may accept these relationships more willingly.

In the 1960s and 1970s, several systematic studies of work conditions were made. For instance, in a retrospective study of two bank groups in Belgium, Kornitzer et al. (1) observed that employees in one group—private banks—had a higher incidence of coronary heart disease than employees in the other group—state-owned banks. This could not be explained by biomedical risk factors (2). The Kornitzer group later discussed the complex relationships among stress, biomedical risk factors, and cardiovascular risk (3). This study was one of the first to indicate a possible relationship between certain kinds of work conditions—work demands (which were higher in the private banks)—and risk of myocardial infarction (MI). Other cross-sectional studies during the late 1950s and 1960s (4–7) indicated that there may be a relationship between excessive overtime work and cardiovascular illness risk; the Hinkle's et al. (8) study of "night college" men in the Bell Telephone Company was the first prospective indication in this direction. During the same time period, there were also studies that indicated a higher incidence of MI among lower level employees in large companies (9). This related to social class observations, and for the first time raised suspicion that psychosocial stress may not be primarily a problem for people with a lot of responsibility, as researchers had tended to believe previously.

During this phase of confusion and lack of theoretical models, sociologists entered the field and several models were introduced—for instance, those of the Michigan School of Sociology (10), and Cooper's (11) comprehensive models for describing the psychosocial aspects of white-collar work. This chapter focuses on the concepts introduced by Karasek, although they do not cover all the aspects of the psychosocial work environment. Karasek introduced his demand–control model, which was an architect's synthesis of the demand (stress) and the lack of control (sociological) research traditions (12). In generating the concept *lack of control*, or *lack of decision latitude* as Karasek labeled it, sociologists had been following traditions from Marx. The question was: Is the worker alienated from the work process? It was assumed that the possibility of utilizing and developing skills (*skill utilization*), a concept developed in work psychology, was closely related to *authority over decisions*. In factor analyses of responses to questions about work content, these two factors appeared to go together; accordingly, they have been added to one another to constitute *decision latitude* (13). The other dimension, *psychological demands*, included qualitative and quantitative demands.

It should be emphasized that the demand–control model was never intended to explain all the work environment-related illnesses. Thus, there was no element of individual variation introduced into its original construction. On the contrary, the model dealt with the way in which work is organized, and the way in which this relates to illness. This simplicity has made the model useful in organizational work. A model that tries to explain "all of the variance" has to be more complicated, and may be scientifically more but educationally less successful than the simple model that was introduced.

According to the model, there is interaction between high psychological demands and low decision latitude. If demands are regarded as the x-axis and decision latitude as the y-axis in a two-dimensional system, and the different combinations of high–low demands and high–low decisions are regarded, four combinations are recognized. The high-demand–low-decision latitude combination is regarded as the most relevant to illness development. Karasek used a drastic analogy to describe this combination: If a person is crossing a street and he or she sees a truck approaching, he or she may speculate that he or she will be able to cross the street without being hit by the truck, if he or she regulates his or her speed appropriately. However, if his or her foot gets stuck in the street, his or her decision latitude diminishes dramatically, and he or she is now in an extremely stressful situation. According to the theory, this kind of situation (not necessarily as dramatic), if prolonged and repeated for a long time, increases sympathoadrenal arousal and, at the same time, decreases anabolism, the body's ability to restore and repair tissues. The combination of high psychological demands and low decision latitude is defined as the *active situation*. In this situation, the worker has more possibility to cope with high psychological demands because he or she can choose to plan working hours according to his or her own biological rhythm, as well as develop good coping strategies, facilitating feeling of mastery and control in unforeseen situations. The low-demand–high-decision latitude situation (relaxed) is theoretically the ideal one, whereas the low-demand–low-decision latitude situation may be associated with risk of loss of skills and, to some extent, psychological atrophy (13).

EMPIRICAL TESTS

Karasek's original hypothesis—that excessive psychological demands interact with lack of decision latitude in generating increased risk of cardiovascular disease (CVD)—was tested in a number of epidemiological studies in the 1980s (11–18). There have been many published prospective or cross-sectional studies. The methodology has varied considerably. The most important distinction is that some studies were using the victims' own descriptions of their work situations, whereas others have used aggregated job descriptive data based on representative workers in the occupations in the population. Both methods have advantages and problems. However, individual traits may be associated with systematically distorted work descriptions, and this systematic distortion may be related to illness risk, with both overestimation and underestimation as possible results. On the one hand, the use of aggregated data gives an opportunity to avoid individual distortion (although, of course, collective distortion may still take place). On the other hand, the use of aggregated data does not allow for variations between worksites. This may lead to substantial underestimation of true associations (14). The underestimation problem in the use of aggregated data is probably a more pronounced problem in estimating the importance of psychological demands because this variable shows relatively small variance among occupations. However, decision latitude shows considerable variance among occupations (13). Even the aggregated methodology has varied across studies. In some studies, the classifications have been based on means for each one of the dimensions from employees in the different occupations in the working population. In others, single questions have represented the dimensions, and several combinations (demand–skill utilization and skill–authority over decisions) have been tested.

A recent epidemiological study in Sweden (21), using one of the aggregated methodologies, merits some interest. In this case, a large number of MI cases were identified by means of the nationwide Swedish death register, and by means of county registers including hospitalizations. Controls stratified with regard to gender, age, and geographical area were selected randomly from the population. Analyses were confined to "occupationally stable" subjects who stayed in the same occupation during the two most recent censuses (which were 5 years apart), and to those who had a first MI (in contrast to subsequent infarctions). Table 6.1 shows the results for men below age 65, and Table 6.2 shows the results for men below age 55. Each of the available questions that are usually included in the demand–control scores has been displayed separately. The results are typical for these kinds of studies, with stronger age-adjusted relative risks among the younger men. The expected pattern with the strongest relative risk in the strain quadrant is observed. The results for women were not as clearly in line with the job strain hypothesis, and it should be pointed out that the job strain hypothesis has been less well documented for women than for men.

True (multiplicative) interactions between psychological demands and decision latitude have only been observed in two studies (15, 16), whereas additive interactions were seen in the others. There is no doubt, however, that the use of

TABLE 6.1

Relative Risk (RR) of a First Myocardial Infarction for Subjects in
Different Types of Occupatons (Men 30–64 years of age who did not
change type of occupation between 1970 and 1975)

Hectic Work Combined With:	Type of Occupation[a]							
	Low Strain[b]		Active		Passive		High Strain	
	RR[c]	95% CI	RR[c]	95% CI	RR[c]	95% CI	RR[c]	95% CI
Monotony	1.0	—	1.0	0.9–1.0	1.2	1.1–1.3	1.2	1.1–1.4
Few possibilities to learn new things	1.0	—	1.0	0.9–1.1	1.2	1.1–1.3	1.3	1.2–1.5
Low influence on planning of work	1.0	—	1.0	0.9–1.2	1.2	1.1–1.3	1.3	1.2–1.5
Low influence on work tempo	1.0	—	1.0	0.9–1.1	1.2	1.1–1.3	1.2	1.1–1.3
Low influence on working hours	1.0	—	1.0	0.9–1.1	1.2	1.1–1.3	1.3	1.2–1.5

Note. From Hammar N, Alfredsson L, Theorell T. Job characteristics and incidence of myocardial infarction. A study of men and women in Sweden, with particular reference to job strain. Int J Epidemiol. In press.

[a]Basis for classification of type of occupation:
Job is above/below median in

proportion reporting:	Low Strain	Active	Passive	High Strain
Hectic work	Below	Above	Below	Above
Decision latitude	Above	Above	Below	Below

[b]Reference category.
[c]Relative risk adjusted for age, county, and calendar year.

TABLE 6.2

Relative Risk (RR) of a First Myocardial Infarction for Subjects in
Different Types of Occupatons (Men 30–54 years of age who did not
change type of occupation between 1970 and 1975)

Hectic Work Combined With:	Type of Occupation[a]							
	Low Strain[b]		Active		Passive		High Strain	
	RR[c]	95% CI	RR[c]	95% CI	RR[c]	95% CI	RR[c]	95% CI
Monotony	1.0	—	0.9	0.8–1.1	1.1	1.0–1.4	1.2	1.0–1.5
Few possibilities to learn new things	1.0	—	1.0	0.8–1.2	1.3	1.1–1.6	1.4	1.2–1.7
Low influence on planning of work	1.0	—	1.1	0.9–1.3	1.3	1.0–1.6	1.6	1.2–2.0
Low influence on work tempo	1.0	—	1.0	0.8–1.2	1.1	0.9–1.4	1.2	1.0–1.5
Low influence on working hours	1.0	—	1.1	0.9–1.3	1.1	0.9–1.7	1.5	1.2–1.8

Note. From Hammar N, Alfredsson L, Theorell T. Job characteristics and incidence of myocardial infarction. A study of men and women in Sweden, with particular reference to job strain. Int J Epidemiol. In press.

[a]Basis for classification of type of occupation:
Job is above/below median in
proportion reporting:

	Low Strain	Active	Passive	High Strain
Hectic work	Below	Above	Below	Above
Decision latitude	Above	Above	Below	Below

[b]Reference category.

[c]Relative risk adjusted for age, county, and calendar year.

the two dimensions together has provided better predictions than using either one of them alone.

As expected, the summary of relative risks of coronary heart disease in employees with, compared to employees without, job strain indicates that studies utilizing self-reported work descriptions have shown higher relative risks (2.0–4.0 vs. 1.3–2.0). Demands have been shown to be relatively more important in studies utilizing self-reported data than in studies utilizing aggregated data. Some of the studies have covered other risk factors, and one of them also covered Type A behavior (17). In general, the adjustment for standard risk factors for CVD does not eliminate the association between the high-demand–low-decision latitude combination and cardiovascular (in most studies clinically verified MI, and in three studies coronary heart disease [CHD]) risk. In one case, the Framingham study (17), the adjustment for other risk factors strengthened the association.

Only one study, the Hawaii Cardiovascular Survey (18), showed no association at all between high demand–low decision latitude and cardiovascular illness risk. Many of the participants in this study were above 55 years of age at the start of the follow-up period. Studies of participants younger than 55 years of age in general have shown stronger associations than those including older subjects. Another observation is that high demand–low decision latitude has proved to be a more powerful predictor of cardiovascular illness risk in blue-collar men than in white-collar men. For instance, a Finnish study (19) included mainly blue-collar workers and showed a strong association. The study by Johnson and Hall (15) included separate analyses of blue-collar and white-collar men that illustrate this point. For further discussion, see Marmot and Theorell (22).

A small, clinical 5-year follow-up study of men in Stockholm below age 45 who had suffered an MI indicated that returning to a job perceived as psychologically demanding and with low decision latitude (particularly low intellectual discretion) may be associated with increased risk of re-infarction death (23). This was true even after adjustment for biomedical risk factors, degree of coronary atherosclerosis, Type A behavior, and education. This finding emphasized the potential importance of this research to cardiovascular rehabilitation.

INTRODUCTION OF SOCIAL SUPPORT TO THE MODEL

There are two recent developments in this field. First of all, Johnson et al. included social support in their theoretical models (24). Their study of CVD prevalence in a large random sample of Swedish men and women indicated that the joint action of high demands and lack of control (decision latitude) is of particular importance to blue-collar men, whereas the joint action of lack of control and lack of support is more important for women and white-collar men. The multiplicative interaction among all three of them (isostrain) was tested in a 9-year prospective study of 7,000 randomly selected Swedish working men. Interestingly, for the most favored 20% men (low demands, good support, good decision latitude), the progression of cardiovascular mortality with increasing age was slow and equally so in the three social classes. In blue-collar workers, however, the age progression was much steeper in the worst isostrain group than in the corresponding isostrain group in white-collar workers.

WORKING LIFE CAREER

The second recent development in the field has involved attempts to use the occupational classification systems to describe the "psychosocial work career." Researchers have pointed out (25) that an estimate of work conditions only at one point in time may provide an imprecise estimation of the total exposure to adverse conditions. Descriptions of all the occupations during the whole work career are obtained for the participants. Occupational scores are subsequently used for a calculation of the "total lifetime exposure." The "total job control exposure" in relation to 9-year age-adjusted cardiovascular mortality in working Swedes was studied. It was observed for both men and women that the cardiovascular mortality differences between the lowest and highest quartiles were twofold even after adjustment for age, smoking habits, and physical exercise. Furthermore, if the person had had several large fluctuations in job control over the years, his or her risk of cardiovascular death during follow-up increased even more—up to almost threefold, compared with the high-control group (26). The index of psychological demands recorded in this study (the index consisted of two questions: Is your work hectic? Is your work psychologically demanding?) did not predict risk of cardiovascular death in the way that was expected. For men, it had no predictive value at all; for women, it predicted significantly in the reverse direction—the higher the psychological demands during the career, the lower the risk. These latter findings may indicate that either the index is not capturing psychological demands, or demands are associated with risk in different ways in the short-term (according to previous studies) compared with the long-term perspective. They also illustrate differences between men and women in the patterns of correlations between psychosocial factors and CVD (27).

NOTES ON PSYCHOMETRIC PROPERTIES

At present, two different forms of the demand–control–support questionnaires are widely used. The first one is an expansion of Karasek's original questionnaire, which was originally based on the American Quality of Employment Survey (QES) studies (28). This has been extensively tested and used, particularly in the United States, but also in central Europe (e.g., in the MONICA studies) and Japan. Not only is the decision latitude scale based on a slightly larger number of questions than the original one, but other scales also have been included, such as social support, physical demands, and personal insecurity.

The second form of the demand–control–support questionnaire has been used mainly in Sweden. It is shorter and does not have as many dimensions as the American one (29). It also uses only four response categories for each question, and a frequency-based rather than intensity-based grading. The tests of internal consistency in Table 6.3 refer to the Swedish version, which has five questions dealing with (mainly quantitative) psychological demands and six questions dealing with decision latitude (four about intellectual discretion and two about authority over decisions).

A few notes on psychometric properties of some of the demand–control–support measures should also be made because they may be of more general interest in the field of psychosocial methodology. We have noticed that the scales measuring the two aspects of decision latitude—*intellectual discretion* and *authority over*

TABLE 6.3
Internal Consistency (Cronbach alpha) in Working Men and Women as a
Function of Psychosocial Variables

Index	Furniture Movers (Men)	Medical Secretaries (Women)	Men (Community Sample)	Women (Community Sample)
Psychological demands	0.70	0.70	0.75	0.80
Intellectual discretion	0.37	0.35	0.54	0.70
Decision latitude	0.48	0.80	0.76	0.77
Social support	0.83	0.86	0.89	0.89

decisions (which together constitute the *decision latitude* scale)—show wide differences among occupational groups (29). Furthermore, analyses of internal consistency show that Cronbach alpha coefficients are high when mixed working populations are studied, but in some cases considerably lower when homogeneous occupation groups are studied. One possible reason for this may be that decision latitude is determined, to a great extent, by the content of work in the occupation, whereas demands and social support reflect local workplace conditions and individual perception to a greater extent. Table 6.3 shows the results of a comparison between random samples of working men and women and two samples of occupations (female medical secretaries and male furniture movers) with regard to internal consistency (Cronbach alpha) and the indices of psychological demands, intellectual discretion, decision latitude, and social support at work (29). For intellectual discretion, it is obvious that the internal consistency is low for both occupational groups. For the total decision latitude scale, the internal consistency is good in the community sample gender groups, but low in the male furniture mover group. In the group of female medical secretaries, the internal consistency of the decision latitude index is high. Similar conclusions were made in a study of another homogeneous group—namely, health care personnel (30). For social support, the internal consistency was good in all groups.

When a comparison was made in the community sample group between 90 men and 90 women, it was found that the correlation pattern differs between the genders. For both genders, there were, as expected, strongly significant positive correlations between intellectual discretion and authority over decisions (men 0.62, women 0.45) and between sleep disturbance and covert coping (men 0.24, women 0.27; both sleep disturbance and covert coping were measured by means of a questionnaire described in the publication [29]). For women, however, there was a significant relationship between psychological demands and covert coping that did not exist for men (women 0.22, men −0.01). For men, there was a strongly significant positive correlation between intellectual discretion and psychological demands (men 0.28, women 0.07), as well as a tendency toward a positive correlation between authority over decisions and psychological demands (men 0.16, women 0.01). No such relationships were found for women.

This reflects what has been found in several studies—namely, that demands tend to be matched by decision latitude in men but not in women (for a discussion see [13]), and also that, in general, the psychophysiological pathways between work environment factors and illness may be different in men and women.

Inconsistent results have been found with regard to the association between job strain and blood pressure. Part of the reason for this may be that job strain is relevant primarily to the blood pressure levels during working hours. In two different studies—one of men who were studied by means of fully automated blood pressure measurements at work, during leisure, and during sleep (31), and a second of female caregivers who were studied by means of self-triggered measurements of blood pressure (32)—we found that job strain was associated with blood pressure during working hours and at rest, but not during leisure hours. In the study of women, a clear association was also observed between job strain and plasma prolactin level when the subject arrived at work in the morning, and plasma prolactin was also significantly associated with blood pressure levels at work. Schnall et al. (33) found clear relationships between job strain and hypertension, and, for the younger subjects in their study sample, between job strain and ventricular hypertrophy, even after adjustment for a number of potential confounders.

SOCIAL REWARD

A model similar to the demand–control model has been developed and tested by Siegrist et al. (34). Their model uses *effort* and *social reward* as the crucial dimensions, and the hypothesis to be tested is that high effort without social reward is pathogenetic. The *social reward* dimension has elements of both decision latitude and social support. In a recently published study of industry workers (34), it was shown that combinations of high effort and lack of reward predicted increased MI risk independently of biomedical risk factors. The relative risk was in the order of 4.0.

A CONCRETE EXAMPLE: THE BUS DRIVER

One area that has developed more specifically than other research endeavors in this field is the study of bus drivers. There is now overwhelming evidence that bus drivers, particularly those driving in inner-city areas, have an excess risk of developing MI (35–37) at an early age compared with other workers. Possible reasons for this excess risk have been explored. It has been shown that standard risk factors cannot explain all of it (38). It has previously been suspected that exposure to carbon monoxide may be of importance, but this seems unlikely (38). Other toxicological exposure may be of importance—for instance, combustion products (39). However, it has been emphasized in recent research that job strain may be an important factor (40), and some physiological consequences of job strain in bus drivers have been explored. Catecholamines (41) have been shown to be elevated in bus drivers who experience a high degree of job strain, for instance. However, more specific hypotheses have also been developed. Belkic et al. (42) found that bus drivers seem to develop an aroused electrophysiological response to "the glare pressor test" more rapidly than others, particularly when instructions simulate a traffic situation (42). It is possible that professional drivers have an accumulated experience of dangerous situations associated with sudden "glares," particularly at night, and that this may be a potent factor explaining why bus drivers develop an excess risk for MI after some years of driving—they become constantly hyperalert during driving, and this may be of importance to several of the risk factors. Accordingly, it seems important to diminish number of driving hours and to improve external conditions for bus driving (e.g., by creating special bus routes, educating pedestrians, and reinventing the conductor). This is an important concrete example of mechanisms operating in a low-control, low-support, and high-demand situation.

PHYSIOLOGICAL MEASUREMENTS

The physiological basis for the associations between psychosocial factors and CHD has been a lively research field during the period. Catecholamines have been suspected of mediating some of the relationship, and during the period it has become possible not only to study urinary excretion (which is still a good way to collect data on sympathoadrenal activity during integrated periods of time), but also the small concentrations that exist during rest in venous plasma. A study by our group recently showed that poor social network and support, as well as a job classified as *boring*, all contribute to an elevated venous plasma adrenaline at rest in the studied 28-year-old men (43). On the whole, however, the main endeavor has been the study of urinary catecholamine excretion (44). Recently, epidemiological studies have shown a correlation between poor social network and high urinary excretion of catecholamines (45), as well as between poor decision latitude and high catecholamine excretion (46). However, it has also been found that sympathoadrenal reactions in different organs may be specific, and accordingly generalizations should not be made in all instances (47).

The possibilities to monitor physiological functions continuously have induced a revolution in this field. For instance, because we can now study heart rate and blood pressure during activity and sleep, we have started to explore how psychosocial factors relate to the development of coronary atherosclerosis, for instance. The lowest heart rate during sleep correlates with degree and progression of coronary atherosclerosis (48, 49). It could be that inability to relax is associated with a high heart rate during sleep, as well as with progression of coronary atherosclerosis.

Similarly, Undén and Orth-Gomér showed that poor social support at work is associated with a high heart rate throughout day and night (50). The interpretations of these associations are not clear, but it is possible that feelings of distress may activate the sympathoadrenal system. The results from a longitudinal study performed by our group (51, 52) indicate that, when working subjects perceive increasing levels of job strain (spontaneous variations were followed at 3- to 4-month intervals during a year), these variations are associated with increasing systolic blood pressure during working hours, as well as decreasing levels of plasma testosterone. The former observation indicates increasing sympathoadrenal arousal and the second one decreasing anabolic activity.

A growing field that relates to catecholamines is also coagulation. For instance, a boring job (or job strain) has been related to high plasma fibrinogen levels (53), and recently lack of reward was shown to be associated with high plasma fibrinogen levels among middle managers (54). The question that arises could be formulated in the following way: To what extent do psychosocial variables associated with both clots and atherosclerosis exist? Certainly the common themes in lack of social support in life in general and lack of possibilities to learn and influence decision at work may be boredom and lack of reward.

Personality

It has been speculated that the association between job strain and risk of CVD could be due to personality differences in the subjective descriptions of the work environment. In some studies, this has been tested empirically in relationship to Type A behavior (17, 23, 33). In these studies, the relationship between job strain and cardiovascular illness risk remained significant even after adjustment for Type A scores. A more thorough study has been made recently, and relationships were found between certain personality traits and the job strain model—for instance, "active jobs" (high demand, high control) were associated with increased Type A scores (55). This study gives us no reason to believe that the relationship between job strain and personality could be explained away by personality traits as confounding factors. However, it should be pointed out that many years of exposure to a nonsupportive job strain situation could enforce personality and behavioral traits that could be coronary prone. It is also possible that such traits interact adversely with job strain. Research in this field has been insufficient so far.

LOCOMOTOR DISORDERS

Another example of a research field that has been exploring the demand–control–support model is that of locomotor disorders. Several studies (unfortunately mostly cross-sectional) have provided data regarding the association between the perceived psychosocial work environment and risk of disorders in neck, shoulders, and low back. The findings are diverging. In some of them, psychological demands, in others, decision latitude, and in others, social support, are important (56). This may simply reflect the differences in exposure to adverse conditions in different groups. Furthermore, in the case of locomotor disorders, we are dealing with less easily defined conditions, and it is sometimes difficult to disentangle different levels in a causal chain. In a recent study by our group (57), psychological demands were shown to be strongly associated with sleep disturbance, plasma cortisol levels, self-reported muscle tension, and pain in the locomotor system. Another recent study indicated that, in female health care personnel in Stockholm, the demand–control model had a relationship with symptoms from the low back region, but no relationship with symptoms from the neck and shoulders (58).

A recent study by our group has shown that pain threshold may be related to the demand–control–support model in a complex way. Randomly selected men and women were asked to fill out questions about these dimensions in the descriptions of their work. Their pain thresholds were measured on six different points in the neck and shoulders, first at rest before anything else happened in the laboratory, second in conjunction with an experimental stress test (the Stroop test), and third after a new resting period. Our analyses indicate that, as expected, the pain threshold increased during acute stress, that those who reported a habitually high level of psychological demands at work had higher pain thresholds than others (i.e., were less pain sensitive than others), and that those who reported a low level of decision latitude in their habitual working situation had a lower pain threshold during experimental stress than others (59). The interpretation of these findings is difficult. It seems plausible that subjects with high psychological demand levels who mobilize energy to meet demands may also repress feelings of pain. This may increase risks of long-term development of pathological changes in locomotor tissues. However, it is also plausible to assume that long-term exposure to low decision latitude may increase the risk of depression (13), and that this could explain why subjects who describe their jobs in these terms are unable to raise their pain thresholds during acute stress situations.

FUTURE RESEARCH GOALS

At present, research in this field has established a possible general model for studying the relationship between the psychosocial work environment and risk of cardiovascular illness development. However, general models are far from applicable to practical preventive work. Energy needs to be devoted to the formulation of more specific models that are applicable to caregivers, bus drivers, industry workers, teachers, and so on.

Few studies have evaluated the effects of work organization changes in line with the theoretical models that have been used. A strict evaluation has turned out to be difficult because attention to individual risk factors and individual counseling concerning them has turned out to be a necessary motivational factor in work organization change processes (13, 60). In line with the quality of working life research, the changes that have been tried are focusing on improved social support and increased decision latitude. One example is to increase the number of structured staff meetings, which enables increased social support as well as improved democracy in decision making in the worksite. Few studies have tried such changes and evaluated them in relation to CVD. One example is a Swedish study that included in its program individual counseling as well as exploration of the work organization and subsequent initiation of changes (61). Interestingly, the program was taken up differently in the four worksites that participated in the experimental program. In one worksite ("active"), the employees were more used to organizational work, and the supervisors were more inclined to be actively engaged in such work than in the other worksites ("passive"). The plasma cortisol levels developed differently in these groups. In both groups, there was a tendency for the cortisol levels to increase initially during the process; subsequently, they diminished in the active group and increased in the passive group. There was also a tendency for plasma testosterone levels to rise more in the active group (in women particularly) than in the passive group, and this increase was still observed at the time of follow-up 4 months after the end of the program (62). We need more research of this kind in the future, in which controlled interventions are explored by means of psychological and physiological methods.

It has become obvious that physical and psychosocial work environment factors could interact in complex ways, and that this has been neglected in previous research. A large-scale, multidisciplinary, case-control study, SHEEP (Stockholm HEart EPidemiology), of all MIs in the greater Stockholm area during a 2-year period has the goal of filling this gap. In the same vein, a large-scale, longitudinal study of several thousand working men and women is just starting in Stockholm. The goal of this study, WOrk environment, Life style and risk Factors for coronary heart disease (WOLF), is to follow the development of biomedical and psychosocial risk factors in different occupations and worksites in Stockholm.

One criticism that has been leveled against the use of the demand–control model has been that there is a relationship between low social class and high risk of developing cardiovascular illness, and that this in itself may explain the association between job strain and cardiovascular illness risk (63). In several studies, however, social class and education have been factors that have been adjusted for, and, despite this, the relationships have remained significant (13). There is a possibility that the relationship between low social class and elevated cardiovascular illness risk may be partly explained by the fact that adverse job conditions are more common in lower socioeconomic strata than in other groups of the population. This should be explored in more detail in future research.

SUMMARY

Several recent studies have shown that the psychosocial work environment is of significance to risk of developing CVD. Of particular importance in the recent development of this field is that theoretical models, such as the demand–control–support model and the social reward model, have been developed. They provide the basis for studies of the interaction between different environmental factors (e.g., between psychological demands and control, and between support and control). Such interactions have been studied in relation to physiological mechanisms of relevance to heart disease, and they have also been used in intervention studies that have focused on work organization factors underlying the perceived work environment.

Many epidemiological studies have explored the association between work environment and risk of heart disease. These studies have supported the hypothesis that the combination of high psychological demands and low decision latitude (small possibility for the individual to control conditions at work) is associated with increased risk of CVD. Direct effects of psychosocial work environment factors on neuroendocrine factors of relevance to CVD risk have been shown, such as high catecholamine output in job strain situations, as well as progressively increasing sympathoadrenal arousal, increasing sleep disturbance, and decreasing anabolism with increasing job strain. Significant relationships between the psychosocial work environment and the accepted cardiovascular risk factors—in particular, smoking habits—have also been shown in some studies. The relationship between job strain and blood pressure is difficult to study, and conflicting results have been found. Some of the inconsistencies in this field seem to have methodological explanations. The relationships between the demand–control model and social class, as well as between the model and gender, are presently being discussed in the literature.

Other disease categories have also been studied using the demand–control–support model. Some relationships between the model and symptoms in the locomotor system have also been found. In this case, the relationships may be different in different strata of the population and different for different outcomes (e.g., low back vs. neck and shoulder symptoms).

Intervention research has shown that the demand–control–support model is educationally useful. It could be used effectively in discussions about improved work conditions. Conversely, explorations regarding the basic dimensions have to become specific for different strata of the workforce, and our measurement instruments have to be improved to make further progress possible.

REFERENCES

1. Kornitzer M, Kittel F, Dramaix M, et al. Job stress and coronary heart disease. Adv Cardiol 1982;19:56–61.
2. Kittel F, Kornitzer M, Dramaix M. Coronary heart disease and job stress in two cohorts of bank clerks. Psychother Psychosom 1980;34:110–23.

3. Kornitzer M, Kittel F. How does stress exert its effects—smoking, diet and obesity, physical activity. Postgrad Med J 1986;62:695–96.

4. Biörck G, Blomqvist G, Sievers, J. Studies on myocardial infarction in Malmö 1935–1954: II. Infarction rate by occupational group. Acta Med Scand 1958;161:21–28.

5. Buell P, Breslow L. Mortality from coronary heart disease in California men who work long hours. J Chronic Dis 1960;11:615–26.

6. Russek HI, Zohman BL. Relative significance of heredity, diet and occupational stress in coronary heart disease among young adults. Am J Med Sci 1958;235:266.

7. Kasanen A, Kallio V, Forsström J. The significance of psychic and socioeconomic stress and other modes of life in the etiology of myocardial infarction. Ann Med Intern Fenn 1963; 52 Suppl 43:1–40.

8. Hinkle LE, Whitney LH, Lehman EW, et al. Occupation, education and coronary heart disease. Science 1968;161:238–48.

9. Pell S, d'Alonzo CA. Acute myocardial infarction in a large employed population: report of six-year study of 1,356 cases. JAMA 1963;185:831–41.

10. Katz D, Kahn R. Social psychology of organizations. New York: Wiley, 1966.

11. Cooper CL, Marshall J. Occupational sources of stress: a review of the literature relating to coronary heart disease and mental ill health. J Occ Psychol 1976;49:11–28.

12. Karasek RA. Job demands, job decision latitude, and mental strain: implications for job redesign. Admin Sci Q 1979;24:285–307.

13. Karasek RA, Theorell T. Healthy work. New York: Basic Books, 1990.

14. Alfredsson L. Myocardial infarction and environment: use of registers in epidemiology [master's thesis]. Stockholm: Karolinska Institute, 1983.

15. Johnson JV, Hall EM. Job strain, workplace social support and cardiovascular disease: a cross-sectional study of a random sample of the Swedish working population. Am J Public Health 1988;78:1336–42.

16. Alfredsson L, Theorell T. Job characteristics of occupations and myocardial infarction risk: effects of possible confounding factors. Soc Sci Med 1983;17:1497–1503.

17. La Croix AZ. Occupational exposure to high demand/low control work and coronary heart disease incidence in the Framingham cohort [dissertation]. Chapel Hill: University of North Carolina, 1984.

18. Reed DM, La Croix AZ, Karasek RA, et al. Occupational strain and the incidence of coronary heart disease. Am J Epidemiol 1989;129:495–502.

19. Hahn M. Job strain and cardiovascular disease: a ten year prospective study. Am J Epidemiol 1985;122:532–40.

20. Karasek RA, Baker D, Marxer F, et al. Job decision latitude, job demands, and cardiovascular disease: a prospective study of Swedish men. Am J Public Health 1981;71:694–705.

21. Hammar N, Alfredsson L, Theorell T. Job characteristics and incidence of myocardial infarction. A study of men and women in Sweden, with particular reference to job strain. Int J Epidemiol 1994;23:277–284.

22. Marmot M, Theorell T. Social class and cardiovascular disease: the contribution of work. Int J Health Services 1988;18(4):659–74.

23. Theorell T, Perski A, Orth-Gomér K, et al. The effects of the strain of returning to work on the risk of cardiac death after a first myocardial infarction before age 45. Int J Cardiol 1991;30:61–7.

24. Johnson JV, Hall EM, Theorell T. Combined effects of job strain and social isolation on cardiovascular disease morbidity and mortality in a random sample of the Swedish male working population. Scand J Work Environ Health 1989;15:271–79.

25. House JS, Strecher V, Metzner HL, et al. Occupational stress and health among men and women in the Tecumseh Community Health Study. J Health Soc Beh 1986;27:62–77.

26. Johnson JV, Stewart W, Hall EM, Fredland P, Theorell T. Long-term psychosocial work environment exposure and cardiovascular mortality: a prospective nested case-control study of randomly sampled Swedish males. Am J Publ Health. In review 1994.

27. Hall EM. Women's work: an inquiry into the health effects of invisible and visible labor [master's thesis]. Stockholm: Karolinska Institute, 1990.

28. Karasek RA. Job content questionnaire. Los Angeles, CA: University of Southern California, 1985.

29. Theorell T, Michelsen H, Nordemar R. Validitetsprövning av indexbildningarna psykiska krav, kontrollmöjligheter (stimulans och påverkansmöjligheter), positiva faktorer (=socialt stöd i arbetet), sömnrubbningar samt dold och öppen coping [Validity testing of indices psychological demands, decision latitude (intellectual discretion and authority over decisions), positive factors (= social support at work), sleep disturbance and covert and open coping]. In: Hagbarg M, Hogstedt C, editors. Metodbeskrivning MUSIC I. Stockholm: Arbetsmiljöinstitutet, 1993.

30. Theorell T, Ahlberg-Hulten G, Jodko M, et al. Att förbättra arbetsmiljön i vård [To improve working conditions in health care]. Stressforskningsrapporter nr 233. Stockholm: National Institute for Psychosocial Factors and Health, 1992.

31. Theorell T, de Faire U, Johnson J, et al. Job strain and ambulatory blood pressure profiles. Scand J Work Environ Health 1991;17:380–85.

32. Theorell T, Ahlberg-Hultén G, Jodko M, et al. Influence of job strain and emotion on blood pressure levels in female hospital personnel during work hours. Scand J Work Environ Health 1993;19:264–69.

33. Schnall PL, Schwartz JE, Landsbergis PA, et al. Relation between job strain, alcohol, and ambulatory blood pressure. Hypertension 1992;19(5):488–94.

34. Siegrist J, Peter R, Junge A, et al. Low status control, high effort at work and ischemic heart disease: prospective evidence from bluecollar men. Soc Sci Med 1990;31(10):1127–34.

35. Alfredsson L, Hammar N, Hogstedt C. Incidence of myocardial infarction and mortality from specific causes among bus drivers. Int J Epidemiol 1992;22:57–61.

36. Rosengren A, Anderson K, Wilhelmsen L. Risk of coronary heart disease in middle-aged bus and tram drivers compared to men in other occupations: a prospective study. Int Epidemiol 1991;20:82–7.

37. Belkic K, Savic C, Theorell T, et al. Mechanisms of cardiac risk in professional drivers. A clinically and ecologically relevant neurocardiologic model. Stockholm: National Institute of Psychosocial Factors and Health, 1992.

38. Söndergård-Kristensen T, Damsgaard MT. Hjertekar-sygdomme og arbeidsmiljö [Cardiovascular diseases and work environment]. Copenhagen: Arbejdsmiljöfondet, 1987.

39. Gustavsson P. Cancer and ischemic heart disease in occupational groups exposed to combustion products. Solna, Sweden: National Institute of Occupational Health, 1989.

40. Hedberg G, Jacobsson KA, Janlert U, et al. Riskindikatorer för ischemisk hjärtsjukdom i en kohort av manliga yrkesförare [Risk indicators for ischemic heart disease in a cohort of male professional drivers]. Stockholm: National Institute of Occupational Health, 1991.

41. Evans G, Carrere S. Traffic congestion, perceived control and psychophysiological stress among urban bus drivers. J Applied Psychol 1991;76:658–63.

42. Belkic K, Ercegovac D, Savic C, et al. EEG and cardiovascular reactivity in professional drivers. The glare pressor test. Eur Heart J 1992;13:304–09.

43. Knox S, Theorell T, Svensson J, et al. The relation of social support and working environment to medical variables associated with elevated blood pressure in young males: a structural model. Soc Sci Med 1985;21:525–31.

44. Frankenhaeuser M, Johansson G. Stress at work: psychobiological and psychosocial aspects. Int Rev Appl Psychol 1986;35:287–99.

45. Eide R. Psychosocial factors and indices of health risks [master's thesis]. Bergen, Norway: University of Bergen, 1982.

46. Härenstam A, Theorell T. Work conditions and urinary excretion of catecholamines—a study of prison staff in Sweden. Scand J Work Environ Health 1988;14:257–64.

47. Hjemdahl P, Fagius J, Freyschuss B, et al. Muscle sympathetic activity and norepinephrine release during mental challenge in humans. Am Physiol Soc 1989;E654–E664.

48. Perski A, Hamsten A, Lindvall K, et al. Heart rate correlates with severity of coronary atherosclerosis in young postinfarction patients. Am Heart J 1989;116(5 Pt1):1369–73.

49. Perski A, Olsson G, Landou C, et al. Minimum heart rate and coronary atherosclerosis: independent relations to global severity and rate of progression of angiographic lesions in men with myocardial infarction at young age. Am Heart J 1992;123(3):609–16.

50. Undén A-L, Orth-Gomér K, Elofsson S. Cardiovascular effects of social support in the workplace: 24 hour ECG monitoring of men and women. Psychosom Med 1991;53:50–60.

51. Theorell T, Perski A, Åkerstedt T, et al. Changes in job strain in relation to changes in physiological state. Scand J Work Environ Health 1988;14:189–96.

52. Theorell T, Karasek RA, Eneroth P. Job strain variations in relation to plasma testosterone fluctuations in working men—a longitudinal study. J Intern Med 1990;227:31–6.

53. Markowe HL, Marmot MG, Shipley MJ, et al. Fibrinogen: a possible link between social class and coronary heart disease. Br Med J 1985;9:291–96.

54. Siegrist J, Peter R. Structural and individual intervention at the workplace. Lessons from socioepidemiologic research. Lecture at the Second International Congress of Behavioral Medicine; 1992 July 15–18; Hamburg.

55. Landsbergis PA, Schnall PL, Deitz D, et al. The patterning of psychological attributes and distress by "job strain" and social support in a sample of working men. J Behav Med 1992;15(4):379–405.

56. Bonger PM, de Winter CR. Psychosocial factors and musculoskeletal disease—a review of the literature. Nederlands: Instituut voor Praeventieve Gezondheidszorg, 1992.

57. Theorell T, Harms-Ringdahl K, Ahlberg-Hultén G, et al. Psychosocial job factors and symptoms from the locomotor system—a multicausal analysis. Scand J Rehab Med 1991;23:165–73.

58. Ahlberg-Hultén G, Sigala F, Theorell T. Social support, job strain and pain in the locomotor system among health care. Stockholm: National Institute of Psychosocial Factors and Health, 1993.

59. Theorell T, Nordemar R, Michélsen H, Stockholm Music Study Group. Pain thresholds during standardized psychological stress in relation to perceived psychosocial work situation. J Psychosom Res 1993;37(3):299–305.

60. Theorell T. Medical and physiological aspects of job interventions. In: Cooper CL, Robertson IT, editors. International review of industrial and organizational psychology. Vol. 8. Chichester: Wiley, 1993:173–92.

61. Eriksson I, Orth-Gomér K, Moser V, et al. KRUstress. Stockholm: Statshälsan, 1991.

62. Theorell T, Orth-Gomér K, Undén A-L, et al. Endocrine markers during a job intervention. Work and Stress. In press.

63. Albright CL, Winkleby MA, Ragland DR, et al. Job strain and prevalence of hypertension in a biracial population of urban bus drivers. Am J Public Health 1992;82:984–89.

Chapter 7

Stressful Work, Self-Experience, and Cardiovascular Disease Prevention

Johannes Siegrist
Institute of Medical Sociology,
University of Düsseldorf

There are at least four important reasons that account for the centrality of work and occupation in advanced industrialized societies. First, having a job is a principal prerequisite for continuous income opportunities. Level of income determines a wide range of life chances. Second, training for a job and achievement of occupational status are the most important goals of primary and secondary socialization. It is through education, job training, and status acquisition that personal growth and development are realized, that a core social identity outside the family is acquired, and that intentional, goal-directed activity in human life is shaped. Third, occupation defines a most important criterion of social stratification in advanced societies. Amount of esteem and social approval in interpersonal life largely depend on type of job, professional training, and level of occupational achievement. Furthermore, type and quality of occupation, and especially the degree of self-direction at work, strongly influence personal attitudes and behavioral patterns in areas that are not directly related to work, such as leisure, family life, education, and political activity (1). Finally, occupational settings produce the most pervasive and continuous demands during one's lifetime, and they absorb the largest amount of active time in adult life. Exposure to adverse job conditions carries the risk of ill health by virtue of the amount of time spent and the quality of demands faced at the workplace. At the same time, occupational settings provide unique options to experience reward, esteem, success, and satisfaction.

To understand the impact of working life on health in general, and on cardiovascular health in particular, it is important to realize that major changes in the working environment and task profiles occurred during the past few decades. Among these changes, the following are of special importance:

1. Fewer jobs are defined by physical demands; more jobs are characterized by psychomentally and emotionally demanding profiles.
2. There is a shortage of labor in the production sector, especially in traditional mass production, whereas more jobs are now available in the service sector.
3. An increasing number of jobs is concerned with information processing (computerization, automatization).
4. Overall, for a large part of the working population, occupational life has become less stable and secure than in earlier times (e.g., due to increased occupational mobility, structural unemployment, and forced retirement).
5. Several demographic and socioeconomic changes have a profound impact on working life, such as women's increasing participation in the labor process and a growing portion of the elderly among the economically active segments of the population.

How do these changes affect human health? More precisely, what are the critical components of the stressfulness of everyday work experience that are affecting human health in general and the cardiovascular system in particular? What subgroups of the labor force are exposed to increased cardiovascular risks as far as specific psychomental and socioemotional stressors are concerned? It is the aim of this chapter to identify new pathways linking adverse occupational conditions to elevated cardiovascular risks. Such pathways are assumed to operate along two lines: via enhanced neurohormonal and autonomic activation triggered by stressful experience, and via health-detrimental behaviors such as increased cigarette smoking or faulty diet.

There is no obvious reason to restrict this question to cardiovascular health. However, taking into account the following arguments, we feel such a restriction is well justified. First, in terms of public health, prevalence and incidence of cardiovascular disease (CVD) in the economically active segments of industrialized societies is of primary concern (2). No doubt it is essential to improve our ability to detect and prevent the risks of premature CVD manifestation. Second, convincing scientific evidence linking stressful experience to cardiovascular dysfunction and disease is now available (3–5). In particular, a specific quality of stressful experience with relevance to the cardiovascular system has been identified: "active distress" (6–9). Unlike Selye's notion of stress as a nonspecific general state of arousal (10), active distress points to the specific quality of emotional and neurohormonal activation following the experience of energy mobilization without success or control, of high cost followed by low gain, and of high effort without reward.

Experimental conditions of sustained active distress were shown to be associated with the progression of coronary atherosclerosis (8), altered lipid metabolism (11), enhanced cardiovascular reactivity (12, 13), and elevated blood pressure (14, 15) in animal studies. Respective evidence in humans derived from psychophysiological, clinical, and epidemiological studies cannot be adequately summarized here (e.g., 3–6, 16, 17). Finally, our own research over the past 12 years has been concerned with cardiovascular risk and disease from both social-epidemiological and psychophysiological perspectives, and a representative selection of respective research findings is discussed in this chapter.

It is difficult to identify pathways linking stressful working conditions to elevated cardiovascular risk at the level of job titles or at the level of conventional measures of socioeconomic status (SES). As Karasek and Theorell pointed out, such measures "appear to be too narrow in their conceptualization of occupational experience to delineate acccurately the mechanisms by which stress-related illness is caused" (18, p. 78). Therefore, theoretical models of stressful occupational experience that successfully identify those critical pathways need to be developed and tested.

One such model, the "job strain model," has proved to be particularly successful and important in this respect (18). This model, developed by Karasek (19) and extended more recently by Karasek and Theorell (18) and Johnson and Hall (20), combines two crucial dimensions of psychosocial working life—*job demand* and *job control*—to predict distress and subsequent coronary risk. Lack of control over how to meet the job's demands and how one can use one's skills defines a state of strain that inhibits learning. Strain-induced inhibition of learning, in turn, further increases strain experiences by impairing the worker's confidence (18). In other words, the model postulates an interaction of demand and decision latitude, as well as demand and skill acquisition on indicators of emotional distress and physiological dysfunction. The stressfulness of these experiences is enhanced under conditions of low social support and high social isolation (20). The empirical evidence of the job strain model in explaining cardiovascular risk and disease is impressive and convincing. Moreover, the model is now increasingly used to guide the design and implementation of preventive programs at the worksite (21).

Despite its outstanding merits, several limitations of the job strain model became evident more recently. For instance, in an increasing number of jobs, especially in service-oriented jobs dealing with humans, task content may not be the single most important dimension of stressful work experience. In such jobs, "burnout" has been linked to intensity of negative emotions even under conditions of high skill discretion and decision latitude (22). An increasing proportion of the workforce is now threatened by a different type of lack of control, which is not primarily related to task profile or work organization, but rather to job career and employment security. In these instances, lack of control over one's occupational status is the critical dimension.

A third critical comment on the job strain model concerns the role of personal coping characteristics in the stressor–strain association underlying the model. It is unlikely that the experience of strain in high-demand and low-decision settings is basically the same in all individuals who are exposed to an identical job condition. Rather, personal coping characteristics were shown to mediate the association between stressor and strain to an impressive degree (e.g., 23–25). Therefore, as Karasek and Theorell (18) pointed out, "a model that considers both individual and environmental factors is clearly necessary" (p. 95).

In keeping with these arguments, we have developed the model of effort–reward imbalance at work. Although linked to the job strain model, this approach has a different focus: the reward structure of work and its potential for self-regulation. The following sections describe its basic underlying ideas, its conceptual definition and measurement, and major empirical results including practical implications for prevention.

EFFORT–REWARD IMBALANCE
AND SELF-REGULATION AT WORK

This approach is based on a synthesis of several theoretical traditions. The first tradition dates back to the early classical writings of Karl Marx (26) and John Stuart Mill (27). Although starting from different assumptions, both writers agreed that, in a private market economy, a principal inequity exists between the hardships and earnings at work, and between the efforts spent and wages and salaries obtained in turn. Mill attributed this imbalance to the intrinsic restrictions of the labor market (e.g., those with low skills have fewer choices), whereas young Marx argued that private ownership by the capitalist destroyed the two basic functions of work for human well-being: the experience of "satisfactory productivity" and the experience of "enjoyment" resulting from this activity. According to Marx, alienation at work and exploitation instead prevent successful "self-confirmation" (26).

To my knowledge, this is the first time a concept has been defined that explicitly links the broader socioeconomic structure of occupational life with important human motivations concerned with self-regulation. Yet the heuristic potential of this concept becomes more evident if we introduce a second theoretical tradition: the sociological inquiry of self-experience.

In this respect, the writings of Georg Simmel (28) and George Herbert Mead (29) are of special interest. Both authors were interested in the way self and social structure are interrelated. According to Mead, the nature of human thoughts and experiences is essentially reflexive. This means that an individual learns to see him or herself in terms of anticipated reactions that significant others display toward him or her in a particular situation. Relevant self-experience is learned as a socially validated experience (29). Although in adult life self-experience may be less dependent on anticipated reactions from significant others, socially validated positive feedback from important reference groups still seems crucial for personal well-being.

But how are the dynamics of socially validated self-experience related to occupational life? In this respect, an important argument was developed by Simmel (28). According to him, socially validated, favorable self-experience depends on the availability of a social status (i.e., on the fact that an individual belongs to society). Simmel argued that social validation always occurs as a normative process (i.e., a process related to social expectations or norms, and to social positions or roles). Occupational status is considered a master status in modern societies. Therefore, successful self-experience, at least for large segments in adult populations, considerably depends on the availability of occupational positions.

Based on the arguments of Mill, Marx, Mead, and Simmel, a research model can now be developed that accounts for the specific stressfulness of occupational life characterized by high effort, inadequate wage, and lack of control over one's occupational status. Under these conditions, two crucial aspects of self-regulation—self-efficacy and self-esteem—may be compromised. The model of effort–reward imbalance assumes that high effort spent at work, in combination with low reward obtained in turn, triggers sustained negative emotions, which in turn activate autonomic neuroendocrine pathways (30). More explicitly, the model depicted in Fig. 7.1 exhibits three characteristics. First, it defines effort at work as a function of two conditions: high extrinsic task demands and high intrinsic motivation (i.e., high level of job involvement). Second, because the focus of this model is on occupational reward, three types of reward are distinguished: money, esteem, and status control (i.e., gratification in terms of promotion prospects, job security, absence of risk of forced downward mobility, and job loss). This latter reward dimension is of utmost importance in terms of stress theory because it points to the powerful threats produced by job loss or degradation on favorable self-experience. The third characteristic of this model can best be explained by referring to the theory of behavioral economics (31). This theory predicts continued behavioral disengagement under conditions of high cost and low gain. Yet the strategy of behavioral economy cannot be successfully applied if the costs produced by disengagement (e.g., the risk of facing downward mobility or being laid off) overweigh the costs of accepting inadequate benefits. Thus, contrary to the theory

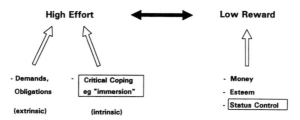

FIG. 7.1. The model of effort–reward imbalance.

of behavioral economics, the model of effort–reward imbalance predicts continued behavioral activity even under conditions of low gain.

Intrinsic coping is defined in terms of a coping pattern termed *immersion*. Immersion defines a cognitive-motivational style of excessive striving and involvement that is continued even under conditions of exhaustion. Immersion reflects an unusually high need for control in individuals—a need to be visible and powerful through tough achievements. It manifests itself as increased irritability, latent hostility, competitiveness, and inability to withdraw from work obligations (30).

METHODS AND STUDY SAMPLES

How is this model measured? In social-science research on work and health, three sources of information are usually available:

1. contextual information derived from independent sources such as administrative data and objective measurements;
2. descriptive information obtained from workers through structured interviews or questionnaires; and
3. evaluative information reflecting subjective appraisal (obtained through interviews and questionnaires).

Although in terms of psychological stress theory subjective appraisal is the crucial component (32), our model explicitly combines the different sources of information. This decision in favor of a triangulation of information is justified next.

The following list of indicators defines the core measures of the effort–reward imbalance at work.

Intrinsic Effort

The coping pattern *immersion* is measured by a psychometric scale termed *need for control* (30). This scale contains 45 dichotomous items. By means of confirmatory factor analysis, two latent factors were repeatedly found: *vigor* and *immersion*. According to our theoretical assumption, the latter factor defines a critical style of coping with demands reflecting frustrated, but continued efforts and associated negative feelings. A high score (upper tertile of the 29 items defining the total factor score immersion, or upper tertile of factor scores on its subscales: [a] need for approval, [b] competitiveness and latent hostility, [c] impatience and disproportionate irritability, and [d] inability to withdraw from work obligations) indicates a critical stage of intrinsic effort.

In addition to this pattern of critical coping with demands, the following indicators of an emotionally distressing state of effort were included: (a) feelings of sustained anger during the past 12 months, (b) feelings of sustained hopelessness during the past 12 months, and (c) distress-induced sleep disturbances (33).

Extrinsic Effort

Contextual information on extrinsic effort varies according to the study population. In our blue-collar study, piece work, shift work, overtime work, and increase of work load due to shortage of labor force were major contextual indicators of extrinsic effort. In the study on middle managers, the number of subordinates was considered a different important contextual indicator of extrinsic effort. Descriptive and evaluative information on extrinsic effort was obtained from ratings concerning frequency and stressfulness of experienced work pressure, interruptions, inconsistent demands, or facing difficult problems.

Occupational Rewards

In addition to contextual information on wages and salaries, the worker's evaluation of payment was assessed. Esteem reward was measured by two items asking about being accepted by supervisors or colleagues, and about receiving help in difficult conditions by supervisors or colleagues. Status control was measured partly by contextual information (e.g., amount of redundancy in the workforce during observation period), partly by description and evaluation (forced mobility, promotion prospects, status inconsistency, job insecurity).

In keeping with the core assumption of the effort–reward imbalance, we focused our analysis on those conditions where at least one indicator of high extrinsic or intrinsic effort and one indicator of low occupational reward were simultaneously present. These conditions were thought to trigger sustained active distress and, subsequently, to impair the cardiovascular system. However, according to the principle of triangulation (34), we did not specify in advance the type of information (contextual, descriptive, evaluative) on which these indicators were based. This was done in accordance with more recent insights into the nature of chronic stress, which is not necessarily confined to recurrent conscious appraisal processes (35, 36).

The two study samples from which the following results were obtained and the research designed are as follows. First, we conducted a 6½-year prospective study of a cohort of 416 male blue-collar workers (ages 25–55, M = 40.8 ± 9.7). All men were free from overt coronary heart disease (CHD) at entry. Medical and psychosocial data were collected at entry and three times during follow-up. Baseline psychosocial measures were used to explain prevalence and change over time in major coronary risk factors, and to predict new clinical events (37–39).

The second study to be reported was a cross-sectional analysis of associations between indicators of effort–reward imbalance at work and major coronary risk factors such as hypertension, elevated fibrinogen, elevated atherogenic lipids, and smoking in a sample of male middle managers (n = 179, ages 40–55, M = 48.5 ± 4.5). This sample was remarkably homogeneous in terms of age and occupational status, and was representative of the total group of middle managers of this age group in the enterprise (40, 41).

RESULTS

The Blue-Collar Study

Table 7.1 contains an overview of major findings of the prospective blue-collar study. Odds ratios derived from logistic regression analyses are given with 95% confidence intervals. In these analyses, the model fit of the most parsimonious model is tested by the likelihood ratio difference test in a bottom–up procedure. Effects of confounding variables on the criterion under study are not presented in this overview.

Findings indicate that two indicators of high effort and two indicators of low reward at work independently predict new coronary events (acute myocardial infarction [AMI], or sudden cardiac death [SCD; ICD 410–414]). The magnitude of these odds ratios is well comparable, although the confidence intervals are quite large. This latter fact may be due to the small number of cases in this sample.

In keeping with our theoretical assumption, we explored the cumulative effect of a simultaneous manifestation of high effort and low reward in cases versus controls. This simultaneous manifestation was present in 38% of future cases, but only in 7.4% of the remaining group. With an odds ratio of 3.42 (combined effect of the two components), there was clear evidence in favor of this assumption.

In a next step, the robustness of findings was explored using the following two strategies. First, the group of cases was extended by including cerebrovascular events (stroke). There is no a priori reason to exclude this type of clinical event from stress-related cardiovascular epidemiology. At least we expected some of the observed effects to be maintained in this enlarged group. As shown in Table 7.1, two of the four indicators remained significant in the most parsimonious model: *immersion* and *status inconsistency* (for further discussion, see Fig. 7.2).

A second strategy aimed to combine the group of clinical cases with the group of subclinical conditions (ECG with signs of advanced ischemic heart disease [IHD], or left-ventricular hypertrophy without meeting criteria of primary endpoints), a group that is frequently excluded from statistical analysis in prospective studies. When combining the clinical and subclinical groups, the combined variable *high effort and low reward*, based on the previously mentioned indicators, produced a highly significant effect (odds ratio 6.15; details not shown). Thus, either strategy contributed to the robustness of reported findings to some extent.

In terms of prevention, it is important to know whether workers characterized by high effort and low reward exhibit elevated coronary risks well in advance of the often fatal first clinical manifestation of IHD. One such indicator is the so-called "coronary high-risk status" (i.e., the co-manifestation of hypertension and atherogenic lipids). A powerful interaction of those two factors to produce IHD was first demonstrated in the Framingham study (42), and was replicated in our much smaller blue-collar cohort (38). Table 7.1 demonstrates independent effects of at least three indicators of high effort and low reward on coronary high-risk status.

TABLE 7.1

Odds Ratios From Multivariate Logistic Regression Analysis Explaining Coronary Risk Factors and Clinical Events by Indicators of Effort–Reward Imbalance at Work in Blue-Collar Workers

Indicator	Odds Ratio	95% CI	Criterion	n
Work pressure (extrinsic effort)	3.45	0.97–12.30	Acute myocardial infarction (AMI) or sudden death (SCD)	263
Immersion (intrinsic effort)	4.53	1.15–17.80		
Status inconsistency (reward, status control)	4.40	1.36–14.20		
Job security (reward, status control)	3.41	0.81–14.50		
Immersion (intrinsic effort)	3.57	1.22–10.47	AMI, SCD, or stroke	314
Status inconsistency (reward, status control)	2.86	1.04–7.80		
Competitiveness (intrinsic effort)	2.79	1.29–6.04	Coronary high-risk status[a]	310
Sustained anger (intrinsic effort)	5.41	1.85–15.83		
Low promotion prospects (reward, status control)	2.71	1.11–6.63		
Job instability (reward, status control)	1.54	0.68–3.49		

Note. From (37–39).

[a]SBP ≥ 160 mm Hg and/or DBP ≥ 95 mm Hg; LDL cholesterol ≥ 180 mg/dl or ratio LDL/HDL cholesterol > 4.0 (for details, see [38]; for further details, see text).

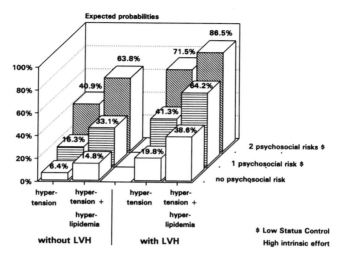

FIG. 7.2. Expected probabilities of cardiovascular events (AMI, stroke) in a 6.5-yr. prospective study (N = 314 blue-collar men), based on multiple logistic regression analysis.

Again, the robustness of findings was further explored by additional analysis. First, the relevant questions measuring effort–reward imbalance entered factor analysis, and a logistic regression was performed using respective factor scores. In terms of odds ratios, results showed even stronger effects (43). Second, the temporal stability of reported findings was checked by replicating the analysis with psychosocial measures derived from a consecutive screening (43).

To demonstrate the potential of improved prediction by combining information on biomedical risk factors and psychosocial risks, expected probabilities for relevant combinations of variables can be calculated using the beta coefficients of the multiple logistic regression analysis (44). One example of this type of analysis is found in Fig. 7.2. In this figure, calculated risk stratification for new cardiovascular events fits with our assumption that the presence of psychosocial risks augments the probability of a cardiovascular event at all levels of biomedical risks, especially if the two components of *high effort* and *low reward* are simultaneously present.

In conclusion, in view of documented excess morbidity and mortality from IHD in lower socioeconomic groups in middle adulthood (45, 46), it is important to know more precisely what psychosocial factors contribute to this excess risk. The model of effort–reward imbalance, as measured in this study, is able to identify some critical conditions related to unfavorable self-regulation in threatening occupational contexts. It is important to note that threats to occupational status control are the only category of reward with explanatory power in this study population. Neither indicators of esteem reward nor measures of financial benefits were predictive. However, indicators of intrinsic effort, especially the coping pattern *immersion*, seem to be more important than indicators of extrinsic effort. It may be that, in this blue-collar group, extrinsic effort did not vary to a sufficient degree to account for differential disease susceptibility. In fact, the group under study was exposed to unusually high levels of work pressure throughout the observation period.

The Middle Managers Study

This study was finished only recently, and most findings so far are unpublished. Therefore, the presentation of some selected results is restricted to a summary overview presented in Table 7.2 (36, 40). In this table, odds ratios are always related to a combined, three-category variable measuring the presence–absence of the two critical components of the model (2 = two indicators [high effort and low reward] are present; 1 = one indicator only is present; 0 = neither indicator is present). It is assumed that Category 2 produces the most powerful effects on the criteria under study. As can be seen from Table 7.2, this assumption holds true in three different respects: in explaining (a) cigarette smoking, (b) elevated level of atherogenic lipids, and (c) arterial hypertension. In these analyses, the effect of relevant confounders was controlled, as was done in the previous study.

Similar findings, not shown in detail here, were obtained with respect to elevated plasma fibrinogen and to the previously mentioned coronary high-risk status. Taken together, these results underline the importance of stressful experience at work in explaining the prevalence of multiple important cardiovascular risk factors in middle adulthood. Moreover, they show that refined theoretical concepts are capable of differentiating those at risk within occupationally homogeneous groups, such as middle managers in a large car-producing enterprise. In accordance with evidence obtained from the blue-collar study, it is the imbalance between high effort and low reward that matters most.

However, there are also some interesting differences between the two studies. First, in middle managers, *esteem reward* is an important variable in addition to *status control*. It should be emphasized that job security in this group is very high, unlike in the case of blue-collar workers. Less dramatic threats, such as forced mobility and lack of esteem reward, may become important sources of distress in this group. Second, extrinsic effort is a powerful predictor of cardiovascular risk in middle managers. Unlike in blue-collar workers, we found considerable variation in extrinsic efforts. For instance, the number of subordinates varied between 7 and 150 men. Taken together, these findings lend support to the strategy of developing measures of occupational stress that, to some extent, can be adapted to the different target groups under study.

IMPLICATIONS FOR PREVENTION

Although the results reported in this chapter need further confirmation, we should nevertheless emphasize that the empirical basis of the blue-collar study covers more than 2,000 person years. Moreover, a second prospective study conducted in a

TABLE 7.2

Odds Ratios From Multivariate Logistic Regression Analysis Explaining Coronary Risk Factors by Indicators of Effort–Reward Imbalance at Work in Middle Managers

Indicator (Combined Variable)	Odds Ratio	95% CI	Criterion	n
Number of subordinates (extrinsic effort)	1.08[a]	0.50–2.34	Cigarette smoking	163
Lack of esteem by colleagues (reward)	4.34[b]	1.50–12.54		
Low promotion prospects (reward, status control)				
Frequent interruptions or high work load (extrinsic effort)	1.87[a]	0.89–3.93	Atherogenic lipids (LDL cholesterol ≥ 160 mg/dl)	168
Lack of help if needed (reward, esteem)	3.33[b]	1.22–9.21		
Frequent interruptions (extrinsic effort)	2.25[a]	0.90–6.00	Hypertension	170
Forced job change (reward, status control)	6.81[b]	1.70–26.60		

Note. From (36, 40).

[a]Indicator of high effort or low reward.
[b]Indicator of high effort and low reward. For further details, see text.

98

different sociocultural setting produced some interesting results that can be interpreted in terms of effort–reward imbalance (47). The relevance of the findings of the cross-sectional study of middle managers is limited because no prospective data are available. Yet additional experimental information on cardiovascular and hormonal reactions to psychomental stress at work substantiates the reported findings (36). To our knowledge, this is the first time the prevalence of a majority of important cardiovascular risk factors is shown to be consistently associated with a set of indicators measuring chronic psychosocial stress.

Implications of these results for prevention are important at least at two levels. First, monitoring and screening activities should be intensified in early and middle adulthood in economically active segments of advanced industrialized societies. Special emphasis should be put on occupational groups defined by high work-related efforts, poor benefits and poor job security, or related threats to status control. It is reasonable to expect the following in these groups: (a) a higher prevalence of important cardiovascular risk factors, (b) a higher proportion of individuals with multiple cardiovascular risks, (c) a lower proportion of individuals who are aware of their risks and/or who follow prescribed medication or other means of risk-factor control, and (d) a higher prevalence of subclinical or clinical IHD. Although the monetary and nonmonetary benefits of such strategies of targeted intervention still have to be demonstrated, it is nevertheless evident that a reduction of the burden of cardiovascular morbidity and mortality in middle adulthood is of primary importance in terms of public health.

A second implication for prevention concerns the design and implementation of intervention activities guided by the model of effort–reward imbalance. Traditionally, intervention with regard to stress at work has focused on individual behavior or small-group processes. These approaches are well justified in view of the documented effects of critical patterns of coping with work demands, and of inadequate interpersonal behavior at the worksite. However, structural measures have to be integrated into successful strategies of behavioral change (48). The importance of structural changes in the work environment was recently elucidated by a series of impressive findings evaluating the effects of job redesign according to the model of job strain (18, 21, 49).

Similarly, measures of structural intervention can be derived from the model of effort–reward imbalance. Here, the following measures are suggested as important targets:

1. Jobs with cumulative exposure to work stressors should be replaced. If not feasible, exposure time should be reduced. It is important to offer jobs to these highly vulnerable groups that are not paid worse (e.g., by introducing mixed-task profiles).
2. High effort at work should be compensated more adequately by wage differentials, flexible payment, and related incentives (e.g., participation in savings). This flexibility is usually lacking in traditional patterns of negotiation between enterpreneurs and trade unions.

3. Additional measures of occupational reward should be promoted, such as more flexible work schedules, time savings, extra-job services (e.g., nursery schools for working mothers, shopping facilities), or investments in job security.

4. Esteem reward should be developed by improving feedback from supervisors and strengthening teamwork across traditional boundaries of hierarchy. In this respect, segmentation of hierarchies may be an important structural prerequisite.

5. Opportunities for job training and requalification need to be strengthened. Counseling activities should be offered to those who lack motivation and to those who anticipate adverse events in their occupational career.

These and related structural measures should be combined with interpersonal and individual intervention. Thus, a new type of preventive effort in the field of occupational psychosocial health becomes evident. With the help of theoretical models, it is hoped that challenges of prevention can be met more successfully in the near future.

REFERENCES

1. Kohn M, Schooler C. Work and personality: an inquiry into the impact of social stratification. Norwood, NJ: Ablex, 1983.
2. Uemura K, Pisa Z. Trends in cardiovascular disease mortality in industrialized countries since 1950. Wld Health Stat Q 1988;41:155–67.
3. Beamish RE, Singal PK, Dhalla NS, editors. Stress and heart disease. Boston: Nijhoff, 1985.
4. Weiner H. Perturbing the organism: the biology of stressful experience. Chicago: University of Chicago Press, 1992.
5. Williams R, Williams V. Anger kills. New York: Times Books, 1993.
6. Henry JP, Stephens PM. Stress, health, and the social environment. Berlin: Springer, 1977.
7. Frankenhaeuser M. Psychoneuroendocrine approaches to the study of emotions related to stress and coping. In: Howe D, editor. Nebraska symposium on motivation. Lincoln, NE: University of Nebraska Press, 1979:209–34.
8. Manuck SB, Kaplan JR, Adams MR, et al. Effects of stress and the sympathetic nervous system on coronary artery atherosclerosis in the cynomolgus macaque. Am Heart J 1988;116:328–33.
9. Siegrist J, Siegrist K, Weber I. Sociological concepts in the etiology of chronic disease: the case of ischemic heart disease. Soc Sci Med 1986;22:247–53.
10. Selye H. The general adaptation syndrome and the diseases of adaptation. J Clin Endocrinol 1946;6:117–96.
11. Sapolski RM, Mott GE. Social subordinance in wild baboons is associated with suppressed high density lipoprotein cholesterol: the possible role of chronic social stress. Endocrinol 1987;121:1605–10.
12. Matthews KA, Weiss SM, Detre T, et al., editors. Handbook of stress, reactivity, and cardiovascular disease. New York: Wiley, 1986.
13. Krantz DS, Manuck SB. Acute psychophysiologic reactivity and risk of cardiovascular disease: a review and a methodologic critique. Psychol Bull 1984;96:435–64.
14. Henry JP. Biological basis of the stress response. Integr Physiol Behav Sci 1992;27:66–83.

15. Koolhaas JM, Fokkema DS, Bohus B, et al. Individual differences in blood pressure reactivity and behavior of male rats. In: Schmidt TH, Dembroski TM, Blumchen G, editors. Biological and psychological factors in cardiovascular disease. Berlin: Springer, 1986:517–26.
16. Marmot M, Elliott P, editors. Coronary heart disease epidemiology. Oxford: Oxford University Press, 1992.
17. Schmidt TH, Dembroski TM, Blumchen G, editors. Biological and psychological factors in cardiovascular disease. Berlin: Springer, 1986.
18. Karasek RA, Theorell T. Healthy work: stress, productivity, and the reconstruction of working life. New York: Basic Books, 1990.
19. Karasek RA. Job demands, job decision latitude, and mental strain: implications for job redesign. Adm Sci Q 1979;24:285–307.
20. Johnson JV, Hall E. Job strain, work place social support, and cardiovascular disease. Am J Public Health 1988;78:1336–42.
21. International Labour Office, editor. Conditions of work digest. Preventing stress at work. Vol. 11, 2. Geneva: 1992.
22. Paine WS, editor. Job stress and burnout: research, theory, and intervention perspectives. Beverly Hills, CA: Sage, 1982.
23. Steptoe A, Appels A, editors. Stress, personal control and health. Chichester: Wiley, 1989.
24. Parkes KR. Personal control in an occupational context. In: Steptoe A, Appels A, editors. Stress, personal control and health. Chichester: Wiley, 1989:21–48.
25. Spector PE. Perceived control by employees: a meta-analysis of studies concerning autonomy and participation at work. Hum Relat 1986;39:1005–16.
26. Marx K. Frühe Schriften. Vol. I. Darmstadt: Wissenschaftliche Buchgesellschaft, 1962.
27. Mill JS. Principles of political economy with some of their applications to social philosophy. London: Routledge & Kegan Paul, 1965.
28. Simmel G. Soziologie [Sociology]. Berlin: Duncker Humblodt, 1958.
29. Mead GH. Mind, self and society. Chicago: University of Chicago Press, 1962.
30. Siegrist J, Matschinger H. Restricted status control and cardiovascular risk. In: Steptoe A, Appels A, editors. Stress, personal control and health. Chichester: Wiley, 1989:65–82.
31. Schönpflug W, Batmann W. The costs and benefits of coping. In: Fisher S, Reason J, editors. Handbook of stress, cognition and health. Chichester: Wiley, 1989:699–714.
32. Lazarus RS. Emotion and adaptation. New York: Oxford University Press, 1991.
33. Siegrist J. Sleep disturbances and cardiovascular risk: a biopsychosocial approach. In: Peter JH, Podszus T, von Wichert P, editors. Sleep related disorders and internal diseases. Berlin: Springer, 1987:173–82.
34. Mechanic D. Medical sociology. New York: The Free Press, 1978.
35. LeDoux JE. Emotion. In: Plum F, editor. Handbook of physiology. Nervous system V, higher function. Washington, DC: American Physiological Society, 1987:419–59.
36. Siegrist J. Soziale Krisen und Gesundheit [Social crises and health]. Göttingen: Hogrefe, 1995.
37. Siegrist J, Peter R, Junge A, et al. Low status control, high effort at work and ischemic heart disease: prospective evidence from blue-collar men. Soc Sci Med 1990;31:1127–34.
38. Siegrist J, Peter R, Georg W, et al. Psychosocial and biobehavioral characteristics of hypertensive men with elevated atherogenic lipids. Atherosclerosis 1991;86:211–18.
39. Siegrist J, Peter R, Motz W, et al. The role of hypertension, left ventricular hypertrophy and psychosocial risks in cardiovascular disease: prospective evidence from blue-collar men. Eur Heart J 1992;13 Suppl D:89–95.
40. Siegrist J, Peter R, Klein D: Der Einfluss von Rauchen und Distress auf die Entwicklung von Herz-Kreislauf-Risiken [Cigarette smoking, distress and cardiovascular risks]. Unpublished manuscript. Institute of Medical Sociology, University of Düsseldorf, 1993.
41. Peter R, Siegrist J, Stork J, et al. Zigarettenrauchen und psychosoziale Arbeitsbelastungen bei Beschäftigten des mittleren Managements [Smoking and psychosocial workload in middle managers]. Soz Prèventivmed 1991;36:315–21.

42. Castelli WP, Anderson KA. A population at risk. Am J Med 1986;80 Suppl 2A:23–32.
43. Peter R. Berufliche Belastungen, Belastungsbewältigung und koronares Risiko bei Industrie-arbeitern [Work stress, coping, and coronary risk in blue-collar workers]. Münster: LIT Verlag, 1991.
44. Hennekens CH, Buring JE. Epidemiology in medicine. Boston: Little, Brown & Co., 1987.
45. Marmot MG, Theorell T. Social class and cardiovascular disease: the contribution of work. Int J Health Serv 1988;18:659–71.
46. Siegrist J. Contributions of sociology to the prediction of heart disease and their implications for public health. Eur J Public Health 1991;1:10–21.
47. Siegrist J, Bernhardt R, Feng Z, et al. Socioeconomic differences in cardiovascular risk factors in China. Int J Epidemiol 1990;19:905–10.
48. Syme SL. Control and health: a personal perspective. In: Steptoe A, Appels A, editors. Stress, personal control and health. Chichester: Wiley, 1989:3–18.
49. Theorell T. Medical and physiological aspects of job intervention. Int Rev Ind Organiz Psychol 1993;8:173–92.

BIOBEHAVIORAL AND PSYCHOSOCIAL FACTORS IN CARDIOVASCULAR DISEASE PREVENTION

Insulin Metabolism, Sympathetic Nervous System Regulation, and Coronary Heart Disease Prevention

Neil Schneiderman
Jay S. Skyler
University of Miami

High blood pressure, elevated serum cholesterol, and advancing age have long been recognized as major risk factors for coronary heart disease (CHD) (1). Unfortunately, knowledge about these risk factors, either alone or in combination, does not predict most new cases of CHD. Moreover, the exact causal relationships between risk factors and CHD are not firmly established. Thus, for example, we know that the risk of atherosclerotic CHD is directly related to blood pressure level (2), but antihypertensive medications, which have been valuable in reducing mortality from stroke and congestive heart failure, have been far less successful in reducing CHD morbidity and mortality (3). This suggests that another variable or other variables may be mediating the relationship between elevated blood pressure and CHD.

The incompleteness of our knowledge concerning CHD risk factors has led to a search for additional risk factors. These include: diabetes mellitus (4), smoking (5), obesity (6), physical inactivity (7), excessive alcohol consumption (8), poor dietary habits (9), and psychosocial variables such as Type A behavior pattern (10), hostility (11), depression (12), excessive fatigue (13), lack of social support (14, 15), occupational stress (16), and low socioeconomic status (SES) (17). Although the search for risk factors has been useful, it is necessary to understand the exact mechanisms by which they operate if we are to maximize our strategies for primary and secondary prevention.

The search for underlying causes of CHD has focused on increased understanding of metabolic mechanisms. In the present chapter, we intend to explore the hypothesis that insulin metabolism (18–21) and stress hormones, including catecholamines (22) and glucocorticoids (23), are importantly involved in the pathogenesis of CHD. We intend further to explore the possibility that an understanding of the parts played by the sympathetic nervous system (SNS), insulin resistance, and hyperinsulinemia will clarify the important role that behavioral interventions can play in both primary and secondary prevention of CHD.

In recent years, a constellation of disorders associated with insulin resistance and hyperinsulinemia has been identified; these appear to be associated with the risk of CHD. This constellation has had several names, among the earliest being glucose intolerance-obesity-hypertension (GOH) syndrome (24), "syndrome X" (21), and the "deadly quartet" (20). The members of the quartet include upper-body obesity, glucose intolerance, hypertriglyceridemia, and hypertension. In the present chapter, we refer to the cluster as the *insulin metabolic syndrome*, and include in it tendencies toward central obesity, hyperglycemia, hypertension, dyslipidemia (hypertriglyceridemia, hyperapobetalipoproteinemia, and low concentration of high-density lipoprotein [HDL] cholesterol), and atherosclerosis. To a lesser extent, hyperuricemia and renal dysfunction may also be involved.

Although the insulin metabolic syndrome has conceptual utility in our comprehension of the pathogenesis of CHD, it is only one part of the story. A more comprehensive understanding of the processes involved must necessarily focus on a variety of behaviors, hormones, hemostatic factors, and aspects of lipid metabolism. Figure 8.1 provides a schematic diagram of how several important intermediate variables appear to relate lifestyle and emotional factors to the development of atherosclerotic coronary artery disease (CAD). Figure 8.2 provides a second schematic diagram depicting how several important intermediate variables (some of which also appear in Fig. 8.1) would also appear to relate lifestyle and emotional factors to coronary morbidity and mortality. It is evident, from examining Figs. 8.1 and 8.2, that insulin metabolism and SNS activity are critical to our comprehension of relationships between behavior on the one hand and CHD morbidity and mortality on the other hand.

LIFESTYLE AND BEHAVIOR

Diet

There is little doubt that total serum cholesterol and its major constituents—low-density lipoprotein (LDL) cholesterol and HDL cholesterol—are strongly related to the risk of CHD. Although levels of circulating lipids and lipoproteins are influenced, to a large degree, by genetic and homeostatic mechanisms (25), dietary factors such as consumption of saturated fats (26) and alcohol (27) play some role in the variability of lipids and lipoprotein. An excess intake of fats and alcohol can also lead to obesity, which, in turn, can lead to an increase in atherosclerosis (28) and hypertension (29).

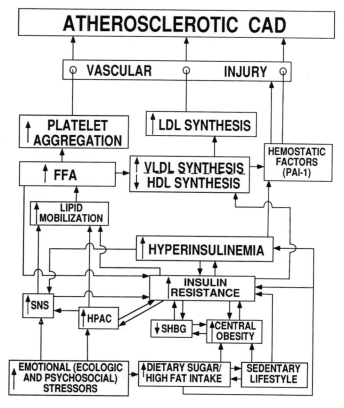

FIG. 8.1. Schematic diagram depicting how several key variables may mediate relationships between emotional and lifestyle factors on the one hand, and coronary artery disease on the other hand. Abbreviations: CAD, coronary artery disease; FFA, free fatty acids; HDL, high-density lipoprotein; HPAC, hypothalamico-pituitary-adrenocortical system; LDL, low-density lipoprotein; PAI, plasminogen activation inhibitor; SHBG, sex hormone binding globulin; SNS, sympathetic nervous system; VLDL, very low-density lipoprotein.

The prevalence of hypertension is 50% greater in people consuming three to five drinks daily and 100% greater in those who have more than six drinks daily, relative to those who consume little alcohol (30). This increased prevalence of hypertension has been linked to increased plasma catecholamines (31) and is independent of weight gain (32). At intake levels of alcohol exceeding 40 gm/day, both systolic and diastolic blood pressure are acutely raised by about 7 mm Hg (33).

Other dietary patterns also tend to influence adrenergic activity. Activation of the SNS is suppressed by caloric restriction (34) and stimulated by overfeeding (35). For example, studies using norepinephrine turnover in rodents to assess SNS activity have shown that overfeeding in rats stimulates SNS activity (36). Similarly, increased body mass index and increased caloric intake have each

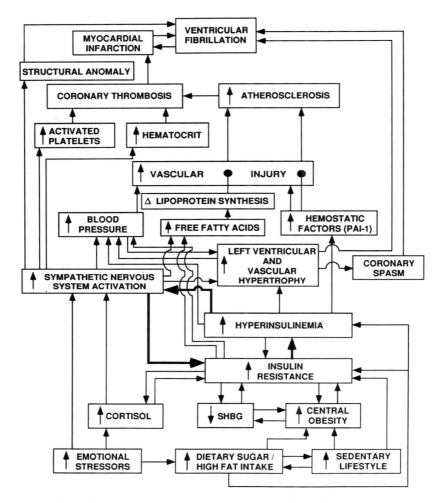

FIG. 8.2. Schematic diagram showing how a number of key variables may mediate relationships between emotional and lifestyle factors on the one hand, and CHD morbidity and mortality on the other hand. Abbreviations: PAI, plasminogen activation inhibitor; SHBG, sex hormone binding globulin.

been associated with elevated urinary norepinephrine excretion in humans (37). Both fats and carbohydrates have stimulatory effects on the SNS (38), whereas protein is without stimulatory effect even when fed in caloric excess (39).

The effects of overeating on SNS activity appear to be mediated by insulin (40) (Fig. 8.1). In the same study that found that body mass index and caloric intake were independently associated with increased urinary norepinephrine excretion, for instance, it was also found that elevated norepinephrine excretion was associated with hyperinsulinemia. This is consistent with the observation that exogenous insulin infusions during the euglycemia insulin clamp result in an increase in plasma norepinephrine (41) and an increase in muscle sympathetic nerve discharge (42).

There is now considerable experimental evidence showing that dietary sugars can contribute both to increased plasma insulin and SNS activity. Thus, for example, dietary sugar induced an increase in catecholamine excretion and blood pressure in spontaneously hypertensive rats (SHR) and Wistar–Kyoto (WKY) control rats, although higher blood pressures were measured in the SHR (43). Similarly, in studies of fructose feeding in Sprague–Dawley rats, it was found that replacement of complex carbohydrates by fructose causes an increase in blood pressure, impaired insulin-stimulated glucose utilization, and elevated serum triglyceride levels (44). This effect was attenuated by aerobic exercise (45). Suppression of insulin secretion by chronic infusion of somatostatin prevented the rise in blood pressure during fructose feeding (46).

The experimental evidence supports the concept that dietary sugar contributes to hyperinsulinemia and, through its effect on insulin, is a mediator of SNS activity. This, in turn, appears to have an impact on both blood pressure and lipid metabolism (Fig. 8.2). When plasma insulin concentration has been assessed in relation to serum lipid status, significantly higher insulin levels have been found in individuals with elevated LDL and very low-density lipoprotein (VLDL) values (47). Thus, relationships have been shown relating diet, obesity, insulin resistance, hyperinsulinemia, and SNS activity, and these in turn have been related to changes in blood pressure and lipid profiles (Figs. 8.1 and 8.2).

Diet–Stress Interactions

Behavioral stressors may also impact on potential CHD risk through the modification of diet (23). Thus, stressors have been shown to influence eating behavior in humans (48) and nonhuman animals (49). Individuals experiencing occupational stress, for example, are more likely to consume alcohol and coffee (50), as well as increased calories, fat, and a greater proportion of calories from fat (51). Job loss has been shown to be related to weight gain (52). Possible relationships among emotional stressors, changes in diet, and an increase in central obesity are depicted in Figs. 8.1 and 8.2, as are the routes by which these variables may contribute to increased coronary risk.

Catecholamines released during emotional stress or exertion can mobilize lipid stores from adipose tissues (Fig. 8.1) (53). The mobilized lipids are hydrolyzed to free fatty acids for energy production in muscular activity (54). Thus, SNS activation, elicited by physical exertion including fight-or-flight reactions, can lead to the effective utilization and rapid removal of free fatty acids from the circulation. When lipid mobilization induced by strong emotion is not accompanied by vigorous activity, however, the free fatty acids are not cleared as rapidly, and may become converted to triglycerides by the liver. These are then circulated in the blood as a component of VLDL (55). Some VLDL remnants become converted into LDL, and are again released into the circulation. It is LDL that is the source of most lipid in atheroma (56). Although alcohol per se cannot be stored as fat, it can serve as an energy source. Thus, when fats and alcohol are consumed as excess calories, fat storage is facilitated.

The manner by which emotional stressors and diet can interact to promote coronary risk has been explored in studies conducted on nonhuman primates (57–59). In most of these studies, groups of cynomolgus monkeys lived in socially stable or unstable environments for up to 2 years. In the socially unstable environment, five- or six-member living groups were periodically distributed. Because cynomolgus monkeys tend to form dominance hierarchies determined by the outcome of aggressive encounters among group members, the periodic reconstitution of living groups led to increases in aggression as new dominance hierarchies were being formed.

In an initial study conducted on male cynomolgus monkeys maintained on a low-fat diet, dominant animals living in the socially unstable environment developed significantly more coronary atherosclerosis than dominant animals in the stable condition, or subordinate animals in either condition (57). The amount of coronary atherosclerosis observed, however, was small, but statistically significant. In contrast, when compared with similarly treated animals maintained on a high-fat diet (43% calories from fat; 0.34 mg cholesterol/calorie), atherosclerosis was much more pronounced in the monkeys fed the high-fat diet (58). Moreover, the atherosclerosis was significantly potentiated by both psychosocial factors (i.e., unstable living environment) and personality (dominance). In this case, the dominant male monkeys (i.e., animals with high social status) living in the unstable environment revealed significantly more coronary artery atherosclerosis than either dominant or subordinate monkeys living in the stable environment, or subordinate monkeys living in the unstable environment.

Epidemiological studies suggest that significant gender differences in CHD risk remain unexplained after adjustment for negative health behaviors (smoking, alcohol consumption), demographic variables, and biological risk factors such as total serum cholesterol, which could be influenced by reproductive hormones (60, 61). Studies conducted on female cynomolgus monkeys living in stable versus unstable environments suggest that the unexplained gender differences in CHD risk may be due to an interaction between biological and behavioral variables (59, 62). In these studies, the animals were maintained on the atherogenic diet.

Female cynomolgus monkeys with low social status (i.e., subordinates) are subjected to more aggression and spend more time alone in social isolation than do the more dominant group members (59, 62). One indication of the stress experienced by the subordinate female monkeys is the hypersecretion of cortisol in response to adrenocorticotropin hormone (ACTH) following dexamethasone suppression (63). Another indication of the stress experienced by these low-status females is their poor ovarian function. In any event, both ovariectomized female monkeys and subordinate females with poor ovarian function revealed coronary artery disease comparable to males, and significantly greater than that shown by nonovariectomized, socially dominant females.

In summary, behavioral factors may, in part, impact on coronary risk through modification of diet. Furthermore, cynomolgus monkeys on high-fat diets show more coronary artery disease than monkeys on low-fat diets. Once placed on high-fat diets, dominant male and subordinate female cynomolgus monkeys living in unstable environments reveal significantly more atherosclerosis than their counterparts living in low-stress environments. The studies on cynomolgus monkeys provide valuable insights into potential interactions among diet, psychosocial stressors, personality, gender, and menstrual status.

Physical Activity

A large body of literature has provided evidence that aerobic fitness is inversely related to blood pressure in both normotensive and hypertensive individuals (64–66). A decrease in SNS activity is associated with increased fitness, as indexed by decreased plasma norepinephrine (67, 68). In obese individuals, both weight loss and exercise decrease blood pressure (69) and insulin resistance (70). In addition, it has been observed that, following a prolonged program of exercise training, reduction in blood pressure was associated with a decrease in insulin resistance as opposed to weight loss (71). Thus, it appears that increasing aerobic fitness may lower blood pressure, in part, through the decrease in insulin resistance that occurs with exercise (71, 72).

Increases in physical activity are also associated with elevations in HDL cholesterol and decreases in triglycerides and LDL cholesterol, which are independent of body weight, diet, and smoking (73). Both cross-sectional (74) and longitudinal (75) studies have shown an inverse relationship between aerobic fitness and insulin resistance. Regular exercise appears to be necessary to maintain insulin sensitivity because deconditioning results in an elevation in insulin response to an oral glucose tolerance test (76) and an increase in insulin resistance (77) within 10 days.

Smoking

Cigarette smoking is a major risk factor for CHD (5). Acutely, smoking stimulates increases in heart rate, blood pressure, and cortisol (78–80). Smoking typically increases in response to stressors (81), and smoking intensity has been associated with personality characteristics such as hostility (82). Relative to nonsmokers, smokers have significantly higher serum concentrations of total cholesterol, triglycerides, and VLDL cholesterol, and lower concentrations of HDL cholesterol (83). The detrimental effects of smoking on HDL cholesterol may be due to acute effects of smoking on increases in free fatty acids, triglycerides, and VLDL cholesterol (84), or to differences in diet and body fat distribution between nonsmokers and smokers (85).

INSULIN METABOLIC SYNDROME

Based on a large epidemiological study of middle-aged persons, Modan and colleagues (24) suggested that hyperinsulinemia may be the underlying factor responsible for the high frequency with which obesity and glucose intolerance coexist in the hypertensive population. Briefly, they noted that prevalence of glucose intolerance was 28% in normotensives, 48% in untreated hypertensives, and 62% in treated hypertensives. The prevalence of hypertension was significantly related to the degree of hyperinsulinemia, and was the same order of magnitude among the obese and the nonobese.

Previously, it had been noted that the incidence of hypertension among the obese approaches 50%, and that a large proportion of hypertensives tend to be obese (86). Investigators also noted that hypertriglyceridemia and low HDL cholesterol are often associated with obesity (87). With such information available, several investigators during the late 1980s called attention to a possible insulin metabolic syndrome (20, 21, 88). More recently, a population-based study examined prevalence rates for central obesity, noninsulin dependent diabetes mellitus (NIDDM), impaired glucose tolerance, hypertension, hypertriglyceridemia, and hypercholesterolemia (89). The investigators observed that hyperinsulinemia was common to these six disorders, which each carry increased risk of CHD (89).

Obesity

Obese adults are nearly twice as likely to be hypertensive as similarly aged nonobese persons (29). Central- or upper-body obesity is a more powerful determinant of blood pressure than overall measures of obesity, such as body mass index (90). Interestingly, several investigators have reported that upper-body fat accumulation is related to glucose intolerance and hyperinsulinemia (91, 92). The increase in pancreatic insulin secretion and hyperinsulinemia is thought to reflect peripheral insulin resistance, with a compensatory increase in insulin secretion to maintain euglycemia (93).

Many of the studies that have examined insulin sensitivity (resistance) have used the euglycemia insulin clamp technique (94). This method involves infusing insulin into subjects at a high, fixed rate to achieve a steady-state plasma insulin concentration. Plasma glucose is then maintained constant (clamped) at euglycemia by virtue of continuous infusion of glucose. Once a steady-state glucose infusion rate is achieved, this is taken as the rate of glucose metabolism (M), less any urinary glucose losses.

Using the euglycemia insulin clamp technique, several investigators have shown that insulin resistance increases as a function of obesity (95). Quantitatively, this insulin resistance mostly affects muscle and involves both nonoxidative and oxidative pathways of glucose disposal (96). Causes of the impairment of insulin-mediated glucose uptake can range from decreased blood flow to target tissue, reduced insulin-receptor concentration, defects in signal transduction, and defects at the level of the glucose-transport system. Because the pancreatic beta cells are able to increase their secretory activity to offset the insulin resistance, however, the net result is a well-compensated metabolic state. The trade-off for glucose tolerance remaining normal is hyperinsulinemia.

Weight reduction in the obese is associated with reduction of blood pressure (86, 97) and a decrease in hyperinsulinemia and insulin resistance (98). A relationship between insulin metabolism and hypertension can also be demonstrated independent of obesity. For example, one study performed euglycemia insulin clamp studies on normotensive, nonobese hypertensive, and obese hypertensive subjects (99). The investigators found evidence of increased insulin resistance in both hypertensive groups, which persisted after adjustment for gender, age, body mass index, and waist–hip ratio.

Dyslipidemia

Dyslipidemia appears to be a consistent feature of the insulin metabolic syndrome (19). Population studies have widely observed positive correlations between insulin and triglycerides and a negative correlation between insulin and HDL cholesterol (100–102). Direct examinations of the relationship between insulin action and plasma lipoproteins have been conducted on Native Americans (103), young White men (104), and individuals with varying degrees of glucose intolerance (105). Briefly, utilizing the euglycemia insulin clamp technique to quantitate insulin resistance and insulin action, investigators have shown that total and VLDL triglyceride concentrations are higher with greater degrees of insulin resistance, whereas HDL cholesterol concentrations are lower with greater degrees of insulin resistance. The relationship between lipoprotein concentration and insulin action appears to be independent of obesity and fasting insulin.

Although controversial, the association between triglycerides and insulin action does not appear to be explicable in terms of direct stimulation of VLDL production by insulin because: (a) studies in isolated hepatocytes have shown that insulin inhibits VLDL secretion (106), and (b) intensive insulin therapy of diabetes generally results in lower plasma triglycerides (107). In contrast, it appears that insulin resistance in adipocytes results in less inhibition of lipolysis and, therefore, increased release of free fatty acids and increased fatty acid flux throughout the splanchnic area (108). The increased availability and delivery of free fatty acids to the liver results in increased VLDL–triglyceride synthesis because free fatty acids are the major substrates for VLDL–triglyceride production

(109). The relationships among free fatty acids, insulin resistance, and VLDL synthesis are depicted in Fig. 8.1.

Stress hormones—including epinephrine, norepinephrine, cortisol, glucagon, and growth hormone—also play a role in the regulation of free fatty acids (23). Each of these hormones stimulates lipolysis, antagonizing the effects of insulin on adipocytes. This, in turn, increases plasma free fatty acid concentrations and delivery of free fatty acids to the liver for VLDL–triglyceride synthesis.

Psychological stressors in the laboratory have been shown to increase the production of stress hormones, free fatty acids, and plasma triglycerides in the absence of changes in total cholesterol concentration (110, 111). Similarly, lipid metabolism can be modulated by a number of other factors including diet, alcohol intake, smoking, obesity, and physical activity (112).

Non-Insulin-Dependent Diabetes Mellitus (NIDDM)

Insulin resistance occurs in 25% of nonobese individuals with normal oral glucose tolerance, in most people with impaired glucose tolerance, and in the majority of patients with NIDDM (21). The extent to which glucose tolerance has deteriorated in these three groups appears to be directly related to the ability of pancreatic beta cells to compensate for the defect in insulin action. Thus, individuals who are insulin resistant, but able to maintain normal oral glucose tolerance, are able to compensate for the insulin resistance by hypersecreting insulin. In contrast, patients with NIDDM are unable to increase their insulin secretory response sufficiently to prevent hyperglycemia.

When a nondiabetic individual becomes obese, insulin resistance is likely to occur, but glucose tolerance can remain normal because the pancreatic beta cells are able to increase their ability to secrete insulin sufficiently to offset the insulin resistance (113). Thus, in this setting, insulin resistance is counterbalanced by an increase in insulin secretion so that glucose tolerance remains fairly normal, with the trade-off being hyperinsulinemia. In genetically susceptible individuals with sustained obesity, it may not be possible to maintain an adequate level of insulin secretion, and thus NIDDM may supervene (18).

Insulin resistance in the obese individual may be either acquired or inherited, whereas insulin resistance in the normal-weight NIDDM individual is genetically transmitted (114). Thus, the incidence of diabetes ranges from 70% to 90% in identical twins, and in the offspring of two diabetic parents (114–116). Among first-degree relatives, the incidence of NIDDM is 30%–40% (116).

Hypertension

A number of population studies have reported positive correlates between fasting plasma insulin and blood pressure (24, 117–119). In general, the relationship has tended to persist after adjustments for obesity and frank diabetes.

Studies using the euglycemia insulin clamp technique have confirmed that hypertensive individuals have greater insulin resistance than normotensive individuals (99, 120). In one study, young untreated hypertensives with normal weight and glucose tolerance were found to have lower insulin sensitivity than normotensive control subjects (120). The study also showed that the decreased insulin sensitivity was a consequence of a reduction in nonoxidative glucose metabolism (glycogen synthesis and glycolysis), with glucose oxidation remaining normal. Results from oral glucose tolerance tests indicated higher levels of both glucose and insulin in hypertensive subjects. In another study using the euglycemia insulin clamp technique, comparisons were made among normotensive, nonobese hypertensive, and obese hypertensive groups (99). Reduced insulin sensitivity was observed in both hypertensive groups, with obese hypertensives showing the most insulin resistance. The insulin-resistance findings persisted after adjustment for gender, age, body mass index, and waist–hip ratio.

Further support for the relationship between insulin metabolism and blood pressure derives from intervention studies relating weight loss and exercise training to reductions in blood pressure. For example, one study reported a strong correlation between decrements in blood pressure and decreases in plasma insulin in obese hypertensive subjects participating in a 12-week weight-reduction program (29). Similarly, a positive correlation was found between decrements in blood pressure and plasma insulin in obese women participating in a 6-month physical training program (71). The correlation between blood pressure and insulin occurred even when body weight remained unchanged.

There are several mechanisms by which hyperinsulinemia, secondary to insulin resistance, could contribute to the development of hypertension. These include renal sodium retention, SNS hyperactivity, smooth muscle hypertrophy, and altered transport and composition of cellular electrolytes.

It has long been known that the prevalence of hypertension tends to be high in societies that consume large amounts of sodium (121). It is also known that hypertension in patients with NIDDM or obesity tends to be associated with elevated total-body sodium content and volume expansion (122, 123). Several studies using the euglycemia insulin clamp have shed light on the potential relationships among sodium handling, insulin metabolism, and blood pressure regulation. In our own laboratory, for instance, we have observed that increases in blood pressure to a moderately high sodium diet (i.e., salt sensitivity) was positively associated with insulin resistance (124). Previous studies by others using the clamp have found that insulin tends to reduce sodium excretion by increasing sodium reabsorption in the distal tubules of the kidney (125, 126). An in vitro study in rabbits has shown that insulin also increases sodium chloride reabsorption in the proximal tubules (127).

Another mechanism by which insulin can cause hypertension involves activation of the SNS (see Fig. 8.2). The overfeeding of carbohydrates or fats in rats has been shown to increase SNS activation and blood pressure (38). Using the euglycemia insulin clamp technique in humans, insulin was shown to cause a dose-related increase in norepinephrine level, which was, in turn, related to blood pressure (41). Therefore, it appears that the pathways shown in Fig. 8.2—relating insulin resistance, hyperinsulinemia, SNS activation, and increases in blood pressure—may be operative in the development of hypertension.

Still another way by which hyperinsulinemia could be involved in the pathogenesis of hypertension is by stimulation of vascular smooth muscle hypertrophy. Regulation of the systemic circulation can be influenced by a narrowing of the lumen of resistance vessels (128, 129). Insulin may contribute to this process either directly or indirectly through the stimulation of growth factors, including insulin-like growth factor (130, 131). Interestingly, receptors for insulin-like growth factor-1 and insulin have been identified in blood vessels (132).

Finally, hyperinsulinemia may alter the activity of one or more sodium (Na^+) pumps, which are present in the cell membranes of arteriolar smooth muscle cells. For instance, this could lead to the intracellular accumulation of Na^+, which, in turn, would sensitize arteriolar smooth muscle cells to the pressor effects of norepinephrine and angiotensin II (133–135).

A particular cell membrane pump that has been implicated in the pathogenesis of hypertension is the Na^+–Hydrogen (H^+) exchanger (136). The Na^+–H^+ pump has been linked to calcium (Ca^{2+}) exchange (133, 137). Moreover, hyperinsulinemia is known to augment Na^+–H^+ exchange (138).

Several observations support the Na^+–H^+ exchanger hypothesis. First, the Na^+–H^+ exchanger is the only established genetic marker for essential hypertension (139). Second, augmented Na^+–H^+ activity occurs in the platelets and leukocytes of hypertensive patients (140, 141). Third, intracellular free Ca^{2+} is increased in the erythrocytes of hypertensives (133). Fourth, erythrocyte Na^+–H^+ countertransport is significantly greater in hypertensive than in nonhypertensive subjects (142).

In summary, numerous studies have documented relationships between fasting plasma insulin and blood pressure level, and between insulin resistance and hypertension. Although the exact mechanisms relating insulin metabolism and hypertension are not known, considerable evidence suggests that hyperinsulinemia—secondary to insulin resistance—may increase blood pressure through increased renal sodium retention, altered transport of cellular electrolytes, smooth muscle hypertrophy of arteriolar resistance vessels, and/or augmented SNS activation. However, as indicated in Fig. 8.2, the relationship between insulin metabolism and increased blood pressure is likely to be complex because hyperinsulinemia not only stimulates SNS activity (143), but increases in SNS activity can lead to further insulin resistance (144), setting up the basis for a positive feedback loop. Moreover, as shown in Fig. 8.1, elevated levels of plasma free fatty acids can inhibit insulin-stimulated glucose uptake (145), and SNS activity stimulates the production of free fatty acids (144), thus creating yet another potential loop. Such loops may have implications for the progressive nature of hypertension.

SYMPATHETIC NERVOUS SYSTEM

Although insulin metabolism appears to play a major role in the relationship between behavioral variables on the one hand and CHD on the other hand, the role of the SNS in both etiology and pathogenesis of CHD also deserves consideration. As shown in Figs. 8.1 and 8.2, SNS activity is important in the production of free fatty acids, increases in blood pressure, vascular and left-ventricular hypertrophy, platelet activation, and induction of ventricular fibrillation. Although the interactions between the SNS and insulin metabolism largely preclude considering either factor in isolation, it is likely that, in some instances, focus could be placed on SNS activation as an etiological cause. Thus, at least in some instances, increased sympathetic tone may be the primary mechanism underlying the increase of both plasma insulin values and arterial blood pressure (22).

Recently, Julius and colleagues (146) emphasized that SNS-induced skeletal muscle vasoconstriction can negatively impact on glucose extraction in skeletal muscle, which is the site of insulin resistance in both NIDDM (147) and hypertension (148). Julius (22) pointed out that: (a) insulin resistance is associated with inadequate postprandial skeletal muscle vasodilation (149), (b) beta blockers decrease cardiac output and are associated with decreased insulin sensitivity in hypertension (150), (c) exercise training improves microcapillarization and positively influences insulin sensitivity (92), and (d) vasodilator drugs improve insulin sensitivity in hypertension (151).

Increased SNS tone could also provide a primary mechanism in atherogenesis. As previously described, SNS activity may increase plasma triglycerides through its effect on lipoprotein lipase (152). The SNS may also induce insulin resistance by stimulating free fatty acid production, thereby increasing production of VLDL–triglyceride with a consequent decrease of HDL synthesis. By stimulating alpha-adrenergic receptors, the SNS may also influence the catabolism of LDL cholesterol (153).

To the extent that high SNS tone may contribute to the initiation of hypertension (22), certain features of such hypertension are likely to contribute to increased CHD risk. For example, an increase in SNS tone can promote coronary thrombosis (see Fig. 8.2) by increasing platelet aggregation (154) and hematocrit values (22).

As shown in Fig. 8.2, SNS activation may also lead to left-ventricular hypertrophy. Norepinephrine stimulated hypertrophy of myocardial cells, for example, appears to be produced by an alpha-1-adrenergic response (155). Similarly, an increase in SNS tone appears to be a trophic factor in vascular hypertrophy (156). Ingestion of large quantities of alcohol can also lead to acute blood pressure elevations (33), elevated plasma catecholamines (31), and hypertension (30).

Julius and his collaborators have provided considerable evidence that increased SNS drive is particularly strong in the early phases of the hypertensive process. Thus, by using selective autonomic blockades, they have shown an increase in both cardiac beta-adrenergic (157) and vascular alpha-adrenergic (158) drive.

Particularly in young patients with borderline hypertension, a "hyperkinetic" circulation may be involved, in which increases may occur in plasma nor-epinephrine, heart rate, and cardiac output (159). In contrast, as hypertension becomes more established, the prolonged pressure load causes hypertrophy in the resistance vessels (160), and the blood pressure elevation is sustained by an increase in total peripheral resistance (161). As Julius pointed out, the pattern of hyperkinetic circulation shown by many hypertensives at rest is compatible with the hemodynamics of a sustained defense reaction (22).

SYMPATHETIC NERVOUS SYSTEM AND STRESS

To understand interactions among stressors, the SNS, and cardiovascular disease (CVD), it is necessary to consider characteristics of the organism, the environment, and organism–environment interactions (i.e., behavior). Page's (162) mosaic theory of blood pressure regulation implies that the hereditary factors that underlie hypertension consist of a spectrum of variants more or less randomly mixed in the genetic coding of human reproduction. The development of selectively bred animal strains has provided the means to examine some of the putative variants that might contribute to human hypertension. The most widely used animal model for studying genetic factors in hypertension has been the SHR.

Tonic increases in blood pressure among SHR begin at about 6 weeks of age, develop rapidly over the next several months, and achieve a high, sustained hypertension before 6 months of age. Young SHR, like borderline hypertensive humans, display a "hyperkinetic" circulation reminiscent of the defense reaction (e.g., high heart rate and cardiac output) (163). These young SHR show greater increases in SNS activity, plasma catecholamines, and cardiovascular reactivity when subjected to flashing lights, loud noises, vibrations, physical restraint, or cold temperature. In contrast to the young SHR, older SHR, much like chronic hypertensive humans, reveal normal or reduced cardiac output, but elevated total peripheral resistance.

Although the basis of SHR hypertension is clearly genetic, experiential factors can influence the hypertensive phenotype. For example, cross-fostering SHR pups to WKY normotensive mothers can attenuate the subsequent resting blood pressure of adult SHR (164). Alternatively, socially isolating SHR from the time of weaning until 7 months of age results in lower baseline blood pressure relative to that observed in group-reared SHR, although both groups reveal comparable cardiovascular responses to acute stressors (163).

The borderline hypertensive rat (BHR) is a first-generation cross between the SHR and the WKY (165). This animal model develops marginally elevated blood pressure under usual cage conditions, but develops frank hypertension when either chronically stressed or fed a high-sodium diet (166). The stress-induced hypertension can be blocked by exercise (167). Thus, the data from the

SHR and BHR provide evidence for genetically based, SNS mediated hypertension that is modifiable by environmental influences.

Although patients with sustained hypertension show greater responsiveness to psychophysiological stressors in the laboratory than do normotensive individuals (168), interpreting such findings can be problematic because the vasculature of such patients may be hypertrophic. In contrast, findings that the normotensive offspring of parents with hypertension reveal greater cardiovascular responsiveness than the normotensive offspring of normotensive parents (169, 170) suggest that the increased responsiveness is antecedent to the development of hypertension. Interestingly, twin studies have shown that monozygotic twins are significantly more alike than dizygotic twins in their blood pressure and heart rate responses to psychological stressors (171). Thus, it would appear that genetic influences presumably involving SNS mediation operate on cardiovascular responses to psychological challenge in humans as well as animal models.

A psychosocially stressful environment can also lead to the development of cardiovascular pathology. Henry and coworkers developed an excellent murine model of stress-induced hypertension (172) and arteriosclerosis (173). The mouse strain selected remains normotensive if reared in the typical laboratory colony. In contrast, if initially reared in isolation and then placed in a special group habitat designed to increase social and territorial fighting, the mice develop progressive and eventually irreversible increases in blood pressure. This hypertension is, in part, mediated by increases in the adrenal medullary enzymes, tyrosine hydroxylase, and phenylethanolamine N-methyltransferase (173). The hypertension involves heightened activity of the renin-angiotensin-aldosterone system, and can be prevented by long-term administration of beta-adrenergic antagonists (172, 174). Relative to control animals, the psychosocially stressed mice also show more severe arteriosclerotic degeneration of the intramural coronary vessels, as well as myocardial fibrosis and interstitial nephritis (173). Thus, it appears that the cardiovascular pathology induced by the psychosocial stressors is related, in part, to long-term SNS arousal.

As previously seen, socially unstable environments can promote coronary atherosclerosis in nonhuman primates; this is influenced by diet, personality, and gender (57–59, 62). Interestingly, long-term maintenance of monkeys on the beta-adrenergic antagonist propranolol significantly attenuates the atherosclerosis of dominant male monkeys living in unstable groups and fed an atherogenic diet (175). The amelioration is not associated with concomitant changes in social behavior or hierarchical associations, but is consistent with the view that decreased sympathetic tone attenuates stress-induced atherosclerosis.

A relationship between social instability and hypertension has also been shown in humans. In one study conducted in the United States, unstable residential neighborhoods in the city of Detroit were defined in terms of high crime, divorce/separation, and residential transiency rates, as well as the low SES of the residents (176, 177). A major finding of the study was that, after adjustment for age and weight, subjects living in the high-stress area had a greater risk of being hypertensive than those living in low-stress areas. When considered together, the human and animal studies relating psychosocial instability to cardiovascular disorders are consistent with the view that activation of the SNS appears to be involved.

Various personality traits have also been related to cardiovascular pathology. Recall, for example, that in cynomolgus monkeys living in unstable environments and fed an atherogenic diet, dominant males (58) and subordinate females (59) had the most atherosclerosis. Human epidemiological studies have further suggested that behavioral traits may be associated with CHD. The Western Collaborative Group Study (WCGS) reported that Type A behavior was associated with almost a twofold increase in risk for CHD after multivariate adjustment for other risk factors (178). Type A individuals were characterized as hard driving, achievement oriented, excessively involved in their jobs, impatient, time oriented, competitive, and showing considerable potential for hostility.

Questions concerning the risk-factor status of Type A arose when large prospective studies of persons at high risk for CHD failed to confirm Type A as an independent risk factor (179–181). Inconsistency of results among trials, as well as a lack of specificity in identifying individuals at elevated risk, led to the examination of specific components of the heterogeneous Type A construct. Soon after the initial WCGS findings were published, a reanalysis of the data showed that the best discriminator between a subset of cases and controls was hostility (182). More recently, the hostility component was found to predict CHD mortality over the long-term follow-up of the WCGS sample (183), even though the global Type A behavior pattern did not (184). Other long-term prospective studies, using the Cook–Medley Hostility scale, have also shown an association between hostility scores and CHD mortality (11, 185). Similarly, a large epidemiological study in Finland confirmed an association between hostility and CHD mortality among men with a history of hypertension and heart disease (186).

The mechanism by which hostility may convey risk remains speculative, but a relationship between hostility and SNS arousal appears to exist. A study of white-collar male and female employees in Sweden, for example, studied relationships between hostility on the one hand and cardiovascular/neuroendocrine activity on the other hand (187). No relationship was found between total Type A scores and reactivity in the workplace, but men with high hostility scores showed greater reactivity than men with low hostility scores on measures of systolic blood pressure, heart rate, cortisol, norepinephrine, and epinephrine. Furthermore, women and men who were high in hostility had significantly higher LDL cholesterol than women and men low in hostility.

Although anger expression seems to be associated with CHD, anger suppression paradoxically appears to be associated with hypertension and its sequelae. For instance, a study of factory workers observed that job stress was related to the prevalence of hypertension, but only among those who suppressed their anger

(188). Also, a prospective epidemiological study found that suppressed anger predicted mortality among hypertensives over a 12-year follow-up period (189). Anger suppression has also been associated with exaggerated blood pressure reactivity in the laboratory (190). The paradoxical finding that both anger expression and anger suppression are related to cardiovascular disorders is resolvable when one considers that: (a) the two variables represent separate factors, rather than two poles in the same dimension (191); (b) both variables represent responses to perceived stressors; and (c) several alternative biological pathways, only some of which may involve elevated blood pressure, can contribute to CHD. In any event, it appears that hostility (either suppressed or expressed) may contribute to the development of CVD through activation of the SNS.

Although hostility and Type A appear to be the psychological variables most often associated with CHD, other psychological states, such as depression (192), have also been implicated. In Gothenburg, Sweden, for example, admission to a psychiatric hospital for depression was associated significantly with the subsequent development of MI (193). A large epidemiological study in the United States also reported that depressive symptoms and perceived helplessness were associated with CHD mortality (194). Interestingly, several studies have observed increased plasma norepinephrine levels in depressed patients (195, 196). Norepinephrine spillover from synapses has also been found to be elevated in patients with primary depressive illness (197). Thus, it appears that the association between depression and CHD may involve activation of the SNS.

IMPLICATIONS FOR CORONARY
HEART DISEASE PREVENTION

The evidence suggests that insulin metabolism and activation of the SNS play central mediating roles in the development of CHD. Moreover, positive feedback loops involving increased activation of the SNS and insulin metabolism may provide a particularly pernicious mechanism leading to accelerated development of disease processes. Of particular relevance to the present chapter is the role that emotional stressors; diets high in alcohol, sugar, and fats; and a sedentary lifestyle may have on a constellation of variables that appear to contribute to CHD development.

To the extent that emotional stressors, poor diet, and lack of physical exercise contribute to the pathogenesis of CHD, management of stress, a healthy diet, and the promotion of physical activity should provide the cornerstones for the primary and secondary prevention of CHD. The complex interrelationships depicted in Figs. 8.1 and 8.2 suggest that the interrelations among behavioral risk factors are complex, and that focusing on a single risk factor at a time without regard to others may be ineffective.

The problem of dealing with obesity is illustrative. As previously described, hypertension, NIDDM, and dyslipidemia are each associated with obesity.

Weight loss can improve each of these conditions. Such programs have been launched and may initially prove successful. The major problem with weight-reduction intervention programs, however, has been in maintaining the weight loss (198). Unfortunately, most weight-loss programs are based solely on reducing food intake, and these do not work well after the target weight is achieved. Even programs that have used behavioral strategies, such as social support and cognitive behavior modification in conjunction with diet, have had disappointing results.

Improving health outcomes in the obese involves dealing with multiple variables simultaneously. Successful management includes attention to diet, physical activity, and emotional behavior. Aerobic exercise, of course, facilitates the metabolism of excess calories. However, depression can be a barrier to exercise. Perhaps equally important, emotional stressors and a sedentary lifestyle may maintain central obesity by promoting insulin resistance (Figs. 8.1 and 8.2). Interestingly, aerobic exercise training in a multicomponent maintenance program has shown promise in enhancing the efficacy of behavior therapy in the treatment of obesity (199). The research that we have reviewed also suggests that composition of the diet, as well as total calories, are important.

Perhaps the most controversial aspect of lifestyle modification for the prevention and treatment of CHD or its precursors is the use of stress-management techniques, including relaxation training. Thus, for example, a number of relaxation-training techniques have been used in the treatment of hypertension with mixed results. Although clinically significant results have been obtained in several studies (200–202), others have failed to show a significant effect from relaxation training (203). On the basis of a meta-analysis of studies conducted prior to 1987, it appears that behavioral interventions provide modest benefit with regard to diastolic blood pressure, but not systolic blood pressure (204).

Any of several factors could account for the discrepancies among studies examining the effects of relaxation training in the treatment of hypertension. These include patient selection, intervention procedure chosen, and/or design of individual studies. To the extent that behavioral interventions such as relaxation training decrease blood pressure by reducing SNS activity, behavioral treatment approaches should be most effective in individuals with high levels of sympathetic tone. Some evidence exists that the hypertensive patients who respond best to progressive muscle relaxation have higher heart rates and plasma norepinephrine values prior to treatment (205, 206).

To the extent that antihypertensive medications alone have not been extremely successful in reducing CHD morbidity and mortality, the conceptualization of antihypertensive treatment may need some reconsideration. If one looks at the relationship of hypertension to obesity, hyperglycemia, and dyslipidemia, a multimodal approach to treatment may be useful under some conditions. Thus, decreasing alcohol consumption, increasing aerobic activity, decreasing the ingestion of fats and sugar, and participating in some form of stress management, perhaps including relaxation training, could go hand in hand with antihypertensive medications. Many physicians believe that, once placed on antihypertensive medications, patients should remain on them for life. However, it may be reasonable, through multimodal therapy, to have as a therapeutic objective the eventual removal of some patients from medication.

The reduction of perceived stress, which in some cases may involve relaxation training, would also appear to be useful in secondary prevention. Available evidence suggests that efforts to reduce the hostile, competitive, and impatient behaviors of post-MI patients (207, 208), or to provide social support (209, 210), lead to improved prognosis in CHD. To the extent that such variables as *depression* are linked to MI (193), or CHD more broadly (194), behavioral interventions known to alleviate depression, either alone or in combination with pharmacotherapy, deserve consideration. Interestingly, selective serotonin uptake inhibitors not only ameliorate depression, but also decrease SNS activation (211), appetite (212), and anger/aggression (213).

Although a multimodal approach to intervention appears to be called for in individuals with clearly established disease, it may also be useful in primary prevention among high-risk individuals. It has long been known, of course, that consummatory behaviors such as smoking and poor diet contribute to CHD risk, and that modifying these behaviors can reduce risk (214, 215). In the Oslo, Norway study, for instance, which was a randomized, controlled clinical trial conducted on 12,000 high-risk men, counseling procedures produced a 45% reduction in tobacco usage, a 20% reduction in triglycerides, and a 13% reduction in cholesterol in an intervention group relative to a control group (215). The rate of MI and sudden death was 47% lower in the intervention group. Although not all studies have shown convincing effects of changing diet on CHD morbidity and mortality (216), the preponderance of evidence favors the view that weight loss and decreasing the ingestion of saturated fats and alcohol in high-risk individuals can impact favorably on CHD morbidity and mortality.

The matter of patient adherence is of considerable concern in intervention studies designed to decrease CHD risk. Average rates of compliance with antihypertensive medication, for instance, have been about 65%, even with one-a-day regimens (217). Many patients fail to take their medication at all, however, and erratic adherence is not unusual.

When one considers the complexity involved in changing diet, increasing exercise, and reducing stress, it would seem that patient adherence could be a major problem. However, major population studies, such as the North Karelia, Finland trial and the Oslo, Norway trial, suggest that multimodal interventions can be effective (214, 215). The keys to the more successful intervention studies appear to be credibility, social validation, and manageability. Thus, recommendations that come from a prestigious and credible source, such as the medical establishment, have a reasonable chance of being followed. Furthermore, if those about them, including major role models, are seen as adhering to a regimen, those for whom the adherence messages are intended may be more likely to participate. Also, if adherence is geared toward the physical capacities of those involved, and the demand is not too rigorous, the possibility of success is improved. Thus, regimens that avoid lengthy stress-reduction procedures, starvation diets, and excessive exercise demands may require longer to achieve their goals, but may be more likely to obtain adherence.

In summary, the studies reviewed in this chapter suggest that emotional stressors (including unstable environments), poor dietary practices (including alcohol abuse and excessive ingestion of fats and sugar), and a sedentary lifestyle can combine and interact to promote the pathogenesis of CHD. We have emphasized the roles that insulin metabolism and activation of the SNS play in mediating the relationships between behavioral variables on the one hand and CHD morbidity and mortality on the other hand. Throughout our discussion, we emphasized how emotional stressors, poor diet, and a sedentary lifestyle set the stage for a cluster of health problems, including obesity, hypertension, NIDDM, and dyslipidemia. Although genetic factors play a major role in each of these conditions, the expression of these conditions is heavily influenced by behavioral factors. Just as the pathogenesis of these disorders is related to behavioral variables, a multimodal behavioral approach to primary and secondary prevention could make a major contribution to reductions in CHD morbidity and mortality.

REFERENCES

1. Dawber TR, Meadors CF, Moore FE. Epidemiological approaches to heart disease. The Framingham Study. Am J Public Health 1951;41:279–90.
2. MacMahon S, Peto R, Cutler J, et al. Blood pressure, stroke, and coronary heart disease: Part 1. Prolonged differences in blood pressure: prospective observational studies corrected for the regression dilution bias. Lancet 1990;335:765–74.
3. Collins R, Peto R, MacMahon S, et al. Blood pressure, stroke, and coronary heart disease: Part 2. Short-term reduction in blood pressure: overview of randomised drug trials in their epidemiological context. Lancet 1990;335:827–38.
4. Stamler J, Epstein FH. Coronary heart disease: risk factors as guides to preventive action. Prev Med 1972;1:27–48.
5. U.S. Department of Health and Human Services. The health consequences of smoking: cardiovascular disease. A report of the surgeon general. Washington, DC: Department of Health and Human Services, Public Health Service, Office on Smoking and Health; 1983 DHEW Pub. No. (PHS) 84-50204.
6. Donahue RP, Abbott RD, Bloom E, et al. Central obesity and coronary heart disease in men. Lancet 1987;1:821–23.
7. Paffenbarger RS, Wing AL, Hyde RT. Physical activity as an index of heart attack risk in college alumni. Am J Epidemiol 1978;108:161–75.
8. Hennekens CH, Rosner B, Cole DS. Daily alcohol consumption and fatal coronary heart disease. Am J Epidemiol 1978;107:196–200.
9. Shekelle RB, Shyrock AM, Paul PO, et al. Diet, serum cholesterol, and death from coronary heart disease—The Western Electric Study. N Eng J Med 1981;304:65–70.
10. Rosenman R, Brand R, Jenkins C, et al. Coronary heart disease in the Western Collaborative Group Study: final follow-up of 8.5 years. JAMA 1975;233:872–77.

11. Shekelle RB, Gale M, Ostfeld AM, et al. Hostility, risk of CHD, and mortality. Psychosom Med 1983;45:109–14.

12. Ahern DK, Gorkin L, Anderson JL. Biobehavioral variables and mortality or cardiac arrest in the Cardiac Arrhythmia Pilot Study (CAPS). Amer J Cardiol 1990;66:59–62.

13. Appels A, Mulder P. Excess fatigue as a precursor of myocardial infarction. Eur Heart J 1988;9:758–64.

14. Orth-Gomér K, Rosengren A, Wilhelmsen L. Lack of social support and incidence of coronary heart disease in middle-aged Swedish men. Psychosom Med 1993;55:37–43.

15. Ruberman W, Weinblatt E, Goldberg J, et al. Psychosocial influences on mortality after myocardial infarction. N Eng J Med 1984;311:552–59.

16. Karasek RA, Baker D, Marxer F, et al. Job decision latitude, job demands, and cardiovascular disease: a prospective study of Swedish men. Am J Public Health 1981;71:694–701.

17. Marmot M. Socioeconomic determinants of CHD mortality. Int J Epidemiol 1989;18:S196–S202.

18. DeFronzo RA, Ferrannini E. A multifaceted syndrome responsible for NIDDM, obesity, hypertension, dyslipidemia, and atherosclerotic cardiovascular disease. Diab Care 1991;14:173–94.

19. Howard BV, Schneiderman N, Falkner B, et al. Insulin, health behaviors, and lipid metabolism. Metabolism 1993;42(Suppl):25–35.

20. Kaplan NM. The deadly quartet: upper-body obesity, glucose intolerance, hypertriglyceridemia and hypertension. Arch Intern Med 1989;149:1514–20.

21. Reaven GM. Role of insulin resistance in human disease: Banting lecture. Diabetes 1988;37:1595–1607.

22. Julius S. Sympathetic hyperactivity and coronary risk in hypertension: Corcoran lecture. Hypertension 1993;21:886–93.

23. Brindley DN, McCann BS, Niaura R, et al. Stress and lipoprotein metabolism: modulators and mechanism. Metabolism 1993;42(Suppl):3–15.

24. Modan M, Halkin H, Almog S, et al. Hyperinsulinemia: a link between hypertension, obesity and glucose intolerance. J Clin Invest 1985;75:809–17.

25. Breslow JL. Lipoprotein transport gene abnormalities underlying coronary heart disease susceptibility. Ann Rev Med 1991;42:357–71.

26. Arntzenius AC, Kromhout D, Barth JD, et al. Diet, lipoproteins, and the progression of coronary atherosclerosis. N Eng J Med 1985;312:805–11.

27. Castelli WP, Doyle J, Gordon T, et al. Alcohol and blood lipids: The Cooperative Lipoprotein Phenotyping Study. Lancet 1977;2:153–55.

28. Armstrong DB, Dublin LI, Wheatley GM: Obesity and the relation to health and disease. JAMA 1951;147:1007–14.

29. Sims EAH. Mechanisms of hypertension in the overweight. Hypertension 1982;4 Suppl 3:III43–III49.

30. Klatsky AL, Friedman GD, Siegelaub AB, et al. Alcohol consumption and blood pressure: Kaiser-Permanente multiphasic health examination data. N Eng J Med 1977;296:1194–1200.

31. Kaysen G, Noth RH. The effects of alcohol on blood pressure and electrolytes. Med Clin N Am 1984;68:221–46.

32. Friedman GD, Klatsky AL, Siegelaub AB. Alcohol, tobacco and hypertension. Hypertension 1982;4 Suppl III:143–50.

33. Maheswaran R, Gill JS, Davies P, et al. High blood pressure due to alcohol: a rapidly reversible effect. Hypertension 1991;17:787–92.

34. Young JB, Landsberg L. Suppression of sympathetic nervous system during fasting. Science 1977;196:1473–75.

35. Young JB, Landsberg L. Stimulation of the sympathetic nervous system during sucrose feeding. Nature 1977;269:615–17.

36. Young JB, Saville E, Rothwell NJ, et al. Effect of diet and cold exposure on norepinephrine turnover in brown adipose tissue in the rat. J Clin Invest 1982;69:1061–71.

37. Troisi RJ, Weiss ST, Parker DR, et al. Relation of obesity and diet to sympathetic nervous system activity. Hypertension 1991;17:669–77.
38. Landsberg L, Young JB. Insulin-mediated glucose metabolism in the relationship between dietary intake and sympathetic nervous system activity. Int J Obes 1985;9:63–8.
39. Kaufman LN, Young JB, Landsberg L. Effect of protein on sympathetic nervous system activity in the rat: evidence for nutrient-specific responses. J Clin Invest 1986;77:551–58.
40. Landsberg L. Hyperinsulinemia: possible role in obesity-induced hypertension. Hypertension 1992;19(Suppl):151–155.
41. Rowe JW, Young JB, Minaker KL, et al. Effect of insulin and glucose infusions on sympathetic nervous system activity in normal man. Diabetes 1981;30:219–25.
42. Anderson EA, Balon TW, Hoffman RP, et al. Insulin increases sympathetic activity but not blood pressure in borderline hypertensive humans. Hypertension 1992;19:621–27.
43. Fournier RD, Chiueh CC, Kopin IJ. Refined carbohydrate increases blood pressure and catecholamine excretion in SHR and WKY. Am J Physiol 1986;250:E381–E385.
44. Hwang IS, Ho H, Hoffman BB, et al. Fructose-induced insulin resistance and hypertension in rats. Hypertension 1987;10:512–16.
45. Reaven GM, Ho H, Hoffman BB. Attenuation of fructose-induced hypertension in rats by exercise training. Hypertension 1988;12:129–32.
46. Reaven GM, Chang H, Hoffman BB, et al. Resistance to insulin-stimulated glucose uptake in adipocytes isolated from spontaneously hypertensive rats. Diabetes 1989;38:1155–60.
47. Burke GL, Webber LS, Srinivasan SR. Fasting plasma glucose and insulin levels and their relationship to cardiovascular risk factors in children: The Bogalusa Heart Study. Metabolism 1986;35:441–46.
48. Robbins TW, Fray PJ. Stress-induced eating: fact, fiction or misunderstanding? Appetite 1980;1:103–33.
49. Robbins TW, Everitt BJ, Sahakian BJ. Stress-induced eating in animals. In: Cioffi LA, James WPT, Van Etallie TB, editors. The body weight regulatory system: normal and disturbed mechanisms. New York: Raven, 1981:289–97.
50. Conway TL, Vickers Jr RR, Ward HW. Occupational stress and variation in cigarette, coffee, and alcohol consumption. J Health Soc Behav 1981;22:155–61.
51. McCann BS, Warnick GR, Knopp RH. Changes in plasma lipids and dietary intake accompanying shifts in perceived workload and stress. Psychosom Med 1990;52:97–108.
52. Morris JK, Cook DG, Shaper AG. Non-employment and changes in smoking, drinking, and body weight. Br Med J 1992;304:536–41.
53. Heindel JJ, Orci L, Jeanrenaud B. Fat mobilization and its regulation by hormones and drugs in white adipose tissue. In: Masoro EJ, editor. International encyclopedia of pharmacology and therapeutics. Pharmacology of lipid transport and atherosclerotic processes. Oxford: Pergamon, 1975:175–373.
54. Zierler KL, Maseri A, Klassen D, et al. Muscle metabolism during exercise in man. Trans Am Phys 1968;81:266–68.
55. Schonfeld G, Pfleger B. Utilization of exogenous free fatty acids for the production of very low density lipoprotein triglyceride by livers of carbohydrate-fed rats. J Lipid Res 1971;12:614–21.
56. Miller GJ. High density lipoproteins and atherosclerosis. Ann Rev Med 1980;31:97–108.
57. Kaplan JR, Manuck SB, Clarkson TB, et al. Social stress and atherosclerosis in normocholesterolemic monkeys. Science 1982;220:733–35.
58. Kaplan JR, Manuck SB, Clarkson TB, et al. Social stress, environment and atherosclerosis in cynomolgus monkeys. Arteriosclerosis 1982;2:359–68.
59. Shively CA, Kaplan JR, Adams MR. Effects of ovariectomy, social instability and social status on female Macaca fascicularis social behavior. Physiol Behav 1986;36:1147–53.
60. Wingard DL, Suarez L, Barrett-Connor E. The sex differential in mortality from all causes and ischemic heart disease. Am J Epidemiol 1983;117:19–26.

61. Matthews KA. Interactive effects of behavior and reproductive hormones on sex differences in risk for coronary heart disease. Health Psychol 1989;8:373–87.

62. Adams MR, Kaplan JR, Clarkson TB, et al. Ovariectomy, social status, and atherosclerosis in cynomolgus monkeys. Arteriosclerosis 1985;5:192–200.

63. Kaplan JR, Adams MR, Koritnik DR, et al. Adrenal responsiveness and social status in intact and ovariectomized Macaca fascicularis. Am J Primatol 1986;11:181–93.

64. Hickey N, Mulcahy R, Bourke GJ, et al. Study of coronary risk factors related to physical activity in 15,171 men. Br Med J 1975;3:507–9.

65. Erikssen J, Forfang K, Jervell J. Coronary risk factors and physical fitness in healthy middle-aged men. Acta Med Scand 1981;645(Suppl):57–64.

66. Paffenbarger RS, Wing AL, Hyde RT, et al. Physical activity and incidence of hypertension in college alumni. Am J Epidemiol 1983;117:245–57.

67. Kiyonaga A, Arakawa K, Tanaka H, et al. Blood pressure and hormonal responses to aerobic exercise. Hypertension 1985;7:125–31.

68. Nelson L, Jennings GL, Esler MD, et al. Effect of changing levels of physical activity on blood-pressure and haemodynamics in essential hypertension. Lancet 1986;2:473–76.

69. Reisin E, Frohlich ED, Messerli FH. Cardiovascular changes in obesity after weight reduction. Ann Intern Med 1983;98:315–19.

70. Golay A, Felber JP, Dusmet M. Effect of weight loss on glucose disposal in obese and obese diabetic patients. Int J Obes 1985;9:181–90.

71. Krotkiewski M, Mandroukas K, Sjöstrom L, et al. Effects of long-term physical training on body fat, metabolism and blood pressure in obesity. Metabolism 1979;28:650–58.

72. Jennings GL, Deakin G, Dewar E, et al. Exercise, cardiovascular disease and blood pressure. Clin Exp Hypertens Theo Prac 1989;11:1035–52.

73. Thompson PD, Cullinane EM, Sady SP. Modest changes in high-density lipoprotein concentration and metabolism with prolonged exercise training. Circulation 1988;78:25–34.

74. Hollenbeck C, Haskell W, Rosenthal M. Effect of habitual physical activity on regulation of insulin-stimulated glucose disposal in older males. J Am Geriatr Soc 1985;33:273–77.

75. DeFronzo RA, Sherwin RS, Kraemer N. Effect of physical training on insulin action in obesity. Diabetes 1987;36:1379–85.

76. Heath GW, Gavin III JR, Hinderliter JM. Effects of exercise and lack of exercise on glucose tolerance and insulin sensitivity. J Appl Physiol 1983;55:512–17.

77. King DS, Dalsky GP, Clutter WE. Effects of exercise and lack of exercise on insulin sensitivity and responsiveness. J Appl Physiol 1988;64:1942–46.

78. Benowitz NL, Kuyt F, Jacob P. Influence of nicotine on cardiovascular and hormonal effects of cigarette smoking. Clin Pharm 1984;36:74–81.

79. Kerschbaum A, Pappajohn DJ, Bellet S. Effect of smoking and nicotine on adrenocortical secretion. JAMA 1968;203:275–78.

80. Robertson D, Tseng C-J, Appalsamy M. Smoking and mechanisms of cardiovascular control. Am Heart J 1988;115:258–63.

81. Epstein LH, Perkins KA. Smoking, stress, and coronary heart disease. J Cons Clin 1988;56:342–49.

82. Scherwitz LW, Perkins LL, Chesney MA. Hostility and health behaviors in young adults: The CARDIA Study. Am J Epidemiol 1992;136:136–45.

83. Craig WY, Palomaki GE, Haddow JE. Cigarette smoking and serum lipid and lipoprotein concentrations: an analysis of published data. Br Med J 1989;298:784–88.

84. Brischetto CS, Connor WE, Connor SL, et al. Plasma lipid and lipoprotein profiles of cigarette smokers from randomly selected families: enhancement of hyperlipidemia and depression of high-density lipoprotein. Am J Cardiol 1983;52:675–80.

85. Barrett-Connor E, Khaw KT. Cigarette smoking and increased central adiposity. Ann Intern Med 1989;111:783–87.

86. Kannel WB, Brand N, Skinner Jr JJ, et al. The relation of adiposity to blood pressure and development of hypertension. Ann Intern Med 1967;67:48–59.

87. Foster CJ, Weinsier RL, Birch R. Obesity and serum lipids: an evaluation of the relative contribution of body fat and fat distribution to lipid levels. Int J Obes 1987;11:151–61.

88. Ferrannini E, DeFronzo RA. The association of hypertension, diabetes and obesity: a review. J Nephrol 1989;1:3–15.

89. Ferrannini E, Haffner SM, Mitchell DB, et al. Hyperinsulinemia: the key feature of a cardio-vascular and metabolic syndrome. Diabetologia 1991;34:416–22.

90. Blair D, Habicht J-P, Sims EAH, et al. Evidence for an increased risk for hypertension with centrally located body fat and the effect of race and sex on this risk. Am J Epidemiol 1984;119:526–40.

91. Kissebah AH, Vydelingum N, Murray R, et al. Relation of body fat distribution to metabolic complications of obesity. J Clin Endocrinol Metab 1982;54:254–59.

92. Krotkiewski M, Björntorp P, Sjöström L, et al. Impact of obesity on metabolism in men and women: importance of regional adipose tissue distribution. J Clin Invest 1983;72:1150–62.

93. Olefsky JM, Kolterman OG, Scarlett JA. Insulin action and resistance in obesity and nonin-sulin-dependent type II diabetes mellitus. Am J Physiol 1982;243:E15–E30.

94. DeFronzo RA, Tobin JD, Andres R. The glucose clamp technique: a method for quantifying insulin secretion and resistance. Am J Physiol 1979;6:E214–E223.

95. Bonadonna R, Groop L, Kraemer N, et al. Obesity and insulin resistance in man: a dose response study. Metabolism 1990;39:452–59.

96. DeFronzo RA. Lilly lecture 1987: the triumvirate: b-cell, muscle, liver: a collusion responsible for NIDDM. Diabetes 1988;37:667–87.

97. Kempner W, Newborg BC, Peschel RL, et al. Treatment of massive obesity with rice/reduction diet program: an analysis of 106 patients with at least 45 kilograms weight lost. Arch Intern Med 1975;135:1575–84.

98. Olefsky J, Reaven GM, Farquhar JW. Effects of weight reduction on obesity. Studies of lipid and carbohydrate metabolism in normal and hyperlipoproteinemic subjects. J Clin Invest 1974;53:64–76.

99. Pollare T, Lithell H, Berne C. Insulin resistance is a characteristic feature of primary hyper-tension independent of obesity. Metabolism 1990;39:169–74.

100. Orchard TJ, Becker DJ, Bates M. Plasma insulin and lipoprotein cholesterol concentrations: an atherogenic association? Am J Epidemiol 1983;118:326–27.

101. Zavaroni I, Dall'Aglio E, Alpi O, et al. Evidence for an independent relationship between plasma insulin and concentration of high density lipoprotein cholesterol and triglyceride. Atherosclerosis 1985;55:259–66.

102. Modan M, Halkin H, Fuchs Z, et al. Hyperinsulinemia—a link between glucose intolerance, obesity, hypertension, dyslipoproteinemia, elevated serum uric acid and internal cation imbal-ance. Diab Metab 1987;13:375–80.

103. Abbott WGH, Lillioja S, Young AA. Relationships between plasma lipoprotein concentrations and insulin action in an obese hyperinsulinemic population. Diabetes 1987;36:897–904.

104. Garg A, Helderman JH, Koffler M. Relationship between lipoprotein levels and in vivo insulin action in normal young white men. Metabolism 1988;37:982–87.

105. Laakso M, Edelman SV, Olefsky JM, et al. Kinetics of in vitro muscle insulin-mediated glucose uptake in human obesity. Diabetes 1990;39:965–74.

106. Sparks CE, Sparks JD, Bolognino M. Insulin effects on apolipoprotein B lipoprotein synthesis and secretion by primary cultures of rat hepatocytes. Metabolism 1986;35:1128–36.

107. Howard BV. Lipoprotein metabolism in diabetes mellitus. J Lipid Res 1987;28:613–28.

108. Fujioka S, Matsuzawa Y, Tokunage K. Contribution of intra-abdominal fat accumulation to the impairment of glucose and lipid metabolism in human obesity. Metabolism 1987;36:54–9.

109. Reaven GM, Mondon CE. Effect of in vivo plasma insulin levels on the relationship between perfusated free fatty acid concentration and triglyceride secretion by perfused rat livers. Horm Metab Res 1984;16:230–32.
110. Carlson LA, Levi L, Oro L. Plasma lipids and urinary excretion of catecholamines in man during experimentally induced emotional stress, and their modification by nicotinic acid. J Clin Invest 1968;47:1795–1805.
111. Fredikson M, Blumenthal JA. Serum lipids, neuroendocrine and cardiovascular response to stress in healthy type A men. Biol Psychol 1992;34:45–58.
112. Cowan LD, Wilcosky T, Criqui MH. Demographic, behavioral, biochemical, and dietary correlates of plasma triglycerides: Lipid Research Clinics Program Prevalence Study. Arteriosclerosis 1985;5:466–80.
113. Felber J-P, Ferrannini E, Golay A, et al. Role of lipid oxidation in pathogenesis of insulin resistance of obesity and type II diabetes. Diabetes 1987;36:1341–50.
114. Newman B, Selby JV, King MC, et al. Concordance for type 2 (non-insulin-dependent) diabetes mellitus in male twins. Diabetologia 1987;30:763–68.
115. Barnett AH, Eff C, Leslie RD, et al. Diabetes in identical twins: a study of 200 pairs. Diabetologia 1981;20:87–93.
116. Kobberling J, Tillil H. Empirical risk figures for first-degree relatives of non-insulin-dependent diabetics. In: Kobberling J, Tattersal R, editors. The genetics of diabetes mellitus. London: Academic, 1982:201–10.
117. Pyorala K, Savolainen E, Kaukola S, et al. Plasma insulin as coronary heart disease risk factor: relationship to other risk factors and predictive value during 9-1/2 year follow-up of the Helsinki policemen study population. Acta Medica Scand 1985;701(Suppl):38–52.
118. Fournier AM, Gadia MT, Kubrusly DB, et al. Blood pressure, insulin, and glycemia in nondiabetic subjects. Am J Med 1986;80:861–64.
119. Wing RR, Bunker CH, Kuller LH, et al. Insulin, body mass index, and cardiovascular risk factors in premenopausal women. Arteriosclerosis 1989;9:479–84.
120. Ferrannini E, Buzzigoli G, Bonadonna R, et al. Insulin resistance in essential hypertension. N Eng J Med 1987;317:350–57.
121. Tobian L. Salt and hypertension. In: Genest J, Kuchel O, Hamet P, et al., editors. Hypertension. New York: McGraw-Hill, 1983:422–32.
122. Feldt-Rasmussen B, Mathiesen ER, Deckert T, et al. Central role for sodium in the pathogenesis of blood pressure changes independent of angiotensin, aldosterone and catecholamines in type 1 (insulin-dependent) diabetes mellitus. Diabetologia 1987;30:610–17.
123. Mujais SK, Tarazi RC, Dustan HP, et al. Hypertension in obese patients: hemodynamic and volume studies. Hypertension 1982;4:84–92.
124. Marks JB, Thompson NE, Ironson GH, et al. Sodium intake affects blood pressure in insulin resistant subjects. Diabetes 1994;43:100 (Abstract).
125. DeFronzo RA, Cooke CR, Andres R, et al. The effect of insulin on renal handling of sodium, potassium, calcium and phosphate in man. J Clin Invest 1975;55:845–55.
126. Skott P, Hother-Nielsen O, Bruun NE, et al. Effects of insulin on kidney function and sodium excretion in healthy subjects. Diabetologia 1989;32:694–99.
127. Baum M. Insulin stimulates volume absorption in the rabbit proximal convoluted tubule. J Clin Invest 1987;79:1104–09.
128. Mulvany MJ. Pathophysiology of vascular smooth muscle in hypertension. J Hypertension 1984;2 Suppl III:413–20.
129. Folkow B. Cardiovascular structural adaptation: its role in the inhibition and maintenance of primary hypertension: Volhard lecture. Clin Sci 1978;55:3s–22s.
130. Kleinman KS, Fine LG. Prognostic implications of renal hypertrophy in diabetes mellitus. Diab Met Rev 1988;4:179–89.
131. Froesch ER, Schmid C, Schwander J, et al. Actions of insulin-like growth factors. Ann Rev Physiol 1985;47:443–67.

132. King GL, Goodman D, Buzney S, et al. Receptors and growth promoting effects of insulin and insulin like growth factors on cells from bovine retinal capillaries and aorta. J Clin Invest 1985;75:1028–36.

133. Blaustein MP. Sodium ions, calcium ions, blood pressure regulation, and hypertension: a reassessment and a hypothesis. Am J Physiol 1977;232:C165–C173.

134. Hermsmeyer RK. Vascular muscle membrane cation mechanisms and total peripheral resistance. Hypertension 1987;10 Suppl 1:20–2.

135. Dominiczak AF, Bohr DF. Vascular smooth muscle in hypertension. J Hypertension 1989;7:S107–S115.

136. Mahnensmith RL, Aronson PS. The plasma membrane sodium-hydrogen exchanger and its role in physiological and pathophysiological process. Circ Res 1985;56:773–88.

137. Erne P, Hermsmeyer K. Intracellular vascular muscle Ca^{2+} modulation in genetic hypertension. Hypertension 1989;14:145–51.

138. Moore RD. Stimulation of Na:H exchange by insulin. Biophys J 1981;33:203–10.

139. Camussi A, Bianchi G. Genetics of essential hypertension: from the unimodal-bimodal controversy to molecular technology. Hypertension 1988;12:620–28.

140. Ng LL, Dudley C, Bomford J, et al. Leucocyte intracellular pH and Na^+/H^+ antiport activity in human hypertension. J Hypertension 1989;7:471–75.

141. Livne A, Veitch R, Grinstein S, et al. Increased platelet Na-H exchange rates in essential hypertension: application of a novel test. Lancet 1987;1:533–36.

142. Orlov SN, Postnov IY, Pokudin NI, et al. $Na^+–H^+$ exchange and other ion-transport systems in erythrocytes of essential hypertensives and spontaneously hypertensive rats: a comparative analysis. J Hypertension 1989;7:781–88.

143. Christensen NJ, Gundersen HJG, Hegedus L. Acute effects of insulin on plasma noradrenaline and the cardiovascular system. Metabolism 1980;29:1138–45.

144. Krieger DR, Landsberg L. Mechanisms in obesity-related hypertension: role of insulin and catecholamines. Am J Hypertension 1988;1:84–90.

145. Ferrannini E, Barrett EJ, Bevilacqua S, et al. Effects of fatty acids on glucose production and utilization in man. J Clin Invest 1983;72:1737–47.

146. Julius S, Gudbrandsson T, Jamerson K, et al. Hypothesis: the hemodynamic link between insulin resistance and hypertension. J Hypertension 1991;9:983–86.

147. DeFronzo RA, Gunnarsson R, Bjorkman O, et al. Effects of insulin on peripheral and splanchnic glucose metabolism in noninsulin-dependent (type II) diabetes mellitus. J Clin Invest 1985;76:149–55.

148. Natali A, Santoro D, Palombo C, et al. Impaired insulin action on skeletal muscle metabolism in essential hypertension. Hypertension 1991;17:170–78.

149. Baron AD, Laakso M, Brechtel G, et al. Mechanism of insulin resistance in insulin-dependent diabetes mellitus: a major role for reduced skeletal muscle blood flow. J Clin End Metab 1991;73:637–43.

150. Pollare T, Lithell H, Morlin C, et al. Metabolic effects of diltiazem and atenolol: results from a randomized, double-blind study with parallel groups. J Hypertension 1989;7:551–59.

151. Pollare T, Lithell H, Selinus I, et al. Application of prazosin is associated with an increase of insulin sensitivity in obese patients with hypertension. Diabetologia 1988;31:415–20.

152. Pykallsto OJ, Smith PH, Brunzell JD. Determinants of human adipose tissue lipoprotein lipase: effect of diabetes and obesity on basal and diet induced activity. J Clin Invest 1975;56:1108–17.

153. Sacks FM, Dzau VJ. Adrenergic effects on plasma lipoprotein metabolism: speculation on mechanisms of action. Am J Med 1986;80 Suppl 2A:71–81.

154. Ardlie NG, Glew G, Schwartz CJ. Influence of catecholamines on nucleotide-induced platelet aggregation. Nature 1966;212:415–17.

155. Simpson P. Norepinephrine-stimulated hypertrophy of cultured rat myocardial cells is an alpha-1 adrenergic response. J Clin Invest 1983;72:732–38.

156. Hart MN, Heistad DD, Brody MJ. Effect of chronic hypertension and sympathetic denervation on wall/lumen ratio of cerebral vessels. Hypertension 1980;2:419–28.

157. Julius S, Pascual AV, London R. Role of parasympathetic inhibition in the hyperkinetic type of borderline hypertension. Circulation 1971;44:413–18.

158. Esler M, Julius S, Zweifler A, et al. Mild high-renin essential hypertension: neurogenic human hypertension? N Eng J Med 1977;296:405–11.

159. Julius S, Krause L, Schork N, et al. Hyperkinetic borderline hypertension in Tecumseh, Michigan. J Hypertension 1991;9:77–84.

160. Folkow B. Role of vascular factors in hypertension. Cont Nephrol 1977;8:81–94.

161. Lund-Johansen P. Central haemodynamics in essential hypertension at rest and during exercise: a 20-year follow-up study. J Hypertension 1989;7 Suppl 6:S52–S55.

162. Page IH. Pathogenesis of arterial hypertension. JAMA 1949;140:451–58.

163. Folkow B, Hallbeck M. Physiopathology of spontaneous hypertension in rats. In: Genest J, Koiw E, Kuchel O, editors. Hypertension: physiopathology and treatment. New York: McGraw-Hill, 1977:507–528.

164. Cierpial MA, Konarska M, McCarty R. Maternal effects on the development of spontaneous hypertension. Health Psy 1988;7:125–35.

165. Lawler JE, Barker GF, Hubbard JW, et al. The effects of conflict on tonic levels of blood pressure in the genetically borderline hypertensive rat. Psychophysiology 1980;17:363–70.

166. Lawler JE, Sanders BJ, Chen YF, et al. Hypertension produced by a high sodium diet in the borderline hypertensive rat. Clin Exper Hypertens 1987;A9:1713–31.

167. Cox RH, Hubbard JW, Lawler JE, et al. Exercise training attenuates stress-induced hypertension in the rat. Hypertension 1985;7:747–51.

168. Brod J, Fencl V, Hejl Z, et al. Circulatory changes underlying blood pressure elevation during acute emotional stress (mental arithmetic) in normotensive and hypertensive subjects. Clin Sci 1959;18:269–79.

169. Falkner B, Onesti G, Angelakos ET, et al. Cardiovascular response to mental stress in normal adolescents with hypertensive parents. Hypertension 1979;1:23–30.

170. Ditto B. Parental history of essential hypertension, active coping, and cardiovascular reactivity. Psychophysiology 1986;23:62–70.

171. Turner JR, Hewitt JK. Twin studies of cardiovascular response to psychological challenge: a review and suggested future directions. Ann Beh Med 1992;14:12–20.

172. Henry JP, Stephens PM, Santisteban GA. A model of psychosocial hypertension showing reversibility and progression of cardiovascular complications. Circ Res 1975;36:156–64.

173. Henry JP, Ely DL, Stephens PM, et al. The role of psychosocial factors in the development of arteriosclerosis in CBA mice. Atherosclerosis 1971;14:203–18.

174. Henry JP, Vander AJ, Stephens PM. Effects of an angiotensin converting enzyme inhibition on psychosocial hypertension in mice. Clin Sci 1979;57(Suppl):153–61.

175. Kaplan JR, Manuck SB, Adams MR, et al. Inhibition of coronary atherosclerosis by propranolol in behaviorally predisposed monkeys fed an atherogenic diet. Circulation 1987;76:1364–72.

176. Harburg E, Erfurt JC, Chape C, et al. Socio-ecological stressor areas and Black-White blood pressure: Detroit. J Chronic Dis 1973;26:595–611.

177. Harburg E, Efurt JC, Hauenstein LS, et al. Socio-ecological stress, suppressed hostility, skin color, and Black-White male blood pressure: Detroit. Psychosom Med 1973;35:276–96.

178. Brand RJ, Rosenman RH, Sholtz RI, et al. Multivariate prediction of coronary heart disease in the Western Collaborative Group Study compared to the findings of the Framingham Study. Circulation 1976;53:348–55.

179. Shekelle RB, Hulley SB, Neaton JD, et al. The MRFIT behavior pattern study: II. Type A behavior and incidence of coronary heart disease. Am J Epidemiol 1985;122:559–70.

180. Case RB, Heller SS, Case MB, et al. Type A behavior and survival after acute myocardial infarction. N Eng J Med 1985;312:737–41.

181. Shekelle RB, Gale M, Norusis M. Type A score (Jenkins Activity Survey) and risk of recurrent coronary heart disease in the Aspirin Myocardial Infarction Study. Am J Cardiol 1985;56:221–25.

182. Matthews KA, Glass DC, Rosenman RH, et al. Competitive drive, Pattern A, and coronary heart disease: a further analysis of some data from the Western Collaborative Group Study. J Chronic Dis 1977;30:489–98.

183. Chesney MA, Hecker MHL, Black GW. Coronary-prone components of Type A behavior in the WCGS: a new methodology. In: Houston BK, Snyder CR, editors. Type A behavior pattern: research, theory and intervention. New York: Wiley, 1988:168–88.

184. Carmelli D, Swan GE, Rosenman RH, et al. Behavioral components and total mortality in the Western Collaborative Group Study. Paper presented at the meeting of the Society of Behavioral Medicine, San Francisco, April 1989.

185. Barefoot JC, Dahlstrom WG, Williams RB. Hostility, CHD incidence, and total mortality: a 25-year follow-up of 255 physicians. Psychosom Med 1983;45:59–63.

186. Koskenvuo M, Kaprio J, Rose RJ, et al. Hostility as a risk factor for mortality and ischemic heart disease in men. Psychosom Med 1988;50:330–40.

187. Lundberg U, Hedman M, Melin B, et al. Type A behavior in healthy males and females as related to physiological reactivity and blood lipids. Psychosom Med 1989;51:113–22.

188. Cottington EM, Matthews KA, Talbot D, et al. Occupational stress, suppressed anger, and hypertension. Psychosom Med 1986;48:249–60.

189. Julius M, Harburg E, Cottington EM, et al. Anger-coping types, blood pressure, and all-cause mortality: a follow-up in Tecumseh-Michigan (1971–1983). Am J Epidemiol 1986;124:220–33.

190. Jorgensen RS, Houston BK. Family history of hypertension, personality patterns, and cardiovascular reactivity to stress. Psychosom Med 1986;48:102–17.

191. Suarez EC, Williams RB. The relationships between dimensions of hostility and cardiovascular reactivity as a function of task characteristics. Psychosom Med 1990;52:558–70.

192. Dimsdale JE. The effect of depression on cardiovascular reactivity. In: Field TM, McCabe PM, Schneiderman N, editors. Stress and coping across development. Hillsdale, NJ: Lawrence Erlbaum Associates, 1988:215–25.

193. Lindegard B. Physical illness in severe depressives and psychiatric alcoholics in Gothenburg, Sweden. J Affect Dis 1982;4:383–93.

194. Kaplan G. Psychosocial aspects of chronic illness: direct and indirect associations with ischemic heart disease mortality. In: Kaplan R, Criqui M, editors. Behavioral epidemiology and disease prevention. New York: Plenum, 1985:237–69.

195. Lake C, Picker D, Ziegler M, et al. High plasma norepinephrine levels in patients with affective disorder. Am J Psych 1982;139:1315–18.

196. Wyatt R, Portnoy B, Kupfer D, et al. Resting plasma cateacholamine concentrations in patients with depression and anxiety. Arch Gen Psych 1971;24:65–70.

197. Esler M, Turbott J, Schwarz R, et al. The peripheral kinetics of norepinephrine in depressive illness. Arch Gen Psych 1982;39:295–300.

198. Jeffery RW. Weight management and hypertension. Ann Beh Med 1991;13:18–22.

199. Perri MG, McAdoo WG, McAllister DA, et al. Enhancing the efficiency of behavior therapy for obesity: effects of aerobic exercise and a muticomponent maintenance program. J Cons Clin 1986;50:670–75.

200. Agras WS, Southam MA, Taylor CB. Long-term persistence of relaxation-induced blood pressure lowering during the working day. J Cons Clin Psychol 1983;51:792–94.

201. Aivazyan TA, Zaitsev VP, Salenko BB, et al. Efficacy of relaxation techniques in hypertensive patients. Health Psy 1988;7:193–200.

202. Patel C, Marmot MG, Terry DJ. Controlled trial of biofeedback-aided behavioural methods in reducing mild hypertension. Br Med J 1981;282:2005–08.

203. Goldstein IB, Shapiro D, Thananopavarn C, et al. Comparison of drug and behavioral treatments of essential hypertension. Health Psy 1982;1:7–26.

204. Kaufmann PG, Jacob RG, Ewart CK, et al. Hypertension intervention pooling project. Health Psy 1988;7(Suppl):209–24.
205. Cottier C, Shapiro K, Julius S. Treatment of mild hypertension with progressive muscle relaxation: predictive value of indexes of sympathetic tone. Arch Int Med 1984;144:1954–58.
206. McGrady AV, Higgins JT. Prediction of response to biofeedback assisted relaxation in hypertensives: development of a hypertensive predictor profile (HYPP). Psychosom Med 1989;51:277–84.
207. Burell G, Öhman A, Sundin Ö, et al. Modification of the Type A behavior pattern in post-myocardial infarction patients: a route to cardiac rehabilitation. Int J Beh Med 1994;1:32–54.
208. Friedman M, Thoresen CE, Gill JJ, et al. Alteration of type A behavior and its effect on cardiac recurrences in post myocardial infarction patients: summary results of the Recurrent Coronary Prevention Project. Am Heart J 1986;112:653–65.
209. Frasure-Smith N, Prince R. Long-term follow-up of the Ischemic Heart Disease Life Stress Monitoring Program. Psychosom Med 1989;51:485–513.
210. Ornish DM, Brown SE, Scherwitz LW. Can lifestyle changes reverse coronary heart disease? The Lifestyle Heart Trial. Lancet 1990;2:129–33.
211. Verrier RL. Neurochemical approaches to the prevention of ventricular fibrillation. Fed Proc 1986;45:2191–96.
212. Fuller RW, Wong DT, Robertson DW. Fluoxetine, a selective inhibitor of serotonin uptake. Med Res Rev 1991;11:17–34.
213. Newhouse JP. An inconoclastic view of health cost containment. Health Aff 1993;12(Suppl):152–71.
214. McAlister A, Puska P, Salonen J, et al. Theory and action for health promotion: illustrations from the North Karelia Project. Am J Public Health 1982;72:43–50.
215. Hjermann I, Velve-Byre K, Home I, et al. Effect of diet and smoking intervention on the incidence of coronary heart disease. Report from the Oslo Study Group of a randomized trial in healthy men. Lancet 1981;ii:1303–10.
216. Multiple Risk Factor Intervention Trial Research Group. Multiple Risk Factor Intervention Trial: risk factor changes and mortality results. JAMA 1982;248:1465–77.
217. McKenney JM, Slining JM, Anderson HR, et al. Effect of clinical pharmacy services on patients with essential hypertension. Circulation 1973;48:1104–11.

Chapter 9

Psychophysiological Processes in the Prevention of Cardiovascular Disease

Andrew Steptoe
University of London

The prevention of cardiovascular disease (CVD) is a multidisciplinary endeavor involving all the biomedical and social sciences that contribute to behavioral medicine. The purpose of this chapter is to outline the contributions that can be made by psychophysiology. The first section describes the features that characterize psychophysiology, and then reviews the research paradigms that are typically utilized. The remaining sections discuss the relevance of psychophysiological methods to CVD prevention, focusing on three issues: psychophysiological methods in the investigation of etiological processes, the use of psychophysiology in the prediction of vulnerability to cardiac events in people with preexisting coronary artery disease (CAD), and the role of psychophysiology in treatment and rehabilitation programs.

PSYCHOPHYSIOLOGY AND ITS METHODS

A recent authoritative text edited by Cacioppo and Tassinary (1) defined *psychophysiology* as "the scientific study of cognitive, emotional and behavioral phenomena as related to and revealed through physiological principles and events" (p. ix). This is only one of numerous definitions put forward since the discipline of psychophysiology was established some 40 years ago. It is so broad as to accommodate much of behavioral medicine and physiological psychology, as well as psychophysiology as it is currently practiced. But arguing about formal definitions is a frustrating enterprise because it is improbable that a single formulation can be devised that will be satisfactory to all. In the present context, it is more appropriate to take a pragmatic approach, defining the discipline in terms of the types of investigation and methods that psychophysiologists use in cardiovascular behavioral medicine.

Psychophysiological applications to behavioral medicine typically involve the monitoring of physiological functions in relation to concurrent emotional and behavioral states. Originally, psychophysiological studies were confined to the laboratory or clinic, and explored the cardiovascular and neuroendocrine responses to stressors, individual differences in reaction patterns, or changes in physiological function with behavioral interventions. Laboratory studies remain the mainstay of psychophysiology, but the development of ambulatory methods has increasingly led to investigations under everyday or naturalistic conditions. Describing psychophysiology as a method of studying relationships between physical responses and ongoing behavior places no limits on the nature of the physiological processes being monitored. Indeed, one of the characteristics of psychophysiology has been the development of technology to assess more and more sophisticated and precise aspects of cardiovascular function. Studies some 20 years ago, in which heart rate was measured electrocardiographically and accompanied by intermittent registrations of blood pressure or forearm blood flow, have now been superseded by investigations of cardiac output and regional blood distribution (using impedance cardiography and systolic time intervals), renal function and sodium excretion, platelet activation and myocardial function, together with the application of mathematical modeling techniques such as power spectrum analysis. The cardinal element of psychophysiology is that these functions are assessed in response to defined behavioral events, and that studies typically involve repeated measurement of the physiological processes under investigation. In this respect, the psychophysiological approach is distinct from behavioral epidemiology or clinical studies in cardiovascular behavioral medicine. The targets of investigation may be similar (e.g., personality characteristics in relation to blood pressure, or cardiovascular consequences of different work patterns). However, in the behavioral epidemiological study, physiological measures are typically collected under office or clinic conditions on one or a few occasions, whereas psychophysiologists are predominantly concerned with dynamic interrelations between behavior and physiology.

Laboratory Versus Field Assessment

Psychophysiological research in early behavioral medicine was dominated by studies of biofeedback and the voluntary control of blood pressure and heart rate (2). Over the last 15 years, mental stress testing in the laboratory has become the major research paradigm (3). It has involved studies of many clinic and high-risk groups, and assessments of a wide range of physiological processes in response to a variety of conditions, such as problem solving, stress interviews, and information-processing tasks. The methodology of mental stress testing in the laboratory has been thoroughly reviewed in various texts (4, 5). Reservations concerning the reliability of laboratory assessments have largely been allayed by a new generation of investigations, indicating that, provided care is taken with physiological measurement and administration of behavioral stimuli, reliable and consistent response patterns are observed (6, 7).

The last decade has seen the development of lightweight portable blood pressure monitors suitable for ambulatory monitoring from people as they go about their ordinary lives. This has sparked a vigorous debate concerning the relative merits of laboratory psychophysiological assessments as opposed to investigations involving ambulatory monitoring (8). The controversy has been fueled by the observation of many investigators that cardiovascular reactions to laboratory stress tests show only weak associations with blood pressure or heart rate levels assessed with ambulatory measures over the day (9, 10). Because there is evidence that ambulatory measures predict CVD risk independently of clinic readings (11), it has been suggested that laboratory mental stress testing may be irrelevant to cardiovascular etiology.

Space precludes detailed discussions of why associations between laboratory and field may be weak, or the description of studies in which more reliable effects have been observed (12, 13). In the present context, it is more fruitful to consider laboratory and ambulatory techniques as complementary, converging on the same issues through different routes (3). Laboratory and clinic studies have the advantage that psychophysiological measures are obtained under precisely controlled and standardized conditions, and in response to known events. Experimental designs can be used, enabling hypotheses to be rigorously tested. The psychophysiological measures can be more elaborate than those currently feasible in field settings, so that investigators are not confined to parameters such as blood pressure and heart rate. In contrast, ambulatory measures can be used to assess psychophysiological responses to real, everyday events, rather than the contrived situations of the laboratory. Physiological function is linked directly with people's spontaneous experiences in their lives, and the frequency and intensity of their emotions are observed in ways that are not inhibited by the constraints of the laboratory or clinic setting. Up until now, ambulatory studies have been predominantly descriptive in their design; this means that participants are not randomized to the conditions of interest, and that concurrent influences on psychophysiological function (activity, posture, smoking, beverages, etc.) have to be allowed for statistically. One of the major tasks presently facing investigators is the development of analytic methods that will enable the variability in cardiovascular function that is associated with behavioral events and emotional states to be separated from the variability in function that is attributable to physical activity.

PSYCHOPHYSIOLOGY AND ETIOLOGICAL PROCESSES

Research on psychophysiological processes that may be relevant to the etiology of CVD has evolved from basic investigations of psychophysiological responses to mental stress into studies that attempt a more comprehensive understanding of psychosocial risk in the broader context of pathophysiology. This evolution can best be illustrated by studies of psychophysiological aspects of essential hypertension. The first experiments in this area established that a proportion of diagnosed hypertensive patients show elevated blood pressure responses to mental arithmetic in comparison with normotensives, and that reactions are sustained for longer periods following the termination of tasks in patients than in controls (14). This observation has been elaborated in a number of ways. First, detailed hemodynamic studies have been undertaken to investigate the changes in regional blood flow and cardiac function underlying stress-induced modifications in blood pressure. Second, it has been recognized that the type of behavioral challenge is significant, and that actively demanding and engaging conditions elicit hemodynamic responses that are substantially different from those mobilized during stressors such as the cold pressor test (15). Third, studies of hypertensives have been supplemented by experiments involving people with normal blood pressure who are nevertheless considered to be at increased risk for developing the disorder by virtue of their family history, tonic blood pressure level, or race (16–18). Fourth, there has been interest in the psychological characteristics of people at risk for hypertension, with accumulating evidence that individuals who suppress anger and negative emotion may be particularly susceptible (19, 20). These trends have led to psychophysiological studies in which biological predispositions, such as family history, situational factors, and psychological characteristics, are evaluated simultaneously.

A recent study from our laboratory illustrates this approach (21). It was based on the hypothesis that the adolescent offspring of people with elevated blood pressure would show heightened cardiovascular reactions to mental stress only when they were confronted by demanding situations requiring active and effortful coping behavior, and only when they also had tendencies to suppress anger. It was therefore predicted that high-risk children who do not suppress anger would not show heightened cardiovascular adjustments during behavioral challenge. The study involved 60 boys ages 12–16 years. Because studies of family history have been criticized for relying on reports of blood pressure status rather than objective evidence, we measured the blood pressure of all participants' parents in their own homes. On this basis, the boys were classified as *low family risk* (n = 40) and *high family risk* (n = 20). Participants were not told of their risk status; this was done to overcome the problem of "labeling" and to avoid awareness of blood pressure status, which has been shown to influence psychophysiological reactivity (22).

Participants completed the State–Trait Anger Expression Inventory (23), and were classified by binary split on the Anger Inhibition subscale. Interestingly, the distribution of Anger Inhibition scores was comparable in the high and low family-risk subjects. Thus, anger inhibition was not more prevalent among boys at increased biological risk. This procedure resulted in a comparison of four groups: high family-risk subjects who were either high ($n = 10$) or low ($n = 10$) in anger inhibition, and low family-risk subjects who were high ($n = 20$) or low ($n = 20$) in anger inhibition. Blood pressure, heart rate, cardiac baroreflex activity, electrodermal activity, respiration rate, and subjective feelings of tension were then monitored at rest and during performance of two actively challenging tasks: nonverbal mental arithmetic and a frustrating psychomotor task (mirror tracing).

Illustrative results for diastolic blood pressure are shown in Fig. 9.1. It is evident that no tonic differences in diastolic pressure were present at rest. However, when asked to complete the tasks, the high family-risk subjects who reported anger inhibition showed greater diastolic responses. No differences between the responses of the other three groups were observed. Thus, the combination of biological risk with appropriate situational demands and psychological characteristics seems important to the elicitation of heightened cardiovascular reactivity patterns.

The implications of studies of this type for CVD prevention are potentially important. Not only do they help delineate the psychophysiological processes

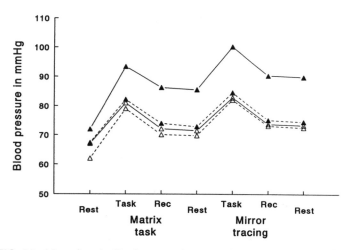

FIG. 9.1. Mean diastolic blood pressure for rest trials (Rest) and during matrix task and mirror tracing task trials. Each task trial is divided into a 5-min. task period (Task) and a 3-min. posttask recovery (Rec) period. The four groups of adolescent boys are designated as follows: high family risk/high anger inhibition: ▲————▲; high family risk/low anger inhibition: Δ————Δ; low family risk/high anger inhibition: ▲- - - - - - -▲; and low family risk/low anger inhibition: Δ- - - - - - -Δ. Note. From (21).

associated with the development of CVD, but they also may be useful in the early identification of people who may be at risk for future CVD. Of course, it is not sufficient merely to target people at increased risk by virtue of family history because only a proportion will go on to develop premature cardiac disease (24). Adding a psychological component to the characterization may help target at-risk people more precisely. However, one can envisage going further by adding a psychophysiological component to risk stratification. It should be noted from Fig. 9.1 that, although the high family-risk anger risk inhibitors as a group showed elevated stress responsivity, there was still substantial variation in the magnitude of responses within this group. It may be that people with propensities to exaggerated stress responsivity are particularly at risk. Evidence supporting this hypothesis comes from longitudinal studies demonstrating that elevated cardiovascular reactivity to actively demanding tasks predicts blood pressure levels in later years (25, 26). Combining knowledge of biological risk with psychophysiological information may allow more precise definition of individuals' overall propensities for psychosocial involvement in CVD risk.

Psychophysiological Modeling of Psychosocial Risk Factors

A second important way in which psychophysiological methods are relevant to understanding etiological processes is through modeling the mechanisms that link psychosocial factors with disease risk. A wide range of psychosocial phenomena—such as social support, socioeconomic status (SES), life stress, and work patterns—have been associated in epidemiological studies with cardiovascular risk. The following question arises: What processes mediate these effects? Health-related behaviors, including smoking and lack of regular exercise, may be responsible in part (27). However, it is often suggested that physiological processes such as neuroendocrine and cardiovascular activation are involved. Therefore, psychophysiological techniques can be used to model the impact of psychosocial factors on cardiovascular function.

An example of this application of psychophysiological methods is in relation to social support. The hypothesis has been tested that social support exerts its influence on disease risk partly through modulating stress-related cardiovascular activity. Over recent years, a series of experiments has been reported in which cardiovascular responses to various behavioral tasks have been compared in people tested either on their own or in the presence of a supportive person or friend. Reductions in cardiovascular responsivity have been observed by several investigators, suggesting that social support does indeed attenuate stress-related physiological function (28, 29). Results are not entirely consistent because effects depend on the extent to which the other person is supportive or evaluative (30). This is understandable because social contacts are known to have both positive and negative effects on health and emotional well-being (31).

Another illustration of the use of psychophysiological methods in modeling psychosocial factors concerns job demands and patterns of work. The evidence that patterns of work influence CVD risk is described elsewhere in this book (see chaps. 4 and 5). The demand–control model suggests that job strain and increased risk may emerge when intense job demands are coupled with low control over how the work is done, as well as limited skill development (32). Psychophysiological studies have shown that cardiovascular and neuroendocrine responses are typically more intense in situations of high as opposed to low task demand. The effects of control over work pace are less well understood. Therefore, we have conducted a series of studies in which cardiovascular and neuroendocrine responses to self-paced (controllable) and externally paced (uncontrollable) tasks in the laboratory were compared. Important aspects of this experimental approach are that people are randomized to self-paced and externally paced conditions, and that work demands are equated in the two groups. Thus, any differences in physiological response are likely to result from variations in controllability, not work demands or individual characteristics. It was hypothesized that if the effects of job strain on disease risk are mediated, in part, by stress-related activation of the cardiovascular system, then people performing tasks under external pacing should show larger blood pressure and heart rate responses than those carrying out the same tasks at the same rate, while being able to choose the pace for themselves.

In one study, 40 healthy men ages 55–65 years were recruited from the local population (33). Each person performed two tasks: a computerized visual problem-solving task, and the mirror tracing task. Half the participants carried out both these tasks at their own pace. The speed at which they performed tasks was recorded, and then was imposed on the externally paced group. For example, the problem-solving task involved showing a series of visual puzzles on a computer screen. The time available to solve each problem in the externally paced condition was the average time to solution recorded in the self-paced group. In this way, exposure to the tasks (or work rate) was equated, but a difference lay in whether subjects had control over task pace.

Table 9.1 summarizes results from this study. It can be seen that the groups did not differ in blood pressure or heart rate at rest. But during tasks, the responses were substantially greater in the externally paced than self-paced conditions. For example, the mean increase in blood pressure during the mirror tracing task was 41.8/19.5 mm Hg in externally paced subjects, compared with 28.1/13.8 mm Hg in the self-paced group. These effects are consistent with the notion that job demands, coupled with low job control, lead to greater cardiovascular stress responsivity than do similar job demands coupled with high job control.

It is probable that, in the next few years, more psychosocial risk factors for CVD will be subject to laboratory analyses of this kind (34). The strategy has already been used extensively in the valuation of individual characteristics such as hostility and Type A behavior (35). Such studies provide evidence that is complementary to behavioral epidemiological data, strengthening the case for serious clinical consideration of psychosocial factors. In addition, they hold out

TABLE 9.1
Control Over Work Pace and Cardiovascular Stress Responses

Variable	Rest	Mirror Drawing	Δ Mirror Drawing	Matrices	Δ Matrices
Systolic blood pressure (mm Hg)					
Self-paced	130.8 ± 26.0	158.9 ± 32.5	28.1	150.7 ± 31.4	19.9
Externally paced	133.4 ± 16.0	175.2 ± 26.8	41.8	167.4 ± 23.8	34.0
Diastolic blood pressure (mm Hg)					
Self-paced	69.0 ± 11.8	82.8 ± 14.6	13.8	78.4 ± 14.4	9.4
Externally paced	73.5 ± 10.0	93.0 ± 14.6	19.5	89.0 ± 12.4	15.5
Heart rate (bpm)					
Self-paced	71.5 ± 10.9	77.5 ± 10.7	6.0	74.4 ± 10.1	2.9
Externally paced	74.4 ± 11.6	83.7 ± 13.0	9.3	79.9 ± 14.1	5.5

Note. From (33). Mean values ± SD and task–rest differences (Δ) averaged over 5-minute trials.

the possibility of more refined risk stratification, facilitating effective allocation of preventive resources.

PSYCHOPHYSIOLOGICAL RESPONSES AND ACUTE CARDIAC EVENTS

One of the most promising avenues of research over recent years has been the discovery of the role of psychophysiological factors in triggering acute cardiac events such as arrhythmia and myocardial ischemia (36). This field has received impetus from studies implicating autonomic mechanisms in the survival of people with CAD. Kleiger and coworkers (37) showed a strong association between depressed heart rate variability and subsequent mortality in postmyocardial in-farction (MI) patients, and this was independent of other risk factors. The pattern has been confirmed in independent studies (38, 39). High resting heart rates have also been shown to predict subsequent sudden cardiac death in epidemi-ological studies, and may be associated with accelerated progression of athero-sclerosis (40, 41). Recently, depression of heart rate variability was observed among patients without CAD who survived sudden cardiac death (42). Inter-estingly, high heart rate levels and low heart rate variability appear to be asso-ciated with psychological depression in patients with CAD (43), and depression is recognized as a predictor of mortality in post-MI patients (44).

The pattern of high heart rate level and low heart rate variability may be a result of low parasympathetic (or vagal) tone. Lown and Verrier (45) showed that low vagal tone predisposes animals with experimental MI to ventricular fibrillation, and that stressful events increase risk of ventricular arrhythmia through this mechanism. As yet, there have been comparatively few psycho-physiological studies in humans of ventricular tachycardia and fibrillation, although Tavazzi, Zotti, and Rondanelli (46) found that serious arrhythmias could be induced using programmed ventricular stimulation during mental stress, but not under control conditions. The largest study concerning stress reactivity and cardiac arrhythmia reported thus far is the Cardiac Arrhythmia Pilot Study (47). In a group of 353 post-MI patients, few associations between cardiac morbidity and responses to mental stress were observed. However, the study only enrolled patients who experienced very high frequencies of premature beats, and therefore may have had an insufficient range to observe correlations between psychophysiological factors and arrhythmia. The stressor was also weak, and elicited only mild cardiovascular activation.

In contrast with the research on ventricular arrhythmias, a great deal of interest has been directed at behavioral stresses as triggers of myocardial ischemia. Rozanski and coworkers (48) assessed 39 patients with CAD using radionuclide ventriculography to image abnormalities of myocardial function during mental arithmetic, public speaking, and various other conditions. Twenty-nine patients showed cardiac wall motion abnormalities during exercise, of whom 21 also showed abnormalities during mental stress. Ischemic responses were greatest during the speech task, even though this was not rated as any more stressful than other stimuli. The level of oxygen demand at which ischemic responses were induced during mental stress was lower than that associated with ischemia during exercise. This suggests that mental stress testing was not simply mimicking exercise in placing high work demands on the heart, but that stress-induced autonomic and neuroendocrine responses were mobilized. It has subsequently been found that hemodynamic responsivity is elevated among patients with CAD who show ischemic and arrhythmic responses during mental stress (49, 50).

Another mechanism that may be relevant is activation of blood platelets and other factors associated with thrombus formation (51). Platelet activation with acute stress has been observed in both healthy adults and patients with CAD (52, 53). The rupture of atherosclerotic plaques and thrombosis has a role in silent ischemia, as well as in stable angina and MI, and may therefore be relevant to stress-induced ischemic episodes (54).

Studies of emotionally induced cardiac ischemia in field settings have not yet been extensively documented. The ambulatory left-ventricular function monitor, known as the VEST, promises to provide valuable information, but is cumbersome at present (55). Ambulatory studies associating electrocardiographic ST-segment changes with behavioral states are beginning to emerge (56). For example, Barry and colleagues (57) monitored ST-segment depression over a 24-hour period and related ischemic episodes with ongoing activities. Adjusting for the time spent in each activity category, it was found that ischemia occurred proportionately more during episodes described as *psychologically stressful* than at other times.

The implications of this psychophysiological research on acute triggers of cardiac events are wide ranging. Psychologically induced myocardial ischemia and arrhythmia are evidently not rare phenomena among people with CAD. It is notable that, in most of the studies reported in the literature, ischemic and arrhythmic episodes were asymptomatic. Many of these ischemic episodes are unrecognized using conventional electrocardiographic indicators. Patients who show large stress-induced cardiovascular responses in the laboratory may be at high risk for future cardiac events. This conclusion is reinforced by the observation in a small study from Manuck and coworkers (58) that post-MI patients who had a serious recurrence over the next few years showed higher blood pressure responses to problem-solving tasks than did those who remained free of recurrence. Prevention of MI and sudden cardiac death among people with recognized CAD would be facilitated if ischemic and arrhythmic responses to standardized stressors were assessed. Such a procedure would allow clinicians to detect which individuals appear unusually susceptible to stress-induced cardiac changes, so that appropriate action might be taken to prevent potentially fatal cardiac crises.

PSYCHOPHYSIOLOGICAL FACTORS
AND RESPONSES TO TREATMENT

The third broad area of application of psychophysiological methods in CVD lies in the areas of treatment and patient management. In this respect, psychophysiological methods may be used in three ways: as methods of treatment, as means to evaluate efficacy of treatment, and as means to predict responses to behavioral treatment.

The psychophysiological treatment par excellence is biofeedback. Biofeedback procedures originated in the psychophysiology laboratory, with techniques being devised to provide feedback of blood pressure or heart rate, in the hope that patients would acquire voluntary control over these functions. After promising early results, disillusion set in with applications of biofeedback to cardiovascular disorders. The evidence that biofeedback led to direct voluntary control over autonomic function was not convincing, the techniques for providing cardiovascular biofeedback were relatively cumbersome, and biofeedback appeared to confer little advantage over simpler techniques, such as relaxation training (59). Methods such as biofeedback of skin temperature or electrodermal activity continue to be used with cardiovascular patients, but these techniques are not employed for their direct impact on cardiovascular activation, but rather as general indicators of relaxation (60, 61).

The use of psychophysiological techniques to evaluate the efficacy of behavioral treatments has been somewhat disappointing. Although some studies of relaxation-based stress management for hypertension have shown reductions of cardiovascular reactivity following treatment, the majority of results has been inconclusive (62). In studies of Type A behavior modification or stress management in patients with CAD, tests of acute cardiovascular responses to mental stressors have shown only limited changes following treatment (63, 64). However, it may be premature to discard psychophysiological methods in this context. One problem is that cardiovascular responses to mental stress have typically been evaluated without providing patients with the opportunity to deploy the coping methods they have acquired during training. It has been assumed that, through some automatic process, stress responsivity would be modified so that no specific instructions were necessary. However, if patients are asked to prepare themselves appropriately for coping with stressors by using the methods they have learned, it is possible that cardiovascular responsivity will indeed be modified (65).

The prediction of which individuals will benefit most from behavioral intervention programs is another important potential application of psychophysiological methods. Thus far, patients with CAD or hypertension have been offered behavioral treatment in a relatively indiscriminate fashion, and little research has been done to identify which people will show the greatest improvement (66). It is possible that psychophysiological methods will prove useful in this respect. For example, Cottier, Shapiro, and Julius (67) found that the hypertensive patients who benefited most from a muscle relaxation program were those with high initial heart rates and norepinephrine levels; somewhat similar results have been reported by others (68). Unfortunately, psychophysiological research in this area is extremely limited so far.

Psychophysiological applications in treatment settings may prove significant to behavioral medicine in the future. In most parts of the world, resources for helping patients with CVD are limited. Therefore, it is necessary to allocate effort where it is likely to reap the greatest rewards. When stress-related aspects of cardiovascular risk are considered, it is logical to assume that preventive programs should be directed at individuals who are prone to experience especially marked stress-induced autonomic and neuroendocrine responses. Psychophysiological methods are central to efforts to identify stress-prone individuals, and to characterize the situations in which they are most at risk.

CONCLUSIONS

This chapter reviewed applications of psychophysiology in three areas that are relevant to the prevention of CVD: the exploration of etiological mechanisms and the early identification of people at increased risk, the role of acute stress responses in the induction of potentially life-threatening episodes of cardiac arrhythmia and ischemia, and the evaluation of the efficacy of behavioral interventions and the prediction of favorable treatment responses. In each area, laboratory and ambulatory psychophysiological methods provide information valuable to decisions concerning the management of individuals and populations, while also contributing to the broader understanding of the relevance of psychosocial factors in CVD.

REFERENCES

1. Cacioppo JT, Tassinary LG. Preface. In: Cacioppo JT, Tassinary LG, editors. Principles of psychophysiology. Cambridge: Cambridge University Press, 1990.
2. Beatty J, Legewie H, editors. Biofeedback and behavior. New York: Plenum, 1977.
3. Steptoe A, Vögele C. The methodology of mental stress testing in cardiovascular research. Circulation 1991;83 Suppl II:14–24.
4. Matthews KA, Weiss SM, Detre T, et al., editors. Handbook of stress, reactivity and cardiovascular disease. New York: Wiley-Interscience, 1986.
5. Schneiderman N, Weiss SM, Kaufmann PG, editors. Handbook of research methods in cardiovascular behavioral medicine. New York: Plenum, 1989.
6. Durel LA, Kus LA, Anderson NB, et al. Patterns and stability of cardiovascular responses to variations of the cold pressor test. Psychophysiology 1993;30:39–46.
7. Kamarck TW, Jennings JR, Stewart CJ, et al. Reliable responses to a cardiovascular reactivity protocol: a replication study in a biracial female sample. Psychophysiology 1993;30:627–34.
8. Pickering TG, Gerin W. Cardiovascular reactivity in the laboratory and the role of behavioral factors in hypertension: a critical review. Ann Behav Med 1990;12:3–16.
9. Harshfield GA, James GD, Schlussel Y, et al. Do laboratory tests of blood pressure reactivity predict blood pressure changes during every day life? Am J Hypertension 1988;1:168–74.
10. Morales-Ballejo HN, Eliot RS, Boone JL, et al. Psychophysiologic stress testing as a predictor of mean daily blood pressure. Am Heart J 1988;116:673–81.
11. Pickering TG. Ambulatory monitoring and blood pressure variability. Philadelphia: Science Press, 1991.
12. Johnston DW, Anastasiades P, Wood C. The relationship between cardiovascular response in the laboratory and in the field. Psychophysiology 1990;27:34–44.
13. Light KC, Turner JR, Hinderliter AL, et al. Race and gender comparisons: II. Predictions of work blood pressure from laboratory baseline and cardiovascular reactivity measures. Health Psychol 1993;12:366–75.
14. Brod J, Fencl V, Hejl Z, et al. Circulatory changes underlying blood pressure elevation during acute emotional stress in normotensive and hypertensive subjects. Clin Sci 1959;18:269–79.
15. Obrist PA. Cardiovascular psychophysiology. New York: Plenum, 1981.
16. Falkner B, Kushner H, Onesti G, et al. Cardiovascular characteristics in adolescents who develop essential hypertension. Hypertension 1981;3:521–27.
17. Murphy JK, Alpert BS, Moes DM, Sones GW. Race and cardiovascular reactivity: a neglected relationship. Hypertension 1986;8:1075–83.
18. Rostrup M, Westheim A, Kjeldsen SE, et al. Cardiovascular reactivity, coronary risk factors, and sympathetic activity in young men. Hypertension 1993;22:891–99.
19. Kahn HA, Medalie JH, Neufeld HN, et al. The incidence of hypertension and associated factors: the Israeli Ischaemic Heart Disease Study. Am Heart J 1972;84:171–82.
20. Cottington EM, Matthews KA, Talbott E, et al. Occupational stress, suppressed anger, and hypertension. Psychosom Med 1986;48:249–60.
21. Vögele C, Steptoe A. Anger Inhibition and family history as modulators of cardiovascular responses to mental stress in adolescent boys. J Psychosom Res 1993;37:503–14.
22. Rostrup M, Ekeberg O. Awareness of high blood pressure influences on psychological and sympathetic responses. J Psychosom Res 1992;36:117–23.

23. Spielberger CD. Manual of the State-Trait Anger Expression Inventory (STAXI). Windsor: NFER-Nelson, 1988.
24. Watt GCM. Design and interpretation of studies comparing individuals with and without a family history of high blood pressure. J Hypertension 1986;4:1–7.
25. Light KC, Dolan CA, Davis MR, et al. Cardiovascular responses to an active coping challenge as predictors of blood pressure patterns 10 to 15 years later. Psychosom Med 1992;54:217–30.
26. Matthews KA, Woodall KL, Allen MT. Cardiovascular reactivity to stress predicts future blood pressure status. Hypertension 1993;22:479–85.
27. Johansson G, Johnson JV, Hall EM. Smoking and sedentary behavior as related to work organization. Soc Sci Med 1991;32:837–46.
28. Kamarck TW, Manuck SB, Jennings JR. Social support reduces cardiovascular reactivity to psychological challenge: a laboratory model. Psychosom Med 1990;52:42–58.
29. Lepore SJ, Allen KAM, Evans GW. Social support lowers cardiovascular reactivity to an acute stressor. Psychosom Med 1993;55:518–24.
30. Allen KM, Blascovich J, Tomarken J, et al. Presence of human friends and pet dogs as moderators of autonomic responses to stress in women. J Person Soc Psychol 1991;61:582–89.
31. Revenson TA, Schiaffino KM, Majerovitz SD, et al. Social support as a double-edged sword: the relation of positive and problematic support to depression among rheumatoid arthritis patients. Soc Sci Med 1991;33:807–13.
32. Karasek RA, Theorell T. Healthy work. New York: Basic Books, 1990.
33. Steptoe A, Fieldman G, Evans O, et al. Control over work pace, job strain and cardiovascular responses in middle-aged men. J Hypertension 1993;11:751–59.
34. Steptoe A. Stress and the cardiovascular system: a psychosocial perspective. In: Stanford CE, Salmon P, editors. Stress: an integrated approach. London: Academic Press, 1993:120–41.
35. Smith TW. Hostility and health: current status of a psychosomatic hypothesis. Health Psychol 1992;11:139–50.
36. Steptoe A, Tavazzi L. The mind and the heart. In: Julian DG, Camm AJ, Fox K, et al., editors. Diseases of the heart. 2nd ed. London: W. H. Saunders, in press.
37. Kleiger RE, Miller P, Bigger T, et al. Decreased heart rate variability and its association with increased mortality after acute myocardial infarction. Amer J Cardiol 1987;59:256–62.
38. Odemuyiwa O, Malik M, Farrell T, et al. A comparison of the predictive characteristics of heart rate variability index and left ventricular ejection fraction for all-cause mortality, arrhythmic events and sudden cardiac death after acute myocardial infarction. Am J Cardiol 1991;68:434–39.
39. Algra A, Tijssen JGP, Roelandt JRTC, et al. Heart rate variability from 24-hour electrocardiography and the 2-year risk for sudden death. Circulation 1993;88:180–85.
40. Perski A, Olsson G, Landou C, et al. Minimum heart rate and coronary atherosclerosis: independent relations to global severity and rate of progression of angiographic lesions in men with myocardial infarction at a young age. Am Heart J 1992;123:609–16.
41. Shaper AG, Wannamethee G, Macfarlane PW, et al. Heart rate, ischaemic heart disease, and sudden cardiac death in middle-aged British men. Br Heart J 1993;70:49–55.
42. Fei L, Anderson MH, Katritsis D, et al. Decreased heart rate variability in survivors of sudden cardiac death not associated with coronary artery disease. Br Heart J 1994;71:16–21.
43. Carney RM, Rich MW, teVelde A, et al. The relationship between heart rate, heart rate variability and depression in patients with coronary artery disease. J Psychosom Res 1988;32:159–64.
44. Frasure-Smith N, Lespérance F, Talajic M. Depression following myocardial infarction: impact on 6 month survival. JAMA 1993;270:1819–25.
45. Lown B, Verrier RL. Neural activity and ventricular fibrillation. N Engl J Med 1976;294:1165–70.
46. Tavazzi L, Zotti AM, Rondanelli R. The role of psychologic stress in the genesis of lethal arrhythmias in patients with coronary artery disease. Euro Heart J 1986;7 Suppl A:99–106.
47. Ahern DK, Gorkin L, Anderson JL, et al. Biobehavioral variables and mortality or cardiac arrest in the Cardiac Arrhythmia Pilot Study (CAPS). Am J Cardiol 1990;66:59–62.

48. Rozanski A, Bairey CN, Krantz DS, et al. Mental stress and the induction of silent myocardial ischemia in patients with coronary artery disease. N Engl J Med 1988;318:1005–12.
49. Krantz DS, Helmers KF, Bairey CN, et al. Cardiovascular reactivity and mental stress-induced myocardial ischemia in patients with coronary artery disease. Psychosom Med 1991;53:1–12.
50. Zotti AM, Bettinardi O, Soffiantino F, et al. Psychophysiological stress testing in post-infarction patients: psychophysiological correlates of cardiovascular arousal and abnormal cardiac responses. Circulation 1991;83 Suppl II:25–35.
51. Markovitz JH, Matthews KA. Platelets and coronary heart disease: potential psychophysiologic mechanisms. Psychosom Med 1991;53:643–68.
52. Grignani G, Soffiantino F, Zucchella M, et al. Platelet activation by emotional stress in patients with coronary artery disease. Circulation 1991;83 Suppl II:128–36.
53. Malkoff SB, Muldoon MF, Ziegler ZR, et al. Blood platelet responsivity to acute mental stress. Psychosom Med 1993;55:477–82.
54. Gurfinkel E, Altman E, Scazziota A, et al. Importance of thrombosis and thrombolysis in silent ischaemia: comparison of patients with acute myocardial infarction and unstable angina. Br Heart J 1994;71:151–55.
55. Kayden DS, Burns JW. Use of ambulatory monitoring of left ventricular function with the VEST. In: Blascovich J, Katkin ES, editors. Cardiovascular reactivity to psychological stress and disease. Washington, DC: American Psychological Association, 1993:201–12.
56. Krantz DS, Gabbay FH, Hedges SM, et al. Mental and physical triggers of silent myocardial ischemia: ambulatory studies using self-monitoring diary methodology. Ann Behav Med 1993;15:33–40.
57. Barry J, Selwyn AP, Nabel EG, et al. Frequency of ST-segment depression produced by mental stress in stable angina pectoris from coronary artery disease. Am J Cardiol 1988;61:989–93.
58. Manuck SB, Olsson G, Hjemdahl P, et al. Does cardiovascular reactivity to mental stress have prognostic value in post-infarction patients? A pilot study. Psychosom Med 1992;54:102–8.
59. Johnston DW, Steptoe A. Hypertension. In: Pearce S, Wardle J, editors. The practice of behavioural medicine. Oxford: Oxford University Press, 1989:1–25.
60. Blanchard EB, McCoy GC, Whittrock D, et al. A controlled comparison of thermal biofeedback and relaxation training in the treatment of essential hypertension: II. effects of cardiovascular reactivity. Health Psychol 1988;7:19–33.
61. Patel C, Marmot MG, Terry DJ. Controlled trial of biofeedback-aided behavioural methods in reducing mild hypertension. Br Med J, 1981;282:2005–8.
62. Johnston DW. How does relaxation training reduce blood pressure in primary hypertension? In: Schmidt TH, Dembroski TM, Blümchen G, editors. Biological and psychological factors in cardiovascular disease. Berlin: Springer-Verlag, 1986:550–67.
63. Roskies E, Seraganian P, Oseasohn R, et al. The Montreal Type A intervention project: major findings. Health Psychol 1986;5:45–69.
64. Sundin Ö, Öhman A, Burell G, et al. Psychophysiological effects of psychological intervention in myocardial infarction patients. Int J Behav Med 1994;1:55–75.
65. Patel C. Yoga and biofeedback in the management of "stress" in hypertensive patients. Clin Sci 1975;28:171–74.
66. Trzcieniecka-Green A, Steptoe A. Stress management in cardiac patients: a preliminary study of predictors of improvement in quality of life. J Psychosom Res 1994;38:101–14.
67. Cottier C, Shapiro K, Julius S. Treatment of mild hypertension with progressive muscle relaxation: predictive value of indexes of sympathetic tone. Arch Intern Med 1984;144:1954–58.
68. McGrady A, Higgins JT. Prediction of response to biofeedback-assisted relaxation in hypertensives: development of a hypertensive predictor profile (HYPP). Psychosom Med 1989;51:277–84.

Chapter 10

Personality Factors and Coronary Heart Disease

Ad Appels
University of Limburg

A medically trained astronaut with behavioral epidemiological sensors from a distant planet who would embark for a scientific expedition to the blue planet would have an exciting and disturbing trip. Approaching the earth, he would see a belt of cardiovascular diseases (CVDs) covering the northern hemisphere somewhere between the 40- and 60-degree latitude, with the exception of an island that turns out to be Japan. Coming closer to this belt, the astronaut has the impression that it moves like a cloud or wave, going from the west to the east. Coming even closer, the observer sees or believes he sees that not all human beings are equally affected by this disease. When the wave starts to rise at a certain place, primarily the richest or best educated subjects seem to be affected. At its apex, the wave afflicts all social classes equally, and at its decline especially the lower social strata. The astronaut believes he sees that a correlation exists between the shape of the wave and a number of sociological and demographic characteristics, such as the number of new factories, the number of people moving from the countryside to a town, and an increased production of food.

When the astronaut leaves his spaceship after landing and makes a trip through the belt, he notes in his diary that coronary heart disease (CHD) is called a *managerial disease* in some countries and a *poor man's disease* in others. He also notes that the disease seems to be less prevalent in societies where people often meet with a large number of friends and more prevalent in societies where life is dominated by clocks and watches. After visiting some hospitals, he notes that people afflicted by the disease seem to be characterized by an aggressive and impatient lifestyle, and by some remarkable habits such as inhaling the smoke of tobacco leaves.

Did the astronaut make correct observations? We do not know. Only careful measurements may give insight into the origins of the cardiovascular epidemic afflicting industrialized countries. In an attempt to understand the origins of CHD, and to obtain control over the major cause of death in the Western world, numerous epidemiological studies have been done. Some of them seem to confirm the remarkable geographic distribution of the coronary epidemic. For example, Swedish scientists have reported large regional variations in mortality rate from ischemic heart disease in mid-Sweden, with a low prevalence in the east and a high prevalence in the west. This difference could not be explained by variation in risk-factor levels (1). A working group of the World Health Organization (WHO) collected information from 35 studies from 17 countries in Europe, covering a total population of 151,923 subjects. The results showed significant geographical differences that could not be explained by the classic somatic risk factors (2). The regional differences are shown in Table 10.1. This table shows that the coronary epidemic has a number of demographic characteristics that are still poorly understood. When behavioral scientists investigate which personality characteristics increase the risk of CHD, they should never forget that these personality characteristics are formed and shaped by the culture in which people live. To understand the coronary-prone behavior patterns, one should also look at the cultural and socioeconomic roots.

SOCIOCULTURAL ASPECTS OF CORONARY HEART DISEASE

How can the association between culture and disease be investigated? How can we measure which values or motives are important in a given culture? One of the things we can do is analyze the stories parents tell their children. Children's books mirror the values of a culture. They tell in a simple way what is considered bad and good. Or, as Margaret Mead once said, "A culture has to get its values across to children in such simple terms that even a behavioral scientist can understand them" (cited in 3).

McClelland used this idea to test the hypothesis that a high level of achievement motivation is connected with the economic progress of a people. Therefore, he did a content analysis of 21 stories from 33 countries for three different

TABLE 10.1
Estimated Coronary Mortality Risk Expressed
as Standardized Mortality Ratio (SMR) in Different European Regions

Region	Men (Ages 40–59 Years)
Northern Europe	116.3
Western Europe	106.9
Southern Europe	99.6
Eastern Europe	88.1

motives: need for achievement, need for affiliation, and need for power. He gave a score to the descriptions of the personality characteristics of the hero of the story. This content analysis was done on children's books from 1925 and 1950. McClelland demonstrated that a high level of need for achievement as a cultural value precedes the economic development of a country (3).

To test the hypothesis that the achievement motive as a cultural index is correlated with CHD, we computed the correlation between this motive and mortality due to CHD, as registered in the statistical yearbooks of the WHO (4). To control for age, the analyses were done for distinct age strata. Table 10.2 presents an example of the computation of the rank order coefficients. Table 10.3 presents the rank order correlations between a nation's level of need for achievement in 1925 and 1950, and mortality from CHD in 1962.

Table 10.3 shows that a high need for achievement as a cultural value is associated with future CHD mortality in the selected countries. (Need for power and affiliation were not associated with CHD.) The table is suggestive, but proves little. It suggests that subjects characterized by high need for achievement are coronary prone. However, it might be that those who are not achievement

TABLE 10.2
Rank Order Coefficients Between Need for Achievement
and CHD Mortality in Men and Women Ages 55–64

Country	Death Rate	Rank	NA	Rank
Austria	287	17	1.57	10
Belgium	298	16	1.00	18
Denmark	401	8	2.00	6
Finland	604	3	1.24	17
France	126	19	0.81	19.5
West Germany	326	12	1.38	12.5
East Germany	373	9	1.38	12.5
Hungary	326	11	1.29	15.5
Greece	108	22	0.38	21
Ireland	464	6	3.19	1
Netherlands	312	15	0.29	22
Norway	368	10	1.33	14
Sweden	313	14	2.19	4
England	438	7	2.10	5
Australia	631	1	2.81	2
New Zealand	602	4	1.48	11
Spain	113	21	0.81	19.5
Canada	540	5	2.67	3
United States	607	2	1.90	7
Japan	120	20	1.77	9
Argentina	316	13	1.86	8
Chile	223	18	1.29	15.5

Note. Rank order correlation = .60 ($p < .01$).

TABLE 10.3
Rank Order Correlations Between a Nation's Level of Need for Achievement
in 1925 and 1950 and Subsequent Mortality from CHD in 1962

| | Need for Achievement | |
Age Group	1925	1950
25–34	.00	−.08
35–44	.37	.25
45–54	.44*	.36*
55–64	.66*	.44*
65–74	.62*	.38*
75+	.54*	.40*

*p < .05.

oriented, but who live in a hard-driving environment, experience problems that put them at risk for CHD. It might also be that lifestyle changes due to greater prosperity underlie the association. What the table shows is that cultural dynamics might be of some help to understand the increase and decline of CHD as a major cause of premature death in industrialized countries.

The CHD epidemic seems to follow a dynamic pattern. Nowadays, CHD is a disease that mainly occurs in the disadvantaged groups—the so-called low socioeconomic status (SES) groups. However, the SES–CHD gradient seems to change over time. This is illustrated by an observation made in the Kaunas–Rotterdam Intervention Study (KRIS) (5). In that study, about 4,000 males from Kaunas (a city in Lithuania) and Rotterdam (a Dutch city) were screened for cardiovascular risk factors in 1972 and then followed for the next 10 years. All subjects were asked whether their father had suffered from CHD. Table 10.4 shows the association between SES and CHD among the fathers and their sons. The table clearly shows that the gradient changed over time. During this change, the gradient necessarily passes a point of zero association. We know from other sources that the Dutch epidemic reached its apex in 1974. Therefore, the SES–CHD gradient observed in the KRIS is rather flat. Later Dutch studies have observed a stronger negative association.

There is little doubt that the SES–CHD gradient is influenced by changes in lifestyle, especially smoking. However, note that the gradient started to change before the mass media campaigns were organized. Within one generation, a number of things may change.

THE PERSON–ENVIRONMENT FIT

An individual is not only influenced by the culture he or she lives in, but also by his or her work environment. In fact, most people are inclined to associate CHD with job stress. Unfortunately, enough of the strength of that belief is

TABLE 10.4
Changing Gradients of Socioeconomic Differences in Coronary Events

Socioeconomic Gradient	Fathers	Sons
	Kaunas	
	Educational Level	
High	1.00	1.00
Moderate	0.74 (0.30–1.72)	0.93 (0.60–1.43)
Low	0.14 (0.06–0.32)	0.72 (0.44–1.19)
	Occupational Level	
High	1.00	1.00
Moderate	0.18 (0.09–0.36)	0.93 (0.65–1.32)
Low	0.15 (0.09–0.28)	*
	Rotterdam	
	Educational Level	
High	1.00	1.00
Moderate	0.91 (0.50–0.92)	1.27 (0.86–1.89)
Low	0.65 (0.48–0.92)	1.37 (0.94–1.99)
	Occupational Level	
High	1.00	1.00
Moderate	0.65 (0.46–0.92)	1.56 (0.99–2.48)
Low	0.60 (0.43–0.84)	1.64 (1.04–2.58)

*Because occupation was classified information in 1972, the cohort could only be divided into *employees* and *workers*.

inversely related to the number of studies supporting that belief. This statement does not mean that job stress is unrelated to CHD, but that good evidence became available only recently.

A strong model for the investigation of the association between job stress and CHD has been developed by Karasek (6). This model predicts that those who have a job that is simultaneously characterized by the presence of high pressure and the absence of the ability to control one's situation are at increased risk for CHD. Empirical findings give support to this model. An interesting amendment to this model has been developed by Johnson (7), who showed that the effects of these structural job characteristics are modified by the presence or absence of social support.

A slightly different model has been developed by Siegrist (8). This model combines sociological and psychological characteristics of a subject. The basic idea of this model is that the work role in adult life defines a crucial link between self-regulatory functions of a person, such as self-efficacy and self-esteem, and the societal structure of opportunities and rewards. In this model, two different sources of job stress are defined: an extrinsic source (the demands on the job) and an intrinsic source (the motivations of the individual worker in a demanding situation). It is the imbalance between high effort spent and low reward obtained that may threaten health.

Siegrist (8) tested this model in a prospective study of 263 blue-collar workers. This cohort was followed for 6.5 years. The findings demonstrate that two indicators of high effort (work pressure, immersion) and two indicators of low reward (status inconsistency, job insecurity) independently predicted new coronary events (Table 10.5). The simultaneous manifestation was present in 38% of future cases, but only in 7% of the remaining group.

Siegrist's (8) model provides a nice illustration of the interaction between environmental characteristics and personality factors upon the risk for CHD—of the importance of an adequate fit between the person and his or her environment. At the same time, this model raises questions. Are the personality factors antecedent to job stress, or are they the consequence of job stress? Will some people experience more stress because of their character, or do some job characteristics evoke personality characteristics (like immersion)? Most epidemiological models are rather static. A dynamic behavioral medicine model, which attends to the development of behavior, might be more adequate. In fact, the model developed by Siegrist resulted from an attempt to describe the coping career of coronary patients. The odds ratios presented in Table 10.5 show the potential strength of such a dynamic model.

Little attention has been given to marriage and the family as an environmental factor of possible relevance, although several case-control studies have observed that marital discord or problems with children might increase the risk for CHD (9). Loss of a spouse and being unmarried have been observed to increase CHD risk. Hence, chronic family problems and lack of social support have an impact on cardiovascular health. It seems that behavioral medicine might further contribute to our understanding of the etiology of CHD and cardiac rehabilitation

TABLE 10.5
Factors Associated With CHD Incidence in a Follow-up Study
of 263 Blue-Collar Workers (Form 6)

Variable	Odds Ratio	95% CI
Low reward		
Status inconstancy	4.40	1.36–14.20
Job insecurity	3.41	0.81–14.50
High extrinsic effort		
High work pressure	3.45	0.97–12.30
High intrinsic effort		
Immersion	4.53	1.15–17.80

by detailed studies of the influence of marital and family support on the risk for a first or recurrent myocardial infarction (MI).

A special issue in the domain of the person–environment fit is the question of whether women who have a paid job are at increased risk for CHD, especially when they have a simultaneous responsibility for homekeeping and children's education. Because most epidemiological studies have been conducted on males only (because of efficiency reasons), there are still little data available. The general impression derived from the literature is that the answer to this rather broad question is probably negative. In general, women who have a paid job are healthier compared with women who restrict their activities to homekeeping. This might reflect a "healthy worker effect." Those who have health problems might be less inclined or able to participate in the labor force. Undoubtedly, more studies are needed to give a detailed answer to health impact of salaried work in women. In these studies, job characteristics, cultural traditions, and social regulations have to be taken into account.

PERSONALITY CHARACTERISTICS

Behavioral medicine has paid much attention to personality characteristics of coronary patients. For a long time, this research has been dominated by the so-called Type A behavior pattern (TABP). This behavior pattern was first described by cardiologists Friedman and Rosenman (10) as: ". . . an action-emotion complex that can be observed in any person who is aggressively involved in a chronic, incessant struggle to achieve more and more in less and less time, and, if required to do so, against the opposing efforts of other things or other persons, (. . .) stemming from a fundamental and irretrievable sense of insecurity about the intrinsic value of the person involved" (p. 1288). Friedman and Rosenman designed a structured interview to assess the presence of this overt behavior pattern. The interview contains some 25 questions, in which subjects are asked how they usually respond to everyday situations—ones that should elicit impatience, hostility, and competitiveness from Type A individuals. During the interview, overt behavior such as particular speech and psychomotor characteristics are also observed. This interview was applied in a large-scale prospective study. It was found that TABP doubled the risk for CHD, controlling for all somatic risk factors.

The positive results of this study caused a tremendous interest in TABP. In the 1970s, numerous case-control studies and two prospective studies reported the same positive results. TABP became the flagship of behavioral medicine. However, as time continued, more negative results were published, and the widely held belief that TABP is an independent risk factor paled.

It is beyond the scope of this chapter to give a full evaluation of Type A research. Some amendments to the original formulation are discussed later. One of the major lessons from TABP research is that associations between behavioral factors and disease may change over time. In the time span of one generation, the culture changes and so do people. (Look at a television series of 25 years ago. You will notice that people smoked more and spoke in a more clipped and aggressive way.) The negative results of the more recent studies do not prove that the original findings were false. In fact, we even witness, in the short history of our Dutch research group, that a case-control study conducted in 1982 had positive results, a case-control study conducted 7 years later had weak positive results, and the most recent study had negative results. It might be that our criteria changed unnoticed during these years. Perhaps cultural changes influenced the toxicity of Type A behavior. It might be that, during the past decades, social support increased, or people became adapted to the requirements of a fast-moving, industrialized society.

TABP includes a number of behavioral characteristics, such as hard drivingness, job involvement, impatience, irritability, and hostility. One of the first amendments (proposed by Dembroski and colleagues [11]) was to look at the components of TABP, instead of the global rating. This amendment makes sense because one component has been found to be very cardiotoxic—namely, hostility.

Hostility refers to behaviors such as becoming angry when waiting in a line, shouting at other drivers, and openly or subtly expressing cynicism. Hostility can be measured by the structured TAPB interview and by some psychological scales. Up to now, the Cook–Medley Hostility scale has been used most widely. This measure has been related to CHD incidence and all cause mortality, as well as angiographically determined CHD severity (see chap. 11, this volume). Although some studies have reported no association between hostility and CHD, I believe that further studies of hostility and CHD are worthwhile because the best designed studies showed positive results.

Another personality characteristic of possible relevance is a state of unusual tiredness, which is experienced by about 65% of all near-future coronary victims. Some investigators have labeled this state as a *flulike unwell-being* because it has some similarities with feelings of general malaise people experience after a serious viral infection. Others have labeled this state as a *pseudoneurasthenic syndrome.* Interviews of a large number of coronary patients and their wives made us believe that the mental state before the occurrence of an acute coronary event is characterized by three major components: unusual tiredness, increased irritability, and feelings of demoralization. Typical wordings of coronary patients describing their prodromal state are: "My body was like a battery which loses its power," or "the well was drying up." The wives of the coronary patients often mentioned increased irritability as the major behavioral change they had noticed. We have labeled this state *vital exhaustion* (VE) because the loss of energy is the most prevalent and dominant characteristic. Others might have labeled this state *depression.* We did not because exhausted subjects usually are not characterized by mood disturbances. They are not sad and tired, but sad because they have no more energy. Exhausted subjects do not lose their self-esteem, and the typical cognitive aspects of depression (I am the cause of my misfortune; whatever I shall do will be unsuccessful; everything I do is a failure) are usually absent. Coronary patients do not blame themselves. They blame others.

The reports of patients might be biased by a search for meaning. They may attribute the feelings of fatigue and general malaise to "stress" and overestimate their significance because the feelings may just reflect clinical heart disease, such as angina pectoris. To check for this alternative explanation, we did a prospective study of 3,877 apparently healthy males ages 40–65 years. This cohort was followed for 4 years. All subjects completed a questionnaire composed of questions derived from the interviews. It was found that VE was predictive of future cardiac events, controlling for all classic somatic risk factors (12).

Although the positive results of this prospective study provide a strong argument that VE is a risk indicator of CHD, the results are not accepted by many cardiologists because it was impossible to control for subclinical heart disease in this large-scale epidemiological study. To test the alternative hypothesis—that feelings of exhaustion are predictive of future cardiac events because they reflect the extent of atherosclerosis, an impaired left-ventricular ejection fraction, or other clinical characteristics—we conducted a prospective study of 127 patients with successful percutaneous transluminal coronary angioplasty (PTCA). This cohort was followed for 18 months (13).

The results of this study show that the extent of atherosclerosis accounted for about 8% of the exhaustion scores. Subsequently successful PTCA resulted in a significant decrease of exhaustion scores. However, most patients remained exhausted after PTCA. Most important, those who were still exhausted 2 weeks after successful angioplasty were at increased risk for a new coronary event (defined as new angina with ischemia, new coronary lesion, repeat PTCA, coronary bypass surgery, MI, or cardiac death) during follow-up, controlling for all subclinical indicators of CHD (13).

PERSONALITY FACTORS AND CHD PREVENTION

Can the knowledge of personality factors that increase the risk for CHD contribute to the primary prevention of CHD? I am afraid that we have to answer this question in a negative way. We have attempted to demonstrate that coronary-prone behaviors have deep sociocultural roots. Furthermore, we lack the tools to influence factors such as hostility or TABP on a population level, if we would wish to do so.

Knowledge of the personality factors may be helpful to obtain a deeper insight into the socioeconomic roots of the coronary epidemic. We have seen that CHD is most prevalent among the lower SES groups. But why? Smoking is more prevalent among lower SES groups. However, that is only part of the explanation.

TABLE 10.6
Relative Contribution of Lifestyle and Personality Factors to the Excess Risk
for Myocardial Infarction of Subjects With Low Educational Status

Factor	Odds Ratio	Percentage Explained
Low SES	2.25	—
Controlled for:		
Smoking	1.76	39
Vital exhaustion	2.09	13
Hostility	1.87	30
Coffee consumption	2.21	3
All behavioral factors	1.51	59

It is known that the SES–CHD gradient remains to be significant after controlling for smoking. Are personality factors also involved?

My colleague C. Meesters is currently working on a PhD dissertation about hostility as a risk factor for CHD. In his study, he compared 98 men (mean age 55.6 years) who were hospitalized because of a first MI with 168 age-matched healthy neighborhood controls. He observed that a low SES was a risk factor for CHD in his series, the odds ratio being 2.25 (this odds ratio is probably an underestimation of the true difference because he used neighborhood controls). Hence, the risk of MI is increased by 125% in low-SES subjects. Controlling for smoking reduced the odds ratio to 1.76, therefore 39% of the excess risk of low-SES subjects (2.25–1.76/125) is due to smoking. Table 10.6 presents the percentages of the excess risk explained by hostility (assessed by the Buss–Durkee scale), coffee consumption, and VE. The most striking finding presented in Table 10.6 is that hostility explains almost as much of the excess risk as smoking does. Together, the four behavioral factors explain about 60% of the SES–CHD gradient. It is beyond doubt that knowledge of personality factors may contribute to secondary prevention. For example, the Recurrent Coronary Prevention Project has shown that those patients who change their Type A behavior pattern are at decreased risk for a recurrent MI (14). The development and implementation of this type of program in health care belongs to the most challenging tasks of behavioral medicine.

REFERENCES

1. Nerbrand C, Olsson L, Svardsudd K, et al. Are regional variations in ischemic heart disease related to differences in coronary risk factors? Eur Heart J 1991;12:309–14.
2. ERICA Research Group. Prediction of coronary heart disease in Europe. The 2nd report of the WHO-ERICA Project. Eur Heart J 1991;12:291–97.
3. McClelland D. The achieving society. New York: Van Nostrand & Reinhold, 1961.
4. Appels A. Coronary heart disease as a cultural disease. Psychotherapy and psychosomatics 1973;22:320–24.

5. Bosma H. A cross cultural comparison of the role of some psychosocial factors in the etiology of coronary heart disease. Follow-up of the Kaunas–Rotterdam Intervention Study [Dissertation]. Maastricht, The Netherlands: University of Limburg, 1994.

6. Karasek B, Theorell T. Healthy work. New York: Basic Books, 1990.

7. Johnson JV, Hall EM. Social support in the work environment and cardiovascular disease. In: Shumaker SA, Czajkowski SM, editors. Social support and cardiovascular disease. New York: Plenum Press, 1994:145–66.

8. Siegrist J, Peter R, Junge A, et al. Low status control, high effort at work and ischemic heart disease: prospective evidence from blue collar men. Soc Sci Med 1990;31:127–34.

9. Falger P, Schouten E. Exhaustion, psychological stressors in the work environment, and acute myocardial infarction in adult men. J Psychosom Res 1992;36:777–86.

10. Friedman M, Rosenman R. Association of a specific overt behavior pattern with blood and cardiovascular findings. JAMA 1959;169:1286–96.

11. Dembroski TM, MacDougall JM, Costa Jr PT, et al. Components of hostility as predictors of sudden death and myocardial infarction in the Multiple Risk Factor Intevention Trial. Psychosom Med 1989;51:514–22.

12. Appels A, Mulder P. Excess fatigue as a precursor of myocardial infarction. Eur Heart J 1988;9:758–64.

13. Kop W, Appels A, Bar F, et al. Vital Exhaustion predicts new cardiac events after successful coronary angioplasty. Psychosom Med 1994;56:281–87.

14. Friedman M, et al. Alteration of type A behavior and its effect on cardiac recurrences in post myocardial infarction patients: summary results of the recurrent coronary prevention project. Am Heart J 1986;112:65–66.

Chapter 11

Coronary-Prone Behaviors, Hostility, and Cardiovascular Health: Implications for Behavioral and Pharmacological Interventions

Redford B. Williams
Duke University Medical Center

Ever since the sudden deaths of Ananias and Saphira after being chastised by St. Peter—as described in the "Acts of the Apostles" in the New Testament of the Christian *Bible*—we have "known" that stress has the potential for profound effects on the heart. However, it was nearly 2,000 years later before two cardiologists, Meyer Friedman and Ray Rosenman, carried out epidemiological studies that pointed to a specific sort of stress—that experienced by persons with the Type A behavior pattern that prospectively confers increased risk of developing coronary heart disease (CHD) (1).

Based on their work, and that of many other research groups, we were poised in the late 1970s to declare Type A an established CHD risk factor (1). However, at that same time, there began to appear several published reports of failures to find Type A predictive of or correlated with CHD outcomes. The most important of these negative studies was the failure by Shekelle et al. (2) to find Type A, as assessed by the structured interview, to predict CHD events in the large-scale Multiple Risk Factor Intervention Trial (MRFIT) study.

Based on these negative studies, as well as a consideration of preliminary data pointing to hostility as a correlate and predictor of CHD, numerous investigators turned their attention to the hostility component as the likely coronary-prone component of the global Type A construct. In this chapter, I first review the epidemiological evidence pointing to *hostility* as a coronary-prone psychological trait. I then review the evidence regarding the biobehavioral mechanisms, whereby hostility may be contributing to the development of CHD, as well as the potential neurobiological basis of the health-damaging biobehavioral characteristics that appear to cluster in hostile persons. I conclude by considering the implications of what we know about hostility and its biobehavioral mechanisms for prevention and treatment of CHD.

EPIDEMIOLOGICAL EVIDENCE

Since the publication (3) of our first article, which specifically focused on hostility as a correlate of coronary artery disease (CAD) severity and found it to be at least as strongly correlated with CAD as Type A behavior, there has been a burgeoning body of research (4, 5) that focuses on the health consequences of hostility.

First of all, Dembroski and colleagues (6) reanalyzed the original MRFIT structured interviews, scoring them for "potential for hostility" as well as other components of Type A behavior, and found that only the hostility component was a significant independent predictor of CHD events, in both univariate analysis and multivariate analysis that controlled for established risk factors. A similar finding emerged from the Hecker et al. (7) reanalysis of the original Western Collaborative Group Study structured interviews. These results from two large-scale prospective studies make clear that the nonhostility components of Type A behavior have been evaluated and found not to be independent predictors of CHD, whereas the hostility component does emerge as a significant independent predictor.

Following the finding that scores on the Minnesota Multiphasic Personality Inventory (MMPI)-based Cook–Medley Hostility scale correlated with CAD severity (3), there have been numerous studies that used archival MMPI data to evaluate the impact of Hostility scores assessed years earlier on subsequent CHD risk, as well as risk of dying from all causes. By and large, these studies have found that high Hostility scores predict increased subsequent risk of both CHD and all cause mortality (8–10), although there have been some negative studies (11–13).

Even considering these negative studies, thoughtful reviews (4, 5) conclude that the weight of the epidemiological evidence—taking into account not only research using the Hostility scale, but also that using other measures of hostility including interview-based assessments (14) and hostility-relevant measures using other instruments (15)—makes a convincing case that something in the general psychological domain of hostility is indeed a precursor of increased risk of CHD, and probably of all cause mortality as well. That case is strengthened further by a consideration of the potentially health-damaging biobehavioral correlates of hostility that have been found in additional studies.

BIOBEHAVIORAL MECHANISMS

A steadily growing number of studies finds increased sympathetically mediated physiological reactivity when angered, particularly by interpersonal conflict, among persons with high hostility levels as assessed by the Cook–Medley Hostility scale or other instruments (see, e.g., 16–18). Preliminary evidence indicates that, in their everyday lives, hostile persons are also experiencing sympathetic nervous system (SNS) hyperreactivity, as indexed by larger daytime increases in urinary catecholamine excretion (19), and decreased beta-adrenergic receptor number on circulating lymphocytes (20).

In addition to this excessive SNS function, there is also evidence that parasympathetic function is diminished in hostile persons, whether parasympathetic function is indexed by a measure of vagal antagonism of sympathetic effects on ventricular repolarization (21), or by the high-frequency component of the heart rate power spectrum (22).

Along with these differences in autonomic balance, which are quite plausible biological precursors of CHD, emerging evidence also suggests that hostile people engage in risky health behaviors that can also contribute to their increased risk of disease. In the University of North Carolina Alumni Heart Study (UNC-AHS)—a follow-up study of over 4,000 former college students who had taken the MMPI as freshmen in the 1960s—those with higher Hostility scores at ages 18–19 were found at age 42 to have higher body mass index, to consume more alcohol, to smoke at a higher rate, and to have a less favorable cholesterol/high-density lipoprotein (HDL) ratio (23).

Similar findings were obtained in a cross-sectional analysis of the association between Hostility scores and risk behaviors in a more heterogenous sample of younger American participants in the CARDIA study: Those with higher Hostility scores were more likely to be smokers, to consume more alcohol, and to consume more calories per day (24). Interestingly, in the CARDIA study, the impact of hostility on smoking behavior was much larger than in the higher socioeconomic status (SES) participants of the UNCAHS, with nearly 30% of those in the highest Hostility quartile being smokers in the CARDIA study versus less than 20% of high Hostility subjects in the UNCAHS who smoke. Although the CARDIA study did not find the increased body mass index as a function of high Hostility scores, which was observed in the UNCAHS, there was a significant increase in daily caloric intake—600 more calories per day in highest compared with lowest Hostility quartiles—in the younger high Hostility scoring CARDIA subjects. Presumably, this increased caloric intake will be expressed in higher body mass index and lipid ratios by the time the CARDIA subjects reach the age of the UNCAHS participants. There was also an increase in waist–hip ratio as a function of increasing Hostility scores among both African-American and White men in the CARDIA study sample.

Taken together, these biobehavioral characteristics associated with high hostility levels form a profile (i.e., increased sympathetic function, decreased parasympathetic function, increased eating, increased smoking, and increased alcohol consumption) that would be expected, over time, to contribute to a wide range of pathogenic processes, including both atherogenesis and tumorogenesis.

How these effects on pathogenesis actually come about remains to be elucidated, but recent research applying knowledge and techniques of cell and molecular biology offers some promising leads. Based on the findings reviewed previously—of increased cholesterol and catecholamine levels clustering in hostile persons, who are also more likely to smoke—Adams (25) hypothesized that stimulation of beta-adrenergic receptors on macrophages might amplify the pathogenic effects of ligation of the macrophage scavenger receptor by oxidized low-density lipoprotein (LDL), and thereby account for the increased CHD and cancer death rates that have been found among hostile persons in epidemiological studies. Recent pilot studies (unpublished) indicate that activation of macrophage beta receptors causes expression of a potentially pathogenic phenotype that is similar in many respects to the phenotype induced by oxidized LDL. Thus, the increased oxidized LDL that would be expected among hostile persons as a result of their high cholesterol levels and increased smoking habit could combine with their increased catecholamines to amplify the expression of a phenotype in macrophages (or their precursors, monocytes) that would increase rates of both atherogenesis and tumorogenesis.

NEUROBIOLOGICAL UNDERPINNINGS

Why do these health-damaging biobehavioral characteristics of increased sympathetic function, decreased parasympathetic function, increased eating, increased smoking, and increased alcohol consumption cluster in persons with high hostility levels? The answer to this question would not only increase our confidence in the biological plausibility of hostility as a health-damaging psychological trait, but it would also point to possible means of ameliorating the harmful effects of hostility on health.

As I proposed elsewhere (26), all of the potentially pathogenic biobehavioral characteristics that cluster in hostile persons, including even their hostility itself, could be the result of a single neurobiological "lesion": decreased function of the neurotransmitter serotonin in the central nervous system. For example, it has been shown that reduced brain serotonin, as indexed by cerebrospinal fluid levels of the serotonin metabolite 5-HIAA, is present in men with a history of aggressive behaviors (27) and in children who go on to develop aggressive behavior problems (28). Stimulation of one class of brain serotonin receptors ($5HT_{1A}$) causes a reduction in sympathetic outflow and an increase in parasympathetic function (29), whereas raising the level of brain serotonin in general by tryptophan loading also decreases sympathetic outflow (30). There is also evidence that serotonin enhancement reduces smoking (31) and eating (32), and that brain serotonin function is reduced in alcoholics (32).

Thus, both hostility and its health-damaging biobehavioral characteristics could be the result of a common neurobiological mechanism: reduced brain serotonin function. It is important to undertake research to evaluate this hypothesis. One approach would be to evaluate the effects of interventions that either enhance (e.g., via administration of the serotonin-releasing agent fenflu-ramine) or reduce (e.g., via administration of a tryptophan-free amino acid drink) brain serotonin function. Depending on the state of brain serotonin turnover and receptors, these interventions would be expected to have different neuroen-docrine and autonomic effects on high- versus low-hostile persons if they were characterized by decreased versus increased brain serotonin release, respectively.

Equally important, confirmation of a reduced brain serotonergic "tone" in hostile persons by such studies would point the way to one approach to ameliorate the health-damaging effects of hostility: serotonergic enhancement using phar-macological agents.

IMPLICATIONS FOR PREVENTION AND TREATMENT

If hostility and its health-damaging biobehavioral concomitants are the result of a functional serotonin deficiency, correction of this situation—via adminis-tration of pharmacological agents that enhance brain serotonin function, either by increasing serotonin turnover or directly stimulating relevant serotonin re-ceptors—could prove to be an effective means of preventing the damage to health that is found in hostile persons. One such class of agents is the selective serotonin reuptake inhibitors (SSRIs), with fluoxetine (Prozac) being the first FDA-approved agent, but followed now by paroxetine (Paxil) and sertraline (Zoloft). In addition to their known antidepressant effects, these agents have also been proposed as an aid to weight loss via their appetite suppressant effects (33) and as a therapeutic agent in alcohol abuse (34). They have also been found to reduce hostile behavior in monkeys (35).

Whatever the ultimate outcome of the research that will be required to test the serotonergic hypothesis of hostility and its health-damaging effects and its implications for pharmacological approaches to prevention and treatment, there can be little question that behavioral approaches to reducing hostility will be a mainstay of prevention and treatment. Although much more research is required to develop and evaluate the impact of behavioral approaches to ameliorate the adverse effects of psychosocial factors on health (36), there is already encouraging preliminary evidence from randomized clinical trials that psychosocial–behav-ioral interventions that reduce Type A behavior (37) or provide social support (38) improve prognosis in patients who have survived a myocardial infarction (MI). In cancer patients, psychosocial interventions that teach patients how to cope more effectively with stress and negative emotions have been found to improve survival (39, 40).

There is ample reason to believe that psychosocial–behavioral interventions designed to enable hostile persons to curb their anger, to have better relationships with others, and to change their cynical negative attitudes to more positive views of the world and the people in it will both improve prognosis once CHD is present and reduce the likelihood of developing premature CHD in the first place. One self-help approach to achieve these behavioral changes in hostile persons is described in a recent book I co-authored with Virginia Williams (41).

What are needed now are large-scale, multicenter, randomized clinical trials that evaluate behavioral, pharmacological (serotonin-enhancement), and combination approaches to the reduction of hostility and its health-damaging biobehavioral correlates in post-MI patients (36). If these trials show hostility control to be effective in improving prognosis, it will be the most direct possible proof that hostility and other psychosocial factors (like depression) are true risk factors. Such an outcome would also constitute a major improvement in the secondary prevention of CHD, with primary prevention trials the next logical step.

SUMMARY AND CONCLUSIONS

1. The psychological trait of *hostility* predisposes to increased incidence of CHD, as well as deaths from all causes.

2. A cluster of biobehavioral characteristics has been identified in hostile persons, which makes a strong case for the biological plausibility of hostility as a factor that would predispose to both CHD and cancer. Exciting new research is beginning to apply the tools of cell and molecular biology to strengthen this case and identify the specific proximate cellular and molecular pathways whereby hostility contributes to pathogenesis.

3. The clustering of a particular set of biobehavioral characteristics in hostile persons also suggests a possible neurobiological basis for this clustering: deficient brain serotonergic function.

4. Both pharmacological (to enhance brain serotonergic function) and behavioral (to improve stress-coping skills and ability to control hostility) approaches should be evaluated in clinical trials aimed first at patients already suffering from both CHD and cancer, and ultimately at healthy persons at high risk due to increased hostility.

ACKNOWLEDGMENTS

This chapter was supported in part by grants from The National Heart, Lung and Blood Institute (HL36587, HL44998), the National Institute of Mental Health (MH70482), and Clinical Research Unit Grant M01-RR-30.

REFERENCES

1. Review Panel. Coronary-prone behavior and coronary heart disease: a critical review. Circulation 1981;63:1199–1215.
2. Shekelle RB, Hulley SB, Neaton JD, et al. The MRFIT behavior pattern study. II. Type A behavior and incidence of coronary heart disease. Am J Epidemiol 1985;122:559–70.

3. Williams Jr RB, Haney TL, Lee KL, et al. Type A behavior, hostility, and coronary atherosclerosis. Psychosom Med 1980;42:539–49.
4. Williams RB. A relook at personality types and coronary heart disease. Prog Cardiol 1991;4:91–7.
5. Smith TW. Hostility and health: current status of a psychosomatic hypothesis. Health Psychol 1992;11:139–50.
6. Dembroski TM, MacDougall JM, Costa Jr PT, et al. Components of hostility as predictors of sudden death and myocardial infarction in the Multiple Risk Factor Intervention Trial. Psychosom Med 1989;51:514–22.
7. Hecker MHL, Chesney MA, Black GW, et al. Coronary-prone behaviors in the Western Collaborative Group Study. Psychosom Med 1988;50:153–64.
8. Barefoot JC, Dahlstrom WG, Williams RB. Hostility, CHD incidence and total mortality: a 25-year follow-up study of 255 physicians. Psychosom Med 1983;45:59–63.
9. Barefoot JC, Dodge KA, Peterson BL, et al. The Cook–Medley Hostility scale: item content and ability to predict survival. Psychosom Med 1989;51:46–57.
10. Shekelle RB, Gale M, Ostfeld AM, et al. Hostility, risk of coronary heart disease, and mortality. Psychosom Med 1983;45:109–14.
11. Hearn M, Murray DM, Luepker RB. Hostility, coronary heart disease, and total mortality: a 33-year follow-up study of university students. J Beh Med 1989;12:105–21.
12. Leon GR, Finn SE, Murray D, et al. The inability to predict cardiovascular disease from hostility scores of MMPI items related to Type A behavior. J Consul Clin Psychol 1988;56:597–600.
13. McCranie EW, Watkins LO, Brandsma JM, et al. Hostility, coronary heart disease (CHD), incidence, and total mortality: lack of association in a 25-year follow-up study of 478 physicians. J Behav Med 1986;9:119–25.
14. Barefoot JC. Developments in the measurement of hostility. In: Friedman HS, editor. Hostility, coping, and health. Washington, DC: American Psychological Association, 1992:13–31.
15. Barefoot JC, Siegler IC, Nowlin JB, et al. Suspiciousness, health, and mortality: a follow-up study of 500 older adults. Psychosom Med 1987;49:450–57.
16. Smith TW, Allred KD. Blood pressure reactivity during social interaction in high and low cynical hostile men. J Beh Med 1989;11:135–43.
17. Weidner G, Friend R, Ficarrotto TJ, et al. Hostility and cardiovascular reactivity to stress in women and men. Psychosom Med 1989;51:36–45.
18. Suarez EC, Williams RB. Situational determinants of cardiovascular and emotional reactivity in high and low hostile men. Psychosom Med 1989;51:404–18.
19. Suarez EC, Williams RB, Harlan ES, et al. Hostility-related differences in urinary excretion rates of catecholamines. Paper presented at the annual meeting of the Society for Psychophysiological Research; 1991 October; Chicago.
20. Shiller AD, Suarez EC, Kuhn CM, et al. Hostility is associated with lymphocyte beta-2 adrenergic receptor/adenylate cyclase activity. Paper presented at the annual meeting of the American Psychosomatic Society; April 1994; Boston.
21. Fukudo S, Lane JD, Anderson NB, et al. Accentuated vagal antagonism of beta-adrenergic effects on ventricular repolarization. Evidence of weaker antagonism in hostile men. Circulation 1992;85:2045–53.
22. Sloan RP, Shapiro PA, Bagiella E, et al. Cardiac autonomic control and hostility in healthy subjects. Am J Cardiol 1994;74:298–300.
23. Siegler IC, Peterson BL, Barefoot JC, et al. Hostility in late adolescence predicts coronary risk factors at mid-life. Am J Epidemiol 1992;136:146–56.
24. Scherwitz LW, Perkins LL, Chesney MA, et al. Hostility and health behaviors in young adults: the CARDIA study. Coronary artery risk development in young adults study. Am J Epidemiol 1992;136:136–45.
25. Adams DO. Molecular biology of macrophage activation: a final, common pathway whereby psychosocial factors can potentially affect health. Psychosom Med 1994;56:316–27.

26. Williams, RB. Neurology, cellular and molecular biology, and psychosomatic medicine. Psychosom Med 1994;56:308–15.

27. Brown GL, Ebert MH, Goyer DC, et al. Aggression, suicide and serotonin: relationships to CSF mine metabolites. Am J Psychiatry 1982;139:741–46.

28. Kruesi MJP, Hibbs ED, Zahn TP, et al. A 2-year prospective follow-up study of children and adolescents with disruptive behavior disorders: prediction by cerebrospinal fluid 5-hydroxyindoleacetic acid, homovanillic acid, and autonomic measures? Arch Gen Psychiatry 1992;49:429–35.

29. Saxena PR, Villalon CM. Cardiovascular effects of serotonin agonists and antagonists. J Cardiovasc Pharmacol 1990;7:S17–S34.

30. Verrier RL. Neurochemical approaches to the prevention of ventricular fibrillation. Fed Proc 1986;45:2191–96.

31. Gawin FH, Compton M, Dych P. Buspirone reduces smoking. Arch Gen Psychiatry 1989;46:288–89.

32. Levine LR, Enas GG, Thompson WL, et al. Use of fluoxetine, a selective serotonin uptake inhibitor, in the treatment of obesity: a dose-response study. Int J Obes 1989;13:635–45.

33. Ballenger J, Goodwin FK, Major LF, et al. Alcohol and central serotonin metabolism in man. Arch Gen Psychiatry 1979;36:224–27.

34. Sellers EM, Naranjo CA. Therapeutic use of serotonergic drugs in alcohol abuse. Clin Neuropharmacol 1986;9:60–2.

35. Raleigh MJ, McGuire MT, Brammer GL, et al. Serotonergic mechanisms promote dominance acquisition in adult male vervet monkeys. Brain Res 1991;559:181–90.

36. Williams RB, Chesney MA. Psychosocial factors and prognosis in established coronary artery disease: the need for research on interventions. JAMA 1993;270:1860–61.

37. Friedman M, et al. Alteration of type A behavior and its effect on cardiac recurrences in post-myocardial infarction patients: summary results of the Recurrent Coronary Prevention Project. Am Heart J 1986;12:653–65.

38. Frasure-Smith N, Prince R. Long-term follow-up of the Ischemic Heart Disease Life Stress Monitoring Program. Psychosom Med 1989;51:485–513.

39. Spiegel D, Bloom JR, Kraemer HC, et al. Effect of psychosocial treatment on survival of patients with metastatic breast cancer. Lancet 1989;2:888–90.

40. Fawzy FI, Fawzy NW, Hyun CS, et al. Malignant melanoma. Effects of an early structured psychiatric intervention, coping, and affective state on recurrence and survival 6 years later. Arch Gen Psychiatry 1993;50:681–89.

41. Williams RB, Williams VP. Anger kills: seventeen strategies for controlling the hostility that can harm your health. New York: Times Books, 1993.

Chapter 12

New Behavioral Risk Factors for Coronary Heart Disease: Implications for Intervention

Margaret A. Chesney
University of California–San Francisco

Behavioral interventions to reduce coronary heart disease (CHD) morbidity and mortality target the standard risk factors, such as cigarette smoking, and the more recently recognized coronary-prone behaviors, such as hostility. There is increasing evidence that low socioeconomic status (SES), depressive symptoms, and social isolation should be added to the list of targets for interventions because these factors are associated with increased risk for adverse health outcomes, including CHD. The purpose of this chapter is to draw attention to these new behavioral or psychosocial risk factors, and to explore implications for behavioral interventions. The first three sections of this chapter briefly highlight the evidence that each of these psychosocial factors is associated with CHD risk, and sketch out the potential role that intervention could play in diminishing that risk. In the final section, a new intervention—Coping Effectiveness Training—is described. This intervention, based on stress and coping theory, is designed to train individuals to cope with environmental and social stressors, increase social support, and manage negative mood states. As such, Coping Effectiveness Training (CET) is an approach that may be applicable to addressing the new behavioral risk factors for heart disease.

SOCIOECONOMIC STATUS AND CORONARY HEART DISEASE

A positive association between SES and health has existed for centuries (1, 2). Individuals of lower SES status experience greater morbidity and mortality from almost every disease than those of higher status. Persuasive arguments have been made to place SES on the behavioral medicine, epidemiology, and clinical research agendas (3–6). Despite these arguments, researchers have been slow to identify the relative contribution of specific socioeconomic factors on morbidity and mortality (7).

Socioeconomic Status and Coronary Heart Disease: Evidence of a Relationship

Coronary heart disease (CHD) is the leading cause of death among adult women and men. With the extensive contribution that CHD makes to morbidity and mortality, it follows that lower SES would be associated with increased risk of heart disease. This association is most clearly demonstrated in a series of studies of British civil servants conducted by Marmot and his colleagues (8–10; see also chap. 3, this volume). They found a gradient between SES and health that extends from the lower levels to and within the upper levels of social class. When the various components of SES—including income, education, and occupational status—are studied, the results are strikingly consistent across populations. For example, in a recent report of a 30-year follow-up of the Charleston Heart Study, education was more strongly associated with mortality from heart disease than was race (11). The effects due to SES are so consistent that they confound the results of clinical research investigating other risk factors. Given its importance, it is curious why more attention has not been focused on the relationship between SES and CHD. Perhaps it is because the relationship is not specific to heart disease, or because the specific mechanisms underlying the relationship are unknown. Nevertheless, it is shortsighted to not address the link between heart disease and SES, particularly when it has been shown that SES accounts for significant variance in the association between CHD and other risk factors, including elevated blood pressure and cigarette smoking.

The mechanisms by which lower SES exerts its influence have been the topic of considerable discussion (4–6). Efforts to explain the impact of SES on health cite, among other factors, the association between social class and varying rates of individual health behaviors, differential environmental exposures, and availability of accessible quality care (4). Although each of these factors shows a gradient across SES levels that parallels the gradient between SES and heart disease, each—taken separately or in combination—fails to explain the relationship between SES and heart disease. This had led some (5) to conclude that SES may be associated with patterns of factors that have an adverse effect on health, or that SES may be a proxy for other superordinate factors that may be associated with risk, such as *control*. As pointed out by Adler and her associates (6), new methods may be needed to analyze the complex interrelated variables that are integral to the expression of risk associated with various SES levels.

Socioeconomic Status and Coronary Heart Disease: Behavioral Interventions

The goal of this chapter is to heighten awareness among those interested in cardiovascular behavioral medicine of the influence of SES on heart disease, and to raise questions about the implications this relationship has for behavioral interventions. Most CHD intervention studies, including those reported on in this volume, are conducted in samples drawn from groups of higher SES. At the most basic level, behavioral interventions for cardiovascular disease (CVD), including those directed at modifying standard risk factors, should be tested in the populations at greatest risk. This would result in trials among those at the lower levels of SES.

It may be that stress-management interventions are differentially effective at varying levels of SES. Perhaps higher levels of education are needed to comprehend the concepts taught in traditional stress management. Perhaps greater resources and flexibility in work and home schedules are needed to carry out stress-management recommendations. However, it may be that stress-management interventions are more effective, resulting in greater incremental improvements among individuals at lower socioeconomic levels. If this were found to be the case, it might shed light on mechanisms by which SES exerts its adverse health effects. Then the impact of the intervention could be studied, with attention to examining the correlations between changes in variables targeted by the intervention and changes in risk.

Behavioral interventions hold promise for addressing some of the variables thought to be factors in the relationship between social class and risk. Cognitive–behavioral interventions could teach coping strategies that promote self-control, negotiation skills, conflict resolution, and personal empowerment. In addition to these individual-level interventions, behavioral attention could be directed toward environmental factors associated with lower levels of SES. Examples of interventions include making safe exercise facilities for primary prevention and rehabilitation accessible, and modifying norms to increase the use of these facilities across the life span. Community-based interventions to reduce the incidence of acute environmental stressors, such as crime and violence, could also be developed.

Certainly one important point must be made about interventions to reduce the adverse effects of SES on heart disease outcomes. Ultimately, social change is necessary to redress many of the inequities associated with lower SES. It would be easy to focus only on individual interventions, and to avoid the challenge of taking on the adverse health consequences of poverty, lack of education, and unemployment. Although individual intervention is important, behavioral medicine expertise is also needed as the public health community addresses the causes and manifestations of lower SES. A positive step in this direction can be seen with the move that members of the behavioral and clinical medicine communities have taken in defining crime and violence as health problems. Faced with the excessive heart disease rates in less advantaged populations, behavioral medicine has a choice. One alternative is to work only at the individual and group levels, teaching skills for coping with stressors, including those that are social and environmental in origin. The other alternative is to extend and apply effective behavioral strategies toward primary prevention and health promotion at broader societal and environmental levels.

SOCIAL ISOLATION AND CORONARY HEART DISEASE

Low levels of social support, weak social ties, and measures of social isolation are related to adverse health outcomes. A recent review demonstrates that the magnitude of the health risk associated with low social support is equivalent to that associated with cigarette smoking (12). Several studies provide definitive evidence of an association between the lack of social support and heart disease morbidity and mortality.

Social Isolation and Coronary Heart Disease: Evidence of a Relationship

Recently, a 6-year follow-up study of a random sample of 50-year-old men born in Gothenborg, Sweden, in 1933 provided more evidence of the association between social ties and heart disease (13). In this study, 736 men, who were found free from heart disease by physical examination at enrollment into the study, completed questionnaires that included scales providing two indices of social support. One of these indices was *attachment*, a measure of emotional support from very close family and friends. The other index, *social integration*, consisted of a measure of social support provided by each person's social network. Both attachment and social integration were found to be lower in men who developed a major coronary event (either nonfatal myocardial infarction [MI] or death attributed to heart disease) over the 6-year follow-up period than men who did not develop CHD. These two indices of low social support remained significant predictors of CHD events in multivariate analyses controlling for other risk factors.

Two other studies (14, 15) documented the influence of social isolation on prognosis of established coronary artery disease (CAD). Patients participating in the placebo group of the Multicenter Diltiazem Post-Infarction Trial were studied to determine if living alone is an independent prognostic risk factor of a subsequent coronary event in patients with a history of previous acute MI. Living alone at enrollment was an independent risk factor for recurrence over a 1- to 4-year follow-up period in this sample. The majority of these recurrent cardiac events in those who lived alone occurred within the first 6 months post-MI. When the combination of living alone and being in a lower SES level (as indicated by less than 12 years of education) were examined together, the prognostic significance of these factors in combination was higher than either alone. Of clinical significance, this study points out that those living alone represent a relatively large (16.4%) group among post-MI patients (15). Another study (14) examining the importance of social isolation followed 1,368 patients with angiographically documented CAD. In this study, being unmarried without a confidant carried a relative risk of death equal to 3.34 compared with patients who were married, had a confidant, or had both.

The mechanism by which social isolation or lack of social support exerts risk is not known. The association between risk and social isolation may be due to any number of factors—from the unavailability of emergency medical support to the neurohormonal influence of social contact. There is also some suggestion that social isolation is associated with higher risk lifestyles. For example, in the Gothenborg study (13), those showing a lack of social integration were more likely to be cigarette smokers and less likely to exercise.

Social Isolation and Coronary Heart Disease: Behavioral Interventions

Although there have been numerous accounts of the prognostic importance of social support, there are no published accounts of interventions specifically designed to train individuals at risk for CHD in obtaining or maintaining social support. In rehabilitation programs, the provision of direct social support by medical personnel is often a cornerstone of the treatment (16). In behavioral interventions directed toward management of stress-related responses, the direct provision of social support is often given as a rationale for recommending group-based, rather than individual, treatment of patients. Despite these references to social support, behavioral interventions have not placed explicit emphasis on assisting patients to develop social support networks, to use their social networks effectively, or to maintain their social networks over time.

Research is needed to develop and evaluate behavioral interventions designed to address the problems of social isolation. The elevated risk among those living alone or lacking a confidant suggests that various approaches to changing living arrangements or providing confidants may be effective in lowering risk. Approaches to compensate for social support deficit might include the use of visiting health professionals, the creation of housing arrangements that would include rooms for individuals who could provide support or caregiving, and the physical design of multiple family dwellings that would provide privacy while facilitating social integration.

Alternative strategies for addressing social isolation need to be investigated and their relative efficacy determined. New technologies, including the "information superhighways," that will link households in interactive computer and video networks will create extraordinary opportunities for social interaction. While we await these new technologies, research could begin to explore their application for the provision of social support, as well as the delivery of other interventions within behavioral medicine. In addition, interventions being applied today could be augmented to educate individuals of the importance of social support, and to improve skills in seeking and sustaining meaningful supportive relationships. Later in this chapter, an example of such an intervention is presented as part of CET.

DEPRESSION AND CHD

Over the years, depressive symptoms, exhaustion, and emotional drain have been implicated as risk factors for CVD. Maurice Craig was among the first to draw this association when, in 1898, he noted that blood pressure elevation paralleled the clinical course of depression (17). Then, in some of the first major longitudinal studies of CHD mortality, depression would be found to predict death from MI (18–20). Although most of the attention on psychological risk factors was directed toward identifying components of the coronary-prone behavior pattern, a number of studies provided mounting evidence that high levels of depression (21), depressed symptoms and hopelessness (22), psychological stress symptoms (23), and fatigue and exhaustion (24, 25) are associated with increased risk for heart disease.

Depression and CHD: Evidence of a Relationship

Definitive confirmation of a causal link between depressive symptoms and cardiovascular risk has been difficult because much of the research on which these observations were made was retrospective in design, and many of the studies did not use standard assessment procedures to measure depressive symptomatology. However, in the last decade, better designed research has yielded results that underscore the importance of depression in CHD morbidity and mortality. Most notable among this new research portfolio is a prospective study (16) that provides striking evidence of a fivefold greater risk of mortality among depressed, post-MI patients than among their nondepressed counterparts. Unlike previous research, not only was this study prospective in nature but it employed the National Institutes of Mental Health (NIMH) Diagnostic Interview Schedule, which provides a reliable assessment of depression. At the same time that the report of this important study was published, a reanalysis of the Recurrent Coronary Prevention Project (RCPP) (26) was reported. In this reanalysis, depression was found to be an independent predictor of cardiac recurrence and mortality among women.

The proposed link between depression symptoms and CHD extends beyond national borders and is observed in a variety of populations. For example, in Gothenborg, Sweden, admission to the general or psychiatric hospital was associated with increased cardiovascular risk among subjects who resembled mildly depressed patients (27). A further follow-up study of these psychiatric patients revealed that they continued to have an increased rate of MI than controls (28).

The association between depressive symptoms and heart disease is gaining the attention of behavioral medicine, and there is speculation about the mechanism by which depression is linked to increased cardiovascular risk. Supporting the contention that depression is associated with increased atherosclerosis, (a) depression is elevated in patients with angiographically documented heart disease (29), and (b) depression is associated with increased morbidity and mortality in patients with arrhythmias (30). Although confirming the relationship between depression and heart disease, these observations still leave the specific mechanisms to be isolated. One leading proposal is that depression is associated with changes in sympathetic–parasympathetic balance, which may increase arrhythmias (16, 31). In addition, one of the biological theories of depression proposes a dysfunction in serotinergic neurotransmission, which is thought to increase risk through its effects on platelet function (32).

Another set of possible mechanisms by which depression could increase CHD risk involves overt behaviors. CHD may be elevated among those who are depressed because depressed mood is often accompanied by coronary-prone health practices. Specifically, depression is associated with decreased adherence to healthy diet and exercise, and increased use of tobacco. The failure to follow these positive health habits is known to elevate risk for CHD. Still another pathway between depression and CHD may be related to the fact that depression is related to the other stress-related emotional states and social conditions. Perhaps, for some, hostility and anger, or job strain, are personally experienced in conjunction with depressed mood and fatigue. Perhaps, for others, depression may be an effect of social isolation or an emotional state that leads to either social withdrawal or lower social support. Further longitudinal research is needed to fully understand the manner in which depressive symptoms are associated with related psychosocial risk factors, including anger and hostility, job strain, and social isolation.

Depression and CHD: Implications for Intervention

The demonstration that depressive symptoms are associated with increased CHD risk raises questions about the implications for behavioral interventions. For post-MI patients, some have suggested that it may be unethical to *not* intervene to reduce depressive symptoms, given that treatments exist for depression and given the possibility that such interventions would reduce risk and enhance quality of life (31). This position is particularly appropriate for the 15%–20%

of post-MI patients who meet criteria for depression (16). Among the treatment alternatives that should be considered to address depression are interpersonal or cognitive psychotherapy (33) and pharmacological therapies. In addition to traditional drug therapies for depressed mood or symptoms meeting the criteria for clinical depression, the new research on mechanisms linking depression to CHD suggests that selective serotonin reuptake inhibitors may have particular benefit. These agents may not only reduce depression without significant adverse side effects, but may lower CHD risk by decreasing sympathetic arousal (34) and aggression (35), and facilitating smoking cessation (36).

Primary prevention of CHD should also take into account the evidence that depression is predictive of CHD morbidity and mortality. For example, health care professionals could be alerted to this new risk factor, and are encouraged to refer patients for treatment of depressed mood. Individuals who are depressed and have a family history of CVD may be candidates for interventions that address both mood and cardiovascular risk reduction. Cognitive–behavioral therapies that have shown promise in the treatment of depression, both in combination with pharmacotherapy and alone (33), may be particularly appropriate in the context of reducing CHD risk. Such clinical interventions could be integrated as a component in programs that are designed to change standard risk factors such as smoking, as well as programs targeting newer risk factors such as hostility and job strain.

IMPLICATIONS OF THE NEW BEHAVIORAL RISK FACTORS FOR COPING INTERVENTIONS

These three risk factors—SES, social isolation, and depression—all involve psychosocial components and, as noted earlier, are amenable to interventions at a number of levels. The customary level for behavioral interventions is the individual. These new risk factors, particularly SES and social isolation, can also be addressed at the environmental level. In the foregoing sections, attention has been paid to those preventive and ameliorating interventions that could be implemented on a community and societal scale. Environments characterized by joblessness, crime and social distrust, and norms against education can be converted into environments that offer opportunities for jobs promoting positive community changes, encourage social bonds and trust, and promote lifelong learning. In addition, environments can be modified to improve access to resources that are important in reducing risk of disease and restoring physical and psychological well-being. Interventions that diminish barriers between people and enhance social support need be on the behavioral medicine agenda, not necessarily as an alternative, but in addition to individual coping strategies.

Although attention is paid to community-based interventions, additional attention can be paid to addressing these new risk factors at the individual level.

One program that provides a model for individual intervention is Coping Effectiveness Training (CET). This intervention integrates cognitive coping theory with the stress-management and arousal-reduction therapies that are well known to behavioral medicine circles (37). This intervention is currently being tested for its ability to assist patients coping with acquired immunodeficiency syndrome (AIDS). It is described here as an intervention example that addresses these new risk factors, including sources of stress in the social environment, experiences of social isolation within the community, and feelings of depression.

COPING EFFECTIVENESS TRAINING: ONE APPROACH TO REDUCING THE IMPACT OF THE NEW PSYCHOSOCIAL RISK FACTORS

Coping Effectiveness Training (CET) is a group-based intervention that is based on the cognitive theory of stress and coping, while incorporating components of stress management (38, 39). CET provides individuals with a "map" for selecting among coping strategies to prevent or manage stressful situations, enhance support and well-being, and reduce distress. According to the theory underlying this approach, stress is viewed as a "transaction" between the individual and the environment that is personally significant and surpasses the individual's coping strategy. The impact of a stressful transaction is mediated by two processes: the individual's appraisal of the stress and choice of coping.

Appraisal refers to the individual's evaluation of a each stressful transaction in terms of its importance and the extent to which the situation is amenable to change. *Coping* refers to the process by which the individual attempts to manage the demands of the situations appraised as stressful. Coping can be directed to manage or modify the problem that is causing the distress (problem-focused coping), or it can be directed to address the individual's emotional responses to the stressor (emotion-focused coping). The map or "blueprint" taught as part of CET emphasizes "fitting" the coping strategy (i.e., problem- vs. emotion-focused coping) to characteristics of the stressful situations. By contrast, most behavioral or stress-management intervention programs in primary and secondary prevention of CHD teach skills for managing stress, but do not provide any map or blueprint to guide in the selection of strategies to be called on to address the stress individuals experience in their lives (40).

CET, as it is being practiced in programs to assist individuals in coping with chronic stress, is taught during ten 2-hour weekly sessions with groups of 6–10 individuals. In addition to these sessions, group leaders telephone participants to reinforce the CET concept and to problem solve any difficulty participants may have with the program's homework. There is a full-day retreat between the fourth and fifth sessions. To maintain the effects of CET after the initial 10-session training phase, participants meet as a group every 2 months. In the current research evaluating CET, these bimonthly sessions continue for the remainder of a 1-year period. In clinical practice, this maintenance phase might be shortened or extended. CET focuses on teaching the following five elements:

1. *Appraising stressful situations* involves training people to: (a) use their personal affective and behavioral cues to recognize stressful situations, (b) translate general perceptions of stress into specific components, and (c) determine which components of stressful situations are subject to change and which are not.

2. *Training in problem- and emotion-focused coping* teaches cognitive–behavioral skills for both emotion- and problem-focused coping. The skills that comprise emotion-focused coping include relaxation (41–46), cognitive therapy (47, 48), cognitive restructuring (40, 49, 50), and humor (51, 52). The coping strategies that comprise problem-focused coping include problem solving (49–51, 53), decision making (49–51), social and communication skills (41, 42, 45), and negotiation (41, 42, 45, 54).

3. *Matching the coping strategies with characteristics of stressful situations* involves training individuals to match coping strategies with the "changeability" of stressors. Specifically, individuals are trained to apply problem-focused coping strategies to components of stressful situations that are amenable to change. For those components of situations that are not amenable to change, individuals are trained to apply emotion-focused coping strategies. Studies, including those that involve socioenvironmental stressors such as the nuclear accident at Three Mile Island (55), demonstrate that mismatches between the changeability and type of coping increase anxiety and depression (55–58). Individuals are also trained in the skills needed to implement changes in their social environment. For example, if a job with an excessive work load precipitates stress, individuals are trained in the skills necessary to take actions to reduce the work load, and to manage their emotional and physiological reactions to job stress.

4. *Obtaining social support* applies the principle of matching to the use of social support (59). This training is distinguished from the usual concept of perceived social support. Here, individuals are trained in specific skills for identifying the type of social support needed and matching the characteristics of social support sought to the skills or resources of the support provider. For example, if an individual lacks insurance coverage for cardiac rehabilitation and has questions about where to turn, the training would advise him or her to seek out others who are primarily problem focused in their coping. Conversely, if an individual feels depressed and isolated after being alone during a holiday, wants to express these feelings, and wants to be with others, the training would advise him or her to seek out others who are primarily emotion focused in their coping. Lacking such training, the individual might turn for support about his or her isolation to an individual who is primarily problem focused, and thus receive directions about how to plan better for the subsequent year's holiday.

5. *Developing self-efficacy and maintaining the program's effects* are the objectives of the follow-up phase of training. Individuals practice applying their cognitive–

behavioral strategies for coping in different situations, examining situations in which they are unsuccessful in using their new skills, and, over time, enhancing their personal efficacy in coping. This follow-up period also provides an opportunity to reinforce new coping behaviors and prevent relapse—a problem that challenges cognitive–behavioral interventions (60, 61).

CET: Evidence of Efficacy

The CET program is currently being tested in a large, randomized clinical trial. It has also been tested previously in a pilot study of 40 men. The initial pilot study indicated the feasibility of CET, and demonstrated significant effects in decreasing depression and increasing positive morale. These changes in mood were related to changes in coping, which indicated a greater use of planful problem solving and positive reappraisal (adaptive coping), and less use of escape avoidance, self-blame, and confrontive coping (maladaptive coping) (62, 63). Preliminary results from the clinical trial indicate that individuals who received CET are experiencing significantly greater reductions in perceived stress, anger, burnout, and self-blame, and greater increases in social support and coping efficacy than subjects in either of two control groups. The measure of *coping efficacy* designed for this trial assesses skills in the problem-focused coping skills needed for changing stressful social situations. This trial is still underway, therefore additional data on efficacy are forthcoming. The available data indicate that the intervention is applicable for training individuals in managing social stress, increasing social support, and decreasing negative moods. Although preliminary, the evidence suggests that interventions such as CET can be developed to address the new psychosocial risk factors for CHD.

CONCLUSION

There is evidence that low SES, social isolation, and depression should be added to the list of targets for behavioral interventions to reduce CHD morbidity and mortality. The foregoing chapter (a) highlighted the evidence that each of these three behavioral factors is associated with CHD, (b) proposed potential mechanisms underlying these associations, and (c) discussed implications that these new psychosocial factors have for behavioral interventions designed to reduce CHD risk. These new factors are not isolated abnormalities that will be confirmed as independent risk factors in multivariate analyses, but rather are intricately related to existing risk factors. Lower SES is associated with many of the standard risk factors, depression is associated with cigarette smoking and inactivity, and social isolation is associated with hostility. Interventions focused on these new risk factors may hold important clues to the development and patterning of risk profiles, and to their reversal. The social nature of these new risk factors argues for interventions that not only target the individual level, but also strive to make changes to create social environments conducive to health, well-being, and quality of life for all those who dwell with them.

REFERENCES

1. Antonovsky A. Social class, life expectancy and overall mortality. Milbank Mem Fund Q 1967;45:31–73.
2. Syme S, Berkman L. Social class, susceptibility and sickness. Am J Epidemiol 1976;104:1–8.
3. Matthews K. Are sociodemographic variables markers for psychological determinants of health? Health Psychol 1989;8:641–48.
4. Haan M, Kaplan G, Syme L. Socioeconomic status and health: old observations and new thoughts. In: Bunker J, Gomby D, Kehrer B, editors. Pathways to health. Menlo Park, CA: The Henry J. Kaiser Family Foundation, 1989:76–135.
5. Adler N, Boyce W, Chesney M, et al. Socioeconomic inequalities in health. JAMA 1993;269:3140–45.
6. Adler N, Boyce T, Chesney M, et al. Socioeconomic status and health: the challenge of the gradient. Am Psychol 1994;49:15–24.
7. Horowitz J. Toward a social policy for health. N Engl J Med 1993;329:130–33.
8. Marmot M. Socioeconomic determinants of CHD mortality. Int J Epidemiol 1989;18:S196–S202.
9. Marmot M, Shipley M, Rose G. Inequalities in death: specific explanations of a general pattern? Lancet 1984;1:1003–06.
10. Marmot M, Smith G, Stansfeld S, et al. Health inequalities among British civil servants: the Whitehall II study. Lancet 1991;337:1387–93.
11. Keil J, Sutherland S, Knapp R, et al. Mortality rates and risk factors for coronary disease in black as compared with white men and women. N Engl J Med 1993;329:73–78.
12. House J, Landis K, Umberson D. Social relationships and health. Science 1988;241:540–45.
13. Orth-Gomér K, Rosengren A, Wilhelmsen L. Lack of social support and incidence of coronary heart disease in middle-aged Swedish men. Psychosom Med 1993;55:37–43.
14. Williams R, Barefoot J, Califf R, et al. Prognostic importance of social and economic resources among medically treated patients with angiographically documented coronary artery disease. JAMA 1992;267:520–24.
15. Case R, Moss A, Case N, et al. Living alone after myocardial infarction. JAMA 1992;267:515–19.
16. Frasure-Smith N, Lesperance R, Talajic M. Depression following myocardial infarction: impact on 6-month survival. JAMA 1993;270:1819–25.
17. Craig M. Blood pressure in the insane. Lancet 1898;1:1742–47.
18. Lebovitz B, Shekelle R, Ostfeld A, et al. Prospective and retrospective psychological studies of coronary heart disease. Psychosom Med 1967;29:171–265.
19. Paffenbarger R, Wolf P, Notkin J, et al. Chronic disease in former college students. Am J Epidemiol 1966;83:314–28.
20. Thorne M, Wing A, Paffenbarger R. Chronic diseases in former college students: VII. Early precursors of nonfatal coronary heart disease. Am J Epidemiol 1968;87:520–29.
21. Ahern D, Gorkin L, Anderson J, et al. Biobehavioral variables and mortality or cardiac arrest in the Cardiac Arrhythmia Pilot Study (CAPS). Am J Cardiol 1990;66:59–62.
22. Kaplan G. Psychosocial aspects of chronic illness: direct and indirect associations with ischemic heart disease mortality. In: Kaplan R, Crique M, editors. Behavioral epidemiology and disease prevention. New York: Plenum, 1985:237–69.
23. Frasure-Smith N. In-hospital symptoms of psychological stress as predictors of long-term outcome after acute myocardial infarction in men. Am J Cardiol 1991;67:121–27.

24. Hurst J, Crawley I, Morris D, et al. The history: symptoms and past events related to cardio-vascular disease. In: Hurst J, et al., editors. The heart. 7th ed. New York: McGraw-Hill, 1990:122–34.

25. Appels A, Mulder P. Excess fatigue as a precursor of myocardial infarction. Eur Heart J 1988;9:758–64.

26. Powell L, Shaker L, Jones B, et al. Psychosocial predictors of mortality in 83 women with premature acute myocardial infarction. Psychosom Med 1993;55:426–33.

27. Lindegard B. Physical illness in severe depressives and psychiatric alcoholics in Gothenburg, Sweden. J Affective Disord 1982;4:383–93.

28. Appels A. The year before myocardial infarction. In: Dembroski T, et al., editors. Biobehavioral basis of coronary heart disease. Basel: Karger, 1983:18–38.

29. Carney R, Rich M, Freedland K, et al. Major depressive disorders predicts cardiac events in patients with coronary heart disease. Psychosom Med 1988;50:627–33.

30. Kennedy G, Hofer M, Cohen D, et al. Significance of depression and cognitive impairment in patients undergoing programmed stimulation of cardiac arrhythmias. Psychosom Med 1987;49:410–21.

31. Williams RB, Chesney MA. Psychosocial factors and prognosis in established coronary artery disease: the need for research on interventions. [Editorial]. JAMA 1993;270:1860–61.

32. Meltzer H, Arora R. Platelet serotonin studies in affective disorders: evidence of a serotonergic abnormality? In: Sandler M, Coppen A, Harnett S, editors. 5-Hydroxytryptamine in psychiatry. Oxford, England: Oxford University Press, 1991:50–89.

33. Hollon S, Shelton R, Davis D. Cognitive therapy for depression: conceptual issues and clinical efficacy. J Consult Clin Psychol 1993;61:270–75.

34. Verrier R. Neurochemical approaches to the prevention of ventricular fibrillation. Fed Proc 1986;45:2191–96.

35. Berzanyi P, Galateo E, Valzelli L. Fluoxetine activity on muricidal aggression induced in rats by p-chlorophenylalanine. Aggressive Beh 1983;9:333–38.

36. Bowen D, Spring B, Fox E. Tryptophan and high-carbohydrate diets as adjuncts to smoking cessation therapy. J Behav Med 1991;14:97–110.

37. Chesney M, Folkman S. Psychological impact of HIV disease and implications for intervention. In: Zegans L, Coates T, editors. Psychiatric manifestations of HIV disease. Psychiatric Clinics of North America 1994;17:163–182.

38. Antoni MH, Baggett L, Ironson G, et al. Cognitive behavioral stress management intervention buffers distress responses and immunologic changes following notification of HIV-1 seropositivity. J Consult Clin Psychol 1991;59:906–15.

39. Fawzy I, Namir S, Wolcott D. Group intervention with newly diagnosed AIDS patients. Psychiatr Med 1989;7:35–46.

40. Meichenbaum D. Stress inoculation training. Elmsford, NY: Pergamon, 1985.

41. Brown RA, Lewinsohn PM. Participant workbook for the Coping with Depression Course. Eugene: Castalia, 1984.

42. Brown RA, Lewinsohn PM. A psychoeducational approach to the treatment of depression: comparison of group, individual, and minimal contact procedures. J Consult Clin Psychol 1984;52:774–83.

43. Goldfried MR, Trier C. Effectiveness of relaxation as an active coping skill. J Abnorm Psychol 1974;83:348–55.

44. Goldfried M. Anxiety reduction through cognitive-behavioral intervention. In: Kendall PC, Hollon SD, editors. Cognitive-behavioral intervention: theory, research and procedures. New York: Academic, 1979:117–52.

45. Lewinsohn PM, Hoberman HM. Depression. In: Bellack AS, Hersen M, Kazdin AE, editors. International handbook of behavior modification and behavior therapy. New York: Plenum, 1982:397–432.

46. Poppen R. Behavioral relaxation training and assessment. New York: Pergamon, 1988.

47. Beck AT, Rush AJ, Shaw BF, et al. Cognitive therapy of depression. New York: Springer, 1979.

48. Hollon SD, Beck AT. Cognitive and cognitive-behavioral therapies. In: Garfield SL, Bergin AE, editors. Handbook of psychotherapy and behavior change. New York: Wiley, 1989:443–82.

49. D'Zurilla T, Nezu A. Social problem-solving in adults. In: Kendall D, editor. Advances in cognitive-behavioral research and therapy. New York: Academic Press, 1982:201–74.

50. Nezu AM, Perri MG. Social problem-solving therapy for unipolar depression: an initial dismantling investigation. J Consult Clin Psychol 1989;57:408–13.

51. Nezu AM. Efficacy of a social problem-solving therapy approach for unipolar depression. J Consult Clin Psychol 1986;42:847–52.

52. Nezu AM, Nezu CM, Blissett SE. Sense of humor as a moderator of the relation between stressful events and psychological distress: a prospective analysis. J Pers Soc Psychol 1988;54:520–25.

53. Meichenbaum D, Henshaw D, Himel N. Coping with stress as a problem-solving process. In: Krohne HW, Lanz L, editors. Achievement, stress and anxiety. Washington, DC: Hemisphere, 1982:127–42.

54. Fisher R, Ury W. Getting to yes. New York: Houghton-Mifflin, 1981.

55. Collins D, Baum A, Singer J. Coping with chronic stress at Three Mile Island: psychological and biochemical evidence. Health Psychol 1983;2:149–66.

56. Cohen S, Evans G, Stokols D, et al. Stress processes and the costs of coping. In: Cohen S, et al., editors. Behavior, health, and environmental stress. New York: Plenum, 1986:1–23.

57. Forsythe CJ, Compas B. Interaction and cognitive appraisals of stressful events and coping. Cog Beh Ther 1987;11:473–85.

58. Vitaliano PP, DeWolfe D, Maiuro RD, et al. Appraised changeability of a stressor as a modifier of the relationship between coping and depression [Manuscript in preparation]. University of Washington, Seattle, 1989.

59. Thoits PA. Social support as coping assistance. J Consult Clin Psychol 1986;54:416–23.

60. Bandura A. Self-efficacy mechanism in physiological activation and health-promoting behavior. In: Madden J IV, Matthysse S, Barchas J, editors. Adaption, learning, and affect. New York: Raven Press, 1986:229–69.

61. Marlatt GA, George WH. Relapse prevention and the maintenance of optimal health. In: Shumaker S, Schron E, Ockene JK, editors. The adoption and maintenance of behaviors for optimal health. New York: Springer, 1989:44–63.

62. Folkman S, Chesney M, McKusick L, et al. Translating coping theory into intervention. In: Eckenrode J, editor. The social context of stress. New York: Plenum, 1991:239–60.

63. Folkman S, Chesney MA. Coping with HIV infection. In: Stein M, Baum A, editors. Perspectives on behavioral medicine. Hillsdale, NJ: Lawrence Erlbaum Associates. In press.

Part IV

BEHAVIORAL INTERVENTION MODELS IN CARDIOVASCULAR DISEASE PREVENTION

Chapter 13

Health Education at the Individual Level

Gerjo Kok
Harm J. Hospers
Dirk-Jan den Boer
Hein de Vries
University of Limburg–Maastricht

In this chapter, we discuss health education as a strategy for the promotion of health and the prevention of diseases. We focus specifically on health education at the individual level (other chapters of this book describe health education at other levels). First, the concept of *health education* is defined within the broader context of health promotion and prevention. Second, a model is presented on systematic planning and evaluation of health education. Third, psychosocial determinants of health behavior are described, based on social-psychological theories. Fourth, a transtheoretical model of stages of behavior change is presented, illustrated with examples of "tailored" messages. Fifth, we elaborate on health education programs based on attribution theory and relapse-prevention theory because these programs are specific examples of applications for health education at the individual level. Sixth, we focus on systematic large-scale implementation of health education interventions. Finally, conclusions are drawn.

HEALTH EDUCATION AND HEALTH PROMOTION

Green and Kreuter (1) defined *health education* as any planned combination of learning experiences designed to predispose, enable, and reinforce voluntary behavior conducive to health in individuals, groups, or communities. The same authors defined *health promotion* as any planned combination of educational, political, regulatory, and organizational supports for action and conditions of living conducive to health of individuals, groups, and communities. Health education is the educational part of health promotion. Health education is directed at behavior, whereas health promotion is directed at both behavior and environment. Health education focuses on learning and voluntary change. Health promotion involves different strategies, roughly distinguished as: (a) education, (b) availability of provisions and facilities, and (c) regulation and control.

Health promotion and health education are related to prevention. However, *prevention* is a different concept. Prevention is an objective of health care and health policy, whereas health education and promotion are strategies to reach that objective. Prevention can be divided into three types: primary prevention, secondary prevention (or early detection and treatment), and tertiary prevention (or patient care). *Primary prevention* activities try to prevent the disease, *early detection and treatment* activities try to limit the negative consequences of the onset of a disease, and *patient care* activities support patients and their social environment to cope with the disease. In Fig. 13.1, the matrix of health-promotion objectives and strategies is depicted.

We can look at cardiovascular diseases (CVDs) as an example to illustrate the matrix in Fig. 13.1. Primary prevention activities include activities such as prevention of smoking, smoking cessation, lowering fat intake, exercise, and so on. For instance, the different strategies to promote smoking cessation could include education in the form of a smoking-cessation course or a self-help manual. Provisions could include free access to smoking-cessation education, free distribution of nicotine gum, and/or a telephone help line. Regulation would include a ban on smoking ads and/or protection of nonsmokers at the worksite.

Early detection activities could focus on early detection of high blood pressure, followed by early treatment. Educational activities would stimulate people to get themselves screened. Therefore, easy access to blood pressure screening facilities is important (provisions). For some professions, blood pressure screening could be mandatory, or companies could be forced to offer free screening to employees (regulations).

Patient care could involve support for patients who have to undergo an operation. Educational activities are directed at informing the patient about the procedure, helping the patient cope with pain and fear, and promoting compliance with medical treatment. Provisions could include home-care equipment

Health promotion	Primary prevention	Early detection	Patient care
Education			
Facilities			
Regulation			

FIG. 13.1. The matrix of health-promotion objectives and strategies.

and free access to recovery facilities. Finally, regulations could ensure patients' possible reentry into the working process.

In the following, we concentrate on health education, especially at the individual level. However, the matrix has made it clear that health education is a part of health promotion, and can only be effective in an optimal combination of health education at the individual, group, and community levels on the one hand, and other health-promotion strategies such as provisions and regulation on the other hand.

PLANNING AN EVALUATION OF HEALTH EDUCATION

Planned health education requires thorough consideration before action is taken. In stressing the importance of systematic planning, we do not mean to keep health educators from doing, but to stimulate effective action and prevent counterproductive activities. Green and Kreuter (1) presented an excellent integration of different planning ideas in health education and health promotion in their PRECEDE/PROCEED model. We summarize their model by asking 10 questions, including 5 planning questions and 5 evaluation questions (Fig. 13.2). The five planning questions are:

1. How serious is the health problem?
2. Which health-related behavior is involved?
3. What are the determinants of that behavior?
4. Which combination of health-promotion interventions (education, provisions, regulations) might change these determinants and behavior?
5. How can those interventions be implemented?

The five evaluation questions are:

6. Has the implementation been carried out as intended?
7. Have the interventions been executed as planned?
8. Have the determinants of the behavior changed?
9. Has the behavior changed?

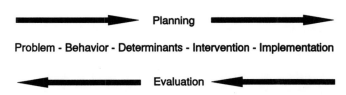

FIG. 13.2. Planning and evaluation of health education and health promotion.

10. Has the problem been lessened?

Insufficient answers to earlier questions weaken the potential of later decisions. We illustrate the application of the planning model by describing a smoking-prevention program (2):

1. *Problem:* Cancer and CVDs are important health problems in most developed countries.
2. *Behavior:* Cancer and CVDs are related to lifestyle. For instance, 35% of all cancer deaths are related to nutrition, 30% to smoking. Preventing younger people from smoking is a relevant behavioral objective.
3. *Determinants:* The most important determinant for the onset of smoking in youth is social pressure from peers, adults, and mass media. Moreover, adolescents often lack the ability to effectively resist social pressure.
4. *Intervention:* The intervention needs to focus on skills to resist social pressure (e.g., in a peer-led school program). Concurrent to that educational program, schools should develop a nonsmoking policy.
5. *Implementation:* Too often potentially effective health education programs are not used by the target organizations. Principals and teachers need to be aware of the availability and advantages of the program. When developing the intervention, this implementation should already be taken into account.
6. *Evaluation:* The evaluation follows the same kind of questioning, but the other way around. The final question is this: Has the problem of cancer and CVDs lessened as a result of the program? It may be clear that such a question is difficult to answer because the outcome effects are too far away in the future. The compromise is to show effects in intermediate indicators (e.g., less smoking in adolescents). To find effects, evaluation needs to start at the beginning of the planning process.

Unfortunately, the 10 steps cited previously are often not given appropriate attention, which is one of the reasons for ineffective prevention activities. The most common mistake people make is jumping from the problem to the intervention without answering the intermediate planning questions. Furthermore, where evaluation is lacking, the ineffectiveness of insufficiently planned interventions may not be noticed. Careful planning can avoid a number of potential pitfalls. We describe these pitfalls in terms of the planning model, and give illustrations from our own experience. All sections are concluded with advice.

Pitfall 1: The Problem

This is the pitfall of developing an intervention for a nonexisting problem. In the Netherlands, a large public campaign was considered to prevent alcohol drinking by pregnant women. However, a careful analysis of the problem indicated that the negative aspects of alcohol drinking by pregnant women were never demonstrated for very low consumption levels (one glass per day or two glasses once a week). Moreover, research showed that few pregnant women consumed more alcohol than that low level. Thus, a large campaign was not appropriate, and the existing educational activities were continued. The advice here is: Always assess the seriousness of a problem and its prevalence.

Pitfall 2: The Behavior

This is the pitfall of developing an intervention addressing behavior that lacks a clear relationship with the problem. In the Netherlands, a public campaign to prevent sports injuries was implemented, despite that we lack sufficient knowledge about the specific behaviors that cause sports injuries. For instance, the relationship between warming up and cooling down on the one hand, and injuries on the other hand, has never been shown convincingly by empirical research. The advice here is: Always be sure that the relationship between the problem and the behavior is clear, and that the behavioral advice is based on that relationship.

Pitfall 3: The Determinants

This is the pitfall of developing an intervention that is based on a misconceived idea about the determinants of the target behavior. The most prominent mistake is the assumption that knowledge about negative effects of a behavior is sufficient to change that behavior: It very seldom is. Smokers know how unhealthy smoking is, but they smoke for other reasons (e.g., relaxation, addiction). The health consequences that make a behavior important for health educators are not necessarily important determinants for the people who conduct that behavior. Another example of this pitfall is a focus on attitudinal aspects of the behavior in terms of advantages and disadvantages, while, for large parts of the target group, the main determinant for their unhealthy behavior is a lack of skills. The advice here is: Always find out what the determinants of the behavior are for the target group, and focus the intervention on that analysis.

Pitfall 4: The Intervention

This is the pitfall of developing an inappropriate intervention. On the health-promotion level, that could be an educational intervention where a more political intervention in terms of policy changes is needed. An example is an educational AIDS-preventive message for IV-drug users promoting the use of clean needles, while access to clean needles is lacking. On the health education level, the error could be choosing the wrong target group or the wrong message. Health education programs tend to reach highly educated people, who need the program least, and often fail to reach lower SES groups, which need the program most. Pretesting the intervention materials is a *must*. The advice here is: Always find out what the best intervention is to realize the objectives and, in case of a health education intervention, how the right people can be reached with the right message.

Pitfall 5: The Implementation

This is the pitfall of developing a potentially effective intervention with an inadequate implementation. In the Netherlands, the Dutch school television developed an AIDS-prevention program for all students ages 12–20 years. Two weeks before the start of the program, one organization of religion-based schools refused to hand out the materials in their schools. It is not important in this respect who is right or wrong about the content of the materials; what is important is that this program failed in terms of implementation. The advice here is: An effective intervention is in itself not sufficient; always find out how the intervention can be adequately implemented on a larger scale.

Pitfall 6: The Evaluation

This is the pitfall of unjustified satisfaction with the intervention, and it involves the failure to evaluate the intervention thoroughly. To expect short-term improvement in the health problems is, in most cases, unrealistic. Yet intermediate indicators should demonstrate changes in relevant behaviors and determinants. For instance, the error could take the form of satisfaction about the large numbers of brochures on the prevention of burn injuries among children that were handed out to mothers, while no notice is taken whether the actual number of injuries has been reduced, the mother's behavior has improved, or even whether the mother's knowledge has increased. The advice here is: Never be satisfied with an intervention until the problem has been reduced, the target behavior has improved, and/or relevant determinants have changed.

For many health educators, this list of pitfalls and advice may seem trivial. Unfortunately, it is not. The errors mentioned are often made, and by sensible people. Time pressure seems to be the main cause for poor planning. Systematically developing answers for all the planning and evaluation questions is rarely feasible. This results in a dilemma: waiting for better answers, or doing the best that one can. We suggest to try the best that one can, but in the meantime also try to find better answers. This is necessary because, as Mullen, Green, and Persinger (3) strongly indicated, the effectiveness of health education is largely determined by the quality of the planning process. Health education practice can be improved by ensuring that health education academics and practitioners have appropriate training in planning, methodology, and experience in applied research (4).

DETERMINANTS OF BEHAVIOR

An important step in the planning process is the analysis of the target behavior determinants. Social-psychological theory and research, fundamental as well as applied, has traditionally provided an important contribution to understanding behavior determinants. Fishbein and Ajzen (5, 6) integrated a series of models from attitude theory and social influence theory in their model of reasoned behavior. Ajzen (7) and other researchers (e.g., 8, 9) added Bandura's *self-efficacy* concept to the determinants model (10, 11), which is now known as the *model of planned behavior* (Fig. 13.3).

Attitudes, social influence, and self-efficacy predict intention, which in turn predicts the behavior. An *attitude* is the combination of all the advantages and disadvantages that people associate with performing the behavior. *Social influence* involves compliance with other people's expectations about behavior, but also the observation of other people's behavior (modeling). *Self-efficacy* is people's estimation about their ability to perform a specific behavior in a specific situation. External variables (variables outside the model), like demographic factors, are supposed to influence behavior via the three determinants and the intention. The relationship between intention and behavior can be influenced by barriers or lack of abilities. The determinants predict behavior via the intention, but self-efficacy can also directly influence behavior. The actual performance of the behavior results in a feedback process that, in turn, influences the determinants. Attitudes, social influence, and self-efficacy are not completely independent from each other. Mostly the intercorrelations are substantial. However, empirical data indicate that measuring each determinant separately improves the prediction of behavior.

The model of planned behavior (7) is not the only model that attempts to describe behavior determinants. Well known in the health education field is the health belief model (6, 7). The health belief model distinguishes three kinds of behavior determinants, which are set in motion by a cue to action: (a) a threat, being the result of susceptibility and severity; (b) factors that facilitate the target behavior; and (c) factors that hinder the target behavior (barriers). Compared with the model of planned behavior, the health belief model focuses on health-related advantages and disadvantages of the target behavior, and not much on other advantages and disadvantages. However, other attitude factors, social influence, and self-efficacy can all be included under facilitating factors and barriers.

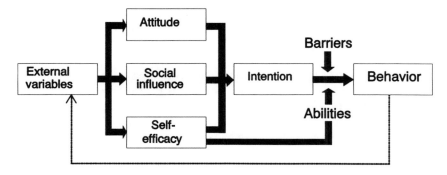

FIG. 13.3. Psychosocial determinants of behavior.

Green and Kreuter's PRECEDE/PROCEED model (1) also contains a determinants model. Green and Kreuter distinguished three types of determinants: predisposing, reinforcing, and enabling factors. Predisposing factors include attitudes, reinforcing factors' social influence, and enabling factors' self-efficacy. However, reinforcing and enabling factors include people's perceptions as well as real facilitating and hindering factors, suggesting other types of health-promotion interventions than just health education.

The following example illustrates the application of the theoretical concepts that we described in the previous section. Schaalma, Kok, and Peters (13) analyzed the determinants of consistent condom use (for AIDS prevention) by adolescents. The authors were interested in possible differences in determinants of behavior between consistent condom users and nonusers. The results show that adolescents who use condoms consistently are more likely to have a positive attitude. More specifically, they are less likely to subscribe to assertions about the unpleasantness of consistent condom use (e.g., unpleasant, interruption, dirty, embarrassed), and they are more likely to acknowledge the necessity of consistent condom use (e.g., good protection, feeling of security, necessary with a well-known partner).

Adolescents who do not consistently use condoms are more likely to perceive a negative social influence with regard to consistent condom use from parents, peers, and, especially, sex partners. They are also less likely to think that most of their peers use condoms in a consistent way because of AIDS.

Regarding self-efficacy assessments, adolescents who claim consistent use are more likely to be confident about their ability to stop making love because of condom use, and about their ability to use condoms while under the influence of alcohol. Furthermore, they are more likely to be confident about their abilities to continue consistent condom use and bring up the subject of condom use because of AIDS to a well-known sex partner.

Thus, attitudes, social influence, and self-efficacy are important determinants of consistent condom use by adolescents. The multiple regression of the three determinants with the behavior was .73, which means that the measured determinants explained 53% of the variance in this behavior. Based on a careful analysis of the determinants of behavior, we can start developing the actual intervention.

STAGES OF BEHAVIOR CHANGE

The amount of theories and empirical data regarding behavior change has reached such a high level that it has become difficult to summarize. Prochaska and DiClemente (14) offered an interesting approach to organizing the available knowledge in their transtheoretical model of stages of change. They distinguished six stages in the process of behavior change (see Fig. 13.4):

1. Precontemplation: People are not aware of the risk related to their behavior.

2. Contemplation: People are aware of the risk, but they are not motivated to change their behavior on short term.
3. Preparation for action: People are motivated to change their behavior in the near future.
4. Action: actual behavior change.
5. Maintainance: continued behavior change.
6. Relapse: lapses, followed by a return to Stage 1, 2, or 3.

The term *transtheoretical* in Prochaska and DiClemente's model indicates that people in different stages of change should be addressed with completely different intervention strategies (i.e., using different theories) because they have different needs. Precontemplators should be made aware of their risk behavior, and should receive information about the advantages and disadvantages of changing their behavior to move to the contemplation stage. Contemplators should be motivated to make concrete plans to change their behavior and to set specific goals. People in preparation should be offered interventions that increase their self-efficacy and abilities, and that promote social support for actual change. People in action should be motivated to maintain their changed behavior. Relapse-prevention techniques should be implemented to avoid relapses in the maintenance stage. Thus, different interventions are needed in different stages of change, targeting different determinants and conditions for behavior change. Theories are available for each stage to assist health educators in designing appropriate interventions (15, 16).

Prochaska and DiClemente's model has been the basis for a number of health education interventions using tailored messages. Tailored messages are based on an individual's stage of change, needs, and circumstances. An example is a study by Skinner, Strecher, and Hospers (17) on physician recommendations for mammography. Women were interviewed about their mammography stage of change, objective and perceived risk status, knowledge and beliefs about breast cancer and mammography, and perceived barriers impeding screening.

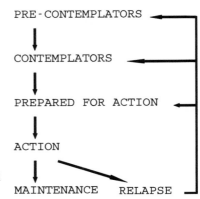

FIG. 13.4. The transtheoretical model of stages of change.

Following the interview, half of the subjects received a standardized message typifying usual care communications. The other half received a tailored message, using desktop publishing techniques, specifically addressing each woman's stage of change, risk status, beliefs, and perceived barriers. The standardized letters addressed a variety of factors that might be relevant to the recipients, whereas the tailored letters addressed only those that, according to the interviews, were relevant for their recipients. The differences in appearance between the standardized and tailored messages were minimized. The results of this study show that tailored messages were more likely to be remembered and were more thoroughly read. Tailored letters resulted in a more favorable mammography status at follow-up for low-income and African-American women.

What specific form should an intervention take? There is no simple way to answer this question. Health educators do not have a "magic bullet"—an intervention that is supposedly effective under all circumstances. On the contrary, interventions that may be effective in one situation can be disastrous in other situations. Interventions have to be developed depending on the target behavior, the target group, the communication situation, and so on. However, there are some general guidelines. Mullen et al. (3) formulated six criteria for the quality of health education interventions:

1. Consonance: the degree of fit between the program objectives and the analyses of the problem and the behavior (see Fig. 13.2).

2. Relevance: the tailoring of the program to the analysis of the psychosocial determinants of the target behavior, and the characteristics of the educational situation as assessed by pretesting or other means.

3. Individualization: the provision of opportunities for the target individuals to have personal questions answered or instructions paced according to their individual progress.

4. Feedback: information given to the target individuals regarding the extent to which improvement is being accomplished.

5. Reinforcement: any component of the intervention that is designed to reward the behavior after the behavior has been enacted (other than feedback).

6. Facilitation: the provision of means for the target individuals to take action and/or means to reduce barriers to action.

IMPROVING SELF-EFFICACY: ATTRIBUTION AND RELAPSE PREVENTION

As we have seen, self-efficacy is a crucial element in health behavior and behavior change. An important question for health education is: Can we improve self-efficacy and thus stimulate the desired behavioral change? During the last decade, there has been an increase in techniques based on attribution theory to improve self-efficacy to induce people to change their behavior (18, 19). Figure 13.5 depicts Weiner's attributional model (20). The model indicates that when outcomes are negative, unexpected, or important, a causal search is started, resulting in causal ascriptions that try to explain the outcomes. For example, a person who attempts to quit smoking but fails might attribute this outcome to a variety of reasons (e.g., low effort, the difficulty of the task, or nicotine dependency). According to attribution theory, perceived causal reasons have an underlying dimensional structure.

Theoretically, three attributional dimensions have been distinguished. The first dimension, *locus of causality*, reflects the extent to which previous outcomes are attributed to causes either internal or external to the person. The second dimension, *stability*, reflects the extent to which previous outcomes are attributed

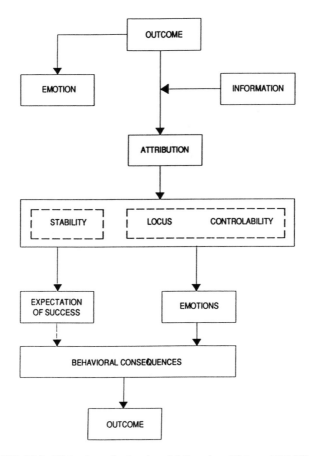

FIG. 13.5. Weiner's attributional model (based on Weiner, 1986 [3]).

to stable or unstable causes. *Stable causes* refer to perceptions that a failure or success was due to immutable, unalterable causes. *Unstable causes* refer to perceptions that a failure or a success was due to causes that are mutable. The third dimension, *controllability*, reflects the extent to which previous outcomes are attributed to controllable or uncontrollable causes. Empirical support is strongest for the dimensions *locus* and *stability*; the support for the dimension *controllability* is weakest. Attribution theory contends that causal ascriptions influence cognitions and emotions related to success and failure. We first describe the cognitive component, and then turn to the emotional component of attribution theory.

Weiner suggested that expectancy of success is determined by the perceived stability of the causes for success and failure. A person attributing a failure to a stable cause (e.g., ability) will have a lower expectancy of success when having to perform the same task again, compared with somebody who attributes a failure on the same task to an unstable cause (e.g., luck). After success, this effect is reversed. The rationale behind Weiner's assumption is this: When there is no reason to expect the cause of failure to change, the cause responsible for the failure will still be present the second time the task is performed. Furthermore, it is assumed that a lowered expectancy of success leads to less adaptive task behavior. Because of the lowered expectation of success, persons invest less energy in the task at hand. This line of reasoning closely parallels Bandura's ideas about self-efficacy (10).

Support for the cognitive component of attribution theory can be found, among others, in a study by Hospers, Kok, and Strecher (21). Hospers and colleagues tested the cognitive component of attribution theory on participants in a weight-reduction program. They measured the number of previous attempts to lose weight, stability of the attributions for previous failure, expectancy of success, and goal attainment. Results of this study are shown in Fig. 13.6.

As hypothesized, goal attainment was positively associated with success expectancy, which, in turn, was negatively related to stability. Furthermore, stability was positively related to the number of former trials. Also, as hypothesized, there was no significant association between the number of previous attempts and goal attainment, nor between stability and goal attainment. These results suggest that it is not the number of former failures people experience that predicts future performance, but rather the way people interpret these failures. The more stable

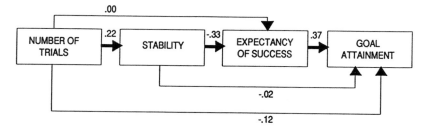

FIG. 13.6. Weiner's attributional model applied to weight reduction.

the cause attributed to failure, the lower the expectancy of success for the next attempts, and hence lower goal attainment.

The relationship between perceptions of locus and controllability on the one hand, and emotions and behavior on the other hand, can be referred to as the *emotional component* of Weiner's attributional theory. It is assumed that different attributions lead to different emotions. An attribution of effort for failure (internal/controllable) will lead to guilt, whereas an attribution of ability for failure (internal/uncontrollable) will lead to shame. There are two kinds of emotions: motivating and debilitating. Motivating emotions lead to a better task performance; debilitating emotions lead to a worse task performance. Guilt is supposed to be motivating, whereas shame is supposed to be debilitating. At the moment, it is empirically unclear which emotions could be termed *debilitating* and which emotions *motivating*.

Interventions based on attribution theory (22) all have a similar assumption: If different attributions lead to different behavioral consequences, it should be possible to change the behavior of people by changing the attributions they make. After failure, an attribution to effort leads to better future task performance than an attribution to, for instance, ability. Preferably, an internal, stable, and uncontrollable attribution for failure should be substituted by an internal, unstable, and controllable attribution. In many instances, this means changing ability attributions for failure at effort attributions. Because of such a change in attribution, people have a higher expectation of success (self-efficacy), which in turn will increase their task performance.

A theory that uses the concepts of *attribution* and *self-efficacy* is Marlatt and Gordon's relapse-prevention theory (23). Relapse-prevention theory explains why people often fail when trying to change a certain addictive behavior (e.g., smoking or drinking). An overview of the theory is presented in Fig. 13.7. A key concept in this theory is the so-called "high-risk situation." A *high-risk situation* is a situation in which people are tempted to return to their former habits. For a smoker who tries to quit smoking, meeting a friend who smokes might be a high-risk situation. To cope with such a situation, people need adequate coping responses. This means that people need to anticipate the situation and know what to do when that situation arises. According to the theory, an absence of an adequate coping response will lead to decreased self-efficacy, which increases the probability of a lapse to previous, undesirable behavior. Because people had decided to quit that previous behavior, the lapse is seen as a failure. Whether an initial lapse results in total relapse is mediated by attributions for that failure. If a lapse occurs, it is important to consider what caused this lapse and what can be done to avoid such lapses in the future. There are causes that a person should not attribute to in this situation (e.g., stable causes like willpower or abilities) because that would result in even lower self-efficacy. Attributions to stable, internal causes will also lead to shame and perceived loss of control.

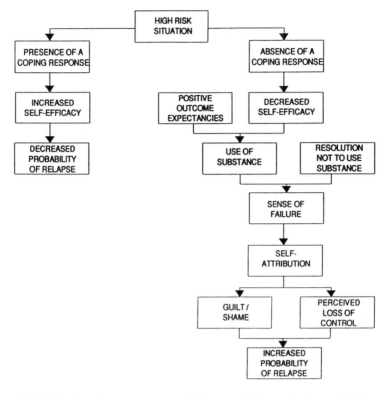

FIG. 13.7. The relapse-prevention model (based on Marlatt & Gordon, 1985 [23]).

For instance, smokers who have decided to quit and find themselves unable to cope with a high-risk situation, resulting in the use of cigarettes, experience a conflict between their commitment to stop smoking and their actions. This conflict could result in a sense of failure, stable and internal attributions, debilitating emotions, and perceived loss of control (lower success expectancies). Thus, attributions to stable, internal causes in this situation will lead to an increased probability of further relapses.

One can conclude from the previously mentioned theories that it is not sufficient to motivate people to adopt healthier behavior; one also has to provide the necessary coping skills to avoid a return to the undesirable behavior. Having an ingrained and automatic coping response will decrease the probability of a relapse because it increases self-efficacy. If, nevertheless, a lapse might occur, it is important that the lapse is attributed to the "right" cause. This means that it should not be attributed to stable causes, but to unstable, controllable causes.

Marlatt and Gordon (23) devised a procedure consisting of four phases to improve their clients' self-efficacy through relapse-prevention training: (a) influencing the frame of reference of the client, (b) searching for high-risk situations and learning coping skills, (c) actually practicing these coping skills, and (d) learning how to handle lapses. The first phase consists of teaching the client that, to master the desired behavior, one has to learn certain skills. For instance, quitting smoking is not a matter of willpower or abilities, but a matter of skills. This replaces ideas like "I am a weakling and I cannot quit smoking by myself" with the idea that one is going to learn the skills to quit smoking. Because self-efficacy is related to experiences of success (10, 20), it is important to state realistic subgoals. One such subgoal could be to stop smoking during the day.

The second phase consists of looking at possible high-risk situations by means of keeping a diary, self-monitoring, or exploring the reasons why previous attempts failed. For each high-risk situation, a coping response should be devised.

Third, it is important to practice these coping responses. One possibility is to actively seek a high-risk situation in a controlled setting and discuss the experiences afterward. The better ingrained and more automatic the coping response, the higher one's self-efficacy and the lower the probability of a lapse.

Finally, if a lapse occurs, it is important to learn from this lapse by examining what caused it and how that situation can be avoided in the future. The attribution is important: People should make unstable and controllable attributions for failure, which in turn motivate them to find a better coping response for that situation. It is not clear whether attributions should be internal or external, but it is clear that attributions should be unstable and controllable. Marlatt and Gordon reported a number of evaluation studies that show the effectiveness of relapse prevention through the training of coping skills.

IMPLEMENTATION

Implementation of a prevention program is an essential part of the health-promotion planning process (24). If we do not ensure implementation, our work has been largely wasted. Relapse programs for weight loss are useless if dieticians do not use them. Underestimating diffusion and adoption barriers is one of the reasons that health education is sometimes ineffective. Although we commonly accept the need for information on determinants of individual behavior, we often fail to recognize that, to develop implementation strategies, we also need information on determinants of institutional behavior, such as adoption of a prevention program by organizations or decision makers within those organizations (24, 25). To illustrate this, we summarize the existing knowledge on the diffusion and adoption of health promotion from three perspectives: (a) features of the innovation that determine adoption, (b) strategies to stimulate adoption, and (c) the importance of a linkage system.

Research in the area of diffusion and adoption, mostly in schools and worksites, suggests a number of features of an innovation (the health-promotion intervention) that determine (non)adoption. These are (24, 25):

Compatibility: When innovations are consistent with the economic, sociocultural, and philosophical value systems of the adopting organization, adoption is more likely to take place.

Flexibility: Innovations that can be unbundled and used as separate components will be applicable in a wider variety of user settings.

Reversibility: If, for any reason, the adopting organization wants to revert to its previous practices, it is desirable that an innovation is capable of termination. Innovations that are not are less likely to be adopted.

Relative advantage: If an innovation appears to be beneficial when compared with current and previous methods, adoption is more likely.

Complexity: Complex innovations are more difficult to communicate and understand, and are therefore less likely to be adopted.

Cost-efficiency: For an innovation to be considered desirable, its perceived benefits, both tangible and intangible, must outweigh its perceived costs.

Risk: The degree of uncertainty introduced by an innovation helps determine its potential for adoption. Innovations that involve higher risk are less likely to be adopted.

Research in the area of intervention strategies to stimulate adoption by organizations, mostly based on social learning theory (10), shows the importance of modeling and incentives (26). Adoption of health-promotion interventions is facilitated by observing other organizations adopt an intervention, as well as by reinforcement in terms of material incentives, social status, or objectives.

Orlandi et al. (24) stressed the need for a linkage system between the resource system that promotes the intervention (e.g., the Anti-Cancer Council) and the user system that is supposed to adopt the intervention (e.g., a worksite). The linkage system should include representatives of the user and resource systems, plus change agents (health educators) who facilitate the collaboration.

CONCLUSIONS

Health education is a strategy for health promotion and disease prevention based on learning and voluntary changes. As such, health education interventions are part of a broader health-promotion policy, and should be developed in combination with other strategies to promote health, such as regulation and creation of provisions. Developing health education interventions is a systematically planned activity, and health educators should be aware of the possible pitfalls that hinder effective planning and evaluation of health education. Research shows that the effectiveness of a health education intervention is largely dependent on the quality of the planning process.

Health education should be based on a thorough analysis of the psychosocial determinants of the target behavior. Different aspects of attitudes, social influence, and self-efficacy determine intention and behavior. It is further crucial to realize that the target population usually has different reasons for behavior than the reasons that motivate health educators to focus on this behavior. The process of behavior change can be described as going through stages. Precontemplators become contemplators who then prepare for action, and after action may become maintainers or relapsers. People in different stages of change need different health education messages. Research shows that tailored preventive messages are more effective than general preventive messages.

Improving self-efficacy is often a crucial objective in health education at the individual level. Self-efficacy is partly determined by attributions people make about successes and failures, and health education interventions are designed to teach people to make unstable, controllable attributions that improve success expectancies and stimulate preventive behavior. Relapse-prevention and re-attribution strategies are specifically designed to teach people the necessary skills to cope with high-risk situations and promote maintenance of behavior change. Potentially effective health education interventions will not be effective if the implementation is not adequately organized. From the start, interventions should be developed in a linkage system between the source system, the target population, and health educators.

REFERENCES

1. Green LW, Kreuter MW. Health promotion planning; an educational and environmental approach. Mountain View, CA: Mayfield, 1991.
2. De Vries H, Dijkstra M, Kok G. A Dutch smoking prevention project: an overview. Hygie 1992;11:14–18.
3. Mullen PD, Green LW, Persinger G. Clinical trials for patient education for chronic conditions; a comparative meta-analysis of intervention types. Prev Med 1985;14:753–81.
4. Kok G, Green LW. Research to support health promotion in practice: a plea for increased cooperation. Health Prom Intern 1990;5:303–08.
5. Fishbein M, Ajzen I. Belief, attitude, intention and behavior. Reading, MA: Addison-Wesley, 1975.
6. Glanz K, Lewis FM, Rimer BK, editors. Health behavior and health education; theory, research and practice. San Francisco, CA: Jossey-Bass, 1990.
7. Ajzen I. Attitudes, personality, and behavior. Milton Keynes, England: Open University Press, 1988.
8. De Vries H, Dijkstra M, Kuhlman P. Self-efficacy: the third factor besides attitude and subjective norm as a predictor of behavior intention. Health Educ Res 1988;3:273–82.
9. Kok G, De Vries H, Mudde AN, et al. Planned health education and the role of self-efficacy: Dutch research. Health Educ Res 1991;6:231–38.
10. Bandura A. Social foundations of thought and action. Englewood Cliffs, NJ: Prentice-Hall, 1986.
11. Strecher VJ, DeVellis BM, Becker MH, et al. The role of self-efficacy in achieving health behavior change. Health Educ Q 1986;13:73–91.

12. Janz NK, Becker MH. The Health Belief Model; a decade later. Health Educ Q 1984;11:1–47.
13. Schaalma H, Kok G, Peters L. Determinants of consistent condom use by adolescents: the impact of experience of sexual intercourse. Health Educ Res 1993;8:255–69.
14. Prochaska JO, DiClemente CC. The transtheoretical approach: crossing traditional boundaries of therapy. Homewood, IL: Dow Jones-Irwin, 1984.
15. McGuire WJ. Attitudes and attitude change. In: Lindsay M, Aronson E, editors. The handbook of social psychology. Vol. 2. New York: Random House, 1985:233–346.
16. Eagly A, Chaiken S. The social psychology of attitudes. Fort Worth, TX: Harcourt Brace Jovanovich, 1993.
17. Skinner CS, Strecher VJ, Hospers HJ. Physician recommendations for mammography: do tailored messages make a difference? Am J Publ Health 1994;84:43–49.
18. Weary G, Stanley MA, Harvey JH. Attribution. New York: Springer, 1989.
19. Den Boer D-J, Kok G, Hospers HJ, et al. Health education strategies for attributional retraining and self-efficacy improvement. Health Educ Res 1991;6:239–48.
20. Weiner B. An attributional theory of motivation and emotion. New York: Springer, 1986.
21. Hospers HJ, Kok G, Strecher VJ. Attributions for previous failures and subsequent outcomes in a weight reduction program. Health Educ Q 1990;17:409–15.
22. Försterling F. Attribution theory in clinical psychology. New York: Wiley, 1988.
23. Marlatt GA, Gordon JR. Relapse prevention; maintenance strategies in the treatment of addictive behaviors. New York: Guilford, 1985.
24. Orlandi MA, Landers C, Weston R, et al. Diffusion of health promotion innovations. In: Glanz K, Lewis FM, Rimer BK, editors. Health behavior and health education; theory, research and practice. San Francisco, CA: Jossey-Bass, 1990:288–313.
25. Rogers E. Diffusion of innovations. New York: The Free Press, 1983.
26. Parcel GS, Erikson MP, Lovato CY, et al. The diffusion of school-based tobacco-use prevention programs; project description and baseline data. Health Educ Res 1989;4:111–24.

Chapter 14

Modification of Health Behavior and Lifestyle Mediated by Physicians

Brian Oldenburg
Queensland University of Technology

Peita Graham-Clarke
University of Sydney

John Shaw
Merck, Sharpe and Dohme

Sheila Walker
National Heart Foundation of Australia (NSW Division)

The practice of clinical and preventive medicine is changing rapidly around the world. Although research leading to the development of new diagnostic techniques and drug treatments has always been part of the experience of physicians, changes within the health care system, and the impact of even broader political and economic changes on this system, will have even more profound effects on the practice of medicine over the next 25 years. The challenge to provide effective and affordable solutions to providing accessible and equitable health care has stimulated great interest in the contribution that can be made by public health and preventive medicine initiatives becoming more integral to the mainstream health care system.

The World Health Organization (WHO) strategy of "Health for All" by the Year 2000 (1) identifies four key goals for the health care systems of all countries: (a) the promotion and facilitation of healthy lifestyles; (b) a reduction in the burden of preventable ill health; (c) the reorientation of health care toward prevention, coupled with appropriate effective care of the sick and disabled; and (d) a health care system that is accessible, equitable, and economically sustainable. To achieve these goals, which have already been incorporated into the health policies of a number of developed countries, primary health care workers, and in particular primary care physicians, will be required to play a more prominent role in helping to prevent disease and promote better health among their patients and the public more generally.

The potential benefits of widespread physician involvement in preventive activities have been argued in the light of supportive evidence, and often assumed evidence, of the efficacy and effectiveness of physician-based interventions. This chapter reviews the current practice of primary care physicians with respect to the prevention of cardiovascular disease (CVD) in developed countries. It is argued here that positively influencing the attitudes, knowledge, and skills of physicians is not enough to improve the current practice of preventive care. Although the physician's office is an ideal and appropriate setting for primary preventive care, the effectiveness of these activities is ultimately dependent on the development and evaluation of effective programs, as well as the institutionalizing of structural supports for their implementation and continued use by physicians.

THE ROLE OF PHYSICIANS IN HEALTH PROMOTION AND DISEASE PREVENTION

Primary care physicians (family physicians or general practitioners) are in a unique position to contribute to disease prevention and facilitate health promotion. In Canada and the United States, over 70% of the adult population reportedly visit their primary care physician for an annual checkup (2). Similarly, studies suggest that over 80% of the Australian population visit a physician at least once in a 12-month period (3). This level of contact is not achieved by any other group of health professionals. Frequent and repeated contact provides a tremendous opportunity for disease-prevention and health-promotion efforts. Indeed, in some developed countries, such as the United States (4), the periodic health examination is already an integral part of clinical practice.

In most developed countries, members of the public have their first point of contact with the health care system with primary care physicians, who are often responsible for providing ongoing care. In the primary care office setting, both the roles and expectations of the physician and patient are conducive to health promotion, and there is the potential to integrate curative, preventive, and health-promotion services (5). Physicians are perceived by the general public as the most reliable and credible source of information on health and advice (6, 7). Patients usually want to receive as much information as possible from their physician (8, 9), and do not wish to attend special programs for help in altering lifestyle behaviors related to smoking and diet (10, 11); health professionals in the mainstream health system are seen as part of the natural environment. Moreover, there is the opportunity to adopt a whole-person approach to care, rather than the disease focus that occurs in most medical specialties. However, although some of the prevention options available to physicians require clinical skills that are already familiar to them, such as screening (or case finding), other options include counseling and education, which require skills that are not necessarily integral to the training of the majority of physicians.

The United Kingdom report, *The Nation's Health: A Strategy for the 1990s* (12), identified 11 public health priorities where the evidence for the effectiveness and support for action was strong. For at least nine of these (tobacco, diet, alcohol, physical activity, sexuality, maternity services, early cancer detection, blood pressure, and immunization), there is a clear and well-defined role for primary care doctors to play. The U.S. *Guide to Clinical Preventive Services* (4) offered a comprehensive assessment of 169 interventions for the prevention of 60 target conditions that can also be appropriately targeted in the primary care setting.

Those physicians who adopt the clinical or "high-risk" approach to prevention tend to concentrate their attention on "the conspicuous segment of disease and risk, seeking to understand and control it as though it were the whole of the problem and failing to recognize its integral links with the state of the population in general" (13, p. 14). It is important to note that the majority of events and deaths due to CVD occur in those with only a moderate elevation of risk (13, p. 14). However, a population strategy aims to promote health and reduce risk among the entire population. As Rose concluded in his recent discussion of the high-risk and population approaches, "preventive medicine must embrace both (perspectives), but, of the two, power resides with the population strategy" (13).

Those health behaviors or components of lifestyle for which evidence is most compelling regarding their importance in the pathogenesis, continuation, and progress of CVD include smoking, dietary behaviors, physical inactivity, poor treatment compliance, some personality and emotional factors, and poor quality relationships and social supports (14). Not only is there substantial epidemiological evidence of an association between such behavioral and lifestyle factors and disease and ill health, but there is also steadily mounting evidence concerning the myriad of social, cultural, and attitudinal factors that are, in turn, determinants of these (14, 15).

Although these lifestyle behaviors, and the determinants of these, are amenable to change, it has only been in the past 20 years that change strategies have been systematically applied to and used to influence such behaviors at individual, group, and community-wide levels. Many developed countries have experienced substantial reductions in death rates due to coronary heart disease (CHD) over the past 30 years. These reductions have occurred in response to both primary preventive efforts and improved pharmacological and other therapies. Manson, Tosteson, Ridker, et al. (16) identified and summarized the extent to which currently available strategies are effective in modifying risk factors for CVD. Based on the best available evidence derived from randomized trials and observational studies, they rated the following: the efficacy of lifestyle change strategies to promote smoking cessation and enhance physical activity as *fair*, a combination of drug and diet therapy for elevated serum cholesterol as *fair to good*, drug treatment of hypertension as *good*, and maintenance of ideal body weight as *poor*. These data are in addition to the many hundreds of controlled intervention studies conducted in a variety of research, clinical, and community settings that have examined the effectiveness of nonmedical interventions in positively influencing health behavior endpoints such as smoking, diet, and physical inactivity. These interventions have included community-wide strategies, programs targeting individuals or groups of individuals in a variety of community settings such as schools and the workplace, and programs that have targeted individuals in clinical settings such as hospitals, community centers, and doctors' offices.

CURRENT PRACTICES AND ATTITUDES OF PHYSICIANS IN CARDIOVASCULAR DISEASE PREVENTION

A number of trends are occurring in developed countries around the world with respect to facilitating physicians' uptake of preventive medicine practices, although it should also be recognized that the pace of change varies markedly among different countries—even among those countries in the European Community (EC). There is increased public awareness of and interest in health behaviors and, more generally, health promotion. As discussed in the previous section, there is increasing evidence regarding the effectiveness of strategies for modifying lifestyle-related risk factors, although, as is discussed later, this evidence is derived mainly from research in nonphysician-based settings. Finally, there are recommendations for the practice of preventive medicine beginning to emerge from a number of expert panels.

Although the majority of family physicians in developed countries like Australia, the United States, and Canada agree that prevention of CVD should be part of their everyday practice, most surveys indicate that, other than screening for hypertension, few actually practice preventive medicine in a planned and coordinated fashion (17–20). For diet and other health behaviors, these surveys demonstrate that knowledge levels are improving, beliefs and attitudes are shifting in the appropriate direction, and that physicians in North America, at least, are becoming more likely to initiate interventions for nutrition, smoking, and, certainly, hypertension. Moreover, the fact that there are more physicians who are engaging in early detection provides at least some evidence that there is an increase in the proportion who are attempting to offer counseling and education directed at prevention.

But lifestyle factors such as smoking are still, in the main, only detected, examined, and acted on in patients who have already developed symptoms or a chronic disease (21). For example, a recent national survey carried out in Australia with over 600 randomly selected primary care physicians (22) indicated that over 80% of the sample believed that their role should include screening for CVD risk factors among all their patients, and giving lifestyle recommendations to their patients. Yet the latter activity was primarily carried out with those patients who were at high risk and motivated to change. Nevertheless, among Australian physicians at least, there has been a significant increase in physicians' confidence with respect to lifestyle change in their patients: from only one third of a sample of physicians in 1983 to over two thirds in this recent survey.

In summary, most doctors undoubtedly remain primarily disease oriented, and they see responding to the immediate "symptomatic" needs of their patients as their major responsibility. Other doctors simply believe that, regardless of any preventive role they might wish to fulfill, they do not have sufficient time, adequate skills, or economic incentives to provide such services.

A recently reported survey of 400 primary care physicians in Missouri, of whom 74% responded, collected information concerning their CVD-control efforts (23). Over 80% of the physicians ranked cigarette smoking and hypertension as having a "large effect" on CVD, with diabetes, a high-fat diet, overweight, and elevated blood cholesterol all being ranked in the same way by over 50% of the physicians. Sedentary lifestyle was ranked as important by only one quarter of the physicians. The most frequently performed CVD-prevention activities were blood pressure screening, general physical examinations, and tobacco education, respectively. Virtually all of these physicians reported knowing their own "usual" blood pressure, almost half reported a predominantly sedentary lifestyle, and, although one third was former smokers, less than 10% reported being current smokers.

In a review of studies on nutrition in primary medical care, Glanz and Gilroy (24) reported that those physicians who were more likely to engage in nutritional counseling believed in the efficacy of diet and dietary counseling, and had confidence in their ability to effectively change their patients' eating patterns. They found substantial variations in the screening, treatment, and management of patients with blood lipid abnormalities. Moreover, they found that there was substantial variation between guidelines for clinical management of elevated cholesterol and the actual practices of physicians. Furthermore, the studies did not show improvements in practice over time, and specific training in screening and detection did not lead to modification of medical practice in regard to recognition or management of nutritional problems.

Studies that have investigated the risk factors and health behaviors of physicians (25, 26) have generally found low rates of smoking, relative to the general population, as well as better adherence to guidelines for preventive care among those who have a healthier personal diet and weight within an acceptable range (27–29).

BARRIERS TO PREVENTIVE MEDICINE IN CLINICAL PRACTICE: ATTITUDES, KNOWLEDGE, AND SKILLS

Although a recent survey of primary care physicians in North Carolina indicated that over 95% agreed that physicians should assist asymptomatic patients in reducing behavioral risk factors (30), a range of important barriers to CVD-prevention activities were identified, including lack of time for counseling and inadequate reimbursement.

There is a complex array of factors that determine whether physicians become actively engaged in screening for risk factors and initiating lifestyle change programs, as well as the quality of such activities and the maintenance of them in the long term. The barriers to health promotion and preventive medicine in general practice have been the subject of a considerable amount of research and discussion, and they can be categorized as either *constraints* that relate to practitioners' attitudes, knowledge, and skills, or *structural barriers* (31–34). A recent review (35) concluded that most preventive strategies in primary care were based on merely "giving advice." The authors cautioned that this had the potential to alienate some patients who had sought medical advice for an unrelated reason, and that this might undermine the patient–doctor relationship. It is important to consider the availability of efficacious and feasible interventions, and the acceptability of these to patients. However, both of these points are discussed in more detail in subsequent sections.

A variety of structural (or environmental) factors can influence the practice of preventive care. In those countries where physicians are reimbursed according to fee for service, procedural medicine and specialized services are often financially more rewarding. Medical students in most countries receive minimal training in preventive medicine; they do not get the opportunity to observe medical practices that are set up for this activity. In most developed countries still, doctors do not see an acknowledged and well-accepted role for preventive medicine (36). Physician practices are generally not set up to facilitate the practice of preventive medicine along with other, more traditional medical interventions.

Many of the barriers that impede the conduct of preventive medicine arise from the attitudes and beliefs of physicians, and these need to be considered, as do physicians' actual levels of knowledge and skills. As is clear from some of the survey research discussed in the previous section, there is tremendous variability in the knowledge levels, attitudes toward prevention, and skill levels of physicians. There are some generalized beliefs held by some physicians that can be a major impediment to the effective conduct of preventive medicine and lifestyle change programs. These include the view that encouraging lifestyle change is an invasion of privacy, represents solicitation of additional services, and is unrewarding (36). Related to the latter attitude is the perception that the rewards derived from achieving larger effects with a relatively small number of individuals is more desirable than achieving much smaller amounts of change with larger numbers of individuals. Doctors' expectations of success for lifestyle change programs, in particular, are often based more on their experience of treatments for acute medical problems, rather than on a more realistic view of what is possible to achieve with most patients. As Chapman recently suggested (37), in relation to minimal intervention smoking-cessation programs, few doctors would continue to prescribe a drug that "failed" 95% of the time. He stressed the importance of doctors not working in isolation, but rather working in ways consistent with secular trends in the wider community and changing public policy.

Although some of the preventive options available to physicians require clinical skills that are already familiar to them, such as screening (or case finding), many others involve counseling and education, which require skills that are not integral to their training. As a consequence of inadequate training at both undergraduate and postgraduate levels, they lack the skills and confidence required to implement lifestyle change strategies appropriately. In any case, as pointed out by Hart (38), prevention is seen by many doctors as an essentially "administrative task" that does not require any specific clinical skills and that, furthermore, if practiced would interfere with the treatment of symptomatic disease.

These many barriers influence physicians' management of risk factors in a variety of ways, particularly when examined in the light of patients' views about the role of their doctor. For example, detection and treatment of high blood pressure is well accepted by both physicians and patients in most industrialized countries. Counseling with regard to smoking cessation is becoming a well-accepted activity for physicians in a number of countries, particularly in North America and Australia, but is probably less well accepted by some patients. Cholesterol and lipid lowering by dietary approaches, in particular, is a confused area for patients and physicians alike because of the previous emphasis on dietary cholesterol and data on all cause mortality following lipid-lowering treatment. Additionally, in the absence of conclusive trial data on the benefits of cholesterol reduction, both doctors and patients have a degree of skepticism.

It should be clear from the discussion so far that, although the case for doctors in primary health care becoming more involved in the prevention of CVD is strong, surveys of current practice and the many barriers that exist demonstrate that this is a particularly difficult challenge, and much progress is still to be made. It is important to identify what might be possible in the setting of primary care, and then to identify how better programs can be developed, implemented, and disseminated in a way that maximizes their impact and effectiveness. This area of preventive and behavioral medicine poses a great challenge and opportunity to physicians and other health professionals who are involved in the delivery of services within primary health settings.

BEHAVIOR CHANGE IN THE CLINICAL SETTING

Over the past 20 years, much has been learned about the steps involved in lifestyle change and how best to apply these to preventive programs being carried out in clinical settings (39). A key challenge has been to develop and implement programs that are sufficiently intensive, but have sufficient program reach to impact on large sections of the community through a variety of settings (39). For behavioral researchers and psychologists who, in the past, have focused their endeavors on the development of maximally intensive, efficacious interventions, which maximize change within the individual, this has not been an easy task.

Implicit in this redefining of the nature of lifestyle change is a shift away from viewing lifestyle change from a purely clinical, or "high-risk," perspective toward that of a more population-based approach.

This is a more difficult challenge when examined in the light of the substantial amount of evidence indicating that health behaviors, such as those related to smoking, diet, and physical activity, are resistant to long-term modification. Even where clinicians are able to initiate a lifestyle change program, failure by patients to adhere is a major problem that often impedes a successful outcome (40–42). Most reviews of the field have found that at least one third of all patients fail to comply with any recommended regimen (43–45). Where the recommendations relate to changing lifestyle, such as exercise, dietary change programs, and smoking, the rates are even higher, where poor maintenance and relapse in the longer term are very common (46–47).

Glanz, Lewis, and Rimer (48) stressed the importance of using theories and models to help explain the determinants of behavior, as well as how to develop more effective ways to influence behavior. However, it is becoming increasingly clear that a variety of theories and models are needed to understand the development and modification of complex behaviors. Moreover, it is likely that the relevance and implications of these need to be considered in relation to the different stages involved in the lifestyle change process and individuals' readiness to change. Such a "stages of change" framework is important with respect to the development and implementation of effective lifestyle change programs in clinical settings such as primary care.

THE STAGES OF CHANGE FRAMEWORK

The idea that lifestyle change occurs in a number of steps is not new. Horn and Waingrown (49) and Cashdan (50), among others, discussed this many years ago. However, perhaps more than any other researchers, the work of Prochaska and DiClemente (51, 52) formally identified the dynamics and structure of change that underlie both self-mediated and clinically facilitated lifestyle change. Alternate versions of their staged model have been proposed by Beitman (53), Brownell, Marlatt, Lichtenstein, et al. (54), Dryden (55), and Marlatt and Gordon (56).

Prochaska and DiClemente (51, 52) identified five overlapping and interactive stages that an individual moves through when initiating an attempt to modify some aspect(s) of his or her lifestyle:

1. Precontemplation stage. At this point, lifestyle issues are not high on an individual's "personal agenda," and he or she is not considering the benefits of lifestyle change. A precontemplator is not convinced that the negative aspects of a health behavior outweigh the positive. Moving ahead to the next stage

appears to be dependent on three factors: taking "ownership" of the problem, increasing awareness of the negative aspects of the problem, and accurately evaluating one's ability and capacity to change.

2. Contemplation stage. At this point, an individual begins to consider the benefits of lifestyle change, and maybe even intends to take some action to change, but he or she has not yet acted on this intention. A contemplator is evaluating options.

3. Preparation stage. An individual in this stage is ready to change and is keen to take action, thus needs to set goals and priorities.

4. Action stage. During this stage, the person begins to engage in active attempt(s) to change or modify some aspect of his or her life. An action individual requires the skills to use the key strategies to change habitual patterns of behavior and adopt a healthier lifestyle.

5. Maintenance stage. If an individual makes it to this stage, he or she has done so by continuing to actively make changes to his or her lifestyle. However, during this ongoing maintenance phase, the individual often experiences one or more episodes of relapse. Relapse is the norm in most lifestyle change attempts.

Using this framework, the challenge for physicians in primary health settings is to assist the progress of their patients through the "stages of change," and to use strategies and techniques that take account of both the needs of patients and their readiness to change. For those who are not ready to change, the goal of intervention is then to increase patients' motivation to make a change attempt. Glanz (57) discussed the three major types of strategies that are appropriate for use in clinical settings: instructional, motivational, and behavioral. The use of these different strategies is not mutually exclusive; in very structured lifestyle change programs, at least, use of all strategies has been associated with greater lifestyle change. How this might best be achieved by the application of increasingly well-accepted lifestyle change principles is outlined in the remainder of this section.

Brownell et al. (54) suggested that long-term lifestyle change involves three basic stages. Stage 1 involves motivating, preparing, and advising the patient to change (the Preparation stage). Stage 2 (the Action stage) involves the initial lifestyle change efforts. Stage 3 (the Maintenance stage) is characterized by attempts to help the patient consolidate initial changes and build on these in the longer term. In a project currently being carried out in Australia (58, 59), a cardiovascular risk-reduction program delivered by general practitioners and directed at smoking cessation, dietary change, and moderate increases in levels of physical activity has been developed according to these three stages. Some of the goals, tasks, and strategies that have been incorporated into this program are outlined next. Most of the strategies incorporated in this program were evaluated and shown to work in a variety of research, clinical, and other settings.

The Preparation Stage

Although there is no completely validated model of the factors that influence behavior, and more particularly lifestyle change, the health belief model, as originally proposed by Rosenstock and modified by Becker and Maiman (60), provides a useful framework for considering how to initiate the change process with patients. Doctors are often able to influence the decision-making process and help individuals weigh up the pros and cons of making significant lifestyle changes. The importance of exploring with patients the benefits and costs associated with lifestyle change has been discussed by a number of authors, in particular, Ockene, Sorensen, Kabat-Zinn, et al. (61).

A person's motivation to change is also influenced by what Becker and Maiman (60) called "cues to action." These can be many and varied, but include other concurrent symptoms the patient may have, illness in other family members or friends, information being disseminated through the media, social influences, and so on. Again, physicians are often able to use these "cues to action" to influence patients to consider their health and how their risk of CVD may be reduced by a lifestyle change such as quitting smoking. Of course, doctors often have contact with individuals during times when they are most amenable to shifting from the Precontemplation stage to the Contemplation stage, and also from the Contemplation stage to the Action stage.

Of course, there are many factors that impact on the lifestyle change process and an individual's preparedness and commitment to change. Consequently, there are many different theories and models that can be usefully applied to this and subsequent stages of the lifestyle change process (48). The family, work, and social environments are all critical to the lifestyle change process—not just simply as "cues for action," but in a much more general way. Given that these are the contexts in which behavior occurs, it is hardly surprising that the complex interrelationships between a person's behavior and his or her social environment can act as both enhancers and impediments to changing lifestyle. Social learning theory, as articulated by Bandura (62), attempts to characterize these interactions. Within this model, behavior is assumed to be influenced not only by the consequences of behavior, as these are interpreted by the individual, but also by our "expectancies." The latter are influenced, in turn, by our beliefs about the relationship between our behavior and the environment, our beliefs about how our actions affect particular outcomes, and whether we believe we are competent to perform the behavior required to achieve a given outcome. Bandura labeled this latter construct as an individual's *self-efficacy*.

Strategies that are directed at increasing a person's level of motivation and self-efficacy are very important, yet physicians often assume that providing information by itself will be a sufficient inducement to change. Nevertheless, helping the person understand the importance of lifestyle change by providing high-quality educational materials, encouraging patients to monitor their lifestyle or part of it so they gain a greater understanding of the lifestyle issues to be addressed, and identifying barriers and enhancers to change are all strategies that can increase the likelihood that an individual will move from Precontemplation to Contemplation.

In summary, the strategies that can be most usefully applied during this stage include:

- Assess risk factors for CVD and the lifestyle, and other determinants of these.
- Provide personalized feedback to the patient.
- Improve patient knowledge and understanding.
- Identify and deal with barriers to change.
- Work with patient to develop a plan for change.
- Involve other family and social supports where possible.

The Action Stage

The challenge in the Action stage of any lifestyle change program is to provide patients with the skills and resources that they require to initiate changes and maintain and build on these in the longer term. Perceived ability to change, or self-efficacy, has been shown to be a good predictor of achieving success in many different lifestyle areas, including smoking cessation, weight control, and becoming physically active (63). Once an individual is keen and committed to move into the Action stage, there is a variety of strategies that have been shown to be effective in helping people achieve significant lifestyle change. Examples of some of the different types of self-management strategies include setting goals, modifying the environment, changing the consequences of behavior, and developing a new and healthier lifestyle. These are discussed in detail in a number of other publications (64, 65).

This approach to lifestyle change is very broad and, if implemented appropriately, will inevitably incorporate elements of many different models, including Social Learning Theory, Health Belief Model, and health education theory. People often embark on a lifestyle change program for idiosyncratic reasons, and with these can go an almost limitless range of unrealistic or irrational beliefs. These can include unrealistic beliefs about how quickly success is likely to occur, and that any setback will inevitably lead to total program failure.

There is an increasing number of valuable printed and audiovisual programs, usually available at a nominal cost from public sector and other health agencies in many developed countries. Although some individuals can follow through self-instructional programs on smoking and other health behaviors by themselves, most will also benefit from some additional support and attention to a number of the points being highlighted here, for each of the three stages of the lifestyle change process.

The Maintenance Stage

Long-term maintenance is the most difficult and often the most neglected aspect of lifestyle change programs. Although many lifestyle intervention studies have shown short-term changes, relapse is a major problem in most areas of lifestyle change. A number of years ago, Farquhar (66) suggested that maintenance of lifestyle change involves, at least in part, the ongoing use of the same motivation-enhancing and behavioral self-management strategies that are used during the Preparation and Action stages.

The work of Marlatt and Gordon (56) demonstrated that the downward spiral into relapse and eventual program failure often follows a minor "slip" or relapse episode. Following on from their research, Marlatt and Gordon developed a method of promoting maintenance called *relapse-prevention training*. As part of this approach, individuals are taught to distinguish between a slip and a relapse. They are also taught to preempt such slips, and to develop coping and other strategies for dealing with these before they arise. Indeed, such strategies can be built into the Action stage of the program.

Long-term maintenance is probably also assisted by use of the following three strategies identified by Brownell et al. (54). The first of these involves ongoing contact with a health professional, but probably at a reduced frequency, over a long period of time for monitoring, feedback, and revision. The second suggestion is that community-based peer-directed or professionally directed support groups can provide continuing opportunities for education and social networking outside of the clinical setting. The third approach involves encouraging patients to take up other programs and make other changes to their lifestyle that will be supportive of a generally healthier lifestyle.

THE EFFICACY AND EFFECTIVENESS OF PHYSICIAN-BASED LIFESTYLE CHANGE INTERVENTIONS

Despite a general consensus in the literature that educational and behavior change strategies can impact on health outcomes by reducing individuals' risk of CVD, it is not entirely clear how effective physicians can be in achieving this end, using the types of strategies just outlined.

Smoking Cessation

Numerous randomized trials have been conducted around the world that have supported the effectiveness of physician-administered smoking-cessation interventions. In fact, the positive results from these trials have provided much of the impetus for physician-based interventions for other health behaviors. A variety of strategies have been tested, including patient education, motivation enhancement, use of nicotine gum and/or nicotine patches, and behavioral interventions. Reported results range from 5% for minimal interventions, including brief advice (67), to 36% for structured, intensive, behavioral counseling and follow-up (68).

Exactly what constitutes the most effective physician-based method (in terms of maximum cessation rate, physician uptake rate, compliance, dropout, and recidivism) is difficult to determine, given the many differences between the studies. Reviews of the literature suggest that brief advice provided by physician is more favorable (in terms of cessation rates) than no advice. In addition, the more time spent by the physician and the greater the intensity of the program, the higher the cessation rate. Additional materials—such as nicotine chewing gum and self-help booklets for patients—and follow-up visits also improved the outcome measure. Multiple intervention modalities to deliver individual advice on multiple occasions, along with other measures that improve patients' motivation such as personalizing the risk, also appear to enhance successful outcome (69–73).

As outlined by Ockene (71), the physician's role with smokers, at the very least, is to educate them about their risk for heart disease and then advise them of the need to stop smoking. Physicians who then wish to go the next step are able to help patients plan an approach to quitting smoking. Interventions can be relatively brief, using available and effective self-help materials now available in most countries through nongovernment organizations involved in the prevention of heart disease and cancer (74).

Managing Hypertension

Treatment of hypertension is chiefly carried out by physicians using pharmacological interventions, yet there remains doubt as to whether this is the most effective or most desirable treatment for all patients. Nonpharmacological approaches or lifestyle modifications for hypertension include weight reduction, increased physical activity, and dietary interventions (moderation of sodium and alcohol intake). Lifestyle change has generally been used as an adjunctive therapy for hypertension. However, in terms of primary prevention, lifestyle change can obviously be of benefit, and lifestyle factors have been used as the basis for the development of nonpharmacological intervention strategies in the prevention of high blood pressure (75). Other preventive strategies that have been suggested for hypertension control, but for which there is limited supportive evidence, include stress management, calcium and magnesium supplements, fish oils, fiber, and alterations in macronutrient consumption (76).

In terms of secondary prevention in those who already have elevated blood pressure, lifestyle change has not been conclusively shown to reduce morbidity and mortality; however, it may reduce the amount of medication required (77) and improve the effectiveness of pharmacological therapy. There is obviously also a role for behavior change strategies in helping patients on pharmacological therapy to enhance their degree of compliance.

Excess body weight is closely correlated with increased blood pressure. In patients who are more than 10% above their ideal weight, weight reduction has been shown to reduce blood pressure (78). Weight reduction in overweight, hypertensive patients also enhances the blood pressure-lowering effects of anti-hypertensive medications, and can significantly reduce other heart disease risk factors.

Exercise is a potentially effective means of reducing blood pressure, but has received less attention than other nondrug methods, such as weight reduction and restriction of alcohol and sodium. Sedentary and unfit normotensive individuals have a 20%–50% increased risk of developing hypertension compared with their more active peers (79). Regular aerobic activity can reduce systolic blood pressure in hypertensive patients by approximately 10 mm Hg (80). Significant reductions in blood pressure have also been observed with only modest increases in physical activity.

The other dietary modifications that have been studied in relation to hypertension are moderation of dietary sodium intake and alcohol consumption. Epidemiological observations and clinical trials support an association between sodium intake and blood pressure. Populations with a low average sodium intake also have a low average blood pressure (81). There have been a number of trials that support a reduction in blood pressure in response to modification of sodium intake. A recent review of trials of sodium reduction and blood pressure showed that moderate sodium restriction in hypertensive individuals can lead to significant reductions in both systolic and diastolic blood pressure in the short term (82). The impact of sodium modification on blood pressure may vary between individuals (e.g., patients with hypertension are more sensitive to changes in dietary sodium than patients without hypertension) (83). Excessive alcohol intake can raise blood pressure and cause resistance to antihypertensive therapy (84).

Increasing Physical Activity

The evidence concerning the effectiveness of counseling to increase exercise and health outcomes related to this has many limitations and shortcomings. Most of the research has been conducted in specific settings with select populations, and has focused on the evaluation of only short-term outcomes such as compliance with exercise recommendations. The generalizability of these findings to the general population is largely unknown.

Few studies have evaluated the effectiveness of physical activity counseling by primary care physicians. Limited support for the effectiveness of primary care physicians in activity counseling has been gathered from studies that have involved only one physician and one patient population (85). For example, Mulder found that a family practice physician was effective in helping patients initiate and sustain an exercise program (86). More recently, however, Lewis and Lynch (87) formally evaluated the effectiveness of brief, exercise advice giving by 24 family medicine residents from one medical center. The investigators reported that, although physicians in the control group were likely to give exercise advice to their patients, physicians in the intervention group gave twice as much advice. After 1 month, patients given exercise advice reported significant increases in exercise duration, but no change in frequency.

The impact of a physician-based counseling intervention as part of a multiple risk-factor program was examined as part of the Insure Project on Lifecycle Preventive Health Services. The investigators reported that the intervention had a positive impact on both physicians and patients, although the results were not significant. Data from the Insure project indicated that 35.9% of patients at one of the intervention clinics began a regular physical activity program, whereas only 28.2% of patients from the control clinic had done so (88).

Many health-related benefits can be associated with physical activity; these include decreased CVD risk and improvements on virtually all risk factors. The optimal amount of exercise required to achieve such benefits is not certain, but the benefits are likely to be attainable with more modest increases in physical activity than was believed even 5 or 10 years ago. Physicians can play an important role in encouraging patients to increase their level of physical activity by providing, where necessary, a medical clearance, and then counseling them on how to establish and maintain an exercise program. Regular, rather than occasional and vigorous, activities should be encouraged, building these into established daily routines.

Reducing Weight and Lowering Lipids

Physicians have an important role to play in screening and managing lipid abnormalities and weight problems. Over the past 10 years, there has been an increase in consensus and policy recommendations regarding the benefits of healthy eating patterns (89, 90). Currently, in the United States at least, there is a recommendation that places nutrition education in all routine health care contacts (4). However, at this stage, there is a paucity of intervention trials examining the effectiveness of physician-based nutrition programs. A recent report (91) showed that an intensive dietary advice program to lower saturated fat intake with physicians and dietitian support produced a 5% fall in total cholesterol. This reflects what is probably achievable by physicians in primary care settings.

The U.S. National Cholesterol Education Program guidelines (92) provide a sound basis on which to provide nutritional interventions in primary care. These guidelines incorporate a thorough patient assessment, treatment, monitoring, and follow-up. Glanz (93) discussed four models of patient nutrition counseling:

(a) brief physician advice, (b) brief individual physician counseling, (c) brief counseling with referral for comprehensive individual counseling, and (d) brief counseling with referral for group education, either one session or long term. In addition to outlining what each of these approaches entails, Glanz identified a number of other issues that need to be addressed by physicians, including the importance of collaborating with other health professionals—in particular, dietitians—and the use of appropriate office systems. The latter is discussed in more detail in a later section.

Multiple Risk-Factor Intervention

Multiple risk-factor interventions for prevention and reduction of risk factors for CVD have been studied over the past two decades. The rationale is based on the multiplicative nature of heart disease risk factors, the fact that risk factors generally occur in groups, and the assumption that success in reducing one risk factor will assist success with other risk factors (13). The results from multiple risk-factor interventions, to date, have been inconclusive.

Although there have been a number of community-based trials where physicians have been important providers of care, it is difficult to ascertain the specific contribution made by physicians. The Insure Project on Lifecycle Preventive Health Services is an example of physician involvement in a community-based trial. The project was a 3-year feasibility study involving the planning, implementing, and evaluation of preventive health services in primary medical care (94). After 12 months, those patients in the intervention group were more likely to report positive changes, including increase in physical activity, weight loss, and decreased alcohol consumption, with no significant difference in smoking-cessation rates. Thus, the authors concluded from their results that risk-factor education and counseling by primary care physicians can improve patients' short-term health-related behavior (95).

The Challenge of Lifestyle Change in Clinical Settings

As this overview of the research demonstrates, there have been relatively few well-conducted efficacy or effectiveness intervention trials of cardiovascular risk reduction in the primary care setting, except in the area of smoking cessation, and many questions remain unanswered. More research is required to more adequately evaluate the efficacy, effectiveness, and efficiency of physician-based interventions. This inevitably involves developing better dissemination and implementation strategies. Although many of the features of the setting in which physicians work make such a setting a promising arena for health-promotion and lifestyle change programs, a variety of factors acting as barriers to the effective adoption, implementation, and ultimate institutionalization of such programs have also been identified in this chapter. There has been relatively little progress made in most countries in terms of such programs becoming well integrated into "routine" practice. A range of possible strategies is discussed in the next section.

STRATEGIES FOR IMPROVING PHYSICIANS' PREVENTIVE CARE

Many of the barriers to implementing physician-delivered interventions can be overcome, and physicians can acquire the skills necessary for effectively implementing lifestyle change programs. Such interventions can be brief and take no longer than the average length consultation if they are structured and well organized, and if physicians use properly evaluated and professionally developed self-help materials. Research has shown that patients respond positively to such programs (96, 97). The remainder of this section considers some of the recently investigated strategies for overcoming barriers to the conduct of preventive medicine in the physician's office. However, it is only possible to give an overview of the range of possible strategies, which are discussed in more detail elsewhere (98).

Practice-based strategies to encourage the practice of preventive care and improve its effectiveness can be classified according to whether they are "provider oriented," "patient oriented," or "office oriented." Provider-oriented interventions attempt to affect the quantity and quality of preventive care by influencing the provider's knowledge, attitudes, and skills. The most commonly used strategies in this regard have included the use of flowsheets or checklists, reminder notices, chart stickers and alerts, audit with feedback, posters in waiting and examination areas, and specially developed clinician handbooks or manuals.

In addition to the use of program materials, including printed booklets and audiovisual programs, a variety of other specific strategies and materials have been evaluated in clinical settings as a means to motivate patients, encourage their involvement, and promote maintenance of change. These patient-oriented interventions have included patient reminders, minirecord cards, questionnaires and checklists, posters, and other audiovisual materials.

Interventions that build nursing and office staff involvement into the delivery of preventive care have great potential, but have not been subjected, to date, to much research. Certainly, the U.S. Preventive Services Task Force (4) and other recently produced guidelines have emphasized the importance of other health professionals being involved in the provision of preventive care. Nurses, psychologists, nutritionists (or dietitians), and a range of other health professionals have many of the skills that are so important for setting up lifestyle change programs and delivering preventive care to individuals. Moreover, the training that these groups have undergone, particularly in the case of psychologists and nutritionists, has generally placed more emphasis on preventive approaches and the delivery of such programs. However, the structure and practice of primary care varies greatly between countries, and this needs to be taken into account when considering the potential of such approaches and ways to implement programs with other health professionals.

Although there is increasing evidence of the value of these "office-based" strategies, there is little information concerning the extent to which these are actually being used in the "real world." With the increasing consensus regarding preventive care guidelines, it is appropriate that many of these office interventions are actually introduced into practice, and the following principles can be used to guide practice:

1. Primary care professionals should utilize some form of a tracking system, which ideally should be computerized.
2. A variety of interventions should be used to take account of the particular needs of the practice and the characteristics of the patient population. Ease of use and cost of implementation and practice are important issues to consider.
3. Wherever possible, nursing and other staff should be involved, and this should be formalized to become part of routine practice.
4. Strategies and efforts directed at stimulating patient interest and awareness, motivation, and ongoing involvement are vital to the long-term success of physicians' initiatives in this area.

The Report of the U.S. Preventive Services Task Force (4) identified the key strategies that have been demonstrated to enhance the effectiveness of counseling concerning behavioral change:

- Develop a therapeutic alliance
- Counsel all patients
- Ensure that patients understand the relationship between behavior and health
- Help patients assess the barriers to behavior change
- Gain commitment from patients to change
- Involve patients in selecting risk factors to change
- Use a combination of strategies
- Design a behavior modification plan
- Monitor progress through follow-up contact
- Involve office and other health care staff

It is necessary to sound a note of caution regarding guidelines. Not only is it difficult to disseminate them, and achieve widespread uptake and use, but, perhaps even more important, there are some practical and conceptual difficulties with them (99). By reflecting expert opinion, they may formalize unsound practice and risk standardizing practice around the average, which is not necessarily best practice. Moreover, this may stifle innovation and prevent the individualizing of an approach for each particular patient.

As has been raised on a number of occasions throughout this chapter, most physicians are not trained in preventive care. There is a need for the medical curriculum to take this into account. Topics and other preventive medicine skills also need to be addressed in postgraduate degrees and in continuing and professional education of physicians once they are working in the community. It is appropriate to sound a note of caution at this point. In contrast to the small number of efficacy trials that have been conducted with primary care or family physicians, there has been a large number of studies conducted that attempt to formally evaluate many of these strategies. However, the results have not been overwhelmingly impressive, and our ability to identify firm conclusions is constrained by many methodological limitations, which have been discussed by Glanz and Gilboy (24), among others.

Finally, it is important to come back to the perspective of the health care system and consider other possible incentives that can be used to encourage physicians to engage in and practice preventive medicine. Providing physicians with the appropriate skills while they are still medical students is part of this, but there is also the vexed question of how such activities can be paid for, and which is the best and most efficient reimbursement mechanism.

SUMMARY

There are tremendous opportunities for physicians and other health professionals to become much more actively involved in the provision of health-promotion and disease-prevention programs as a normal part of their clinical practice. The efforts of health professionals occur in a community context, where there are many other health-promotion efforts occurring through the workplace, the media, and community settings. At any point in time in the general community, there is tremendous movement through the stages of change, in the areas of smoking, diet, and a variety of other health behaviors, with a small proportion of individuals motivated and attempting to make changes. More often than not, these are self-initiated changes that are prompted by the media, legislative changes, initiatives in the workplace, and so on. Health professionals have an opportunity to promote, prompt, and support the need for these changes occurring in the wider community. Viewed in this community context, enhancing the health of the population obviously does not involve just health professionals; rather, there is a need for a variety of approaches and strategies throughout the whole community to be directed at developing personal skills, creating supportive environments, refocusing health-related services, increasing community involvement and participation, and developing health public policy (100).

REFERENCES

1. World Health Organization. Global strategy for health for all by the year 2000. Geneva: Author, 1981.
2. Wilensky GR, Bernstein A. Contacts with physicians in ambulatory settings: rates of use, expenditures, and source of payments. Washington, DC: U.S. Department of Health and Human Services, 1983.
3. Australian Institute of Health Welfare. Australia's health 1992. Canberra: Australian Government Publishing Service, 1992.
4. Report of the U.S. Preventive Services Task Force: guide to clinical preventive services. An assessment of the effectiveness of 169 interventions. London: Williams & Wilkins, 1989.
5. Stott NCH, Davis RH. The exceptional potential in each primary care consultation. J Royal Coll Gen Practit 1979;29:201–05.
6. Glynn TJ, Manley MW, Cullen JW, et al. Cancer prevention through physician intervention. Semin Oncol 1990;17:391–401.
7. Ford AS, Ford WS. Health education and the primary care physician: the practitioner's perspective. Soc Sci Med 1983;17:1505–12.
8. Waitzkin H. Information giving in medical care. J Health Soc Behav 1985;26:81–101.
9. Faden RR, Becker C, Lewis C, et al. Disclosure of information to patients in medical care. Med Care 1981;19:718–33.
10. Fiore M, Novotny T, Lynn W, et al. Methods used to quit smoking in the United States. Do cessation programs help? JAMA 1990;263:2760–65.
11. Ockene JK. Toward a smoke-free society. Am J Pub Health 1984;74:1198–1200.
12. Jacobson B, Smith A, Whitehead M. The nation's health. A strategy for the 1990s. London: Kings Fund, 1991.
13. Rose G. The strategy of preventive medicine. Oxford: Oxford University Press, 1992.
14. Strecher VJ, De Vellis BE, Becker MH, et al. The role of self-efficacy in achieving health behavior change. Health Educ Q 1986;13:73–91.
15. Gochman DF. Health behavior: emerging research perspectives. New York: Plenum, 1988.
16. Manson JE, Tosteson H, Ridker PM, et al. The primary prevention of myocardial infarction. N Engl J Med 1992;326:1406–16.
17. Wechsler H, Levine S, Idelson R, et al. The physicians role in health promotion—a survey of primary care practitioners. N Engl J Med 1983;308:97–100.
18. Orleans CT, George LK, Houpt J, et al. Health promotion in primary care: a survey of US family practitioners. Prev Med 1985;14:636–47.
19. Sobal J, Valente C, Muncie H, et al. Physicians' beliefs about the importance of 25 health promoting behaviors. Am J Public Health 1985;75:1427–28.
20. Mittlemark M, Luepker R, Grimm R, et al. The role of physicians in a community-wide program for prevention of cardiovascular disease: the Minnesota Heart Health Program. Public Health Rep 1988;103:360–65.
21. Dickinson J. Preventive activities in general practice [dissertation]. Newcastle, Australia: University of Newcastle, 1989.
22. Ruth D, Cockburn S, Farish S, et al. General practitioners' reported practices and beliefs concerning the prevention of cardiovascular disease: findings from a survey of Australian general practitioners. In: Doessel DP, editor. General practice evaluation program: the 1992 work-in-progress conference. Canberra: Australian Government Publishing Service, 1993:419–24.

23. Jorge NE, Brownson RC, Smith CA, et al. Cardiovascular disease control efforts among primary-care physicians—Missouri, 1990. MMWR 1992;41:906–09.
24. Glanz K, Gilroy MB. Physicians, preventive care, and applied nutrition: selected literature. Acad Med 1992;67:776–81.
25. Nutbeam D, Catford JC. Modifiable risk factors for cardiovascular disease among general practitioners in Wales. Public Health 1990;104:353–61.
26. Wells KB, Lewis CE, Leake B, et al. Do physicians preach what they practice? A study of physicians' health habits and counseling practices. JAMA 1984;252:2846–8.
27. Shea S, Gemson DH, Mossel P, et al. Management of high blood cholesterol by primary care physicians: diffusion of the National Cholesterol Education Program Adult Treatment Panel guidelines. J Gen Intern Med 1990;5:327–34.
28. Shea S, Basch CE, Zybert P. Correlates of internists' practices in caring for patients with elevated serum cholesterol. Am J Health Promotion 1990;4:421–28.
29. Price JH, Desmond SM, Krol RA, et al. Family practice physicians' beliefs, attitudes, and practices regarding obesity. Am J Prev Med 1987;3:339–45.
30. Center for Disease Control and Prevention. Counseling practices of primary-care physicians—North Carolina, 1991. MMWR 1992;41:565–68.
31. Freymann JG. Medicine's great schism: prevention versus cure: an historial interpretation. Med Care 1975;13:525–36.
32. Nutting PA. Health promotion in primary medical care: problems and potential. Prev Med 1986;15:537–48.
33. Lurie N, Manning WG, Peterson C, et al. Preventive care: do we practice what we preach? Am J Public Health 1987;77:801–04.
34. Ward JE, Gordon J, Sanson-Fisher RW. Strategies to increase preventive care in general practice. Med J Australia 1991;154:523–31.
35. Rollnick S, Kinnersley P, Stott N. Methods of helping patients with behaviour change. Br Med J 1993;307:188–90.
36. Leeder S, Oldenburg B, Wise M, Hawe P, Nutbeam D. Pathways to better health. (National Health Strategy Issues Paper No. 7). Canberra: Australian Government Publishing Service, 1993.
37. Chapman S. The role of doctors in promoting smoking cessation. Br Med J 1993;307:518–19.
38. Hart JT. Prevention of coronary heart disease in primary care: seven lessons from three decades. Fam Prac 1990;7:288–94.
39. Oldenburg B. Promotion of a healthy lifestyle: integrating the clinical and public health approaches. Int Rev Health Psychol. In press.
40. DiMatteo MR, DiNicola DD. Achieving patient compliance. New York: Pergamon, 1982.
41. Becker MH, Maiman LA. Strategies for enhancing patient compliance. J Comm Health 1980;6:113–35.
42. Becker MH. Patient adherence to prescribed therapies. Med Care 1985;23:539–55.
43. Blackwell B. Patient compliance. N Engl J Med 1973;289:249–53.
44. Davis MS. Physiologic, psychological, and demographic factors in patients' compliance of doctors' orders. Med Care 1968;6:115–22.
45. Stimson GV. Obeying doctors' orders: a view from the other side. Soc Sci Med 1974;8:97–104.
46. Carmody T, Senner J, Malinow M, et al. Physical exercise rehabilitation: long term drop out rate in cardiac patients. J Beh Med 1980;3:163–68.
47. Dunbar J, Stunkard AJ. Adherence to diet and drug regimen. In: Levi R, Rifkind B, Dennis B, et al., editors. Nutrition, lipids and coronary heart disease. New York: Raven Press, 1974:391–423.
48. Glanz K, Lewis FM, Rimer BK, editors. Health behavior and health education: theory, research and practice. San Francisco: Jossey-Bass, 1989.
49. Horn D, Waingrow S. Some dimensions of a model for smoking behavior change. Am J Pub Health 1966;56:21–26.

50. Cashdan S. Interactional psychotherapy: stages and strategies in behavioural change. New York: Grune & Stratton, 1973.

51. Prochaska JO, DiClemente CC. Stages of change and the modification of problem behaviors. In: Hersen M, Eisler RM, Miller PM, editors. Progress in behavior modification. Sycamore, NY: Sycamore Press, 1992:183–218.

52. Prochaska JO, DiClemente CC, Norcross JC. In search of how people change: applications to addictive behaviors. Am Psychol 1992;47:1102–14.

53. Beitman BD. The structure of individual psychotherapy. New York: Guilford, 1986.

54. Brownell KD, Marlatt GA, Lichtenstein ER, et al. Understanding and preventing relapse. Am Psychol 1986;41:765–82.

55. Dryden W. Eclectic psychotherapies: a critique of leading approaches. In: Norcross JC, editor. Handbook of eclectic psychotherapy. New York: Brunner/Mazel, 1986.

56. Marlatt GA, Gordon JR, editors. Relapse prevention: maintenance strategies in the treatment of addictive behaviors. New York: Guilford, 1985.

57. Glanz K. Patient and public education for cholesterol reduction: a review of strategies and issues. Patient Educ Couns 1988;12:235–57.

58. Oldenburg B, Graham-Clarke P, Walker S, et al. CVD risk reduction in general practice. Preliminary research findings. Sydney: National Heart Foundation, 1991.

59. National Heart Foundation. Helping patients to make a fresh start (a manual). Sydney: Author, 1993.

60. Becker MH, Maiman LA. Socio-behavioural determinants of compliance with health and medical care: recommendations. Med Care 1975;13:10–24.

61. Ockene JK, Sorensen G, Kabat-Zinn J, et al. Benefits and costs of lifestyle change to reduce risk of chronic disease. Prev Med 1988;17:224–34.

62. Bandura A. Self efficacy: toward a unifying theory of behavior change. Psychol Rev 1977;84:191–215.

63. Strecher VJ, De Vellis BE, Becker MH, et al. The role of self-efficacy in achieving health behavior change. Health Educ Q 1986;13:73–91.

64. Oldenburg B, Gomel M, Graham-Clarke P. Cardiovascular risk reduction through lifestyle change in clinical settings. Ann Acad Med 1992;21:114–20.

65. Ockene IS, Ockene J. Prevention of coronary heart disease. London: Little, Brown, 1992.

66. Farquhar JW. The American way of life need not be hazardous to your health. New York: Norton, 1978.

67. Russell MA, Stapleton J, Jackson PB, et al. District programme to reduce smoking: effect of clinic supported brief intervention by general practitioner. Br Med J 1987;295:1240–44.

68. Richmond R, Austin A, Webster IW. Three year evaluation of a programme by general practitioners to help patients stop smoking. Br Med J 1986;292:803–06.

69. Richmond R, Heather N. General practitioner interventions for smoking cessation: past results and future prospects. Behav Change 1990;7:110–19.

70. Kottke TE, Battista RN, DeFRiese GH, et al. Attributes of successful smoking cessation interventions in medical practice. A meta-analysis of 39 controlled trials. JAMA 1988;259:2882–89.

71. Ockene JK. Smoking intervention: a behavioral, educational, and pharmacologic perspective. In: Ockene IS, Ockene, J, editors. Prevention of coronary heart disease. London: Little, Brown, 1992:201–30.

72. Fiore MC, Novotny TE, Pierce JP, et al. Methods used to quit smoking in the United States: do cessation programmes help? JAMA 1992;263:2760–65.

73. Ockene JK. Physician-delivered interventions for smoking cessation: strategies for increasing effectiveness. Prev Med 1987;16:723–37.

74. U.S. National Cancer Institute. Manual for physicians. Bethesda, MD: Author, 1989.

75. Trials of Hypertension Prevention Collaborative Research Group. The effects of non-pharmacologic interventions of blood pressure of persons with high normal levels: results of the Trials of Hypertension Prevention, Phase 1. JAMA 1992;267:1213–20.

76. Joint National Committee on Detection, Evaluation, and Treatment of High Blood Pressure. The fifth report of the Joint National Committee on Detection, Evaluation, and Treatment of High Blood Pressure (JNC V). Arch Intern Med 1976;153:154–83.

77. Little P, Girling G, Hasler A, et al. A controlled trial of a low sodium, low fat, high fibre diet in treated hypertensive patients: effect on antihypertensive drug requirement in clinical practice. J Human Hypertens 1991;5:175–81.

78. Schotte DE, Stunkard AJ. The effects of weight reduction on blood pressure in 301 obese patients. Arch Intern Med 1990;150:1701–04.

79. Blair SN, Goodyear NN, Gibbons LW, et al. Physical fitness and incidence of hypertension in healthy normotensive men and women. JAMA 1984;252:487–90.

80. World Hypertension League. Physical exercise in the management of hypertension: a consensus statement by the World Hypertension League. J Hypertens 1991;9:283–87.

81. Intersalt Cooperative Research Group. INTERSALT: an international study of electrolyte excretion and blood pressure: results for 24 hour urinary sodium and potassium excretion. Br Med J 1988;297:319–28.

82. Cutler JA, Follman D, Elliott P, et al. I. An overview of randomised trials of sodium reduction and blood pressure. Hypertens 1992;17 Suppl 1:127–133.

83. Sullivan J. Salt sensitivity: definition, conception, methodology, and long-term issues. Hypertens 1992;17 Suppl 1:161–168.

84. World Hypertension League. Alcohol and hypertension—implications for management: a consensus statement by the World Hypertension League. J Human Hypertens 1991;5:1854–56.

85. Campbell MJ, Browne D, Waters WE. Can general practitioners influence existing exercise habits? Controlled trial. Br Med J 1985;290:1044–46.

86. Mulder JA. Prescription of home exercise therapy for cardiovascular fitness. J Fam Prac 1981;13:345–48.

87. Lewis BS, Lynch WD. The effect of physician advice on exercise behavior. Prev Med 1993;22:110–21.

88. Harris SS, Caspersen CJ, DeFriese GH, et al. Physical activity counselling for healthy adults as a primary preventive intervention in the clinical setting. Report for the U.S. Preventive Services Task Force. JAMA 1989;261:3590–98.

89. National Research Council. National Academy of Sciences. Diet and health: implications for reducing chronic disease risk. Washington, DC: National Academy Press, 1989.

90. Thomas P. Health-care professionals: strategies and actions for implementation. In: Thomas P, editor. Improving America's diet and health: from recommendations to action. Washington, DC: National Academy Press, 1991:168–83.

91. Hunninghake DB, Stein EA, Dujovne CA, et al. The efficacy of intensive dietary therapy alone or combined with lobastatin in outpatients with hypercholesterolemia. N Engl J Med 1993;328:1213–19.

92. National Cholesterol Education Program Expert Panel. Report on detection, evaluation, and treatment of high blood cholesterol in adults. Arch Intern Med 1988;148:36–69.

93. Glanz K. Nutritional intervention: a behavioral and educational perspective. In: Ockene IS, Ockene JK, editors. Prevention of coronary heart disease. Boston: Little, Brown, 1992:231–66.

94. Logsdon DN, Rosen MA, Demak MM. The Insure Project on Lifecycle Preventive Health Services. Public Health Rep 1982;97:308–17.

95. Logsdon DN, Lazaro CM, Meier RV. The feasibility of behavioural risk reduction in primary medical care. Am J Prev Med 1989;5:249–56.

96. Bertakis KD. The communicating of information from physician to patient: a method for increasing patient retention and satisfaction. J Fam Pract 1977;5:217–22.

97. Ockene JK, Kristeller JK, Goldberg R, et al. Increasing the efficacy of physician-delivered smoking interventions: a randomized trial. J Gen Intern Med 1991;6:1–8.

98. Solberg LI, Kottke TE, Brekke ML. The prevention-oriented practice. In: Ockene IS, Ockene J, editors. Prevention of coronary heart disease. London: Little, Brown, 1992:469–92.

99. Delamothe T. Wanted: guidelines that doctors will follow: implementation is the problem. Br Med J 1993;307:218.

100. World Health Organization. The Ottawa Charter for Health Promotion. Health Promotion International, 1986;1(4):iii–v.

Chapter 15

Behavioral Medicine Interventions in Secondary Prevention of Coronary Heart Disease

Gunilla Burell
University Hospital–Uppsala

For people who work in the context of giving patients advice on health and lifestyle, it often comes as a surprise that patients do not do as they are told. Studies show that compliance is often discouragingly low, even to simple medical prescriptions. There is an obvious and straightforward answer to why patients do not apply the wisdom of physician advice to their daily lives—they do not have the necessary behavioral skills. Knowing what is right does not automatically make one do the right thing. Theoretical knowledge has fairly little impact on people's daily behavior. It is a well-known fact, from studies of congruence between attitudes and behavior, that the importance of motivation may be overestimated as an influence on what people actually do. Considering that the changes required in disease prevention are often quite complex when it comes to behavior and lifestyle change, this should not come as a surprise. *Disease prevention* could therefore be defined as a professional activity aimed at initiating and enhancing the development of behavioral skills in patients—skills necessary to preserve and sometimes improve health. *Secondary prevention* can be defined as such an activity aimed at patients with existing documented disease.

For patients with coronary heart disease (CHD), the purpose of secondary prevention is to combine medical, surgical, and behavioral strategies, methods, and techniques to slow down or stop the progression of the disease. By this means, postponement or avoidance of further manifestations of the disease is hopefully achieved. Thus, secondary prevention may prolong or improve positive effects of acute interventions. All secondary preventive interventions should be viewed as active ways to influence and treat the disease.

This chapter focuses on behavioral programs intended to develop and reinforce everyday life skills, such as coping with stress, conflicts, and negative emotions, and improve problem solving related to everyday stress and distress.

TARGET PATIENT POPULATIONS

Every CHD patient for whom risk factors and behaviors that can be influenced are identified should be offered some secondary prevention program. In relation to behavior change programs, the most appropriate selection procedure is to describe the program type to patients, and to accept every patient that expresses a personal interest in the targets of the program. Patients are generally adequate in recognizing the changes they need to make. Design and content must be adapted to the patient's risk profile, age, and gender. For those still employed, an important focus is on skills necessary for the work situation, such as stress management, communication, and problem solving.

TIMING OF SECONDARY PREVENTION PROGRAMS

Secondary prevention may focus on the early phase after a coronary event (re-habilitation) or on long-term restoration and maintenance of function. Thus, for instance, a rehabilitation program may aim to restore physical, psychological, and social functions (e.g., after a myocardial infarction [MI]), whereas the goal of more long-term secondary prevention is to develop behavioral strategies to avoid recurrence. In practice, long-term secondary prevention programs may be appropriately implemented whenever the disease risk has been identified. Therefore, behavioral change programs do not necessarily presuppose that the patient has already suffered an MI or gone through coronary bypass graft surgery (CABG). The principles and methods of behavior change tend to be quite similar regardless of where the patient is in the "disease career"; only the motivation and the need to emphasize immediate coping skills may differ.

PSYCHOLOGICAL RISK FACTORS FOR CORONARY
HEART DISEASE

A number of studies have demonstrated Type A behavior to be a risk factor for CHD (1). This behavior pattern is characterized by impatience, a sense of chronic time urgency, hostile competitiveness, and a proneness toward anger and hostility (2). In 1979, after reviewing existing studies, the Review Panel on Coronary-Prone Behavior and Coronary Heart Disease drew the conclusion that Type A behavior is an independent risk factor of the same magnitude as cigarette smoking, hypertension, and high serum lipid levels (3). Whether this relationship holds in high-risk populations has been debated (4). However, when Type A behavior is modified in CHD patients, the risk of recurrence can be reduced (5, 6). This treatment study also showed "emotional arousability" components of Type A behavior to be related to recurrence after MI (7).

Other factors have been shown to increase disease risk. Booth-Kewley and Friedman (8), in a meta-analysis, synthesized results from a large number of studies on the association between CHD and various personality and psychological factors. The general conclusion was that a number of negative emotions and states are significantly related to increased risk of CHD. Thus, a coronary-prone person is someone with one or more negative emotions: depressed, anxious and worried, aggressively competitive, easily frustrated, angry, and/or hostile. Recently, Frasure-Smith (9) demonstrated that depression entailed a fivefold increase in mortality after MI.

Important research has also been presented on the phenomenon of "vital exhaustion" (10, 11)—a state of extreme and long-term exhaustion or burnout that has often been shown to precede an MI, especially in younger patients. This state of burnout, where bodily functions eventually collapse, could be the consequence of incessant and relentless hard-driving behavior (Type A behavior), especially if coupled with negative emotions such as frustration and isolation.

The importance of social network has been demonstrated by Orth-Gomér (12). Blumenthal et al. (13) at Duke University showed that Type A persons with poor social support had more severe coronary occlusions, compared with Type A persons with good social support. It is conceivable that social and emotional support, to some degree, can be protective against the negative effects of stress and everyday pressures.

The issue here is whether such factors can be the target of secondary prevention programs. Research findings indicate that they do have an impact on recurrence risk, and that they are amenable to change. The most systematic interventions have focused on Type A behavior, and such an approach has been shown to reduce recurrence risk to less than half (5, 6).

EFFECTS OF BEHAVIORAL INTERVENTIONS

Programs that have been described in the research literature have more often included post-MI patients than post-CABG surgery patients. The two most important studies, however, included or focused on surgery patients (5, 6, 14). The behavioral principles that constitute the basis for these programs are the same for patients with different manifestations of CHD. That is, most components of the programs are similar regardless of whether they concern post-MI or post-CABG patients, patients with angina pectoris, or high-risk patients. Improved quality of life, decreased anxiety, and modification of stress behaviors are some well-documented effects. A lifestyle change study by Ornish et al. (14) achieved positive effects on indices of disease such as angina pectoris and coronary stenoses. By reducing Type A behavior, Friedman et al. (6) achieved a significant reduction of cardiovascular mortality and morbidity, compared with patients randomized to a control group treatment. In a randomized study of 49 male post-MI patients, significant reductions of Type A behavior were achieved, and these results were maintained at a 1-year follow-up (15). Patients in Type A treatment groups in this study also showed significantly lower resting heart rate after 1 year of treatment, fewer ventricular extra beats, and fewer cardiovascular events during the total study period (16). In an ongoing randomized study by Burell and collaborators (17), including male and female post-CABG surgery patients, significant differences in survival and cardiovascular events were demonstrated between patients in behavioral group treatment and control patients in routine care. In summary, behavioral programs have been shown to influence quality of life, morbidity, and mortality.

EXAMPLES OF INTERVENTION

The Recurrent Coronary Prevention Project (RCPP)(5, 6) demonstrated significant effects on cardiac morbidity and mortality through behavior modification. The aim of the program was to study whether Type A behavior in post-MI patients could be altered, and thereby if cardiac events could be reduced. Eight hundred and sixty-two male and female post-MI patients under the age of 65 were randomly assigned either to a control section, which received group cardiac counseling, or an experimental section, which received both group cardiac counseling and Type A modification. The cumulative 4.5-year cardiac recurrence rate was 12.9% in the experimental patients who received Type A modification, which was significantly less ($p < .005$) than the recurrence rate of 21.2% observed in the control patients. The outcome was related to a significant decrease in Type A behavior among the experimental patients. Long-term follow-up has shown maintained effects on Type A behavior reduction and decreased recurrence rate (6).

Analysis of patients in the RCPP who had undergone CABG showed that surgery patients who received Type A modification suffered significantly fewer cardiac recurrences than surgery patients in the control condition. The same was evident for patients taking beta-blocking drugs: The combination of drugs and Type A modification was superior to drugs and control group cardiac counseling. These results point to the possibility of obtaining synergistic effects from combined treatments.

In a study by Ornish et al. (The Lifestyle Heart Trial) (14), 48 patients with coronary artery disease (CAD) were randomly assigned to either a lifestyle change program or routine medical care. The lifestyle intervention was a combination of the following: a less than 10% fat vegetarian diet, smoking cessation, physical excercise, stress-management techniques (e.g., relaxation, meditation, stretching), and group discussions. No lipid-lowering drugs were given. The groups met twice a week for 1 year. Patients in lifestyle intervention groups increased time of physical exercise from 11 to 38 minutes a day, and the use of stress-management techniques from 5 to 82 minutes a day. Feelings of meaning and well-being increased significantly in the intervention groups, whereas anger and hostility decreased. A 91% reduction of angina pectoris (AP) was obtained in the experimental groups, whereas the control patients reported a 165% rise in frequency of angina. Quantitative angiography showed a statistically significant difference in coronary stenoses. Patients in group treatment exhibited a decrease from 40.0% to 37.8%, whereas in the control patients there was an increase from 42.7% to 46.1%.

The Lifestyle Heart Trial provided evidence that, at least for some patients with CAD, it may be possible to achieve regression of coronary atherosclerosis by a comprehensive lifestyle and behavior change program, without use of lipid-lowering drugs.

Two studies by Burell investigated the feasibility of a secondary prevention behavioral modification program in affecting Type A behavior (15) and cardiac morbidity and mortality (17). In these studies, no selection of patients was made based on social and educational background, but the study samples were representative of the ordinary hospital CHD population. The main objective of the first study (Heart and Lifestyle) was to develop and evaluate a Type A modification group treatment. Forty-nine male post-MI patients under the age of 65 were randomized to group treatment consisting of either Type A modification or cardiac counseling. The treatment period was 1 year. Main outcome measures were assessments of Type A behavior, psychological well-being and quality of life, blood lipids, and cardiac symptoms and function. The results showed significant group differences in Type A behavior, which were maintained at 1-year follow-up. Changes of Type A behavior were associated with improved cardiac functioning.

In an ongoing study by Burell and collaborators, 261 male and female post-CABG surgery patients were randomly assigned either to a 1-year behavioral group intervention or a routine care-control condition. The intervention included Type A behavior modification; problem solving; and ability to cope with pain, anxiety, and distress. The length of treatment was 1 year, plus follow-up sessions in the second and third years. Treatment content and methods included homework assignments; self-monitoring techniques; behavioral drills; cognitive restructuring; and use of audio, film, and written material. The treatment was administered during the first and second years after CABG surgery. At 5–6.5 years postsurgery, there was a statistically significant difference in total mortality between patients in behavioral groups and control patients, as well as in total cardiovascular events (e.g., cardiac death, MI, reoperation, and angioplasty).

This study is consistent with the RCPP study in showing that survival and cardiac events after CABG surgery can be influenced by a behavioral intervention program aimed to improve stress management and coping in everyday life.

POSSIBLE MECHANISMS

Increased coping ability as a psychological mechanism may explain a patient's improved quality of life. The person learns to recognize and predict his or her own reactions, and therefore cope with pain and symptoms more adequately, which decreases anxiety. The person learns to solve interpersonal and other problems more constructively, which reduces stress and depression and improves social and emotional networks. The person develops the ability to identify and change negative cognitive patterns, resulting in more positive expectations and trust in the future and in his or her own competence. Improved knowledge about him or herself and development of new skills enhance the person's feelings of self-efficacy.

It is not quite clear how behavior change can affect medical endpoints. However, it has been shown that individuals who exhibit the Type A behavior pattern show more pronounced psychophysiological reactivity during laboratory stress (18). Such findings are supported by studies that show a relationship between mental stress and silent ischemia (19). The increased secretion of catecholamines associated with Type A behavior may result in both immediate and long-term extra demands on the cardiovascular system. When a patient learns to prevent and more adequately handle challenging and provocative situations in everyday life, sustained sympathetic nervous system arousal is decreased.

Depression is another possible mechanism because depression entails an increased risk for both first MI (8, 20) and worsened prognosis when the disease is manifest (9, 21). High levels of depression have been associated with increased risk for cardiovascular disease (CVD), and this relationship persists after controlling for age, gender, and initial health status. Increased plasma norepinephrine has been suggested as a mechanism by which depression could lead to increased cardiovascular risk (22). Improved coping leading to positive reinforcement of new behaviors may affect the depressive mood that many post-MI and post-CABG patients suffer from, thereby achieving hormonal and immunological changes that are favorable for CHD prognosis.

HOW TO IMPROVE COMPLIANCE

Compliance is facilitated by continuity, long-term follow-up, systematic use of supportive group dynamics, new learning in small and concrete steps, and, of course, the fact that patients feel the program is relevant to their particular problems. The effect of modeling cannot be overestimated. Rehabilitation and more long-term secondary prevention are most effectively done in a group setting.

By being in a similar situation and sharing experiences, patients learn from each other, and an empathetic and enthusiastic group leader becomes an important model. Behavior change techniques should be applied to make some immediate rewards possible. The general and long-term goal of health and well-being in the future may not have much impact on patients' daily behavior. Therefore, the social reinforcement and support of a group may be an important immediate incentive for initiating and practicing behavior change. Long-term strategies must also be built into the program for generalization and maintenance. Components of the program should use multiple techniques and modalities: teaching, discussions, use of audio and visual material (e.g., tapes, films, slides), specific assignments to work on in the group setting and at home, and so on. The purpose is to actively involve every participant. An obvious requirement that deserves attention is for the program to be entertaining.

A long-term program is needed to achieve behavior change that will be maintained and have an impact on disease processes. Friedman et al. (5, 6) used a total treatment time of 4.5 years. A crossover design was used to provide treatment for some of the control patients. For the control subjects subsequently entering into treatment, the treatment period was compressed to 1 year. This procedure also achieved significant reductions of Type A behavior and recurrence. The Ornish et al. (14) lifestyle program was a 1-year intervention, as were the two programs by Burell (15, 17), with some follow-up sessions during the second and third years.

At present, a 1-year treatment period seems to be the minimum time required to change behavior patterns that have been habitual for many years. The previously mentioned programs share the emphasis on practice and behavioral exercises that should be applied in patients' everyday lives. Learning new habits to the extent that they become natural and automatic requires time. Most patients are willing to stay in these types of programs for a year or more.

Further disease prognosis is influenced by the degree to which patients adhere to the program and acquire and apply new knowledge and skills. Friedman et al. (5, 6) showed that attendance in group sessions was related to recurrence risk. This relationship was evident for patients in Type A modification groups, but not in control groups. This observation shows that this was not a nonspecific contact effect, but dependent on the specific components of the Type A modification program.

This effect was also demonstrated in the Ornish et al. lifestyle program (14), which consisted of physical exercise, stress-management techniques, group discussions, and a low-fat vegetarian diet. The more time that patients spent applying the program in everyday life, the more regression of coronary atherosclerosis was achieved.

Thus, patients can be told that they have the choice with respect to the effects they want to accomplish for themselves. The more time and effort they give the program, the better health and well-being will be achieved.

EXPERIENCES OF WOMEN WITH CORONARY
HEART DISEASE

The increased incidence of CHD in younger women, which has been reported in some studies, is currently attracting much interest. When more women seek and need care for cardiac symptoms, it becomes evident that there is a substantial lack of knowledge about female risk profile, adequate diagnostic procedures, and the best way to treat women with CHD.

Post-MI women, relative to men, have more anxiety, depression, and sexual dysfunction (23). Women have a worse prognosis in certain respects, they are less likely to attend cardiac rehabilitation programs (23, 24), and they drop out more frequently. Because most programs are group based and gender mixed, women find themselves to be the minority in rehabilitation activities that are much accommodated to men's needs.

The kind of daily stress that women experience, and that may be associated with increased CHD morbidity, can largely be labeled *relationship stress*: double work load from family chores and professional work, multiple and conflicting roles, a heavy burden from taking care of significant others, and socioemotional exhaustion. Frankenhaeuser's (25) study of male and female superiors pinpointed this situation. She demonstrated that women's catecholamine secretion increased after their work day outside the home ended. In contrast, catecholamine levels in men decreased in the evening. For women, the "second job" awaits in the evening. They may care for others, but not for themselves. Gender roles, high demands that women put on themselves, and women's tendency to give personal health and other needs relatively low priority, all taken together, may prevent women from paying attention to themselves and seeking adequate medical help. Added to this is the experience of many women with CHD of being ashamed of their heart disease, and the frustration of inadequate encounters with the medical system. Also, many women give but do not receive much social support. Women with CHD often report that they feel lonely and have nobody in whom to confide.

In summary, for women with CHD, anxiety, depression, low self-esteem, personal demands for perfectionism, burdens of care for several significant others, and social exhaustion seem to be common. The pressure and burdens of life for men are more related to work demands and social isolation. Therefore, what men and women must learn to cope with differs, as do their reactions to the disease. This emphasizes the need, in many instances, for separate programs for men and women.

SUMMARY

The objectives of behavioral secondary intervention programs are to achieve lifestyle change and create skills that can prevent disease manifestations and symptoms, and promote health and well-being. The goal is to develop long-term behavioral strategies that are learned, practiced, and applied during most phases of the disease. Continuity, long-term follow-up, relevance, and adequate educational principles facilitate learning, generalization, and maintenance. Such programs should be cost-effective because they can reduce morbidity. Behavioral medicine education and training seems to be the most adequate background for professionals responsible for these interventions. Programs for male and female patients need different emphases and profiles. Such programs have been shown to affect psychological well-being, quality of life, risk factors, morbidity, and mortality.

REFERENCES

1. Nunes EV, Frank KA, Kornfeld DS. Psychologic treatment for the Type A behavior pattern and for coronary heart disease: a meta-analysis of the literature. Psychosom Med 1987;48(2):159–73.
2. Friedman M, Rosenman RH. Type A behavior and your heart. New York: Fawcett Crest, 1974.
3. The Review Panel on Coronary-Prone Behavior and Coronary Heart Disease. A critical review. Circulation 1981;63:1199–1215.
4. Matthews KA, Haynes SG. Type A behavior pattern and coronary disease risk: update and critical evaluation. Am J Epidemiol 1986;123:923–60.
5. Friedman M, Thoresen CE, Gill JJ, et al. Alteration of Type A behavior and its effect on cardiac recurrences in postmyocardial infarction patients: summary results of the Recurrent Coronary Prevention Project. Am Heart J 1986;112(4):653–65.
6. Friedman M, Powell LH, Thoresen CE, et al. Effect of discontinuance of Type A behavioral counseling on type A behavior and cardiac recurrence rate of post myocardial infarction patients. Am Heart J 1987;114(3):483–90.
7. Powell LH, Simon SR, Bartzokis TC, et al. Emotional arousability predicts sudden cardiac death in postmyocardial infarction men. Circulation 1991;83:722.
8. Booth-Kewley S, Friedman HS. Psychological predictors of heart disease: a quantitative review. Psychol Bull 1987;101(3):343–62.
9. Frasure-Smith N, Lespérance F, Talajic M. Depression following myocardial infarction. JAMA 1993;270(15):1819–25.
10. Falger PRJ. Behavioral factors, life changes, and the development of vital exhaustion and depression in myocardial infarction patients. Int J Beh Dev 1983;6:405–25.
11. Appels A, Otten F. Exhaustion as precursor of cardiac death. Br J Clin Psychol 1992;31:351–56.
12. Orth-Gomér K, Undén AL, Edwards ME. Social isolation and mortality in ischemic heart disease. A 10-year follow-up study of 150 middle-aged men. Acta Med Scand 1988;224:205–15.
13. Blumenthal JA, Burg MM, Barefoot J, et al. Social support, type A behavior and coronary artery disease. Psychosom Med 1987;49:331–40.
14. Ornish D, Brown SE, Scherwitz LW, et al. Can lifestyle changes reverse coronary heart disease? The Lifestyle Heart Trial. Lancet 1990;336:129–33.
15. Burell G, Öhman A, Sundin Ö, et al. Modification of Type A behavior patterns in post myocardial infarction patients: a route to cardiac rehabilitation. Int J Beh Med 1994;1:32–54.
16. Sundin Ö, Öhman A, Burell G, et al. Psychophysiological effects of Type A modification in myocardial infarction patients. Int J Beh Med 1994;1:55–75.
17. Burell G, Hansson HE, Åberg T, et al. Positive effect of secondary prevention by behavioral modification after coronary artery bypass graft surgery. A prospective randomized clinical trial. Manuscript submitted for publication.

18. Houston BK. Cardiovascular and neuroendocrine reactivity, global Type A and components of Type A behavior. In: Houston BK, Snyder CR, editors. Type A behavior pattern. New York: Wiley, 1988:212–53.

19. Rozanski A, Bairey CN, Krantz DS, et al. Mental stress and the induction of silent myocardial ischemia in patients with coronary artery disease. N Eng J Med 1988;318:1005–12.

20. Ahern DK, Gorkin L, Anderson JL, et al. Biobehavioral variables and mortality or cardiac arrest in the Cardiac Arrhythmia Pilot Study (CAPS). Am J Cardiol 1990;66:59–62.

21. Carney RM, Rich MW, Freedland KE, et al. Major depressive disorder predicts cardiac events in patients with coronary artery disease. Psychosom Med 1988;50:627–33.

22. Dimsdale JD. The effects of depression on cardiovascular reactivity. In: Field T, McCabe P, Schneiderman N, editors. Stress and coping across development. Hillsdale, NJ: Lawrence Erlbaum Associates, 1988.

23. Eaker ED, Packard B, Wenger NK, et al. Coronary artery disease in women. Am J Obstet Gynecol 1988;158:1553–67.

24. Perk J, Hedbäck B, Jutterdal S. Evaluation of a long-term programme of physical training for out-patients. Scand J Rehab Med 1989;21:13–17.

25. Frankenhaeuser M. The psychophysiology of sex differences as related to occupational status. In: Frankenhaeuser M, Lundberg U, Chesney M, editors. Women, work, and health (pp. 39–61). The Plenum Series on Stress and Coping. Series Editor: Donald Meichenbaum.

Chapter 16

Community Interventions in Cardiovascular Disease Prevention

Pekka Puska
National Public Health Institute–Helsinki

This chapter presents some general principles of community-based intervention programs for cardiovascular disease (CVD) prevention. General objectives concerning both medical and behavioral frameworks are presented. Some relevant behavioral social frameworks for planning and evaluation are reviewed. Major elements of the community program are given. Practical examples as well as the main 20-year results of the North Karelia Project—the first major community-based project for CVD prevention—are given. Finally, some relevant recommendations are suggested.

GENERAL OBJECTIVES

Atherosclerotic CVD is the leading health problem in most industrialized countries, and is a rapidly growing problem in many developing countries. Since World War II, extensive medical research has been carried out to learn about the causes and mechanisms of this disease. Research has involved large epidemiological studies within and between populations, basic biochemical and animal studies, intervention trials, and large-scale community-based prevention studies.

Although much will certainly be learned in the future, much is already known about risk factors and pathological mechanisms. Smoking, elevated serum low-density lipoprotein (LDL) cholesterol, and elevated blood pressure have been shown to be major causal risk factors (1). Key questions are: How can this existing knowledge best be used for effective prevention in real life? How can individuals and populations best be helped for optimal heart health?

Individual or Community Approach?

Several expert groups have pointed out the difference in CVD prevention between the individual's point of view and the population's point of view (1, 2). As far as the individual is concerned, the higher the level of risk factors, the higher the probability of developing the disease. Thus, with higher risk-factor levels, preferably considering the total risk-factor profile, individuals should receive more intensive help.

However, from the population's point of view, the picture is different. Most disease cases in the community do not come from the group of individuals with clinically high risk-factor levels. Most cases come from a large proportion of the population with only slight elevation, usually in several risk factors. Thus, major reduction of the disease rates in the community calls for general risk-factor reduction in the population. Because the needed changes relate closely to the general lifestyles of the community, a community-based approach is needed for an effective reduction of disease rates in the population.

The community approach assumes that the magnitude and nature of the problem precludes a simple and external solution. Instead, the intervention program has to be integrated into the existing social and service structures of the community. Because the problem relates closely to lifestyle, the community needs to decide to organize itself to solve the problem, with the help of experts. Basically, it is a question of promoting social lifestyle changes toward a healthier direction.

Although continuous efforts for new medical and technological advances are still needed, it is obvious that major control of CVD and related diseases is possible with existing knowledge if it can be effectively applied in the population. Although a full consensus on all causal links between health habits and disease are lacking, as it may always be, we have to act on the best currently available knowledge. The history of public health is full of examples of successful actions that are not based on full knowledge of the etiology of the disease concerned.

Success has often been based on effective intervention in some parts of the causal chain that lead to severe manifestations. There is little doubt that smoking cessation; general dietary changes reducing saturated fat and salt intake and increasing vegetable and fruit consumption; as well as a modest increase in physical activity would be beneficial for CVD prevention, as well as health promotion in general.

Carefully evaluated community programs form an important link between basic laboratory and clinical research and the large-scale application of public health programs in society. These programs can thus diminish our uncertainty concerning the effectiveness of such action, inform us about effective use of the existing resources (service and other community resources), and tell us about other possible consequences associated with such interventions. Therefore, carrying out carefully evaluated community programs, such as the North Karelia

Project, serves not only its target area, but also serves as a "pilot" or "demonstration" for wider applications.

The demonstration program implies that the intervention is well conceived and implemented as a planned, systematic program. The program contents are determined by existing medical, epidemiological, behavioral, and social knowledge, and are applied intelligently and adopted to the local community setting. Careful evaluation is carried out to assess the usefulness of the intervention for national or other applications. It includes both continuous monitoring and formative evaluation to guide the program, and comprehensive summative evaluation to assess the overall results.

Thus, a key feature of the community program is that it simultaneously applies medical and epidemiological knowledge to identify the health problems and select health objectives, and behavioral and social knowledge to design the actual program contents and activities. This implies an interdisciplinary approach both in planning and implementing the evaluative research (see Fig. 16.1).

Epidemiological/Medical Framework

The main health goal—control of the CVD epidemic—implies major action to reduce the burden of the disease, including primary prevention, treatment, rehabilitation, other secondary prevention, and related research. However, major success in controlling a chronic disease can only be based on primary prevention because intervention after the clinical stages have been reached will only have a limited impact. Thus, the greatest potential in controlling CVD lies in primary prevention: the "mass epidemic" should be tackled by "mass prevention."

For primary prevention, the choice of the main risk factors to be intervened upon is based on the international literature (usually emphasizing the major role of smoking, serum cholesterol [related to dietary habits], and blood pressure). This information has to be matched with information on the prevalence of these factors in the target population. In addition to these "classical risk factors," other possible factors such as physical inactivity, obesity, and psychosocial factors prevalent in the area have to be considered.

Once the risk factors have been agreed on in a program, choices still need to be made concerning the intervention strategy. The "high-risk" (or "clinical" or "focused") approach attempts to identify those people with high risk-factor levels and to intervene on them. The "community" (or "population" or "public health") approach attempts to modify the general risk-factor profile of the whole population.

Although an individual's risk of CHD increases with increasing risk-factor levels (a fact of obvious relevance for clinical practice), it is critical to realize that high-risk individuals produce only a small proportion of the disease cases that occur in the community. Most cases arise among people with only moderate elevations, but usually in several risk factors. This is because the people with

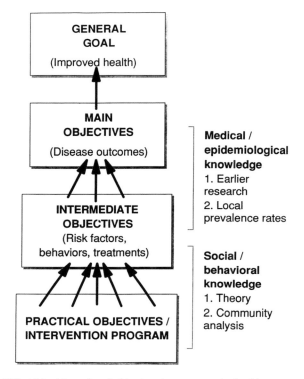

FIG. 16.1. Hierarchy of objectives in a community health program.

moderate risk outnumber the few really high-risk individuals. Thus, major reduction in the number of disease cases in the community can only occur if the
general risk-factor levels can be modified in this great majority—in practice, in
the whole population.

The clearly greater potential of the community approach compared with the
high-risk approach in reducing the CHD rates in the community has been
demonstrated by modeling the different approaches and using the data from the
North Karelia Project, as in Fig. 16.2 (3). This point has also been well described
by Rose (4). The North Karelia Project results also show that lifestyle changes
in the community are not well predicted by people's initial risk-factor levels,
hence further reducing the usefulness of the high-risk approach (5) (see Fig.
16.2).

Thus, from the epidemiological point of view, major reductions in the disease
rates in the community can only be achieved by widespread reduction in the
levels of the multiple risk factors. This implies community-wide efforts to promote
lifestyles that are likely to reduce the risk of CVD. Such lifestyle changes are
also likely to prevent several other noncommunicable diseases, to be safe, and
to promote health in general.

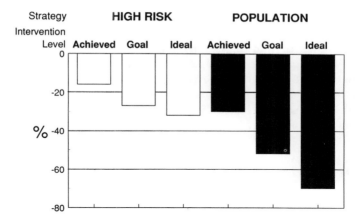

FIG. 16.2. Projected changes in CVD death rates with the high-risk and population risk-factor modification strategies. The high-risk strategy focuses on the population in the top 10% of the risk distribution, and the population strategy addresses the entire population.

The Behavioral/Social Framework

Once the aim of the program has been defined to promote healthy lifestyle and risk-factor changes in the community, the task enters the realm of the behavioral and social sciences. Medical practice has long been based on the assumption that, after identification of the behavioral agents leading to diseases, merely informing the subjects (giving them information) is enough to change the situation. Numerous studies and everyday practice show that this is seldom the case. Behavior is embedded in the social and physical environment in a complex way.

Reference can also be made to the old wisdom of public health: the totality of host, agent, and environment. Much of the work concerning prevention of chronic diseases has concentrated on the link between the agents (risk factors) and the host (man). But actually, many, if not most, of the great achievements in public health have involved major emphasis on the environment. This link to the environment applies to control of CVD, and is a major rationale behind the community approach.

The disease agents (behaviors/risk factors) of heart disease are largely determined by social forces and other environmental factors. Any major progress in influencing the disease rates has to deal with the environmental forces and structures. The natural, most effective way to change a population's risk-factor levels is to work through the community: The community should be the major target, rather than its individuals.

Although the task of influencing people's behaviors and lifestyles is in the domain of social and behavioral sciences, a major problem has been the lack of a unifying theory to serve as a guide. Program- and action-oriented people often feel frustrated by the inability of behavioral and social scientists to tell them what they should do. Despite this, there are sound behavioral and social-science principles to guide our way in planning, implementing, and evaluating community-based health programs. Reference can be made to the old wisdom: "There is nothing so practical as good theory."

The following text briefly describes four theoretical, somewhat overlapping, frameworks for behavioral change. Finally, a model is presented that unifies these approaches in a community-based health program.

RELEVANT BEHAVIORAL/SOCIAL FRAMEWORKS

Behavior Change Approach

This social-psychological approach deals with the determinants of an individual's behavioral changes, and is based on Bandura's (6) work on the process of learning. New behaviors tend to originate, at least on trial bases, from change exposure to powerful models; external and self-enforcement and cognitive control are the consequent determinants of continued new behaviors. This approach also includes elements of the classical field theory of Lewin (7), and the behavioral intention model of Fishbein (8).

In another article, a framework compatible with this approach has been described in greater detail, using examples from the various activities in North Karelia (9). This model emphasizes that program planning and evaluation should include the following key steps to help individuals modify their behavior:

1. Improved preventive services to help people identify their risk factors and provide appropriate attention and services.
2. Information to educate people about the relationship between behaviors and their health.
3. Persuasion to motivate people and promote the intentions to adopt the healthy action.
4. Training to increase the skills of self-management, environmental control, and necessary action.
5. Social support to help people maintain the initial action.
6. Environmental change to create the opportunities for healthy actions and to improve unfavorable conditions.
7. Community organization to mobilize the community for broad-ranged changes (through increased social support and environmental modification) to support the adoption of the new lifestyles in the community.

Concerning persuasion (one of the key steps in the model), the North Karelia Project has emphasized the credibility of the message source (World Health

Organization [WHO], government, academic expert opinion, health motives, etc.), various "affective" aspects (reference to the petition, "county pride," international interest, etc.), and contents of the message that anticipate the counterarguments and match with the local culture. The aim is often to inspire "community action for change," in which people would participate not necessarily for their own sake, but for the sake of the joined action, familiar and close to the people (thus emphasizing incentives other than those related to their long-term disease risk).

As in the Stanford "Three Community Study" (10), the North Karelia Project has placed great emphasis on various efforts to teach practical skills for change (e.g., smoking-cessation techniques, ways to buy and cook healthier foods). In the latter regard, close cooperation with the local housewives' association has proved most valuable. Various activities are carried out simultaneously to provide social support, to create better environmental possibilities (e.g., production and marketing of healthier foods), and ultimately to organize the community to better meet these needs.

The Communication–Behavior Change Approach

The task of introducing new behaviors into the community is basically achieved by communication: mass communication and interpersonal communication. A project communicates its messages through mass media to the population, in addition to its direct communication to various community leaders. In addition to Bandura's (6) social learning theory, the classical communication–persuasion model of McGuire (11), its modification by Flay et al. (12), and the belief–attitude–intention model of Ajzen and Fishbein (13) provide a well-documented theoretical background for this approach.

The North Karelia Project has developed a model, especially in connection with the national TV health education programs of the project (14–16), that recognizes the various steps of behavioral change—from exposure and attention, through comprehension and persuasion, to action and maintenance of new behaviors. Furthermore, the model takes into account the factors that relate to the communicated message and community-related factors that influence the various steps of behavioral change. By carefully observing the different aspects of the model in the planning of the message, and by paying attention or even trying to influence these factors in the community (e.g., increased social interaction) accordingly, the likelihood of positive results increases (see Fig. 16.3).

The task of influencing behavior through mass communication is extremely difficult because of the complex process involved. The rule is that, with many, often conflicting, communication messages, people basically tend to maintain their well-established habits. But with well-designed media interventions in suitable social conditions, efforts can be achieved that are limited in relative terms, but, due to the large audience, may be large in absolute terms, and thus give a favorable cost–effect ratio.

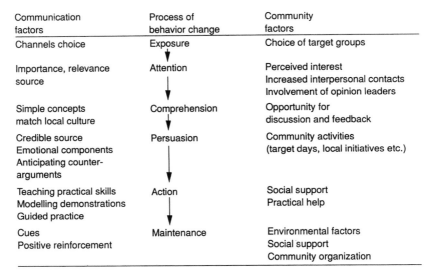

Communication factors	Process of behavior change	Community factors
Channels choice	Exposure	Choice of target groups
Importance, relevance source	Attention	Perceived interest Increased interpersonal contacts Involvement of opinion leaders
Simple concepts match local culture	Comprehension	Opportunity for discussion and feedback
Credible source Emotional components Anticipating counter- arguments	Persuasion	Community activities (target days, local initiatives etc.)
Teaching practical skills Modelling demonstrations Guided practice	Action	Social support Practical help
Cues Positive reinforcement	Maintenance	Environmental factors Social support Community organization

FIG. 16.3. Model of communication–behavior change process in community intervention setting, as used in the planning and evaluation of the North Karelia Project TV programs.

Innovation–Diffusion Approach

New lifestyles are innovations that diffuse with time through the natural networks in the community's members. This diffusion, causing social change, occurs through communication over time. The innovation–diffusion theory argues that mass media are more effective in creating knowledge of innovations and are useful for "agenda-setting" purposes, whereas interpersonal channels are more effective in actually changing attitudes and behaviors. The innovation process occurs in four stages (note the similarity to the previous approach): (a) knowledge, (b) persuasion, (c) decision, and (d) confirmation.

The innovation–diffusion theory classifies people on the basis of their innovativeness as innovators: early adopters, early majority, late majority, or laggards. The social structure has several norms (system effects) that have a strong influence on the rate of diffusion. Early adopters and a greater diffusion rate are more likely to occur in modern rather than traditional community norms. The early adopters usually have the greatest social influence in the community, and are thus in key positions to influence a wider adoption of the innovation. An agent of change is a professional who attempts to influence this innovation–decision process. Three main types of innovation decisions have been suggested: (a) optional decisions (made individually), (b) collective decisions (made by consensus), and (c) authority decisions (made by a superordinate power).

These central principles of innovation–diffusion theory have been developed mainly by Rogers (17). The theory is well supplemented by the classical idea of the two-step flow of new ideas and attitudes through opinion leaders (18). This simplified model holds that new ideas, often originating from mass media, are mediated and modified by certain opinion leaders, and most people are then influenced by interpersonal contacts with these opinion leaders. Opinion leaders can be identified through their particular expertise or position, or they can be informal and indistinguishable by formal criteria. Opinion leaders can either favor or resist the innovation–diffusion process.

The innovation–diffusion principles are of great relevance for many community health programs. A health project is based on certain health innovations that the project—as change agent—tries, through communication, to spread through the social network to the members of the community. The diffusion time is an essential element of the approach. Diffusion can be facilitated by the skillful use of theoretical principles of the communication process. The degree of community resistance (system effect) also has an obviously important role.

Community Organization/Social Policy

Broad-ranged and permanent changes in the community can only be achieved through the existing community structures. Every community has a complex network of social organizations, both official and unofficial, that exercises great influence over individuals' behaviors and lifestyles. The community organization approach emphasizes efforts to influence individuals through changing organizations to meet the desired ends. The concept of *community organization* involves both community self-development (the community initially detecting a problem and organizing itself to cope with it) and outside influences needed to promote the reorganization.

Community organization strategies are important for effective community-based prevention and health-promotion programs (19). For instance, in the case of the North Karelia Project, community organization has been critical. The community petition provided a favorable climate for community reorganization. However, the project team provided the external impetus and resources for change in the community. In doing so, the principles of persuasion and the change agent's role have been of central importance.

The impact of the efforts depends largely on the degree to which the existing community organizations find the proposed actions fitting their particular needs. Therefore, for community self-development to be successful, the program must offer incentives for the proposed collaboration.

It is important for the project team, throughout the program (but with greatest intensity in the beginning), to have close contact with many representatives of community organizations. For example, in the case of the North Karelia Project, the project team has been in close, and often personal, contact with the representatives of the mass media (newspapers, radio), with people of health and other services (administrators, doctors, nurses, teachers, social workers, schools, etc.), with business leaders (dairies, sausage factories, bakeries, groceries, etc.), with key persons of voluntary organizations (heart association, housewives' organization, labor organizations, sports organizations, etc.), and with local political decision makers (county and municipal leaders). Through these contacts, practical and feasible ways can be shown to collaborate, while recognizing each organization's particular needs. The aim is obviously to have the initiated changes influence the general lifestyle in the community. Successful community organization leads the way to social policy favoring healthy change (20).

Unified Model

The approaches described earlier have been unified in Fig. 16.4 to show the behavioral/social model of community intervention found to be most relevant to the North Karelia Project. The external input from the project affects the community through mass media communication to the population at large (where its effect is mediated through interpersonal communication), and even more so through formal and informal opinion leaders associated with various community organizations to influence the community. This two-pronged emphasis is aimed at increasing knowledge, persuading, teaching practical skills, and providing the necessary social and environmental support for the performance and maintenance of these health skills in the population. The acquisition and maintenance of new behaviors ultimately lead to a more favorable risk-factor profile, reduced disease rates, and improved health (see Fig. 16.4).

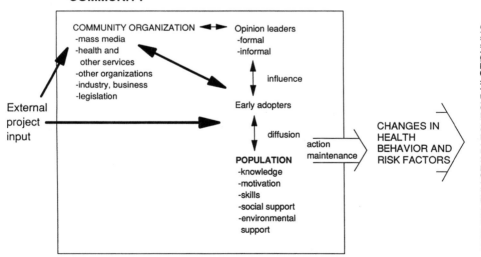

FIG. 16.4. Unified model of community intervention, as used in the North Karelia Project.

ELEMENTS OF A COMMUNITY PROGRAM

The practical framework of the community program consists of three components: (a) planning, (b) intervention program implementation, and (c) evaluation. Although they ideally occur in time sequentially, as listed, in many cases these elements take place simultaneously as the project proceeds (see Fig. 16.5).

Planning

The major elements in the project planning are: (a) definition of objectives, (b) community analysis, (c) establishment of the project organization, and (d) the preparatory steps. The main objectives of the program are usually set by the objective and/or perceived health needs of the community. The intermediate objectives are designed on the basis of the available medical/epidemiological knowledge concerning how to influence the health problem(s). The practical objectives and actual intervention measures should then be based on careful analysis of the community, and on understanding the strategic determinants of the intermediate objectives.

To the greatest extent possible, the community analysis ("community diagnosis") should provide a comprehensive understanding of the situation at the start of the program (21). It should provide the basis for selecting priorities and appropriate methods for the intervention, and it should indicate how continuous follow-up should be carried out to help guide the activities. Already existing data from previous studies, statistics, and expert opinions should be collected

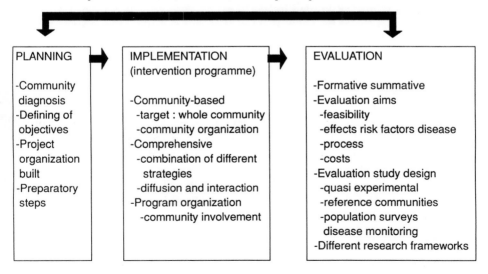

FIG. 16.5. The major elements in the community-based project.

and reviewed. Later on, the results of a baseline survey can also be used to complement the picture.

Important information for the community analysis includes epidemiological information from the area: the mortality and morbidity rates of the different possible health problems of the total population and various subgroups, and the prevalence rates of the possible factors influencing these diseases in the target population. Features of the geography, demography, and socioeconomic factors of the community should be reviewed. Information needs to be obtained about the various lifestyles related to the risk factors, about the various community features influencing these behavior complexes, about the community leadership and social interaction/communication channels, and about other factors relevant to the behavioral/social framework.

Because much of a program's success depends on the support of the population, information is needed on how people and their representatives see the problem, and how they feel about the possibilities of solving it. Because the program depends on the cooperation of the local decision makers and health personnel, their opinions and attitudes are also to be surveyed at the outset. The community resources and service structure also need to be considered before deciding on the actual forms of program implementation.

The establishment of a project organization and the preparatory steps for launching the program also need to be carefully planned. In the project organization, an enthusiastic and competent leadership, with appropriate institutional backup, is needed. The project team needs both professional skills and good contacts with several important sectors of the community. For the community to feel ownership of the project, a good representation from the community in terms of leadership is essential.

Implementing the Intervention Program

The goal is systematically to implement the program according to its aims and principles. Within the overall framework of the program, its actual implementation often needs to be sufficiently flexible to adjust in response to opportunities in the community. Integrating the program into the community social organization is important because, in so doing, the participation of the community and the availability of community resources can be strengthened. Thus, the project usually sets the objectives and develops the general framework, whereas the activities are mainly carried out by the community. The program catalyzes this work by providing materials, training, necessary official support, mass media support, and follow-up.

The program activities should usually be simple and practical to facilitate enactment in a large community. Instead of highly sophisticated services to a few people, simple basic services are often provided to the largest possible population. This eases information dissemination and personnel training. Integration of the intervention measures not only saves the project resources, but avoids duplication and overlapping activities as well, and thus means better use of community resources.

To identify and mobilize community resources, the program should work closely with community agencies and voluntary organizations. Thus, participation in preventive activities should form part of the regular work of the health professional, not simply an extra job or hobby. On many occasions, a community program can combine authority decisions with training and motivation of personnel. Close, personal contact between the project team and the local health personnel is important to help motivation and compliance.

The use of the large network of other organizations and opinion leaders can encourage population participation. Many organizations can appreciate being able to contribute to the success of an important health project. Numerous personal contacts need to be made, local problems discussed, and possibilities for practical contributions reviewed. The population's interest and support generated by the activities can be mediated by the mass media to establish further intervention activities.

Because the motivation and support of the general population forms a cornerstone for the project intervention, much of the practical work is often carried out by lay people and voluntary organizations. In some cultures, trained and motivated public health nurses can be an important personnel group. The role of medical doctors is, at its best, very important, but in many programs they act as medical experts within the general framework.

Evaluation

Evaluation can be divided into internal and formative versus external and summative evaluation. *Internal evaluation* is carried out during and within the program to give rapid feedback to the program workers and management. An overlapping concept is *formative evaluation*, which provides data during the program about the experience with the various program components, and thus helps further to develop ("formulate") the program. The *summative evaluation* of the program assesses over a given time the overall effects and other results, usually by an expert group in some way external to the daily community work. The evaluation aims can, as done in the North Karelia Project, be divided into assessment of the program:

1. Feasibility/performance
2. Effects (behaviors and risk factors, disease rates)
3. Process
4. Costs
5. Other consequences (22)

Feasibility/Performance

The program feasibility or performance evaluation assesses the extent to which it is possible to implement the planned activities (i.e., what actually happens in the community). This concerns the amount of resources that the project has available, how they are used in the community, and how well the activities reach the target populations.

A feasibility evaluation is especially important in a large and comprehensive program, where the community carries out the activities in a large geographical area. Before the question of effects can be meaningfully addressed, the actual intervention must be defined. Results of the feasibility assessment can be based on a log of activities, on statistical data within the community, or on survey and other data (project statistics) collected during and after certain program periods.

Effect

Program effect evaluation is carried out to assess whether and to what extent the main and intermediate objectives are achieved. Thus, indicators of the different objectives need to be defined and measured in the community at the outset and after the given program period. The effect assessment should especially answer these two questions: Did the program cause changes in target behaviors and risk factors (and other possible indicators of intermediate objectives)? If so, were these changes associated with changes in CVD (or other disease) rates?

Because the program target is usually the whole community, information is collected to represent the whole population. For prevalence data (behaviors, risk factors), a representative population sample is usually surveyed at the outset and at the main summative evaluation points. Independent, cross-sectional population samples are preferred so that the baseline measurements or selective loss at follow-up would not influence the findings of the subsequent follow-ups. Relatively large sample sizes are used to detect changes in risk-factor means that would be small for individuals, but meaningful for the population as a whole. Large sample sizes also enable interesting subgroup analyses.

Comparison of baseline and follow-up survey results reveals the changes that take place in the target community during the program period. However, the changes during several years could be partly or completely due to reasons other than the intervention program. Thus, a reference area is often used. A reference area should be as similar to the program area as possible ("matched"), but without the input of the program. This study design can be called *quasiexperimental*, because it represents the situation in which the study can control the experimental intervention and the choice of the reference area, but not the allocation of units to experimental and reference ones (23).

The baseline and follow-up surveys should be carried out simultaneously in the program and reference areas, and with strict adherence to identical methodology and sampling procedures. There are several problems concerning the use of reference area. One is that a major national program is likely to also have an impact in the reference area.

In the case of the North Karelia Project, after the first 5-year period, the project was obliged to help national intervention measures (such as the national TV programs). Also in the reference area, a new university (with medical school) was established in the same year as the project started. Such factors tend to influence health behavior and risk factors in the reference area, and cannot easily be taken into account in the formal effect evaluation. Thus, the given results can often be considered as conservative estimates of the effects.

With major community programs, mortality rates are collected by disease category and analyzed for the different area. Regression-based trends are usually calculated to eliminate the random annual variation. Additional information for the assessment of disease changes can concern hospital discharge data or special disease register.

Process

The process evaluation concerns both the change trends with time during the program and changes in the intervening variables. The former examines when the changes actually took place during the period, whereas the latter relates to the behavioral/social framework adopted and definition of the intended intervening (independent) variables. Measurement of these factors gives a picture of how the change process in the community leads or does not lead to the desired behavioral and risk-factor changes.

Cost

The cost evaluation assesses the total project resources and how they are allocated. In addition, efforts can be made to assess the community costs. This can concern both total community costs or, specifically, the extra costs involved for the community. In addition to the direct community costs, attempts can be made to estimate the indirect community costs and savings.

Other Consequences

In a major national pilot program, attempts also should be made to assess consequences of the program other than those intended. If the program involves the community deeply and leads to changes in lifestyle, it is quite possible that this process may lead to other changes as well. For example, non-CVD health effects may occur. Positive or negative consequences may take place in people's symptoms and subjective health. Socioeconomic, social, and emotional consequences, either positive or negative, may appear. Some of these aspects can be assessed using data from the population surveys.

Community Programs as National Demonstration Projects

The previous text discussed the general nature of community-based projects in CVD prevention. In principle, a community-based project can vary from a relatively restricted academic study or local effort to a rather major project with strong national involvement. The North Karelia Project or the WHO/CINDI demonstration projects definitely fall into the latter category (24).

One advantage of an intervention program in a small community is that an intensive intervention reaching every inhabitant could be used. However, there are also major disadvantages: Many important environmental decisions can only be made at a higher level—at a provincial or often national level. This concerns both legislation and private action, such as the food industry. Another disadvantage would be smaller applicability of such experience on a national level.

In the larger national demonstration projects, the aim is to take a rather large community (county, province, or other large geographically defined area), in which the comprehensive intervention is implemented in a well-conceived way and with careful evaluation. In addition to innovative educational interventions, community organization and major environmental modifications are applied—measures that could possibly be implemented nationally.

Because it may often be difficult to nationally implement many of the needed, often innovative, and somewhat contradictory measures, they are first tested in a "pilot" area. Thus, the national pilot area, with proper evaluation, gives good information on feasibility, effects, and other experiences of such action. When several of the measures are implemented in an integrated and comprehensive way in the same area, a national pilot area gives information on the overall experiences of this kind of intervention package, in which several activities implemented at the same time may support each other.

Thus, the term *pilot* means implementation first in a restricted area and later on, if experiences are positive, nationally. The terms *demonstration* and *model* connote that the preventive activities are done in a more planned and "better" way in that area—to demonstrate or show how to do it well and what the experiences are. Thus, national activities and activities in the demonstration area may take place at the same time and support each other, as in the usual case with many demonstration projects in the industrialized countries. Actually, many demonstration projects first started as a "pilot" activity, but later on clearly became more of a "demonstration" for ongoing national activities (25).

The advantage of demonstration projects is that we can demonstrate the work and learn about the experiences on a more limited scale first. At the same time, the demonstration projects give information on the results and experiences, and thus are powerful sources of inspiration, training, and intellectual resources for national action.

A major practical advantage of the national projects is their visibility. Instead of trying to convince the national decision makers or attract the national media with theoretical arguments, reference can be made to a practical example: "Look how it is done there. Prevention is possible and it works." In summary, a national demonstration project is used to:

- test the different methods of disease control when applied at the same time and in a systematic way in the same community;
- evaluate the feasibility, effects, and other experiences; and
- be a source of public and professional inspiration, visibility, training, and other intellectual resources.

For a national demonstration project to be useful and effective, two important rules should be observed. First, the project should obviously be professionally well planned, implemented, and evaluated. Second, an effective national demonstration project should have good support of the national health authorities, as well as close operational links with them. Thus, communication should continually go both ways. This ensures that relevant national aspects are well considered in the demonstration project, and that the decision makers are familiar and well informed about the experiences concerning national decisions.

As to the national application of the demonstration projects, experience has shown that it does not happen as is commonly thought. In theory, one would first test the intervention package, which would then be neatly given over for national implementation. Instead, in real life, national development takes place all the time, and a good demonstration project gives useful know-how for national development continuously, and particularly when needed. Naturally, major summative evaluation results merge at certain points of time and are of particular importance.

Figure 16.6 shows the overall use of the national demonstration program. A major national health program, with relevant medical information and public desire for change, can be tackled using a carefully designed and evaluated demonstration program. This, in turn, gives valuable information on the possibilities for prevention and health promotion in the given society. The practical results and visible experiences through general diffusion of ideas and national decisions guide the national action (see Fig. 16.6).

EXPERIENCES FROM THE NORTH KARELIA PROJECT

General Background

The North Karelia Project was launched in 1972 in response to a public petition to reduce the extremely high CVD rates in this province of Eastern Finland. Previous epidemiological studies and growing public awareness were important backgrounds. The aim of the North Karelia Project has been to carry out a

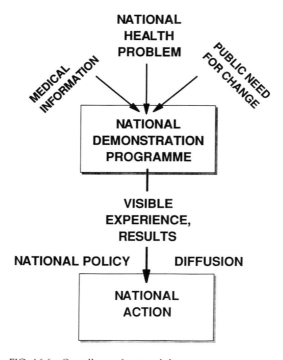

FIG. 16.6. Overall use of national demonstration programs.

well-planned and comprehensive intervention, using both medical knowledge of risk factors and relevant behavioral/social theories for promoting healthy changes in the community. The intervention targets were chosen using available epidemiological knowledge on risk factors and information on their occurrence in the local population.

The major objective of the program in North Karelia has been to decrease the mortality and morbidity rates of CHD and other CVD and chronic diseases, but also to promote the general health of the entire population in the area. Special emphasis has been put on middle-aged men. Primary prevention has been the key through general reduction of the well-known risk factors: smoking, high serum cholesterol levels, and high blood pressure. A central aim has been to promote lifestyles that reduce risk-factor levels and promote health, especially healthy nutrition and nonsmoking.

The practical intervention activities have been integrated into the existing service structure and social organization of the area. The role of the project has been to define the objectives, to train, to coordinate and promote the activities, as well as to assess the results, while most of the actual work has been done by the community. Thus, community involvement and people's participation are emphasized.

In the intervention, practical skills have been taught, social support for change provided, and environmental modifications arranged as part of the comprehensive community organization for healthy change. Previously described theoretical frameworks have been applied in planning and evaluation.

Evaluation

A large baseline survey was carried out in spring 1972 in North Karelia and in the initial reference area. Occurrence of risk factors and related behaviors, as well as their background, were assessed. Thereafter, the special intervention was started in North Karelia. Because of the good experiences and national pressures, the project became actively involved in the national risk-factor reduction activities after the initial 5 years (since 1977), thus also influencing the initial reference area.

After 10 years of the project, the scope of the program was enlarged to include a more integrated prevention of major noncommunicable diseases (NCD) and promotion of health. This was associated with the respective WHO programs ("Inter-Health" and "CINDI," Countrywide Integrated Noncommunicable Disease Intervention). At the same time, major activities were launched to prevent risk factors in youth. Also, the national involvement continued. After the 15-year survey, a decision was made to further intensify the CHD prevention by increasing activities to reduce cholesterol levels and smoking rates (see Fig. 16.7).

The assessment of the effects on people's lifestyles and risk factors has been based on repeated independent surveys of large representative population samples

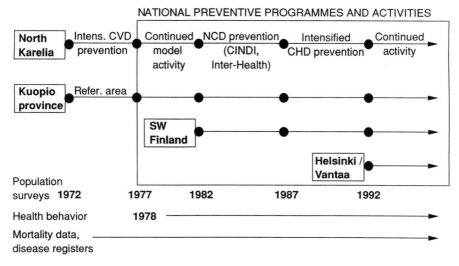

FIG. 16.7. General design of the effect evaluation of the North Karelia Project (developed later to national chronic disease and risk-factor monitoring system).

in North Karelia and in the reference area at the outset (spring 1972), and after successive 5-year periods (1977, 1982, and 1987).

Later, the developments in North Karelia also were compared with the development in the rest of Finland. The risk-factor surveys, initially serving the evaluation of the North Karelia Project, have gradually been developed to serve national health behavior and risk-factor monitoring. The disease rates in North Karelia have been monitored by special MI and stroke registers, recently in the framework of the FINMONICA Project (Finnish part of the WHO MONICA Project).

Intervention Examples

Lay Leader Program.   In the mid-1970s, over 800 lay opinion leaders were systematically recruited and trained in North Karelia to promote risk-reducing and health-promoting lifestyles in their environment and social contacts. The innovation–diffusion approach was the theoretical background for this activity. Several years later, this program was evaluated. The conclusion was that the use of lay leaders made a significant contribution to the overall impact of the project (26).

TV Programs.   Since 1978, a number of major national TV series have been broadcast as collaboration between the North Karelia Project and Finnish TV 2. In the planning, attention has been paid to relevant theories of communication—behavior change. Table 16.1 lists the series broadcast so far.

The feasibility of this activity has been good, and the viewing rates have been high—also among lower socioeconomic and high-risk population groups. The absolute effects, and thus the cost–benefit ratio, have been high, and the secondary impacts have been obvious (16, 27).

Quit and Win Contests.   In connection with the last two "Stop Smoking" TV series, major national "Quit and Win" contests have been organized. These were based on the idea to increase community participation and incentives for

TABLE 16.1
List of TV Series Prepared by the North Karelia Project

Series	Year	Number of Series (appr. 30–45 minutes each)
"Stop Smoking"	1978	7
"Stop Smoking"	1979	8
"Keys to Health"	1980	10
"Keys to Health"	1982	15
"Keys to Health"	1984–1985	15
"Stop Smoking"	1986	8
"Stop Smoking"	1989	9

positive action. In the first contest, over 16,000 Finnish smokers participated. The 6-month abstinence rate of the participants was approximately 20%. The second contest was organized jointly between Finland and Estonia. The general experience was quite favorable (28). However, with time such contests cannot be repeated too often.

Youth Projects. A major aim in preventive health work should be prevention of unhealthy lifestyles or better promotion and maintenance of healthy lifestyles in childhood and adolescence. As part of the general community intervention, schools in North Karelia have been involved in many ways (e.g., the most popular ice hockey team of the province has played with the SMOKE-FREE symbol). Since 1978, two major youth projects have been carried out for more systematic and innovative school-based interventions (29) involving all schools for Grades 7–9 in the province.

Worksite Interventions. Several different worksite interventions have been carried out in North Karelia as part of the project. In the 1970s, several campaigns took place at worksites. In the 1980s, a carefully planned worksite intervention study was carried out (30). Thereafter, a larger worksite activity has been implemented using a number of worksites as demonstration sites for dissemination and community organization.

Collaboration with MARTTA (Housewives') Organization. Because influencing dietary habits has been a central aim of the North Karelia Project, close collaboration with the MARTTA housewives' organization has taken place. This organization is very influential in the rural and semirural areas, especially concerning adoption of new cooking habits. In addition to broad continuous collaboration, several specific collaborative programs have been carried out: "The Parties for Long Life" in the 1970s, "The Happy Hearts' Evening" in the 1980s, and a weight-reduction campaign in the early 1990s. All these programs have concerned thousands of housewives and their families.

Collaboration with Food Industry and Supermarkets. Since the beginning of the North Karelia Project, much collaboration has taken place between the food industry and the project. In the 1970s, this concerned especially promotion of low-fat dairy products with the dairies, promotion of low-fat sausages with the local sausage factory, and, in the late 1970s, reduction of salt in several food items. Many collaborative campaigns have also taken place with the supermarkets and their chains.

In the late 1980s, intensive activities were carried out to promote further changes in diet to lower the still high cholesterol levels. In this activity, much collaboration took place between the project and the industry making vegetable-oil containing products. A major breakthrough was initiation and promotion of the domestic rapeseed oil.

Berry Project. In the 1980s, the project started a major collaborative program to promote the consumption of local berries. This activity has been sponsored by the ministries of agriculture, interior, and commerce. The aim has been to increase the consumption of the healthy and nutritious local berries. In addition to this direct objective, a major aim has been to provide berry farming as a substitute for dairy farming in the area (31).

Twenty-Year Results

The survey results on lifestyles and risk factors show major changes in North Karelia during the first 10 years (1972–1982), and smaller changes in the reference area. From 1982 to 1987, the changes in risk factors were smaller, but again in 1987–1992 greater changes took place. Particularly great have been the changes in smoking among men, and in dietary habits associated with a major reduction in the average serum cholesterol level. In 1972, nearly 90% of men in the area used butter (predominantly saturated fat) on their bread, whereas that proportion in 1992 had reduced to only 20%. Most people now use various mixtures with vegetable oil—mainly heart-healthy rapeseed oil, grown in Finland.

From 1972 to 1992, among men ages 30–59 years in North Karelia, the prevalence of smoking changed from 52% to 32%, the mean serum cholesterol from 7.1 mmol/l to 5.8 mmol/l, and the mean blood pressure from 147/92 mm Hg to 143/84 mm Hg. The reductions in the risk factors during the original project period (1972–1977) were significantly greater in North Karelia than in the reference area. Thereafter, the decline in risk factors has been much the same in North Karelia and the other areas, with increasing decline in the cholesterol levels in 1987–1992 and somewhat greater continued decline in men's smoking in North Karelia (see Fig. 16.8).

After the three preprogram years (1969–1971), the age-adjusted CHD mortality rates (men, ages 35–64 years) declined in North Karelia steeply in the 1970s (−3.0% per year) and even more steeply in the 1980s (−4.1% per year). In 20 years, the age-adjusted mortality rate among men ages 35–64 years in North Karelia has reduced for all CVD 46%, for CHD 46%, for cancer 45%, and for all causes 37% (linear model-based change, 1969–1990). The decline in North Kalelia in the 1970s was significantly greater than in other parts of Finland. The national CHD rates started to decline at the end of the 1970s. After 20 years, the decline in all of Finland reached that of North Karelia (see Fig. 16.9).

Evaluation has also indicated other favorable changes in North Karelia (e.g., a net reduction in CVD-related disability rates, and improved subjective health of the North Karelian population as a consequence of the program). Cancer mortality declined nearly in a parallel way in North Karelia and all of Finland

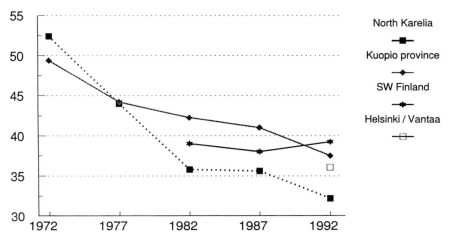

FIG. 16.8. Percent of smokers among 30- to 59-year-old male population in North Karelia and other areas of Finland in 1972–1992.

in the 1970s, whereas in the 1980s the decline in North Karelia (−4.3% per year) was significantly greater than that in all of Finland (−2.1% per year).

Throughout the 20-year period, the feasibility of the program has been good. This has been the case despite that, at least in the early years, the health service resources were scarce and the community norms rather traditional and thus resistant to lifestyle innovations.

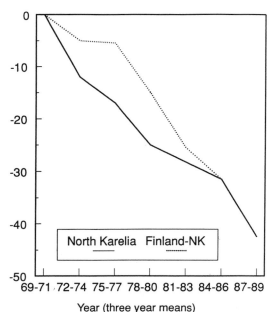

FIG. 16.9. Percent decline in age-adjusted CHD mortality from the preprogram period (1969–1971) among men (ages 35–64 years) in North Karelia and the rest of Finland.

Local health services and health personnel have cooperated well, and have thus formed a firm backbone to the activities. Numerous community organizations have contributed in various ways over the years. Because the project activities have been integrated into the existing services and community organizations, and people's participation has been a key feature, the overall costs of the program have been modest.

Conclusions

The experiences and results of the North Karelia Project support the idea that a well-conceived, determined, and comprehensive community-based program, based on sound epidemiological considerations and relevant behavioral/social principles and theories, can have a major impact on lifestyles and cardiovascular risk factors, and that such a development is associated with reduced CVD rates and improved health in the community. The experiences also show that major practical demonstration projects can be a strong tool for a favorable national health-promotion strategy.

RECOMMENDATIONS

- Preventive community programs should pay attention to the well-established principles and rules of general program planning, implementation, and evaluation.
- Preventive community programs should be concerned with both appropriate medical/epidemiological frameworks to select the intermediated objectives, and with relevant behavioral/social theories in designing the actual intervention program.
- Good understanding of the community ("community diagnosis"), close collaboration with various community organizations, and full participation of the people are essential elements of successful community intervention programs.
- Community intervention programs should combine well-planned media and communication messages with broad-ranged community activities involving primary health care, voluntary organizations, food industry and supermarkets, worksites, schools, local media, and so on.
- Community intervention programs should seek the collaboration and support from both formal community decision makers and informal opinion leaders.
- Successful community intervention programs need to combine sound theoretical frameworks with dedication, persistence, and hard work.

- A major emphasis and strength of a community intervention program should be attempts to change social and physical environments in the community more conducive to health and healthy lifestyles.
- Major community intervention programs can be useful for a target community, but can also have broader impact as a national demonstration program. For this, proper evaluation should be carried out and results disseminated.

REFERENCES

1. World Health Organization. Prevention of coronary heart disease. Report of a WHO Expert Committee. Tech Rep Ser 678. Geneva, 1982.
2. WHO. Community prevention and control of cardiovascular diseases. Geneva: Report of a WHO Expert Committee; 1986. Tech Rep Ser 732.
3. Kottke TE, Puska P, Salonen JT, et al. What if we forget about mass control of coronary risk factors? Projected effects of high risk versus population based prevention strategies in coronary heart disease. Am J Public Health 1985;121:697–704.
4. Rose G. Strategy of prevention: lessons from cardiovascular disease. Br Med J 1982;282:1847–1951.
5. Salonen JT, Heinonell OP, Kottke TE, et al. Change in health behavior in relation to estimated coronary heart disease risk during a community-based cardiovascular disease prevention programme. Int J Epidemiol 1981;10:343–54.
6. Bandura A. Social learning theory. Englewood Cliffs, NJ: Prentice-Hall, 1977.
7. Lewin K. Field theory in social science. New York: Harper & Row, 1951.
8. Fishbein M, Ajzen J. Belief, attitude, intention, and behavior: an introduction to theory and research. Reading, MA: Addison-Wesley, 1975.
9. McAlister A, Puska P, Salonen JT, et al. Theory and action for health promotion: illustrations from the North Karelia Project. Am J Public Health 1982;72:43–50.
10. Farquhar JW, Maccoby N, Wood PD, et al. Community education for cardiovascular health. Lancet 1977;1:1192–95.
11. McGuire WJ. The nature of attitudes and attitude change. In: Lindsay G, Aronson E, editors. Handbook of social psychology. Vol. III. Reading, MA: Addison-Wesley, 1969: .
12. Flay BR, Ditecco D, Schlegel RP. Mass media in health promotion. Health Educ Q 1980;7:127–43.
13. Ajzen I, Fishbein M. Understanding attitudes and predicting social behavior. Englewood Cliffs, NJ: Prentice-Hall, 1980.
14. Puska P, McAlister A, Pekkola J, et al. Television in health promotion: evaluation of a national program in Finland. Int J Health Educ 1981;24:238–50.
15. Puska P, Wiio J, McAlister A, et al. Planned use of mass media in national health promotion: the "Keys to Health" TV program in 1982 in Finland. Can J Public Health 1985;76:336–42.
16. Puska P, McAlister A, Niemensivu H, et al. A television format for national health promotion: Finland's "Keys to Health." Public Health Reps 1987;102:263–69.
17. Rogers E. Diffusion of innovations. New York: Free Press, 1983.
18. Katz E, Lazarsfeld P. Personal influence: the part played by people in the flow of mass communications. New York: Free Press, 1955.
19. Bracht N, editor. Community organization strategies for health promotion. Beverly Hills, CA: Sage, 1990.
20. Milio N. Promoting health through public policy. Philadelphia: F.A. Davis, 1981.

21. Haglund B. Community diagnosis. A theoretical model for prevention in primary health care. Scand J Primary Health Care 1983;1:12–19.
22. Puska P, Tuomilehto J, Salonen J, et al. The North Karelia Project: evaluation of a comprehensive community programme for control of cardiovascular diseases in North Karelia, Finland 1972–1977. Copenhagen: WHO/EURO, 1981.
23. Campbell DT, Stanley JC: Experimental and quasi-experimental designs for research. Chicago: Rand McNally, 1963.
24. Puska P. CINDI demonstration projects for national policy development. Can J Cardiol 1993;9:43D–44D.
25. Puska P, editor. Comprehensive cardiovascular community control programmes in Europe. Copenhagen: World Health Organization; 1988. WHO EURO Reports and Studies 106.
26. Puska P, Koskela K, McAlister A, et al. Use of lay opinion leaders to promote diffusion of health innovations in a community programme: lessons learned from the North Karelia Project. WHO Bull 1986;64:437–46.
27. Korhonen H, Niemensivu H, Piha T, et al. National TV smoking cessation program and contest in Finland. Prev Med 1992;21:74–87.
28. Korhonen H, Puska P, Lipand A, et al. Combining mass media and contest in smoking cessation. An experience from a series of national activities in Finland. Hygie 1993;12:15–18.
29. Vartiainen E, Tossavainen K, Viri L, et al. The North Karelia Youth Programs. Ann NY Acad Sci 1991;623:332–49.
30. Puska P, Niemensivu H, Puhakka P, et al. Results of a one-year worksite and mass media based intervention on health behaviour and chronic disease risk factors. Scand J Soc Med 1988;16:241–50.
31. Kuusipalo J, Mikkola M, Moisio S, et al. The East Finland Berry and Vegetable Project: a health-related structural intervention programme. Health Promotion 1986;1:385–91.

Chapter 17

Healthy Public Policy:
Getting Governments Onside

Michael O'Connor
International Organisation of Consumers Unions

Scientists often complain about governments failing to give due prominence to the former's discoveries when forming public policy. Yet it is not true that governments are blind to science. Governments do what suits their ideological bias or what they are pressed to do, and that includes their attitudes toward science and technology. Indeed, science itself is not apolitical. Therefore, scientists, especially those whose work is not in favor with government, sometimes decide that they have to take part in the political arena if they want their work to lead to some practical result. Nowhere is this more true than for the effects of psychosocial factors on health. The essence of this important research has major implications for public and commercial policy—from the way jobs are designed to how social welfare systems work.

In this chapter, public policy means the policies of governments—international, national, regional, and local—which impact on the public. As such, they are subject to change by democratic processes. The author has spent some years working on turning the discoveries of science into public policy. It may be a darker art than the pursuit of truth, but it is one we ignore at our peril. If we cannot get governments "onside" (i.e., on *our* side), if we cannot get them to support healthy public policy, then all our scientific work may be wasted, gathering dust on library shelves. More to the point, the public will suffer needlessly.

There are two points, however, that should be borne in mind when interpreting this chapter. First, the precise methods one uses to persuade governments to adopt healthy public policy vary widely from country to country. For example, what works well in the United States may be totally inappropriate in Japan.

This author's experience is based mainly in the United Kingdom (UK), although this is supplemented by recent work for the World Health Organization (WHO) in the former communist countries of central and eastern Europe. In the UK, conflict between the community, or sections of it, and government is common. We are used to joining pressure groups, campaigning, and demonstrating for our cause. In other countries, such as in Scandinavia, conflict seems less overt, and pressure groups are currently less common. There seems to be a view that, "if something needs doing then the government will surely do it." Despite these political–cultural differences, this chapter aims to show that there are some basic concepts that apply widely.

Second, the author writes from experience in a particular part of British culture: as a civil servant working mainly in the English Department of Health (with duties including being private secretary to the Minister of Health), but also in a joint unit of the Treasury and Cabinet Office. However, this experience also includes being the director of a pressure group, the Coronary Prevention Group, thus being both a campaigner and a target of campaigns. The perspective has thus been gained on both sides of the fence.

STARTING OUT: ORGANIZATION AND STRATEGIC PLANNING

If you want to change government policy, good organization and strategic planning are essential for two reasons. First, great individuals can sometimes change a government's policies on their own, but this is rare. It is far more common and healthier for people to come together to bring about change. Some of what follows may appear to be relevant only to large organizations, but it also applies to smaller initiatives. Second, changing government policy is rarely achieved overnight. Good policy is not adopted by accident, and advocates for health are not usually pushing at an open door. On the long march, it is all too easy to get lost if you do not have a route map. If you have not brought the appropriate provisions, you may perish en route. You need to organize and plan campaigns, and there are several steps that need to be considered.

Situation Analysis

Public interest campaigns frequently start out from a perception that "something is wrong" and "something needs to be done." This is not to denigrate this approach; it is the common human response to situations we know are wrong, but do not have the immediate resources to solve. Yet if we wish to build an effective strategy, we need to have a clearer picture of where we are now before we decide where we want to go. This process has been called *environmental scanning*, and it has two major advantages.

The first is that a clear idea of the problem gives a better understanding of the solutions. It is important to look at the problem as well as the context in which it is situated. Thus, the problem may be part of some wider social malaise, and an environmental scan may lead you to consider whether you are addressing the real problem. The problem may also reflect changing political, economic, and social factors. In these circumstances, the situation being tackled may be getting better or worse, and your plans need to take this into account. This analysis may also alert you to allies who can support your cause.

The second main advantage of environmental scanning relates more to the process than the result. It is unlikely, and inadvisable, that you will set about changing government policy on your own. You will need co-workers. Some will be recruited along the way, but you will also need some at the start. It is vital that you reach a consensus, at the outset, on what problems you are addressing. All too often campaigns come to grief later on when the originators argue over what problem they were trying to address at the outset. The environmental scanning process helps people come to a common view on the nature of the problem.

Vision, Mission, Goals, and Review

The environmental scanning process naturally leads to the next step: the articulation of a vision, the statement of a mission, the setting of goals, and progress review mechanisms.

Vision. We live in a changing world, and campaign plans must be flexible enough to deal with those changes. Yet there is a need for a fixed point of reference. Otherwise, you are liable to be buffeted by the winds of change, and to lose your identity and sense of purpose. A vision is a set of guiding principles. It is a description of the world as you want it to be, and the kind of organization you want to create to achieve that future. People should consider any goal or strategy by asking, Will this help us achieve our vision? It should be motivating and inspiring. It should be shared by everyone working on the campaign. It should attract people to your cause. People should want to share the vision.

Mission. A vision on its own can seem abstract, sometimes unrealistic, and even pious. A mission statement answers the question, What does your organization do to achieve this vision? It defines the scope of your work for the medium to long term. It must be short—no longer than two sentences. It must be simple. A wide range of people must be able to look at it and say, "I know what they are about." It must be feasible to convey credibility. It should be reflected in everything the campaign produces (e.g., leaflets, letterhead).

Goals. So far we have been describing the world as we want it to be and what we want to achieve; now for a more difficult part—setting goals. Goals are commitments to action to achieve the mission, and these should be in line with the vision. There are many goals that could be chosen. The existence of a vision and a mission helps the choice to some extent, but there is still a multiplicity of options; choosing between them can cause destructive friction within an organization. There is no easy way around this problem. The temptation is to please everyone and adopt a large number of diverse goals. Although some negotiation is necessary, it is important to make goals coherent, mutually reinforcing, and not too numerous or onerous for the organization to handle.

A useful discipline in choosing your goals is a SWOT analysis (i.e., looking at the Strengths and Weaknesses of your case, at the Opportunities offered in your campaign, and the Threats you are likely to face). Your goals should be chosen to build on your strengths, take advantage of the opportunities offered, counter the weaknesses, and meet the threats. It is possible to turn threats into opportunities, but also vice versa. Never ignore the weak points in your case. It may be uncomfortable to address them, but they are the issues that your opponents will seize on, and you must have as convincing an answer as possible. Moreover, these are likely to be critical issues for the undecided among those you are trying to convince. Never try to win only the support of your natural friends. The SWOT analysis also helps set priorities. It is not possible to do everything at once, and a clear understanding of the timing of opportunities and threats will help you set priorities.

Review Mechanisms. However well you plan your campaign, you will not be able to predict everything. You must build in a way of reviewing progress that involves all your colleagues. Without unnecessarily opening up the fundamentals for debate, this process should be capable of leading to a change in direction or tactics if necessary.

GETTING GOING: STRATEGIES

So far, much of what has been said is general good advice about processes, but the next topic—strategy—is dealt with a little differently. The next section considers not just the importance of setting a strategy, but also some key strategic choices you might face. Strategies are detailed action plans to achieve your goals. They refer to the action you need to take today and in the near future. They cannot be set in stone; they need to be flexible to take into account any new or unexpected developments, but they must give clear instructions to those who are running the campaign.

Working Inside or Outside Government?

For many people, there is no option of working inside government, but health professionals are sometimes afforded access as experts on various consultative committees. You may decide that, in your context, this offers a good way forward.

In the countries of central and eastern Europe, for example, it seems that various professional institutes have good access to ministers, and it may be that they can exert considerable power. However, a real problem for them is the instability of government, and, in the long run, they might be better advised to organize in the community. Conversely, the power of senior medical figures in France has done much to improve the government's position on tobacco. Yet on the whole, there are difficulties in relying heavily on working within government.

Governments respond to pressure. The kind of pressure that leads to policy change is a measure of the health of democracy in a country. In the ideal democracy, such pressure would be visible and representative of the needs of a broad range of citizens. In reality, however, the pressure is often covert and represents narrow groups and interests. Thus, public health is in the interests of the whole community, but is sometimes against the interest of powerful vested interests. If the debate is held in private, the health arguments with their inherent democratic benefits may not win. However, if politicians have to debate these issues in public, they are more likely to serve the interests of the public. Tobacco is a good example.

In the UK, the first strong evidence of a link between smoking and lung cancer emerged in 1951. Despite strong pressure from some doctors on Ministry of Health Committees, the government waited until 1954 to acknowledge the risk, and then did so only in vague terms. The evidence mounted during the 1950s, but still government action was weak. Key UK medical professionals became frustrated at the lack of progress, and in 1961 persuaded an independent body—the Royal College of Physicians—to issue a report on the dangers of smoking. It attracted enormous publicity, and forced the government to take much tougher action. The lesson is clear. The government could ignore the advice given by doctors in private, but once the doctors organized outside government the effect was electric.

Of course, all effective campaigns probably include an element of working on both the inside and outside tracks. At the beginning of a campaign, you might be working mainly outside government. Yet as time goes on, and pressure mounts to such an extent that politicians see that they have a real problem, you may need people who can work discreetly inside government. They can broker the deal that may give you most of what you want, but that you might face difficulty in suggesting yourself.

Winning Support

If you decide to work outside government, you will still need to win the support of politicians. You have to be sensitive to the agenda of individual politicians and parties. An effort must be made to locate your issue within their agenda. With left-wing parties, you might couch your case in terms of social justice and equity. The right wing may be more receptive to arguments from the position of ensuring informed choice and enabling markets to work more efficiently. Every political party has a "hot button" that you must try to find. Once they hear you talking their kind of language, they are more likely to give you a hearing. This poses a challenge to some campaigners. Sometimes you will have your own pronounced political views, but if you cannot deal amicably with politicians who see life from a different perspective, you may not be able to communicate your point as effectively as you would wish. Diplomacy and tact are skills to acquire, and they need not reduce the force with which you put your case.

In some cases, you may have direct access to politicians, but it is more likely that you will need to create wider pressure than you can exert personally. You will need to build your constituency. It is important that you build the widest possible group. Apart from the obvious truth—that there is strength in numbers—a wide grouping also makes it clear that yours is not a narrow sectional interest. It is all too easy for government to dismiss movements that they can portray as a small, self-interested group. If you can get others on your side, you will magnify your effect.

Building a Coalition

Coalition building is difficult, but worthwhile. The aim is to find partners who share your vision and at least some of the campaign goals. It is important to be aware of the difference between coalitions and networks of organizations, which come together for the purpose of sharing information about a common issue. Although sharing information is useful, it does not have the same power as organizations working in coordination. Coalitions should be brought together for a specific goal over a limited time period.

The coalition should be as wide as possible. When drawing up potential members, one should consider unlikely allies. Organizations that may have little in common, or have been antagonists in the past, may find something to share. This kind of unlikely partnership can be powerful in convincing politicians because it illustrates the breadth of a coalition. Politicians are not able to brand a coalition as "the same old bunch of fellow travelers" in these circumstances.

Particular attention should be paid to those organizations that individual politicians are likely to listen to. It is all too easy, when forming a coalition, to recruit one's friends. The key politicians may not have the same friends. Right-leaning politicians may listen more to business people, and left-leaning politicians may listen more to trade unionists. On the whole, you should take great care not to seem to be associated with one particular party. Sometimes pressure groups contain people who regard public interest campaigns as party politics by another means. This may be fun for them, but it is not best designed to achieve the organization's vision. Some organizations may support your cause, but because they are too conservative they may not feel comfortable taking a public stand by joining the coalition. This should not mean they are excluded. They should be made to feel wanted and needed. A way should be found for them to make a contribution. They may be critically important when you are nearing your goal. Because of their more independent position, they may be able to deal directly with government and act as a "go-between," but one who is still basically supportive of your goal.

Coordination of coalitions is a time-consuming and skillful business. The coordinator can be based on a member organization, but this can cause difficulties if that organization is then seen as owning the alliance. If an independent organization is set up to carry out the coordination, the question of whether it needs a public face should be considered. Two advantages of a public profile are that it provides a focus for media attention and it attracts helpful publicity when it is launched. However, the coverage afforded to a coordinating agency may be less impressive than the appearance of a large number of independent agencies making similar points.

A balance needs to be struck between helpful publicity and the possibility that its existence threatens the identity of some coalition members. This can partly be avoided if the coalition has a real job to do (i.e., it is set up to achieve a specific goal). Where there is an unfocused coalition, the coordinating agency can start to take on a life of its own. Particular care must be taken by coalition members to ensure that kudos is afforded to the members, and not the coalition as a whole or the coordinating agency. Column inch envy is all too common and dangerous.

Frequently in campaigning there is a need to act rapidly. Care should be taken not to create bureaucratic procedures so that decisions take a long time. The aim must be to build sufficient trust among organizations, such that day-to-day decision making can be delegated to a small group.

A word of caution is needed about coalitions from one who believes in them. They can become the most horrendous battleground of competing egos and rival organizations, and can do more to block progress than your enemies ever believed possible. Good coalition design and choosing the right people to facilitate it are essential. You should take advice from people who are experienced in such an endeavor.

Media Advocacy

The position of the media varies widely from country to country, therefore one must be cautious in describing what appear to be successful strategies. Access is very different, as is the tendency for the media to criticize government. However, in every country, the media is a major opportunity for those who want to change government policy. Technological changes are allowing more and more people to have access to more and more media channels, and this may offer many opportunities for public interest campaigners. However, the ownership of these multiplying media channels may be becoming more concentrated—often in the hands of multinational moguls with little national loyalty or interest in citizens' rights. This is not the place to debate the structure of the media, but many would agree that, whatever the structure, the media represent a major element in any campaign strategy. The question is how to use it to best advantage.

If you ever believed that facts win arguments, abandon that illusion now. Communication wins arguments. If your target does not hear your message, your case is lost. More to the point, there may be people who oppose you—often with more resources—and if they use the media better than you do, it will leave you with a large mountain to climb.

Earlier this chapter referred to the "dark arts" of persuading governments to change policy. If persuasion is dark, some people regard working with the media as the blackest art of all. Many of us may secretly harbor the desire to be media stars, but if we are sensible we recognize the difference between satisfying our vanity and serving our cause. There is a mystique about the media, but it is one we have to overcome.

The starting point is, once again, deciding on who you want to reach. Does your strategy depend on reaching a mass audience, or are you trying to reach a specific group? This decision should help you target particular media and programs or journals. Once you know what media you are after, you can target particular journalists. Find out who they are, and learn how to spell their names correctly. Court them. Cultivate a symbiotic relationship. The first time you speak to them should not be the day you want them to run your story. Organize a lunch at your office, get them to meet your staff, and understand your issue before you want to launch a story. If you are lucky, they may spot a story you have not thought of and run a "special."

Learn how to write a press release. Many newsworthy press releases get rejected because they do not "look right." On average, a journalist will spend a few seconds scanning your press release. If he or she cannot see something that grabs him or her in the first few seconds, the press release will end up in the bin. This mirrors the way readers scan newspaper stories. Remember, good journalists are looking for news; although they may be sympathetic to your cause, they do not want to be used as a mouthpiece. Therefore, only issue a press release when you have something newsworthy to say. Do not send out a press release every week just to let journalists know you are still alive. Cultivate a snappy line in quotes. As a public issues activist, you may get a lot of coverage not on your own press release, but by giving a one-line quote in a relevant story, such as a related initiative by the government. However, you should avoid becoming known as somebody who will give a quote on anything.

Invest in media training. There are tried and tested techniques for getting your point across on television and radio. Although you should encourage a number of people to do media work (and it is very dangerous for one member of a coalition to attract too much media), choose a media spokesperson who enjoys the work and is good at it. From time to time, you may find yourself on television or the radio debating with someone who does not share your point of view. In these circumstances, media training is very important. At all times, try to wrest the initiative from your opponent. He or she will want to give prominence to certain aspects of the issue under discussion, and you will want to highlight other points. For example, on smoking bans in the workplace, the tobacco industry will always say that bans infringe people's rights, but you will want to concentrate on the health consequences of passive smoking. The debate will be won by the person who is most successful in framing the issue. Your aim is to have the audience members go away thinking they have been listening to a debate about the damage done by passive smoking. Your opponent will want them to remember a debate on restricting people's rights. You must realize that people rarely listen or watch closely. They just notice the headlines.

Lobbying: Choosing the Right Person and Level

Government exists at many levels, and you need to decide the level at which it is appropriate to act. In some cases, it will be local; in other cases, decisions will be taken at an international level. Lobbying at an international level requires international organization. Otherwise, it is all too easy to be seen to be expressing a narrow national interest. You need to get together with like-minded organizations from other countries.

In Europe, the need for lobbying at an international level has grown. The development of the European Community (EC) means that if you want to change something you must make your voice heard not only in the Hague or London, but also in Brussels and Strasbourg. The new amendments proposed at Maastricht offer important opportunities for those concerned with health. Once the Maastricht Treaty is ratified, public health will be included in the Treaty of Rome for the first time.

Once you have found the right level, you also need to find the right person. Clearly, the central criterion is to get to the person with power; but in complex organizations such as governments, although power is with the politicians, others also have influence (e.g., civil servants). From personal experience as a civil servant, it is surprising how people sometimes underestimate an official's influence, and therefore misjudge their approach. For example, some do not realize that ministers have little time for detailed thinking, and that it could pay real dividends to influence the official. *Influence* here means providing information, ideas, and arguments—not a hard sell, which makes most civil servants highly suspicious and defensive. A constructive relationship with civil servants should be based on mutual trust and benefit.

On other occasions, the influence of the civil servant is overestimated. Campaigners attribute the minister's ideas to his official, and begin to see the official as the problem, rather than focusing on the minister's political imperatives. It is important to realize the difficulty for civil servants when dealing with campaigners. The civil servant and the minister perform an intricate dance. The minister has the power and takes responsibility for decisions, and so anything that the civil servant says in public can be taken as reflecting the minister's view. Hence, civil servants are loath to talk in public. Yet if this leads to a failure to discuss policy with outside interests, it results in failure to develop policy. Once again, it is important to establish an arrangement in which civil servants feel free to talk openly.

Civil servants also come across campaigners who are frustrated politicians. They seem to be taking up issues merely to "bash" the government, and would perhaps be secretly dismayed if government started to agree with them. This "hidden" motive is all too easy to spot, and does little to encourage government to listen. One sometimes also finds people who complain about a problem, but have no solution to offer. It can be argued that it is for government to find solutions, but it is far more effective to say: This is a problem, here is a solution.

How Not to Do It

This section concludes with an amusing piece by Byron Kennard (1), who put his tongue firmly in his cheek and described some of the ways to ruin a coalition.

1. Forget your origins. Social movements often start in humble, obscure, or disreputable circumstances. When the movement gets successful and these originators become embarrassing, dump these people and put the campaign in the hands of highly paid slick careerists.

2. Get serious about your work. I mean real serious. Work too hard, and put in extremely long hours. Practice looking grim and depressed. If possible, grow morbid. When you have mastered all this, persist in calling your colleagues' attention to your martyrdom.

3. Motivate others by applying guilt. If a group is working to save endandered species, attack it for its insensitivity to the poor. If they are working to help the poor, attack them for their insensitivity to endangered species.

4. Talk a lot about the need to cooperate and share, but for heaven's sake don't actually do it. What you should actually do is dominate.

5. Whatever you do, never share any credit. It is perfectly clear that the whole thing was your idea in the first place, and that nobody living or dead contributed anything important. If, through some terrible miscarriage of justice, other people in the movement begin to receive credit, try to grab it from them.

6. Remember that intensity of commitment is best measured by the amount of incivility that you display. Never be on time for meetings, and talk as much and as loudly as possible when you get there. Try to change the agenda, and insist that old points that have been resolved should be revisited. Leave the meeting early without helping to clear up the coffee cups or put the room in order.

7. Avoid doing any real work while creating the impression that you are giving your all. Try to be put in charge, but do not deliver on any of your own commitments.

Such people are not entirely mythological, but thankfully they are not too common. The most striking thing is how these descriptions also summarize the exact opposite of the ideal campaigner. Some of the best campaigners are those who truly do share, who facilitate others, and who make things happen, rather than engage in destructive displays of vanity and long, involved theorizing leading to nothing other than wasted time and lost causes. In this author's experience, it is often women who are the people who get things done while men theorize and posture.

KEEPING GOING: FUNDING AND RESEARCH

Funding

Some people may say, "This is all very well but where does the money come from to run these campaigns?" It is not easy to raise money for trying to change government policy. There are, of course, commercial agencies with vast amounts of money to invest in changing policy, and without vigorous public interest groups there is a danger of the debate becoming badly unbalanced. Yet it is not realistic to expect government to provide significant financial support for public interest groups. Pressure groups are unlikely to bite the hand that feeds them. However, democracy works better when there is a real debate, and society should have an interest in facilitating that debate.

In the UK, charity law inhibits charities from campaigning for a change in government policy. This position has been described by Des Wilson (2), one of the UK's leading public interest campaigners, as "politics [being] entirely the preserve of political parties." Some charities in the UK have found their way around such restrictions, but current rules still pose a significant barrier to getting involved in public policy. Lack of clarity about the rules can also lead to over-cautious behavior. Yet if all health charities committed themselves to public policy issues, they could do much to improve the prospects of persuading governments to adopt healthy public policies.

Indeed, it can be argued that they have responsibility to do so, but many charities in the UK still resist getting involved. They mainly spend money on medical research, and that is the basis on which they raise money. People do, of course, give money because they hope that a cure will be found for cancer or heart disease before they contract it. But is there not a duty on behalf of those accepting such money, and indeed soliciting it on this basis, to point out that it is highly unlikely that medical science will be able to do much for people who continue to smoke, eat unhealthfully, or take insufficient exercise? Furthermore, people's ability to take healthy decisions can be enhanced by appropriate public policy. That health is affected by public policies has long ceased to be a controversial issue. It is a short step from there to devoting a meaningful sum to designing and advocating healthy public policy.

Some charities might fear that getting involved in public policy might be unpopular with donors. Evidence from Canada suggests this is not true. The Canadian Cancer Society asked a representative sample of their donors the following question: As you may know, new federal laws have been passed that restrict tobacco advertising and promotion. The tobacco industry has mounted a legal challenge to these laws. Would you be willing or not to give money to the Canadian Cancer Society to help it defend the new law? Only 35% said no.

The questionnaire went on to ask: If you were to donate to the Canadian Cancer Society for this special activity, would your support for their regular fundraising be likely to increase, decrease, or remain the same? Only 2% said it would decrease. The public was then asked about its perception of where the society spends its money and where it should be spent. The public thought the society spends 12% of its money on public issues advocacy, and that 9% was the desired level. In fact, the Canadian Cancer Society spends only 0.5% of its budget on public issues advocacy.

On the basis of experience of cancer and heart societies, there seems to be marked differences in their perception of their role in the public policy arena. For example, the Philippines Heart Foundation sees its role as promoting higher standards among cardiologists and supporting poor patients who cannot afford operations. Yet in the United States and Australia, the heart foundations are openly involved in lobbying for changes in public policy. In fact, the American Heart Association has a 12-person team based in Washington, DC, that takes up public issues, although this in part reflects the particular position of lobbying in U.S. politics. In Europe, the Dutch and Danish Heart Foundations make a significant contribution to public education and public policy work. Together with the British Heart Foundation, they are the major funders of the European Heart Network, which was set up in Brussels a few years ago to advance public policy issues within the European Union. This was an exciting initiative, and other organizations, such as the International Union Against Cancer, now also have lobbyists in Brussels. This may be an evolutionary process for medical organizations, moving from funding training to supporting research, through public education, and then to include public issues advocacy.

Research

Approaching the end of this chapter, there are some final areas we need to address. Before we can hope to advocate changes in public policy with any possibility of success, we need to know what constitutes policies that promote health. We know smoking is bad for your health; so is poor nutrition and lack of exercise. On another level of analysis, we know poverty is bad for your health. The social tensions and uncertainties that haunt many citizens of the former communist countries are also prejudicial to health. The challenge is to formulate strategies that will overcome these problems, and then convince governments to take action.

We need to ask ourselves if we know the answers. As advocates for public health, we get into deep political water when tackling some of the major issues such as poverty, but we cannot avoid these questions. If we are to have any hope of success, we need to make sure that we have good evidence for the success of our strategies. In the UK, there is sometimes a certain cynicism about health-promotion campaigns. People ask, Does it really work? If we want to persuade governments to adopt healthy public policy, we need to be able to answer that question convincingly.

Evaluation. The answer to the question, Does it work? is not always easy. Any attempt to change complex patterns of human behavior tends to be difficult to evaluate. The number of parameters we are dealing with is huge, and the tools at our disposal are often blunt instruments. However, we must never use this as an excuse not to evaluate health-promotion programs, and not all health-promotion work is well evaluated.

A survey carried out by the UK Coronary Prevention Group, and funded by the UK Health Education Authority, looked at 64 cardiovascular disease (CVD)-prevention projects in 29 European countries. The results showed an enormous diversity of commitment to evaluation. Some built in complex evaluation procedures from the outset, but others believed that health-promotion campaigns were justified on the basis of the experience that has been gathered internationally over the last 20 years. Although this "act of faith" may be justified, how will these projects continue or expand if they cannot show their success? The English Health Education Authority has a policy of spending 10% of program costs on evaluation; it could be argued that this is money well spent.

Health-Promotion Research. Even if all prevention programs were properly evaluated, there may still be a problem with convincing governments because there is simply not enough research carried out regarding how we can help people adopt a healthier lifestyle. This is the perennial cry of researchers everywhere, but it is no less true for that. It is not an easy area to research, and sometimes health professionals regard it as a "soft" area—lacking the prestige of the "harder" scientific disciplines. Worse still, it offers little opportunity for private profit, and therefore the commercial sector rarely provides funds.

CONCLUSION

The chapter ends by posing this question: Do we want to be active in persuading government to adopt healthy public policy? This author hopes the answer is a vigorous yes.

Health professionals have high credibility with the public and with government, and this means it is vital that they are involved with campaigns. Some health professionals are not comfortable stepping outside a rigorous scientific discipline. They fear getting tangled up in a political world where principles are few and personal ambitions are many. Even if you do not feel that way, it is likely that at least some of your colleagues will be concerned about campaigning openly.

In the UK, we have found that nongovernmental organizations (NGOs) represent one of the best ways for health professionals to make a contribution to changing policy. Such groups are sometimes staffed by nonhealth professionals who are experts in lobbying government, yet rely heavily on the credibility and guidance of health professionals. NGOs have developed, and are developing, in different ways in each country, and they offer good opportunities to make an impact on public policy.

The prize of public health is important, and your role as health professionals is crucial. Frederick Douglass (3), a man who fought for the abolition of slavery in the United States, nicely summarized the choices we must face: "If there is no struggle, there is no progress. Those who profess to favor freedom and yet deprecate agitation are people who want crops without ploughing up the ground. They want rain without thunder and lightening. . . . Power concedes nothing without a demand. It never did and it never will. People might not get all they work for in this world, but they must certainly work for all they get."

ACKNOWLEDGMENTS

I thank Mike Pertschuck and the Advocacy Institute in Washington for many of the ideas in this chapter, and Jeanette Longfield for editing the speech on which the chapter is based.

REFERENCES

1. Kennard B. Not man apart. (Quoted in Doing it ourselves.) International Organisation of Consumer Unions, 1988.
2. Wilson D. Pressure: The A to Z of campaigning in Britain. London: Heineman, 1988.
3. Douglass F. Life and times of Frederick Douglass. New York: Collier Books, 1962.

Part V

SUMMARY AND CONCLUSIONS

Chapter 18

Blending Traditions:
A Concluding Perspective on
Behavioral Medicine Approaches to
Coronary Heart Disease Prevention

Neil Schneiderman
University of Miami

Kristina Orth-Gomér
Karolinska Institute

This book represents an attempt to describe the contemporary context for behavioral medicine approaches to coronary heart disease (CHD) prevention. Almost two decades ago, a small group of distinguished health scientists developed and shaped the concept of *behavioral medicine* into the following classical definition: "Behavioral Medicine is the interdisciplinary field concerned with the development and integration of behavioral and biomedical science knowledge and techniques relevant to the understanding of health and illness and the application of this knowledge and these techniques to prevention, diagnosis, treatment and rehabilitation" (1).

In examining the contents of the present volume, several things become evident with regard to the classical definition. First, the health scientists who formulated the definition were prescient in anticipating the progress that would be made in using an interdisciplinary approach to study and deal with chronic disease and its prevention. Second, the definition of *behavioral medicine* needs to be expanded to include not only the integration of biomedical and behavioral science knowledge, but also sociocultural and psychosocial knowledge. Thus, it is clear from reading the present volume that understanding and progress in CHD prevention requires knowledge about social class, social relations, and personality factors, as well as pathophysiology and principles of behavior change.

A third thing that may become evident from reading this book is that behavioral medicine approaches are important for health promotion as well as disease prevention. Because good health is not merely the absence of disease (2), there is a need to apply behavioral medicine procedures to maintain and improve well-being and productive functioning. Particularly in societies with aging populations, programs involving diet, exercise, and attention to psychosocial factors can help keep people productive longer. In this respect, getting people to quit smoking will not only decrease the risk of cancer and CHD, but will help keep people physically active and in good health, and thus improve the quality of their lives for a longer period of time.

Based on these observations, we suggest that a more contemporary definition of *behavioral medicine* might read: "Behavioral medicine is the interdisciplinary field concerned with the development and integration of biomedical, behavioral, psychosocial, and sociocultural science knowledge and techniques relevant to the understanding of health and illness, and the application of this knowledge and these techniques to disease prevention, diagnosis, treatment, rehabilitation, and health promotion."

It is conceivable that an amended definition could define *behavioral medicine* as a "multidisciplinary" as well as an "interdisciplinary" field, but this might not be particularly useful. *Interdisciplinary* means that an individual or group develops skills in more than one discipline to work at the interface of a problem. *Multidisciplinary* means that two or more individuals, trained in separate disciplines, may attempt to solve a particular problem without departing from their own disciplinary framework.

An example of an interdisciplinary framework is described by Oldenburg and collaborators (chap. 14, this volume), in which a physician trained to attend to the symptomatic needs of the patient also develops some knowledge and skills in health promotion and disease prevention. An example of a multidisciplinary solution is one in which a physician makes a diagnosis of borderline emphysema and simply refers the patient to a nurse, health educator, or clinical psychologist for smoking-cessation treatment. Although it is not incumbent on every physician to become an expert in smoking cessation, weight reduction, and so on, Oldenburg and his colleagues point out that physicians can develop a therapeutic alliance, ensure that patients understand the relationship between behavior and health, gain commitment from patients to change, and facilitate patients working with appropriate health care staff. These activities together constitute an example of behavioral medicine in action. Similarly, in behavioral medicine research, a scientist initially trained in one discipline should learn a sufficient amount about other disciplines to be able to work synergistically with other investigators.

As indicated in the definition of *behavioral medicine*, the field is concerned with the integration and application of knowledge obtained from diverse disciplines. The knowledge base in each discipline is not necessarily equivalent, and the experience of scientists and practitioners of behavioral medicine using concepts and techniques from various disciplines has been variable.

Some of the behavioral medicine approaches to disease prevention have been extensively investigated, well documented, and firmly established, whereas other approaches have been less well researched and scientifically evaluated. On the one hand, smoking-cessation programs have become well established and have shown considerable effectiveness. Recognition of the proper motivational stage of the patient or subject has proved essential and helped increase the effectiveness of these programs (chap. 14, this volume). On the other hand, attempts to influence such complicated issues as stressful work situations or malfunctioning social networks are still exploratory. Methodologies that have been developed in these areas have not yet shown an effect on disease endpoints, although they have demonstrated favorable influences on traditional risk factors such as lipids and blood pressure (chaps. 5, 6, 7, this volume).

Perhaps one of the most desirable goals in decreasing morbidity and mortality rates would be to minimize the social gradient of disease. Unfortunately, even in countries such as Sweden, where social class differences in real income have narrowed substantially since World War II, no decrease in the social gradient of disease has been observed. The data obtained thus far indicate that the gradient cannot be explained solely by differences in material assets or access to health care; this poses a substantial challenge to behavioral medicine research.

An important issue to be raised in any frontier science is *when* to apply new knowledge. As Weiss points out (chap. 2, this volume), we may achieve promising results in clinical studies, but, until such findings are replicated in large-scale clinical trials representative of the condition under study and the population at risk, we must consider such interventions as exploratory. Moreover, the issue in behavioral medicine is complicated by the fact that we are dealing with multiple risk factors; the mechanisms underlying their interaction are, to a large extent, unknown.

Although the conceptual problems faced by behavioral medicine approaches to CHD prevention are formidable, they should not daunt us in our search for both mechanisms and clinical applications. Nor should incomplete knowledge concerning mechanisms paralyze us in our scientific attempts to prevent disease. Thus, for example, following an epidemic of cholera in London during 1854, John Snow capitalized on his knowledge that water mains from two different water companies provided water from separate sources to houses along the same streets. Snow therefore ascertained the total number of houses supplied by each water company, calculated cholera death rates associated with each company's service, and compared them with each other, as well as those in the rest of London (3). Based on the large differences in cholera death rates associated with water from the two separate companies, Snow inferred the existence of a "cholera poison" transmitted by polluted water. In an apocryphal story, Snow has been credited with conducting a "controlled clinical trial" by removing the handles from the pumps in the affected area. Perhaps less dramatically, but more salient, long before Semmelweiss and Pasteur proposed their hypotheses about bacteria and microbes and Robert Koch identified the cholera vibrio in 1883, Snow's research led to "preventive" legislation that compelled the London water companies to filter their water by 1857. This provides an example of the type of scientific research—community—government initiative advocated by Puska (chap. 16, this volume) and O'Connor (chap. 17, this volume).

Similarly, it should be noted that the decreases in CHD morbidity and mortality rates, which have occurred in Western Europe and the United States during the second half of this century, began long before we had any clinical knowledge concerning the effects of low-density lipoproteins or the role of platelets in thrombotic and vascular disease. Thus, it would appear that, although the search for mechanisms and underlying factors that explain observed associations with disease need to be intensified, the use of behavioral medicine interventions can prove useful before we fully understand the underlying mechanisms of disease. Just as we need basic research to describe disease etiology and mechanisms, we need equally strong, scientifically based efforts to intervene against and prevent disease.

CHANGING THE ENVIRONMENT AND BEHAVIOR

Important issues and strategies concerning behavioral medicine approaches to CHD prevention derive from two traditions. One has linked changes in the environment to improved health outcomes. The other has linked these outcomes to changes by individual people in their behaviors. Neither approach is incompatible with the other. Moreover, because *behavior* can be defined as the interaction between an organism and its environment, behavioral medicine may be conceptualized in terms of the study of relationships between organism—environmental interactions and health outcomes.

An early example of changes in the environment leading to improved health can be seen in the circumstances surrounding Snow's research, which found evidence that "cholera poison" was transmitted by polluted water (3). In this case, the environmental solution consisted of filtering the water. In the more contemporary world, scientific identification of cigarette smoking as a major health risk has led to legislation to discourage smoking (e.g., increase the cigarette tax, restrict smoking in public places). To the extent that occupational stress has been linked to CHD morbidity and mortality rates, some efforts have been made to change the work environment (chaps. 6 and 7, this volume). In terms of coronary rehabilitation, attempts have been made to change the psychosocial environment by developing social support networks (chaps. 5 and 15, this volume).

A strong tradition also exists linking behavior change techniques to risk-factor reduction and CHD prevention. Impressive programs have been developed to produce and maintain smoking cessation (4), whereas more modest results have been obtained for decreasing dietary fat and cholesterol (5) and treating obesity (6) and alcohol abuse (7). The Oslo Heart Study in Norway (8) demonstrated that behavioral interventions could reduce multiple risk factors and decrease the incidence of CHD. Behavioral interventions have also been used in CHD rehabilitation programs (chap. 15, this volume). In the Recurrent Coronary Prevention Project (RCPP), Friedman et al. (9) used behavior modification techniques to decrease Type A behavior, and found that reinfarction rates were reduced to half of the rates observed in those who received usual cardiological care. Thus, it would appear that behavioral medicine approaches that focus on changing behaviors and/or the environment can be fruitful.

High-Risk and Population-Based Strategies in Prevention

As pointed out by Orth-Gomér (chap. 1, this volume), two theoretically different approaches have been adopted toward CHD prevention. One of these—the high-risk strategy—is directed toward intervening with individuals who are at high risk for CHD. The second—or population-based—strategy is directed toward reducing risk in an entire population.

Several clinical trials, such as the Oslo Heart Study in Norway (8) and the Myocardial Risk Factor Intervention Trial (MRFIT) in the United States (10), have identified high-risk individuals by screening and then intervened to reduce risk factors and CHD incidence. Both MRFIT and the Oslo Heart Study were successful in demonstrating evidence of risk-factor reduction associated with a significant decrease in CHD incidence when compared with population norms.

Meaningful evaluation of treatment in MRFIT, however, was compromised because many of the "high-risk" men in the control group apparently reduced risk behaviors on their own (10). This appears to have been an instance in which changes in the social environment—some of which may have been induced by media publicity surrounding the trial—confounded the study design. In any event, MRFIT failed to show significant differences between the treatment and control groups. In contrast, the Oslo Heart Study convincingly demonstrated significant differences between the intervention and control groups, both in terms of risk-factor reduction and CHD incidence (8).

One of the major strengths of behavioral medicine is the arsenal of behavior change techniques that have been developed. In some instances, based on the specificity of the problem and patient motivation, the clinical approach may suggest targeting a single unhealthful behavior such as smoking (4). In other instances, such as with the sedentary, overweight, borderline hypertensive patient with moderately elevated cholesterol and triglycerides, a multiple risk-factor intervention program may be preferable. Thus, for example, as pointed out by Schneiderman and Skyler (chap. 8, this volume), improving health outcomes in the obese should include attention to diet, physical activity, and emotional factors. Results from trials such as the Oslo Heart Study suggest that multimodal interventions can be effective (8).

When patients become concerned that they are at high risk, and thus seek help, a window of opportunity is opened for introducing a high-risk intervention strategy. This may occur either within a primary health care office setting (chap. 14, this volume), or within the context of secondary prevention (11, 12) in a cardiological venue (chap. 15, this volume). In either case, the intervention strategy involves using behavioral medicine techniques to change the behaviors of high-risk patients.

In contrast to the high-risk intervention approach, the population-based strategy described in chapter 1 attempts to change the habits of an entire population, including those who are not recognized as being at high risk. Part of the justification for this population-based strategy is that most coronary events and deaths due to cardiovascular disease (CVD) occur in persons with only a moderate elevation of risk (13). In any event, application of a population-based strategy depends on skillful use of the media and community action to communicate and encourage health-promoting knowledge and practices. Examples of this strategy include the North Karelia Project (14) in Finland (chap. 16, this volume) and the Stanford Five City Project (15) in the United States. Once the public accepts the health-promoting knowledge, governments can be encouraged to pass appropriate legislation (chap. 17, this volume) to discourage disease-promoting behaviors such as smoking.

Although the distinction between high-risk and population-based strategies is sometimes framed in terms of attempts to change the individual versus the sociocultural environment, it should be recognized that the efforts to change the environment using a population-based strategy involve the modification of individuals' health behaviors. In this instance, the task of changing behaviors in the community is largely accomplished by communication. As Puska (chap. 16, this volume) points out, the theoretical basis for the behavior change is based on social learning theory (16), communication–persuasion models (17, 18), and the belief–attitude–intention model (19). Thus, it would appear that both high-risk and population-based prevention strategies depend on the application of well-established behavior change techniques.

Empowerment and the Workplace

Marmot and Feeney (chap. 3, this volume) point out that discussions about social inequalities in health have frequently emphasized the issue of poverty or absolute privation. The Whitehall II data that they review, however, indicate that something other than absolute poverty is operative because each grade of British civil servant studied had worse health and a higher mortality rate than the grade above it (20). Syme (chap. 4, this volume) relates this gradient to "control of destiny," or lack of empowerment. According to Syme, the lower one is in the social class hierarchy, the less control one has over the factors that affect life and living circumstances.

Because most premature incidents of CHD occur among the employed, it is hardly surprising that attempts have been made to link stressful working conditions to elevated cardiovascular risk (chaps. 6 and 7, this volume). Thus, Karasek (21) proposed a "job strain" hypothesis that proposes that excessive psychological demands interact with a lack of control (decision latitude) to increase risk of CHD. The job strain hypothesis has been confirmed prospectively (22).

Johnson and his collaborators (23) extended the job strain model to include lack of social support. In a prospective study of 7,000 Swedish working men followed for 9 years, it was found that the joint action of high demand and lack of perceived control was an important predictor for blue-collar men, whereas the joint action of lack of control and lack of social support was a better predictor for white-collar men. According to Theorell (chap. 6, this volume), the joint action of lack of control and lack of social support is also a better predictor for women (chap. 6, this volume).

Although high demand, low decision latitude, and lack of social support appear to be critical elements in relating the workplace to CHD, personal coping characteristics also appear to mediate the association between stressors and strains (24). To the extent that high demand, low decision latitude, and lack of social support depend on individual perceptions, Karasek and Theorell (25) argued that "a model that considers individual and environmental factors is clearly necessary" (p. 95).

Recently, Orth-Gomér and colleagues (26) used the demand–control–support coping model as the basis for a worksite intervention aimed at changing both the work environment and individual behaviors. In this study, Swedish civil servants who self-reported high job stress were voluntarily randomized into either a work stress-reduction intervention or a wait-list control condition.

The intervention program consisted of three components. One component consisted of a 2-day educational course that focused on stress factors at work, reactions to stress in work groups, physiological stress reactions, and methods of coping with stressors and stress reactions. The second component consisted of a personal lifestyle assessment and individually practiced relaxation training. The third component of the stress-management program solicited self-initiatives from workers to improve the worksite situation in terms of demand, decision latitude, and social support without decreasing productivity. The working groups carried out their programs autonomously, but trained health care personnel assisted them in monthly follow-up sessions for the duration of the 8-month program.

Major findings of the study included a significant increase in perceived autonomy in the intervention group, accompanied by an improvement in lipoprotein profile. Although this was a small pilot study, the results suggest that a theory-driven intervention aimed at changing individual and environmental factors in the workplace can improve worker satisfaction, and perhaps also impact favorably on risk-factor status.

The past two decades have witnessed a large increase in workplace health-promotion programs. One of the largest of these has been the Johnson and Johnson LIVE FOR LIFE program in the United States (27). The program was initiated in 1979, and by 1987 covered 31,200 employees in a large number of worksites. Although the program was modified to meet specific needs at each worksite, standard components include: (a) health screening; (b) communications programs (e.g., newsletters) to encourage employee participation; (c) a lifestyle seminar to introduce the program; and (d) a variety of behavior change-oriented programs aimed at smoking cessation, weight control, stress management, blood pressure reduction, nutrition, and fitness. The programs are free of charge and typically occur at the worksite. Strong efforts have been made to change the work environment, with particular attention paid to smoking policies, offering nutritious food, and providing facilities for exercise. Most activities occur on the employees' own time.

A 2-year comparison between LIVE FOR LIFE employees ($n = 1,399$) and control-site employees ($n = 748$) found that the former had significantly: (a) higher smoking-cessation rates, (b) greater weight loss, (c) increased percentages of individuals initiating regular vigorous exercise, (d) lower inpatient costs, and (e) lower absenteeism. Although not directly assessed in the study, it is conceivable that some of the lower inpatient costs and lower absenteeism in the LIVE FOR LIFE subjects may have been related to feelings of empowerment and self-efficacy, as well as behavioral modification of risk factors.

Socioecological and Psychosocial Factors in CHD

Socioecological stressors (chap. 8, this volume), low socioeconomic status (SES; chaps. 3, 4, 12, this volume), social isolation (chap. 12, this volume), and psychosocial factors (chaps. 10, 11, 12, this volume) have been implicated in the development of cardiovascular pathology. Conversely, social support (chap. 5, this volume) and stress-management interventions (chap. 15, this volume) appear to play important roles in primary and secondary CHD prevention.

Psychosocially stressful environments have been linked to hypertension (28) and atherosclerosis (29, 30) in nonhuman animals, and to hypertension (31) and stroke (32) in humans. In cynomolgus monkeys, for example, disrupting the composition of living groups has been shown to promote coronary atherosclerosis; the disease severity is influenced by diet, personality, and gender (29, 30).

Mortality from myocardial infarction (MI) has also been associated with social isolation and high levels of stress (33). The presence of social isolation and high stress together increased the risk of mortality fourfold in men who had a previous heart attack. In a study of post-MI patients, living alone was found to be an independent risk factor for recurrence (34). When the combination of living alone and low SES was examined together, the predictive significance of the two factors in combination was significantly higher than either alone. Thus, it would appear that a stressful living environment, social isolation, and low SES can each contribute to increased cardiovascular morbidity and mortality.

Emotional–behavioral factors have also been associated with CHD (chaps. 8, 10, 11, 12, 15, this volume). In a major prospective investigation, the Western Collaborative Group Study (WCGS) found that Type A behavior was associated in men with almost a twofold increase in risk for CHD after multivariate adjustment for other risk factors (35). Type A individuals were characterized as hard driving, achievement oriented, excessively involved in their jobs, impatient, time oriented, competitive, and showing considerable potential for hostility.

When subsequent prospective studies of persons at high risk for CHD failed to confirm Type A as an independent risk factor (36, 37), questions arose about the specificity and generalizability of Type A. A number of studies have since shown that not all components of the Type A behavior pattern are associated with CHD; reanalysis of the WCGS dataset, for example, showed that the best discriminator between a subset of cases and controls was hostility (38). More recently, the hostility component was found to predict CHD mortality over the long-term follow-up of the WCGS sample, even though the global Type A behavior pattern did not (39). Other long-term prospective studies, using the Cook–Medley Hostility scale, have also shown an association between hostility scores and CHD mortality (40, 41, 42).

Although hostility and Type A appear to be the psychological variables most often associated with CHD, other psychological states, such as depression (43) and vital exhaustion (44), have also been implicated (chaps. 10 and 12, this volume). More than 25 years ago, longitudinal studies found that depression predicted death from MI (45, 46). Recently, a prospective study conducted on post-MI patients found evidence of a fivefold greater risk of mortality among depressed patients (47). Also, in the RCPP, anxiety was associated with rein-farction (48), and depression was found to be an independent predictor of cardiac recurrence and mortality among women (49).

In a quantitative summary (using summary statistics) of the published research through 1984, Booth-Kewley and Friedman (50) found that Type A behavior was reliably associated with CHD, and that the size of the relationship was comparable to traditional CHD risk factors. Furthermore, a meta-analysis of published studies found that higher levels of anxiety, depression, hostility, and aggression were reliably associated with CVD (51). Moreover, the combined effect sizes for anxiety, anger/hostility, anger/hostility/aggression, and depression are of similar magnitude as that observed between Type A and CHD. Thus, it would appear that a number of personality-behavioral variables may be associated with CHD. These psychosocial risk factors seem to be of comparable magnitude to those of traditional risk factors. It also appears that the personality-behavioral variables need to be studied within the contexts of socioecological stressors, social isolation, and low SES.

Just as socioecological stressors and psychosocial factors appear to play a role in the pathogenesis of CHD, the psychosocial environment and behavioral factors seem to have an important role in preventing disease. In a prospective study carried out on 50-year-old Swedish men for a 6-year period, the incidence of MI was found to be more than three times lower in well socially integrated as opposed to poorly socially integrated men (52). Similarly, in a prospective study of older men and women living in three diverse communities in the United States, people who reported extensive social ties—in terms of marriage, relatives, and participation in voluntary community activities—were less likely to die from MI than those with fewer ties during the 5-year study period (53). Among individuals who experienced an MI, those who originally self-reported having multiple sources of social support at the outset of the study were less likely to die from the infarction than those who did not (54).

Although few intervention studies have examined the role of social support in either primary or secondary prevention, this appears to be an area that deserves attention. In a secondary prevention study carried out on post-MI patients in Canada, men in an intervention group received monthly telephone calls from an interviewer (55). If a patient reported having problems, a nurse made a home visit to help the patient cope with the problems. One-year mortality in the intervention group was half that in the usual care-control group. Although one cannot determine from this study how much of the benefit was due to social support, increased professional attention to patient symptoms, or solving problems raised by the patients, the study does support the view that psychosocial interventions can be useful in reducing post-MI mortality. In another secondary prevention trial, the RCPP, which found that an intervention aimed at decreasing Type A behavior reduced reinfarction rates by half, successful decreases in Type A behavior were reportedly accompanied by an increase of support from co-workers and family (9). In chapter 15 of this volume, Burell argues that secondary prevention is probably most effectively done in a group setting because of the social reinforcement and solidarity it provides to group members, as well as the incentive it provides for initiating and practicing behavior change.

The intervention in the RCPP was designed to reduce Type A behavior, particularly hostility and time urgency (9). A recurrence rate of 12.9% was observed in the Type A modification group after 4.5 years, which was significantly less than the recurrence rate of 21.2% observed in a usual cardiological care group (56). The outcome was related to a significant decrease in Type A behavior among the intervention subjects. Thus, it would appear that psychosocial interventions may be useful in the secondary prevention of CHD.

Although the exact pathways by which low SES, socioecological stressors, and social isolation contribute to cardiovascular pathology are presently a matter of speculation, the authors of the present volume present convincing evidence that these sociocultural and psychosocial variables are importantly involved in the pathogenesis of CHD. Similarly, a convincing argument is made for focusing future research on the roles of social support and psychosocial interventions in the prevention of CVD.

BIOBEHAVIORAL FACTORS AND MECHANISMS IN CHD

The present volume focuses attention on the interactive roles played by biomedical, behavioral, psychosocial, and sociocultural variables in the pathogenesis and prevention of CHD. Analysis at each level has helped to identify potential risk factors, and has suggested important approaches to prevention. Results from numerous clinical trials indicate that identification of putative risk factors can contribute to development of prevention strategies. Nevertheless, comprehension of the precise manner by which individual variables cause disease, understanding of the exact interactions that occur among variables, and implementation of efficient intervention studies all require detailed attention to underlying mechanisms. These mechanisms occur not only at the cellular and molecular levels, but also at levels encompassing neurobiological, metabolic, psychophysiological, and psychological functioning, including perception, appraisal, and coping.

Metabolic Factors and CHD

In chapter 8, Schneiderman and Skyler indicate how the search for underlying causes of CHD has focused on increased understanding of metabolic mechanisms. They explore the hypothesis that insulin metabolism and stress hormones, including catecholamines and glucocorticoids, are importantly involved in the pathogenesis of CHD. These factors, in turn, can be linked back to stress responses, diet, and other lifestyle factors.

The literature reviewed by Schneiderman and Skyler indicates that a psychosocially stressful environment can lead to the development of cardiovascular pathology (28–32). In these situations, emotional stressors appear to activate the sympathetic nervous system, which, in turn, can mobilize free fatty acids, elevate blood pressure, activate platelets, increase hematocrit, promote left-ventricular and vascular hypertrophy, facilitate the release and synthesis of plasma cortisol, and increase insulin resistance. The increase in insulin resistance can directly and/or indirectly (through hyperinsulinemia) increase blood pressure, mobilize free fatty acids, promote clotting, facilitate left-ventricular and vascular hypertrophy, and sustain elevated sympathetic nervous system tone. As Schneiderman and Skyler point out, positive feedback loops involving increased activation of the sympathetic nervous system and insulin metabolism may provide a particularly pernicious mechanism leading to accelerated development of the disease process.

As indicated in chapter 8, behavioral stressors may impact on potential CHD risk through modification of diet. For example, individuals experiencing occupational stress are more likely to consume increased amounts of alcohol, coffee, calories, and fat, and a greater proportion of calories from fat. The manner by which emotional stressors and diet can interact to promote coronary risk has been explored in studies conducted in nonhuman primates (29, 30). In these studies, groups of cynomolgus monkeys lived in socially stable or unstable environments for up to 2 years. In the socially unstable environment, five- or six-member living groups were periodically redistributed. Because cynomolgus monkeys tend to form dominance hierarchies, determined by the outcome of aggressive encounters among group members, the periodic reconstitution of living groups led to increases in aggression as new dominance hierarchies were being formed.

In an initial study conducted on male monkeys kept on a low-fat diet, dominant animals living in the socially unstable environment developed more coronary atherosclerosis than dominant animals in the stable condition, or subordinate animals in either condition (57). The amount of atherosclerosis observed was small, but statistically significant. In contrast, when compared with similarly treated animals maintained on a high-fat diet, atherosclerosis was more pronounced in the monkeys fed the high-fat diet (29). Moreover, the atherosclerosis was significantly potentiated by psychosocial factors (i.e., unstable living environment) and personality (dominance). That is, the dominant male monkeys living in the unstable environment revealed significantly more coronary artery atherosclerosis than in the stable environment, or than subordinate monkeys living in the unstable environment.

As indicated in chapter 8, catecholamines released during emotional stress can mobilize lipid stores from adipose tissues. In lean, physically active animals not living on an atherogenic diet, the mobilized lipids are hydrolyzed to free fatty acids for energy production in muscular activity. This can lead to effective utilization and rapid removal of free fatty acids from the circulation. If, as a consequence of the atherogenic diet and an increase in insulin resistance, a high mobilization of lipids does not result in rapid removal of free fatty acids, these acids may become converted to triglycerides by the liver. These are then circulated in the blood as a component of very low-density lipoprotein, some of which ultimately becomes converted into low-density lipoprotein.

In any event, interactions among emotional stressors, a diet including excess calories and fats, and a sedentary lifestyle can interact to promote atherosclerosis and CHD. To the extent that emotional stressors, poor diet, and lack of physical exercise contribute to the pathogenesis of CHD, management of stress, a healthy diet, and the promotion of physical activity should provide a cornerstone for the primary and secondary prevention of CHD.

Psychophysiology

In chapter 9, Steptoe describes how psychophysiological paradigms can be used to study biobehavioral factors that appear to play a role in CHD. Emphasis is placed on psychophysiological methods that can help us understand pathogenic processes, and on the use of psychophysiological procedures that may be of use in the prediction of vulnerability to cardiac events in people with preexisting coronary artery disease (CAD). Psychophysiological methods also appear to be useful in the prediction of future hypertension, and in relating psychosocial factors such as job strain to hypertension and structural changes of the heart.

Psychophysiology has been defined as "the scientific study of cognitive, emotional and behavioral phenomena as related to and as revealed through physiological principles and events" (58, p. ix). Psychophysiological procedures have been useful for studying individuals at increased risk for developing hypertension by virtue of their family history, tonic blood pressure level, or race. Thus, for example, normotensive children of hypertensive parents appear to display greater cardiovascular reactivity to stressful stimuli than normotensive children of normotensive parents (59). There is also evidence that individuals who suppress anger and negative emotions may be susceptible to the development of hypertension (60).

To examine the interaction of biological risk and anger suppression within the context of a stressful situation, a psychophysiological experiment involving mental arithmetic and a frustrating mirror tracing task was performed (61). Family risk of hypertension (present vs. absent) and anger inhibition (high vs. low) were combined in a 2 × 2 factorial design. The high family-risk subjects who reported anger inhibition showed greater diastolic blood pressure responses to the behavioral tasks than did the other three groups. Thus, the combination of biological risk with particular psychological characteristics and appropriate situational demands appears to be important to the elicitation of heightened cardiovascular reactivity patterns.

Studies such as the one just described are potentially important because they can help identify psychophysiological processes that may be associated with the development of CVD. They may also prove useful in the early identification of people who may be at risk for future CVD. This would be useful because only a proportion of individuals with a family history of hypertension go on to develop premature cardiac disease. As Steptoe (chap. 9, this volume) points out, adding both psychological (anger expression) and psychophysiological (cardiovascular reactivity) components to the characterization may help target at-risk people more precisely.

The ability of psychophysiological laboratory studies to predict subsequent hypertension has already been tested. Well-conducted, long-term, prospective studies conducted on young men indicate that cardiovascular reactivity to either a cold pressor test (i.e., immersing a hand in ice-cold water) or a reaction time task involving threat of shock can predict subsequent blood pressure many years afterward. In one study, 910 White male medical students had their pulse rate and blood pressure measured before and during a cold pressor test; blood pressure was assessed again 20–36 years later (62). An association was observed between maximum change in systolic blood pressure and later hypertension, which remained significant after adjustment for study entry age, the Quetelet Index of ponderosity, cigarette smoking, pretest systolic blood pressure, and paternal or maternal history of hypertension.

In a study of young men subjected to a reaction time task, those individuals showing elevated heart rate reactivity to the task revealed elevated heart rate, systolic blood pressure, and diastolic blood pressure levels tonically when tested 10–15 years later (63). The findings remained significant after adjustment for standard risk factors, initial baseline blood pressure, and parental history of hypertension. Thus, the data from the cold pressor and mental stress studies suggest that persons prone to later hypertension manifest an altered physiology at a young age.

An examination of the hemodynamic adjustments of young men subjected to the cold pressor test has indicated that hyperreactors to stimulation have, at baseline, a relatively low cardiac output accompanied by elevated peripheral resistance (64). The hyperreactive blood pressure response is primarily mediated by an increase in total peripheral resistance. Thus, it would appear that the hyperreactivity may represent a central nervous system-mediated adjustment of the cardiovascular system to maintain adequate central perfusion.

Just as psychophysiological procedures appear to be useful in predicting future hypertension, these laboratory procedures also appear to be useful in predicting vulnerability to cardiac events in people with preexisting CAD. In one study conducted on patients with CAD, radionuclide ventriculography was used to image abnormalities of myocardial function during mental arithmetic, public speaking, and physical exercise (65). The level of oxygen demand at which ischemic responses were induced during mental stress was lower than that associated with ischemia during exercise. Thus, mental stress testing appears not simply to be mimicking exercise in placing high work demands on the heart, but appears to mobilize autonomic and neuroendocrine responses that deserve further study. Subsequent studies have also found that hemodynamic responsivity is elevated among patients with CAD who show ischemic (66) and arrhythmic (67) response during mental stress. Thus, it would appear that laboratory psychophysiology investigations may be useful in studying triggers for acute cardiac events.

Psychophysiological investigation, of course, is not only limited to laboratory reactivity experiments. As Steptoe (chap. 9, this volume) points out, ambulatory monitoring permits psychophysiological responses to be related to real, everyday events. This is particularly the case when cardiovascular assessments are used in conjunction with a diary. The diary permits physiological measures to be related to variables such as posture, place, mood, social situation, and the precise activities being engaged in by the subject (68). The use of ambulatory blood pressure-monitoring techniques, in particular, appears to be valuable because they provide information over and above office blood pressure measurements about the relationship between blood pressure and left-ventricular hypertrophy (69) and other hypertensive complications (70).

For instance, ambulatory blood pressure monitoring has been used to examine relationships among job strain, workplace diastolic blood pressure, and left-ventricular mass index (71). After blood pressure screening of 2,556 male employees at various urban worksites, 87 hypertensive subjects and a random sample of 128 control subjects were studied. Job strain was found to be significantly related to hypertension, even after adjustments for age, race, body mass index, Type A behavior, alcohol use, smoking, worksite, 24-hour urine sodium excretion, education, and physical demand level of the job. Subjects with high job strain also had greater echocardiographically determined left-ventricular mass changes. Thus, it appears that job strain may be a risk factor for both hypertension and structural changes of the heart in working men.

Serotonin Deficiency Syndrome

In chapter 11, Williams points out that a number of health-damaging biobehavioral characteristics—including hostility and depression, as well as elevations in eating, smoking, and alcohol consumption—tend to aggregate. Interestingly, these biobehavioral variables, which have been associated with CHD, are also linked to increased sympathetic nervous system activity (chap. 8, this volume) and decreases in the neurotransmitter—serotonin—in the central nervous system (chap. 11, this volume). At least indirect evidence of reduced brain serotonin has been reported for depression (72), hostility (73), increased aggressive and decreased affiliative behaviors in cynomolgus monkeys (74), and alcoholism (75). Conversely, serotonin enhancement has been reported to lower blood pressure in spontaneously hypertensive rats (76); decrease aggression in monkeys (77); and reduce smoking (78), eating (79), and alcohol intake (80) in humans.

The notion of a serotonin deficiency syndrome associated with CHD is interesting and provocative. However, Williams (81) wisely cautioned against too rapidly accepting a "single-lesion" hypothesis because the multiple subtypes of serotonin receptors are known to have opposite effects, and the interaction of the serotonin system with other transmitter systems in the brain is extensive and highly complex. These transmitter systems do not function independently of one another, but interact; cross-talk occurs between second messengers activated by the transmitters.

Despite these reservations, the hypothesis that serotonergic systems may be implicated in a number of behaviors related to CHD is important. In chapter 11, Williams suggests that both pharmacological (to enhance availability of brain serotonin) and behavioral (to improve stress-coping skills) approaches should be evaluated in clinical trials aimed at patients with established CHD. Synergistic relationships between pharmacological and behavioral interventions remain to be explored.

CONCLUSIONS

This volume has explored the rationale for using behavioral medicine approaches to primary and secondary CHD prevention. Our exploration has indicated that understanding and progress in CHD prevention requires knowledge about social class, social relations, and personality factors, as well as pathophysiology, traditional medical practice, and principles of behavior change. To understand and deal with CHD, which is a multifactorially determined disease, an interdisciplinary approach is required. Behavioral medicine offers this approach.

Within this book, we have emphasized how emotional stressors, poor diet, and a sedentary lifestyle set the stage for a cluster of health problems, including obesity, hypertension, noninsulin dependent diabetes mellitus, and dyslipidemia. Although genetic factors play a major role in each of these conditions, their expression is heavily influenced by behavioral factors. Just as the pathogenesis of these disorders is related to behavioral variables, a multimodal behavioral approach to primary and secondary prevention could make a major contribution to reductions in CHD morbidity and mortality.

In this volume, we have described both high-risk and population-based strategies for CHD prevention. A major strength of behavioral medicine is the arsenal of behavioral change techniques that have been developed and are available for interventions with high-risk individuals. These intervention techniques can be directed at either a single unhealthful behavior, such as smoking, or a constellation of factors, such as may be required in patients with the insulin metabolic syndrome. Clinical trials suggest that multimodal interventions can be effective. Both primary care settings and secondary prevention facilities are appropriate for such interventions.

We have mentioned that most coronary events and deaths due to CHD occur in persons with only a moderate elevation of risk. This provides part of the justification for applying a population-based strategy. Studies such as the North Karelia Project, described in this book, have convincingly demonstrated that, by skillful use of the media and community action, primary prevention of CHD can be successfully accomplished.

We have seen herein that social class and stressful working conditions are associated with increased risk of CHD. High job demand, lack of decision latitude, unsatisfactory personal recognition, poor social support, a disparity between high effort expenditure and insufficient reward, and poor coping skills are predictive of increased CHD risk. Intervention studies aimed at changing both the work environment and individual behaviors appear to be promising. Increasing people's feelings of empowerment over important aspects of their lives, including the workplace, may be central to the success of such ventures.

Socioecological stressors, low SES, and social isolation have been implicated in both the pathogenesis of CHD and mortality from MI. Living alone is an independent risk factor for recurrence in post-MI patients. The presence of social isolation and high stress together can increase the risk fourfold in men who have had a previous heart attack. Living alone and low SES also have interactive effects. Thus, it would appear that the combination of social isolation, low SES, and a stressful living environment can be especially devastating in cardiac patients.

Emotional–behavioral factors have also been associated with CHD. Because the correlation between any risk factor and CHD morbidity or mortality is small in the general population, and because specific groups studied tend to be diverse in terms of age, gender, relative risk, sociocultural factors, and sample size, it is hardly surprising that some investigations fail to find significant associations between a specific psychosocial variable and CHD. A quantitative summary of published research, however, has shown that Type A behavior is reliably related to CHD, and that the size of the relationship is comparable to traditional CHD risk factors. Furthermore, a meta-analysis of published studies has found that anxiety, depression, aggressiveness, and hostility are also reliably associated with CHD. The combined effect sizes for these variables are of similar magnitude as that observed between Type A and CHD.

Just as socioecological stressors and psychosocial variables appear to play a role in the pathogenesis of CHD, the psychosocial environment seems to play an important role in preventing CHD. Thus, socially integrated individuals with extensive social networks have a lower incidence of CHD, and, if stricken with MI, are less likely to die. Secondary prevention interventions that decrease Type A behaviors, such as time urgency and hostility, and increase social support and coping skills appear to decrease recurrence and mortality in post-MI patients.

Thus, it would appear that behavioral medicine approaches to the study of CHD and its prevention have much to commend them. Although there are many more questions than answers at this stage of the science, behavioral medicine offers a meaningful way to organize and synthesize the combined biomedical, behavioral, psychosocial, and sociocultural information that makes up the knowledge base concerning CHD and its prevention.

Because of the extensive range of information needed to understand the pathogenesis of CHD and its prevention, behavioral medicine approaches to prevention need to be broad and inclusive, not narrow and exclusive. Fortunately, an increasing number of disciplines are beginning to relate their activities to behavioral medicine approaches; scientists who once boasted of being disciplinary specific have become more comfortable with an interdisciplinary approach.

Within behavioral medicine, there is a need for scientists to understand, respect, and appreciate the fundamentals of the disciplines that contribute to the field. Thus, for example, individuals working within the area of CHD prevention need to know about traditional biomedical mechanisms of disease, as well as communication–persuasion models and behavior modification techniques. Fortunately, a cadre of such individuals has begun to appear in the area of CHD prevention.

REFERENCES

1. Schwartz GE, Weiss SM. Behavioral medicine revisited: an amended definition. J Beh Med 1978;1:249–51.
2. World Health Organization. Preamble. Constitution of the World Health Organization. Geneva: WHO Basic Documents, 1948.

3. Snow J. On the mode of communication of cholera. Snow on cholera. New York: The Commonwealth Fund, 1936.

4. U.S. Department of Health and Human Services. Reducing the health consequences of smoking: 25 years of progress. Washington, DC: U.S. Government Printing Office; 1989. Report of the Surgeon General (DHHS Publication No. CDC-89-8411).

5. Dolecek TA, Milas NC, Van Horn LV, et al. A long term nutrition intervention experience: lipid responses and dietary adherence patterns in the Multiple Risk Factor Intervention Trial. J Am Dietetic Assoc 1986;86:752–58.

6. Stunkard AJ. Perspectives on human obesity. In: Stunkard AJ, Baum A, editors. Perspectives in behavioral medicine: eating, sleeping and sex. Hillsdale, NJ: Lawrence Erlbaum Associates, 1989:9–30.

7. Chaney E, O'Leary M, Marlatt GA. Skill training with alcoholics. J Cons Clin Psychol 1978;46:1092–1104.

8. Hjermann I, Velve-Byre K, Holme I, et al. Effect of diet and smoking intervention on the incidence of coronary heart disease. Report from the Oslo Study Group of a randomized trial in healthy men. Lancet 1981;ii:1303–10.

9. Friedman M, Thoresen CE, Gill JJ, et al. Alterations of Type A behavior and its effect on cardiac recurrences in postmyocardial infarction patients: summary results of the Recurrent Coronary Prevention Project. Am Heart J 1986;112:653–65.

10. Multiple Risk Factor Intervention Trial Research Group. The multiple risk factor intervention trial—risk factor changes and mortality results. JAMA 1982;248:1465–76.

11. Burell G, Öhman A, Sudin Ö, et al. Modification of Type A behavior patterns in post-myocardial infarction patients: a route to cardiac rehabilitation. Int J Beh Med 1994;1:32–54.

12. Ornish D, Brown SE, Scherwitz LW, et al. Can lifestyle changes reverse coronary heart disease? The Lifestyle Heart Trial. Lancet 1990;336:129–33.

13. Rose G. The strategy of preventive medicine. Oxford: Oxford University Press, 1992.

14. McAlister A, Puska P, Salonen J, et al. Theory and action for health promotion: illustrations from the North Karelia Project. Am J Public Health 1982;72:43–50.

15. Farquhar JW, Fortmann SP, Flora JA, et al. Effects of community wide education on cardiovascular disease risk factors: the Stanford Five-City Project. JAMA 1990;264:359–65.

16. Bandura AP. Social learning theory. Englewood Cliffs, NJ: Prentice-Hall, 1977.

17. McGuire WJ. The nature of attitudes and attitude change. In: Lindsay G, Aronson E, editors. Handbook of social psychology. Vol III. Reading, MA: Addison-Wesley, 1969.

18. Flay BR, Ditecco D, Schlegal RP. Mass media in health promotion. Health Educ Q 1980;7:127–43.

19. Ajzen I, Fishbein M. Understanding attitudes and predicting social behavior. Englewood Cliffs, NJ: Prentice-Hall, 1980.

20. Marmot MG, Davey Smith G, Stansfeld S, et al. Health inequalities among British civil servants: the Whitehall II study. Lancet 1991;337:1387–93.

21. Karasek RA. Job demands, job decision latitude, and mental strain: implications for job redesign. Adm Sci Q 1979;24:285–307.

22. Hahn M. Job strain and cardiovascular disease: a ten year prospective study. Am J Epidemiol 1985;122:532–40.

23. Johnson JV, Hall EM, Theorell T. Combined effects of job strain and social isolation on cardiovascular disease morbidity and mortality in a random sample of the Swedish male working population. Scand J Work Environ Health 1989;15:271–79.

24. Spector PE. Perceived control by employees: a meta-analyses of studies concerning autonomy and participation at work. Hum Relat 1986;39:1005–16.

25. Karasek RA, Theorell T. Healthy work: stress, productivity, and the reconstruction of working life. New York: Basic Books, 1990.

26. Orth-Gomér K, Eriksson I, Moser V, et al. Lipid lowering through work stress reduction. Int J Beh Med 1994;1:204–214.

27. Fielding JE. The challenges of work-place health promotion. In: Weiss SM, Fielding JE, Baum A, editors. Perspectives in behavioral medicine: health at work. Hillsdale, NJ: Lawrence Erlbaum Associates, 1991:13–28.
28. Henry JP, Stephens PM, Santisteban GA. A model of psychosocial hypertension showing reversibility and progression of cardiovascular complications. Circ Res 1975;36:156–64.
29. Kaplan JR, Manuck SB, Clarkson TB, et al. Social stress, environment and atherosclerosis in cynomolgus monkeys. Arteriosclerosis 1982;2:359–68.
30. Shively CA, Kaplan JR, Adams MR. Effects of ovariectomy, social instability and social status on female Macaca fascicularis social behavior. Physiol Beh 1986;36:1147–53.
31. Harburg E, Erfurt JC, Havenstein LS, et al. Socio-ecological stress, suppressed hostility, skin color, and Black-White male blood pressure: Detroit. Psychosom Med 1973;35:276–96.
32. Neser WB, Tyroler A, Cassel JC. Social disorganization and stroke mortality in the Black population of North Carolina. Am J Epidemiol 1971;93:166–75.
33. Ruberman W, Weinblatt E, Goldberg JD, et al. Psychosocial influences on mortality after myocardial infarction. N Eng J Med 1984;311:552–59.
34. Case R, Moss A, Case N, et al. Living alone after myocardial infarction. JAMA 1992;267:515–19.
35. Brand RJ, Rosenman RH, Sholtz RI, et al. Multivariate prediction of coronary heart disease in the Western Collaborative Group Study compared to the findings of the Framingham Study. Circ 1976;53:348–55.
36. Shekelle RB, Hulley SB, Neaton JD, et al. The MRFIT behavior pattern study: II. Type A behavior and incidence of coronary heart disease. Am J Epidemiol 1985;122:559–70.
37. Case RB, Heller SS, Case MB, et al. Type A behavior and survival after acute myocardial infarction. N Eng J Med 1985;312:737–41.
38. Matthews KA, Glass DC, Rosenman RH, et al. Competitive drive, Pattern A, and coronary heart disease: a further analysis of some data from the Western Collaborative Group Study. J Chronic Dis 1977;30:489–98.
39. Carmelli D, Swan GE, Rosenman RH, et al. Behavioral components and total mortality in the Western Collaborative Group Study. Paper presented at the meeting of the Society of Behavioral Medicine, San Francisco, March 1989.
40. Shekelle RB, Gale M, Ostfeld AM, et al. Hostility, risk of CHD, and mortality. Psychosom Med 1983;45:109–14.
41. Barefoot JC, Dahlstrom WG, Williams RB. Hostility, CHD incidence, and total mortality: a 25-year follow-up of 255 physicians. Psychosom Med 1983;45:59–63.
42. Koskenvuo M, Kaprio J, Rose RJ, et al. Hostility as a risk factor for mortality and ischemic heart disease in man. Psychosom Med 1988;50:330–40.
43. Dimsdale JE. The effect of depression on cardiovascular reactivity. In: Field TM, McCabe PM, Schneiderman N, editors. Stress and coping across development. Hillsdale, NJ: Lawrence Erlbaum Associates, 1988:215–25.
44. Appels A, Mulder P. Excess fatigue as a precursor of myocardial infarction. Euro Heart J 1988;9:758–64.
45. Lebovitz B, Shekelle R, Ostfeld A, et al. Prospective and retrospective psychological studies of coronary heart disease. Psychosom Med 1967;29:265–71.
46. Paffenbarger R, Wolf P, Notkin J, et al. Chronic disease in former college students. Am J Epidemiol 1966;83:314–28.
47. Frasure-Smith N, Lesperance R, Talajic M. Depression following myocardial infarction: impact on 6-month survival. JAMA 1993;270:1819–25.
48. Low KG, Thoresen CE, Pattillo JR, et al. Anxiety, depression and heart disease in women. Int J Beh Med 1994;1:305–19.
49. Powell L, Shaker L, Jones B, et al. Psychosocial predictors of mortality in 83 women with premature acute myocardial infarction. Psychosom Med 1993;55:426–33.
50. Booth-Kewley S, Friedman HS. Psychological predictors of heart disease: a quantitative review. Psychol Bull 1987;101:343–62.

51. Friedman HS, Booth-Kewley S. The "disease-prone personality": a meta-analytic view of the construct. Am Psychol 1987;42:539–55.

52. Orth-Gomér K, Rosengren A, Wilhemsen L. Lack of social support and incidence of coronary heart disease in middle-aged Swedish men. Psychosom Med 1993;55:37–43.

53. Seeman TE, Berkman LF, Kohout F, et al. Intercommunity variations in the association between social ties and mortality in the elderly: a comparative analysis of three communities. Ann Epidemiol 1993;3:325–35.

54. Berkman LF, Leo-Summers L, Horwitz RI. Emotional support and survival following myocardial infarction: a prospective population-based study of the elderly. Ann Int Med 1992;117:1003–09.

55. Frasure-Smith N, Prince R. Long-term follow-up of the Ischemic Heart Disease Life Stress Monitoring Program. Psychosom Med 1989;51:485–513.

56. Friedman M, Powell LH, Thoresen CE, et al. Effect of discontinuance of Type A behavioral counseling on Type A behavior and cardiac recurrence rate of post myocardial infarction patients. Am Heart J 1987;114:483–90.

57. Kaplan JR, Manuck SB, Clarkson TB, et al. Social stress, environment and atherosclerosis in normocholesterolemic monkeys. Science 1982;220:733–35.

58. Cacioppo JT, Tassinary LG. Preface. In: Cacioppo JT, Tassinary LG, editors. Principles of psychophysiology. Cambridge: Cambridge University Press, 1990:ix.

59. Falkner B, Kushner H, Onesti G, et al. Cardiovascular characteristics in adolescents who develop essential hypertension. Hypertension 1981;3:521–27.

60. Kahn HA, Medalie JH, Neufeld HN, et al. The incidence of hypertension and associated factors: the Israeli Ischemic Heart Disease Study. Am Heart J 1972;84:171–82.

61. Vögele C, Steptoe A. Anger inhibition and family history as modulators of cardiovascular responses to mental stress in adolescent boys. J Psychosom Res 1993;37:503–14.

62. Menkes MS, Matthews KA, Krantz DS, et al. Cardiovascular reactivity to the cold pressor test as a predictor of hypertension. Hypertension 1989;14:524–30.

63. Light KC, Dolan CA, Davis MR, et al. Cardiovascular responses to an active coping challenge as predictors of blood pressure patterns 10–15 years later. Psychosom Med 1992;54:217–30.

64. Peckerman A, Hurwitz BE, Saab PG, et al. Stimulus dimensions of the cold pressor test and the associated patterns of cardiovascular response. Psychophysiology 1994;31:282–90.

65. Rozanski A, Bairy M, Krantz DS, et al. Mental stress and the induction of silent myocardial ischaemia in patients with coronary artery disease. N Eng J Med 1988;318:1005–12.

66. Krantz DS, Helmers KF, Bairey CN, et al. Cardiovascular reactivity and mental stress-induced myocardial ischemia in patients with coronary artery disease. Psychosom Med 1991;53:1–12.

67. Zotti AM, Bettinardi O, Soffiantino F, et al. Psychophysiological stress testing in post-infarction patients: psychophysiological correlates of cardiovascular arousal and abnormal cardiac responses. Circulation 1991;83 Suppl II:25–35.

68. Gellman MD, Ironson GH, Schneiderman N, et al. Sources of variability and methodological considerations in ambulatory blood pressure. In: Schmidt TFH, Engel BT, Blümchen G, editors. Temporal variations of the cardiovascular system. Berlin: Springer-Verlag, 1992:258–71.

69. Devereux RB, Pickering TG, Harshfield GA, et al. Left ventricular hypertrophy in patients with hypertension: importance of blood pressure response to regularly occurring stress. Circulation 1983;68:470–76.

70. Pickering TG, Harshfield GA, Devereux RB, et al. What is the role of ambulatory blood pressure monitoring in the management of hypertension patients? Hypertension 1985;7:171–77.

71. Schnall PL, Piper C, Schwartz JE, et al. The relationship between "job strain," workplace and diastolic blood pressure, and left ventricular mass index. JAMA 1990;263:1929–35.

72. Risch SC, Nemeroff CB. Neurochemical alterations of serotonergic neuronal systems in depression. J Clin Psychiat 1992;53 Suppl 10:3–7.

73. Coccaro EF, Siever LJ, Klar HM, et al. Serotonergic studies in patients with affective and personality disorders. Arch Gen Psychiat 1989;46:587–99.

74. Kyes RC, Botchin MB, Kaplan JR, et al. Extreme aggression and social withdrawal are related to reduced central serotonergic activity in male cynomolgus macaques. Paper presented at annual meeting of the Society for Neuroscience, Anaheim, November 1992.
75. Ballenger J, Goodwin FK, Major LF, et al. Alcohol and central serotonin metabolism in man. Arch Gen Psychiat 1979;36:224–27.
76. Fuller RW, Holland DR, Yen TT, et al. Antihypertensive effects of fluoxetine and 1-5 hydroxytryptophan in rats. Life Sci 1979;25:1237–42.
77. Tompkins EL, Clementa AJ, Taylor DP, et al. Inhibition of aggressive behavior in rhesus monkeys by buspirone. Res Common Psychol Psychiat Beh 1980;4:337–52.
78. Gawin FH, Compton M, Dych R. Buspirone reduces smoking. Arch Gen Psychiat 1989;46:288–89.
79. Levine LR, Enas GG, Thompson WL, et al. Use of fluoxetine, a selective serotonin uptake inhibitor, in the treatment of obesity: a dose-response study. Int J Obes 1989;13:635–45.
80. Sellers EM, Naranjo CA. Therapeutic use of serotonergic drugs in alcohol abuse. Clin Neuropharmacol 1986;9:60–62.
81. Williams RB. Neurobiology, cellular and molecular biology, and psychosomatic medicine. Psychosom Med 1994;56:308–15.

Author Index

R

S

Subject Index

315